AFRICAN HISTORICAL DICTIONARIES
Edited by Jon Woronoff

Historical Dictionary

of

GABON

Second edition

by

David E. Gardinier

African Historical Dictionaries, No. 58

The Scarecrow Press, Inc.
Lanham, Md., & London

British Library Cataloguing-in-Publication data available

Library of Congress Cataloging-in-Publication Data

Gardinier, David E.
    Historical dictionary of Gabon / by David E. Gardinier.—2nd
ed.
       p.   cm.—(African historical dictionaries : no. 58)
    Includes bibliographical references.
    ISBN 0-8108-2768-9 (acid-free paper)
    1. Gabon—History—Dictionaries. I. Title. II. Series.
DT546.15.G37   1994
967.21'003—dc20   93-35490

To my mother and to the memory of my father.

CONTENTS

EDITOR'S FOREWORD—GABON

Gabon, one of Equatorial Africa's most promising states from the outset, became even more attractive once it discovered oil. This commodity, plus significant sources of iron ore, manganese, uranium, and precious woods, gave Gabon an economic boost lacking elsewhere. Due to its modest size and population, it even assumed the dimensions of a mini economic miracle. Unfortunately, as you shall see, the wealth was not evenly spread nor was it always used wisely in the best interests of the nation.

Nonetheless, Gabon has ceased being a backwater and become more prominent in African affairs. Its relations not only with the former colonial power, France, but Europe, America, and the Arab world have grown. Initially its image was enhanced by the strong leadership of President Bongo. As economic and political problems emerged, however, that became more of a hindrance. Just which way Gabon will turn remains uncertain. But this book will certainly help readers understand future events while filling them in on the past. Given the lack of such material in English, it is a particularly useful guide.

This Historical Dictionary of Dr. David E. Gardinier fills an important gap by providing, in a simple and straightforward manner, much of the general data a newcomer would like to have. In some respects, it goes much further and supplies information that would be hard to obtain anywhere else. Certainly the range of leading figures, past and present, make it an exceptional "who's who" of Gabon; the entries on many of its ethnic groups offer unusual insight into its population. Those who wish to know more about Gabon can consult the uniquely complete bibliography.

Dr. Gardinier, a professor of history at Marquette University, has pooled his interests in Equatorial Africa and France to write this volume on Gabon. On the basis of his studies and periodic trips to the region, he has been able not only to collect the necessary information but insert it in a clear and comprehensive framework. This will be appreciated most by those whose first introduction is through the following pages.

Jon Woronoff
Series Editor

PHYSICAL MAP OF GABON

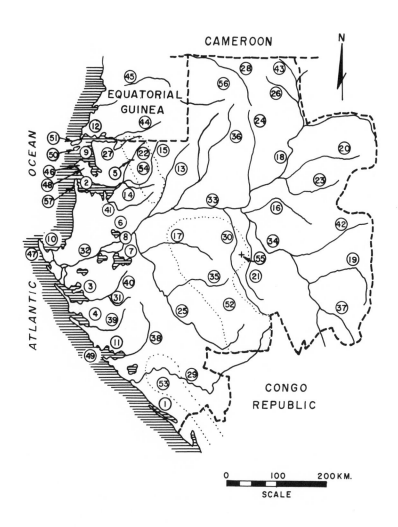

MAP DESIGN - SUSAN R. OHDE

KEY - PHYSICAL MAP OF GABON

BODIES OF WATER

1. BANIO OR MAYUMBA LAGOON
2. ESTUARY
3. FERNAN VAZ LAGOON
4. IGUÉLA LAGOON
5. KINGUÉLÉ FALLS
6. LAKE AZINGO
7. LAKE ONANGUÉ
8. LAKE ZILÉ
9. MONDAH BAY
10. NAZARETH BAY
11. N'DOGO OR SETTÉ-CAMA LAGOON
12. RIO MUNI

RIVERS

13. ABANGA
14. BOKOUÉ
15. COMO
16. DILO
17. IKOY
18. IVINDO
19. LECONI
20. LIBOUMBA
21. LOLO
22. M'BEI
23. MOUNIANGUI
24. MVOUNG
25. N'GOUNIÉ
26. NOUNA
27. NOYA
28. N'TEM
29. NYANGA
30. OFFOUÉ
31. OFOUBOU
32. OGOOUÉ, LOWER
33. OGOOUÉ, MIDDLE
34. OGOOUÉ, UPPER
35. OGOULOU
36. OKANO
37. PASSA OR M'PASSA
38. REMBO N'DOGO
39. REMBO N'GOVE
40. REMBO N'KOMI
41. REMBOUÉ
42. SÉBÉ
43. SINGOUÉ
44. TEMBONI
45. WOLEU

OTHER FEATURES

46. CAPE ESTÉRIAS
47. CAPE LOPEZ
48. CAPE SANTA CLARA
49. CAPE STE. CATHERINE
50. CORISCO ISLAND
51. ELOBEY ISLAND
52. MASSIF DU CHAILLU
53. MAYOMBE MOUNTAINS
54. MONTS DE CRISTAL
55. MONT IBOUNDJI
56. MONT TEMBO
57. POINTE PONGARA

MAP DESIGN-
SUSAN R. OHDE

POLITICAL MAP OF GABON

PROVINCES

1. WOLEU – N'TEM
2. OGOOUÉ – IVINDO
3. ESTUARY

4. MOYEN – OGOOUÉ
5. OGOOUÉ – LOLO
6. OGOOUÉ – MARITIME

7. N'GOUNIÉ
8. HAUT – OGOOUÉ
9. NYANGA

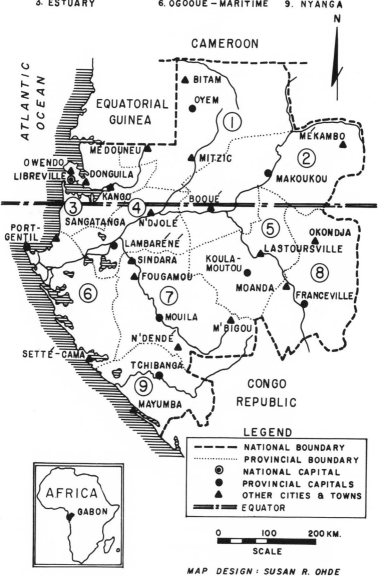

CAMEROON

ATLANTIC OCEAN

EQUATORIAL GUINEA

N

① BITAM
OYEM
MITZIC
MÉKAMBO ②
MAKOUKOU

MÉDOUNEU

OWENDO
LIBREVILLE
DONGUILA
KANGO
BOQUÉ
③
SANGATANGA ④ N'DJOLE
⑤
OKONDJA
LASTOURSVILLE
PORT-GENTIL
LAMBARÉNÉ
SINDARA
KOULA-MOUTOU
⑧
FOUGAMOU
MOANDA
FRANCEVILLE
⑥
⑦
MOUILA
M'BIGOU
SETTÉ-CAMA
N'DENDE
TCHIBANGA
CONGO REPUBLIC
⑨
MAYUMBA

LEGEND

- – – – NATIONAL BOUNDARY
- .... PROVINCIAL BOUNDARY
- ◉ NATIONAL CAPITAL
- ● PROVINCIAL CAPITALS
- ▲ OTHER CITIES & TOWNS
- ═╪═ EQUATOR

AFRICA
GABON

0   100   200 KM.
SCALE

MAP DESIGN : SUSAN R. OHDE

PEOPLES OF GABON

MAP DESIGN - SUSAN R. OHDE

PREFACE TO THE FIRST EDITION

My interest in Gabon originated in 1953 when, as a graduate student at Yale University in the seminar of Professor Harry R. Rudin, I prepared papers on colonial rule in French Equatorial Africa. In 1958, while a student, I published an article in *Current History* on the post-1945 political evolution of the Equatorial African states. After spending the subsequent decade on the political evolution of the French trusteeship territory of Cameroon and the historiography of French colonial rule throughout Africa, I returned in the 1970s to the history of the Equatorial African states, particularly to the development of western education in nineteenth-century Gabon. I have drawn upon material from those researches, most of which are not yet published, for this dictionary. Grants from the Marquette University Graduate School, the Hoover Institution, and the American Philosophical Society enabled me to gather materials in the United States, Europe, and Gabon at various times between 1969 and 1980. A Senior Fulbright Scholarship in Paris during the fall semester of 1979 for a project on education in Francophone Africa gave me the opportunity to secure additional sources and bibliography.

In addition to these institutions, I have received assistance in locating sources and obtaining data from many individuals. In particular, I wish to express my thanks to the following: Dr. David P. Henige, Africana Bibliographer of the Memorial Library, University of Wisconsin, Madison; Rev. Philip Talmage, Mrs. Shirley Arrighetti, Mr. Jack Onufrock, and Mrs. Patricia Bohach of the Marquette University Memorial Library; Mr. Hans E. Panofsky, Mr. Daniel Britz, Mrs. Mette Schayne, and Mrs. Judith Rosenthal of the Herskovits Africana Library of Northwestern University; Professor Brian Weinstein of Howard University; Rev. Leslie King of the Christian and Missionary Alliance, Nyack, New York; Revs. Bernard Noel, Archivist, and Augustin Berger of the Holy Ghost Fathers, Paris; Abbé Jean Moreau and Mlle. Simone Robin of the O.P.M. Library and Archives, Paris; Mlle. J.-M. Léonard, archivist and librarian of the former Société des Missions Evangéliques, Paris; Brothers Macaire Clémenceau, Thouaré-sur-Loire, France, and André Régnier, archivist, Rome, of the Brothers of Saint-Gabriel; Sr. Marie Damien Vallet of the Immaculate Conception Sisters, Rome; Professor Henri Brunschwig, Paris; M. Jean-Hilaire Aubame, Paris; Mlle. Edith Aujames, M. A. Salon, and M. J. Arnaud of the Ministry of Cooperation, Paris.

Dr. Christopher Chamberlin of Washington, D.C., kindly loaned me his dissertation on Gabonese economic history. Professor K. David Patterson of the University of North Carolina at Charlotte, Dr. Henry H. Bucher, Jr., of the African Studies Center at the University of Wisconsin, Madison, and Dr. David Henige read portions of the manuscript. Professor Bruce Fetter of the University of Wisconsin, Milwaukee, shared his extensive knowledge of social change and elite formation in Central Africa. Along with the three readers, he provided encouragement throughout the project. Four research assistants at Marquette University contributed to this dictionary: Lt. Robert McMahon, USN, summarized newspaper sources; Mr. Phillip Chiviges Naylor and Rev. John Steinberger, O.S.M., assembled some of the bibliography; and Mr. Jin Hee-Han typed the original draft.

My wife, Dr. Josefina Z. Sevilla, deserves special credit for suggesting some of the entries and for helping to improve others. She and our children—Kenneth, Annemarie, and Lourdes Marie—gave moral support during my absence gathering materials on three continents and during my presence writing up and typing the results. Eventually I hope to have a book on education in Gabon to dedicate to them, but I would like to dedicate this dictionary to my parents, Mrs. Velma Austin, and the late Kenneth Gardinier, whose sacrifices and encouragement aided the graduate education where my interest in the history of Gabon first developed.

David E. Gardinier
Brookfield, Wisconsin

PREFACE TO THE SECOND EDITION

During the decade since the publication of the first edition of this Historical Dictionary, I have continued to publish articles and chapters concerning missions and education in Gabon. I have drawn upon their data in revising some of the entries for this edition. But the bulk of the revisions and most of the new material derive from an array of new writing on Gabon that equals in volume the publications of the previous 35 years. In particular, I have made a very real effort to provide information that would aid understanding of the recent upheaval in Gabon from a historical perspective. A grant from the Marquette University Graduate School for another project made it possible for me to consult libraries in Paris during April-May 1990. A grant from the African Studies Program of the University of Wisconsin-Madison in the summer of 1991 aided access to French-language periodicals.

As in the case of the first edition, I have received invaluable assistance in locating sources and obtaining data from many individuals. In particular, I wish to express my thanks to the following: Dr. David P. Henige, Africana bibliographer, and the staff of the Memorial Library of the University of Wisconsin-Madison; Rev. Philip Talmage, Mrs. Maria Dittman, and Mrs. Susan Hopwood of the Marquette University Library; the staff of the periodicals section of the Golda Meir Library at the University of Wisconsin-Milwaukee; Mr. Hans E. Panofsky, Mr. Daniel Britz, and Mrs. Mette Schayne of the Herskovits Africana Library of Northwestern University; Rev. David Moore of the Christian and Missionary Alliance in Denver, Colorado; Dr. Michael C. Reed of the University of Washington; Dr. Max Liniger-Goumaz of Lausanne, Switzerland; also, to the following in Paris: Mme. Zofia Yaranga of the Centre d'Etudes Africaines; Mlle. Martine Merthillot, and Mme. Monique Bauer of the Ministry of Cooperation; Mlle. Laurence Porgès and the staff of the Centre de Documentation at the Quai Voltaire; the late M. Robert Cornevin and the staff of the Académie des Sciences d'Outre-Mer; the staff of the International Institute of Educational Planning, UNESCO; Mme. Marie-Christine Held and Mlle. Annemarie Gratiot at the D.E.F.A.P., boulevard Arago; Mlle. Michèle Lesoeur of the Oeuvres Pontificales et Missionnaires.

In Paris also M. François Gaulme, editor-in-chief of *Marchés Tropicaux et Méditerranéens,* provided valuable insights concerning contemporary Gabon. Rev. Jean-François Zorn loaned me his dissertation on the missions of the Société des Missions Evangéliques prior to 1914. Dr. Henry H. Bucher, Jr., of Austin College again drew upon his encyclopedic knowledge of the Mpongwe for my benefit. Professor Bruce Fetter of the University of Wisconsin-Milwaukee shared his extensive knowledge of the historical demography of Central and Equatorial Africa. My wife, Dr. Josefina Z. Sevilla, of the Milwaukee Area Technical College, helped to improve entries on science and medicine. Mr. Stephen Leahy, a research assistant at Marquette University, typed the bibliography and some of the revisions while assembling the manuscript. My wife and children again gave moral support during my absence gathering materials and during my presence writing up and typing the results. They performed some of the tasks that would ordinarily have been mine so that this second edition could see the light of day more quickly.

David E. Gardinier
Brookfield, Wisconsin

NOTE ON SPELLING

The absence of any universally accepted system of transliteration of African names into French or English and the development of variant spellings through the centuries that Europeans have been in Equatorial Africa pose problems for any author who wishes to achieve accuracy and consistency.

Because French is the official language of Gabon, I have used the French transliteration for places and individuals. In the case of variant spellings, I have followed the usage in F. Meyo-Bibang and J.-M. Nzamba's *Notre Pays, Le Gabon* (1975). For the names of some of the Bantu peoples, one is faced with the additional problem of whether to use the basic stem or the plural—e.g., Kota or Bakota. In this case I have chosen the form most widely used in the sources I have consulted. Thus I have found Bakèlè, Bakota, and Bapounou more frequently used than Kèlè, Kota, and Pounou, on the one hand, and Loumbou, Téké, and Vili more often than Baloumbou, Batéké, and Bavili, on the other. To aid the reader, I have given both forms in some cases—e.g., Bakota or Kota, Loumbou or Baloumbou.

NOTE ON GABONESE NAMES

During the 1970s and 1980s a larger number of Gabonese adopted the practice of adding the family name of their mother after that of their father. Thus in the case of Casimir Oyé-Mba, Oyé is the name of his father's family and Mba the name of his mother's family. Some individuals hyphenate the two family names. In such cases the first name is generally that of the father's family but not always. President Bongo continues to use only the family name of his father.

ABBREVIATIONS AND ACRONYMS

ABCFM	American Board of Commissioners for Foreign Missions
ACCT	Agence Culturelle pour Coopération Technique
ACP	African, Caribbean, and Pacific (Countries)
AEF	Afrique Equatoriale Française
AGEG	Association Générale des Etudiants du Gabon
AGP	Agence Gabonaise de Presse
APEEG	Association des Parents d'Elèves et d'Etudiants du Gabon
APSG	Association pour le Socialisme au Gabon
BDG	Bloc Démocratique Gabonais
BEAC	Banque des Etats de l'Afrique Centrale
BEPC	Brevet d'Etudes du Premier Cycle
BGD	Banque Gabonaise de Développement
CAC	Christian Alliance Church
CAR	Central African Republic
CCCE	Caisse Centrale de Coopération Economique
CCFOM	Caisse Centrale de la France d'Outre-Mer
CEEAC	Communauté Economique des Etats de l'Afrique Centrale
CFA	Colonies Françaises Africaines; Communauté Financière Africaine
CFTC	Confédération Française des Travailleurs Chrétiens
CGAT	Confédération Générale Aéfienne du Travail; Confédération Générale Africaine du Travail
CGT	Confédération Générale du Travail
CGT-FO	Confédération Générale du Travail—Force Ouvrière
CICIBA	Centre International des Civilisations Bantu
CIRMF	Centre International de Recherches Médicales de Franceville

CMA	Christian & Missionary Alliance
CMG	Comité Mixte Gabonais
CNTG	Confédération Nationale des Travailleurs Gabonais
COGEMA	Compagnie Générale des Matières Nucléaires
COGES	Comité Gabonais d'Etudes Sociales et Economiques
COMILOG	Compagnie Minière de l'Ogooué
COMUF	Compagnie des Mines d'Uranium de Franceville
COSYGA	Confédération Syndicale Gabonaise
EC	European Community (CE in French)
EDF	European Development Fund (FED in French)
EEC	European Economic Community (CEE in French)
EIB	European Investment Bank (BEI in French)
ENA	Ecole Nationale d'Administration
FAC	Fonds d'Aide et de Coopération
FAO	Food and Agriculture Organization
FEA	French Equatorial Africa
FEANF	Fédération des Etudiants d'Afrique Noire
FESAC	Fondation de l'Enseignement Supérieur en Afrique Centrale
FESYGA	Fédération Syndicale Gabonaise
FIDES	Fonds d'Investissement pour le Développement Economique et Sociale
GEC	Groupe d'Etudes Communistes
IOM	Indépendants d'Outre-Mer
MB	MORENA des Bûcherons
MO	MORENA Originel
MORENA	Mouvement de Redressement National
OAMCE	Organisation Africaine et Malgache pour la Coopération Economique
OAU	Organization of African Unity
OCTRA	Office du Chemin de Fer Transgabonais
ORSTOM	Office de la Recherche Scientique et Technique d'Outre-Mer
PBFM	Presbyterian Board of Foreign Missions
PDA	Parti Démocratique Africain
PDG	Parti Démocratique Gabonais
PGP	Parti Gabonais du Progrès
PUNGA	Parti d'Union Nationale Gabonaise

RDA	Rassemblement Démocratique Africain
RGR	Rassemblement des Gauches Républicains
RNB	Rassemblement National des Bûcherons
RPF	Rassemblement du Peuple Français
RSDG	Rassemblement Social et Démocratique Gabonais
SEDECE	Service de Detection et Contre-Espionage
SEEG	Société d'Eau et d'Energie du Gabon
SHO	Société Commerciale, Industrielle, et Agricole du Haut-Ogooué
SME	Société des Missions Evangéliques
SNBG	Société Nationale des Bois du Gabon
SNEA	Société Nationale Elf-Aquitaine
SOGARA	Société Gabonaise de Raffinage
SOGAREM	Société Gabonaise de Recherches et d'Exploitation Minières
SOMIFER	Société des Mines de Fer de Mekambo
SONADIG	Société Nationale des Investisseurs du Gabon
UAM	Union Africaine et Malgache
UDE	Union Douanière Equatoriale
UDEAC	Union Douanière Economique de l'Afrique Centrale
UDSG	Union Démocratique et Sociale Gabonaise
UDSR	Union Démocratique et Sociale de la Résistance
UGSC	Union Gabonaise des Syndicats Croyants
UNSC	Union Nationale des Syndicats Croyants
UPG	Union du Peuple Gabonais
URAC	Union des Républiques d'Afrique Centrale
USC	Union des Syndicats Confédérés
USG	Union Socialiste Gabonaise

CHRONOLOGY

1472	Portuguese arrive in the Estuary of the Gabon or Como River.
1482	Diego Cam reaches mouth of the Zaire or Congo River.
1760s to 1840s	Atlantic slave trade reaches its height.
1778	Portugal cedes to Spain its claims to the coasts between the Niger and Ogooué rivers.
Feb. 9, 1839 & Mar. 18, 1842	Mpongwe clan heads, Kings Denis & Louis, cede sovereignty to France.
1840s and 1850s	Fang descend northern tributaries of the Como River.
June 22, 1842	American Protestants (ABCFM of Boston) found mission at Baraka in Estuary and open schools.
June 11, 1843	French found post, Fort d'Aumale, in Estuary.
Sept. 28, 1844	French Catholic missionaries (Holy Ghost Fathers) arrive near Fort d'Aumale.
July 31, 1849	Immaculate Conception Sisters of Castres, France, arrive near Fort d'Aumale.
Aug. 1849	French found Libreville as settlement for Vili liberated from slave traders.
Sept. 18, 1852	Benga clan heads at Cape Esterias make treaty with French.
June 1, 1862	Orungu chiefs at Cape Lopez make treaty with French.
Jan. 18, 1868	Nkomi chiefs at Fernan Vaz make treaty with French.
July 27, 1870	American Presbyterians assume the missionary field of the ABCFM.
1874	Dr. Robert Nassau founds Presbyterian mis-

	sion above Lambaréné in the middle Ogooué.
1875–1885	Savorgnan de Brazza explores the Ogooué and Congo Basins.
Jan. 7, 1880	Ntâkâ Truman first Mpongwe ordained a Presbyterian pastor.
Feb. 1881	Catholic missionaries found a post at Lambaréné.
Mar. 12, 1883	Vili chiefs at Loango make treaty with French; Catholic missionaries found a post there.
Dec. 12, 1885	Franco-German treaty fixes frontier with Cameroons.
Apr. 1886	French Congo established with Gabon as autonomous colony.
July 1889	Fang bring first okoumé to Libreville for export to Europe.
1892–1893	Presbyterians transfer their Ogooué missions to French Protestants (SME of Paris).
1893	Société du Haut-Ogooué receives concession over vast areas.
Mar. 15, 1894	Franco-German agreement further defines frontier with the Cameroons.
1894	Jean-Rémy Rapontchombo first Gabonese to earn a *baccalauréat* in France.
1895–1899	Catholics establish missions in the N'Gounié River Basin.
July 23, 1899	André Raponda Walker is the first Gabonese to be ordained a Catholic priest.
1899	Concessionary system extended throughout Gabon.
June 27, 1900	Franco-Spanish convention defines frontier with Spanish Guinea (Rio Muni).
Oct. 1900	Brothers of Saint-Gabriel open the Ecole Montfort in Libreville.
July 1, 1904	Capital of French Congo transferred to Brazzaville.

1907	First public school opens in Libreville.
Jan. 15, 1910	Gabon becomes part of the federation of French Equatorial Africa.
1913	Dr. Albert Schweitzer begins his medical mission at Lambaréné.
1918	Loango coast transferred from Gabon to the Middle Congo.
1918	Jean-Félix Tchicaya and Hervé Mapako-Gnali sent to the Ponty School in Senegal.
1918	Libreville branch of the Ligue des Droits de l'Homme founded.
1921–1934	Forced labor for construction of the Congo-Ocean Railroad.
1922	Léon Mba named Fang canton chief at Libreville.
1922	Laurent Antchouey and Louis Bigmann found *L'Echo Gabonais* at Dakar.
Apr. 15, 1925	Haut-Ogooué Region transferred to the Middle Congo.
1928–1929	Awandji revolt against administrative and concessionary exactions.
1930	World depression hits Gabon and the okoumé industry.
1933	Léon Mba exiled to Ubangi-Shari.
1933	Americans from the Christian and Missionary Alliance enter the N'Gounié River valley.
1935	First Gabonese enroll at the Ecole Renard at Brazzaville.
1935–1936	The Great Revival throughout northern Gabon.
Oct. 1937	François-de-Paul Vané wins election to the Governor-General's Council of Administration.
Sept.–Nov. 1940	Free French defeat Vichy supporters and gain control of Gabon.
1942	Governor-General Félix Eboué creates the first public school with grades seven to ten.

Jan. 30 to Feb. 8, 1944	Brazzaville Conference considers reforms for Black Africa.
Nov. 18, 1945	Jean-Félix Tchicaya elected to the First Constituent Assembly.
Apr. 11, 1946	Forced labor abolished.
May 7, 1946	Black Africans made French citizens.
July 5, 1946	FIDES formed to make public investments in Black Africa.
Oct. 13, 1946	Gabon becomes Overseas Territory of the Fourth French Republic.
Oct. 16, 1946	Haut-Ogooué Region returned to Gabon; Gabon's international boundaries fixed.
Nov. 1946	Jean-Hilaire Aubame first elected to French National Assembly.
Dec. 1946	First elections held for Territorial Assembly.
1947	Comité Mixte Gabonais founded by Léon Mba.
Sept. 1947	Union Démocratique et Sociale Gabonaise founded by Jean-Hilaire Aubame.
Sept. 1953	COMILOG created to exploit the manganese of Franceville (exploitation begins in 1962).
Apr. 1954	Bloc Démocratique Gabonais founded by Senator Paul Gondjout.
1956	SOMIFER organized to exploit the iron of Mékambo.
Jan. 1956	First petroleum produced in Port-Gentil area.
Nov. 1956	Elections for municipal governments with African mayors.
Dec. 1956	Uranium discovered in the Haut-Ogooué (production begins in 1961).
Apr. 1957	First Executive Council with Léon Mba as its top African official.
Sept. 28, 1958	Gabon votes for membership in the French Community; federation of F.E.A. abolished.
Nov. 29, 1958	Gabon becomes an autonomous republic with Léon Mba as prime minister.

1959	Evangelical Church of South Gabon becomes independent.
Feb. 19, 1959	Constitution with a parliamentary system adopted.
June 23, 1959	Gabon organizes a customs union with the three other Equatorial African states.
July 15, 1960	Gabon signs cooperation agreements with France.
Aug. 17, 1960	Gabon becomes independent republic.
Sept. 20, 1960	Gabon admitted to United Nations membership.
Nov. 15, 1960	François Ndong named the first Gabonese Catholic bishop.
Nov. 16–17, 1960	Mba arrests Gondjout, president of the National Assembly, and other ministers despite their parliamentary immunity.
1961	Evangelical Church of Gabon achieves independence.
Feb. 12, 1961	Legislative elections.
Feb. 21, 1961	Constitution with a presidential regime adopted.
Dec. 12, 1961	Gabon organizes FESAC with three other Equatorial African states.
June 1963	Gabon joins the Organization of African Unity.
Jan. 21, 1964	Mba dissolves the National Assembly and orders new elections.
Feb. 17–20, 1964	Military coup leads to French intervention to restore President Mba.
Apr. 12, 1964	BDG wins majority of seats in assembly elections.
Dec. 8, 1964	Gabon forms UDEAC with Cameroon and the three Equatorial African states.
Sept. 4, 1965	Death of Albert Schweitzer at Lambaréné.
Nov. 11, 1966	Mba names Albert Bongo to replace Paul-Marie Yembit as vice president of the government.
Feb. 16, 1967	Constitution amended to create position of vice president of the republic.
Mar. 19, 1967	Mba reelected president and Bongo elected

	vice president of the republic; BDG wins all seats in the National Assembly elections.
Nov. 28, 1967	Death of Mba elevates Bongo to the presidency.
Dec. 13, 1967	Vice presidency of the republic suppressed.
Mar. 12, 1968	After abolishing existing parties, Bongo establishes a single party, the Parti Démocratique Gabonais.
Nov. 9, 1968	Position of vice president of the government reinstituted.
1970s	Thousands of Equatorial Guineans seek refuge from the Macias regime.
Aug. 1970	University of Libreville created.
July 29, 1972	Constitution amended to institutionalize PDG's role in government.
Jan. 18–20, 1973	First Extraordinary Congress of the PDG.
Feb. 25, 1973	Bongo reelected president and a new National Assembly elected.
Feb. 12, 1974	New cooperation agreements signed with France.
Apr. 15, 1975	Constitutional amendments further define institutional role of the PDG in government and create position of prime minister.
1977	Recession linked to downturn in petroleum income begins.
July 1977	Air Gabon created.
July 1978	Expulsion of 11,000 Béninois (Dahomeyans).
Sept. 1978	First section of the Transgabonais Railroad opens to N'Djolé.
Jan. 24–27, 1979	Second Extraordinary Congress of PDG discusses economic crisis.
Mar. 11, 1979	Opening of deep-water port at Owendo.
Nov. 18, 1979	Second Ordinary Congress of the PDG.
Dec. 30, 1979	Bongo reelected president.
Feb. 20, 1980	Legislative elections held.
Dec. 10, 1980	Elections for provincial, departmental, and municipal assemblies held.

Feb. 7, 1981	Opening of Africa No. 1 at Moyabi.
Feb. 8, 1981	New agreement for scientific and technical cooperation signed with France.
Mar. 24–30, 1981	Ten thousand Cameroonians repatriated in the wake of violence emanating from a football match.
August 17, 1981	Constitutional revision makes the prime minister head of government; Bongo relinquishes multiple cabinet posts.
Dec. 1981	Surfacing of opposition party, the Mouvement pour le Redressement National (MORENA).
Feb. 17–18, 1982	Visit of Pope John Paul II.
Nov. 26, 1982	Condemnation of MORENA members to 20 years at hard labor.
1983	Opening of a deep-water port at Port-Gentil.
Jan. 1983	Creation of the International Center of Bantu Civilization (CICIBA).
Jan. 17, 1983	Opening of the Transgabonais to Booué.
Mar. 1983	Third Extraordinary Congress of the PDG takes up the challenge of MORENA; constitutional revision making PDG the sole legal party.
Oct.–Dec. 1983	Crisis in relations with France in wake of publication of *Affaires Africaines*.
Oct. 17, 1983	Creation of the Economic Community of the States of Central Africa (CEEAC).
Dec. 1983	Estates-General of Education summoned to propose solutions to educational problems.
Jan. 1985	Bongo's speech denouncing Lebanese merchants sparks looting of their shops.
Mar. 3, 1985	Legislative elections held.
Aug. 9, 1985	MORENA in Paris forms government-in-exile.
Aug. 11, 1985	Execution of Captain Alexandre Mandja, convicted of plotting to assassinate the president.

Aug. 1985	Discovery of vast new oil reserves at Rabi-Kounga.
1986	Start of a prolonged economic recession linked to downturn in petroleum prices and a weak dollar.
Sept. 1986	Third Ordinary Congress of the PDG.
Nov. 1986	Bongo reelected president.
Dec. 30, 1986	Inauguration of the Transgabonais to Franceville.
1987	Opening of the Scientific and Technical University at Masuku.
June 28, 1987	Local elections held with competing lists within the PDG.
Oct. 7, 1987	Discovery of lode of rare metals near Lambaréné.
Dec. 13, 1988	Discovery of lode of phosphates at Lambaréné.
Dec. 30, 1988	Opening of minerals port at Owendo.
May 1989	Father Paul Mba-Abessolé returns after 12 years in exile for talks with Bongo.
Aug. 1989	Ending of the schism in the Evangelical Church of Gabon.
Oct.–Nov. 1989	Uncovering of two related plots to assassinate the president and overturn his regime.
Jan. 14, 1990	Third Extraordinary Congress of PDG Central Committee reaffirms necessity of one-party regime but creates special commission on democracy.
Jan. 16–20, 1990	Student protests at the Omar Bongo University leave dozens wounded and spark pillaging in the popular quarters of Libreville.
Mar. 1990	Intensification of strikes and popular demonstrations against the policies of the Bongo regime.
Mar. 23, 1990	Opening of national conference involving both PDG and opposition groups to plan reforms.
Apr. 27, 1990	New government headed by Casimir Oyé-

	Mba includes ministers from opposition parties.
May 17–20, 1990	Fourth Extraordinary Congress of PDG.
May 22, 1990	Constitutional amendments restore multi-partyism.
May 23, 1990	Death in suspicious circumstances of opposition leader Joseph Rendjambe produces violent reactions, particularly at Port-Gentil.
May 24, 1990	French military intervention at Port-Gentil to protect French lives and property.
May 29, 1990	Presidential Guard restores order among the African population of Port-Gentil.
June 20–24, 1990	First Congress of MORENA elects Paul Mba president.
Sept. 16, Oct. 21 and 28, 1990	Elections for a new National Assembly, marred by widespread irregularities, result in slight PDG majority.
Nov. 20–21, 1990	New National Assembly containing opposition deputies takes office; Oyé-Mba renamed prime minister.
Dec. 15, 1990	Conviction of the accused in the plots of 1989.
Jan. 21, 1991	Faction of MORENA headed by Father Mba becomes the Rassemblement National des Bûcherons.
Mar. 5, 1991	National Assembly unanimously approves a new semi-presidential constitution.
June 5, 1991	General strike called by opposition parties forces government to accelerate implementation of the new constitution.
June 28, 1991	New government conforming to the constitution invested by the National Assembly; Oyé-Mba remains prime minister.
July 1991	National Assembly creates a nine-member Constitutional Court.
Aug. 1991	Fifth Extraordinary Congress of the PDG.
Oct. 1991	National Assembly establishes the National

	Council for Communications to protect basic liberties.
Oct. 5–7, 1991	Franco-African summit of heads of state held in Libreville.
June 6, 1992	National Assembly passes new labor law permitting strikes and independent unions.
Oct. 1992	Ten thousand illegal immigrants forced to return to Nigeria.

TABLES

TABLE 1.   GABON: NATIONAL BUDGETS, 1960–1980
(in millions of francs CFA)

Year	Functioning	Equipment	Total
1960	4,072	536	4,608
1961	5,104	782	5,886
1962	5,889	1,010	6,899
1963	6,835	2,362	9,197
1964	7,957	2,554	10,511
1965	8,587	3,405	11,992
1966	10,858	1,939	12,797
1967	11,534	2,903	14,437
1968	12,116	4,484	16,600
1969	12,736	5,061	17,797
1970	14,218	5,785	20,003
1971	16,661	7,862	24,523
1972	19,227	11,776	31,003
1973	22,213	14,730	36,943
1974	27,081	20,663	47,744
1975	44,185	107,263	151,448
1976	58,717	134,396	193,113
1977	84,582	171,210	255,792
1978	226,000	63,800	289,800
1979	238,000	90,000	328,000
1980	221,710	92,000	313,710
1981	275,200	136,000	411,200
1982	282,500	193,700	476,200
1983	332,300	250,400	582,700
1984	360,200	338,800	699,000
1985*	220,700	403,500	715,000
1986*	248,500	367,900	687,400
1987*	211,000	97,300	369,200
1988*	207,000	66,200	341,900
1989*	202,000	68,600	347,200
1990*	216,000	89,000	341,500
1991	223,000	77,000	434,000
1992	219,000	74,000	398,000 (est.)
1993	234,000	85,000	398,500 (est.)

*Annual totals include amounts for debt service, which were as follows: 1985 41,200; 1986 47,200; 1987 52,800; 1988 68,600; 1989 76,600; 1990 36,500. The budget deficits, financed by foreign loans, were as follows: 1985 83,500; 1986 184,700; 1987 105,700; 1988 95,300; 1989 88,600; 1990 48,000.
Sources: 1960–1966 [723]; 1967–1973 [1373]; 1974–1977 [698]; 1978–1980 [661, 680]; 1981–1991 [65, 1365]. (Bracketed numbers refer to the Bibliography.)

TABLE 2.   GABON: VALUE OF EXPORTS AND IMPORTS, 1960–1978
(in millions of francs CFA)

Year	Exports (f.o.b.)	Imports (c.i.f.)
1960	11,826	7,829
1961	13,627	8,853
1962	14,627	10,067
1963	18,125	11,875
1964	22,540	13,742
1965	25,905	15,425
1966	25,920	16,384
1967	29,516	16,585
1968	30,714	15,875
1969	36,663	20,127
1970	33,610	22,139
1971	51,829	26,810
1972	50,297	34,106
1973	63,925	36,977
1974	234,900	85,450
1975	201,921	100,529
1976	272,449	120,237
1977	329,800	176,001
1978	295,300	139,200
1979	377,000	113,100
1980	523,900	179,700
1981	597,000	228,000
1982	709,000	237,000
1983	762,000	276,000
1984	891,000	320,000
1985	876,700	384,000
1986	372,000	339,000
1987	386,600	220,000
1988	356,100	235,700
1989	518,700	239,800
1990	675,400	209,200

Sources: 1960–1966 [723]; 1967–1972 [1373]; 1972–1976 [1308]; 1977–1978 [1364]; 1978–1990 [1364,1365]. Statistics after 1966 exclude gold and trade with the members of UDEAC. (Bracketed numbers refer to the Bibliography.)

TABLE 3.   GABON; PRODUCTION OF FUELS AND MINERALS, 1960–
1980 (in thousands of metric tons for petroleum & manganese; metric tons for
uranium; kilograms for gold; & thousand cubic meters for natural gas)

Year	Petroleum	Natural Gas	Manganese	Uranium	Gold
1960	800	7,451	—	—	550
1961	774	6,700	—	969	475
1962	827	8,790	203	1,161	507
1963	890	8,612	637	1,317	1,111
1964	1,058	9,457	948	1,288	1,130
1965	1,264	10,647	1,275	1,644	1,155
1966	1,447	11,493	1,268	1,599	1,071
1967	3,444	17,422	1,147	1,452	910
1968	4,642	24,871	1,254	1,371	513
1969	5,030	25,000 (est.)	1,377	1,388	443
1970	5,364	25,000	1,453	1,077	501
1971	5,785	30,539	1,866	1,274	421
1972	6,304	34,460	1,936	523	355
1973	7,598	39,449	1,919	1,412	349
1974	10,202	45,624	2,119	1,713	227
1975	11,315	47,429	2,220	1,766	131
1976	11,325	239,417	2,280	1,297	
1977	11,070	684,277	2,080	1,850	
1978	10,600	61,900	1,661	1,407	
1979	9,800	61,000	2,300	1,100	
1980	8,900	72,000	2,163	1,050	
1981	7,650	78,000	1,488	1,022	
1982	7,800	82,000	1,506	970	
1983	7,850	81,000	1,862	1,006	
1984	8,725	65,000	2,110	940	
1985	8,630	71,000	2,330	969	
1986	8,300	72,000	2,510	900	
1987	7,760	73,000	2,590	794	
1988	7,970	73,000	2,250	929	
1989	10,227	87,600	2,250	862	
1990	13,494	85,700	2,214	709	
1991	13,493 (est.)			679	

Sources: 1960–1966 [723]; 1967–1977 [1308]; 1978–1990 [1364, 1365]. (Bracketed
numbers refer to the Bibliography.)

TABLE 4.   GABON: EXPORTABLE PRODUCTION OF FOREST AND
AGRICULTURAL PRODUCTS, 1960–1979
(in metric tons for okoumé, cocoa, coffee, & palm oil; in cubic meters for ozigo)

Year	Okoumé	Ozigo	Cocoa	Coffee	Palm Oil
1960	736,673	47,000	2,578	655	384
1961	782,000	45,000	4,022	712	307
1962	700,000	35,000	2,442	540	425
1963	761,000	54,000	3,742	730	555
1964	821,000	72,000	4,021	847	1,067
1965	794,000	53,501	3,778	366	1,146
1966	787,000		3,832	244	1,103
1967	750,000		4,794	306	1,123
1968	842,000		4,091	267	1,374
1969	927,983	59,542	5,050	292	1,890
1970	922,245	68,326	5,176	486	326
1971	1,023,939	66,025	6,095	485	155
1972	1,141,216	96,213	5,031	642	
1973	1,081,011	138,323	3,733	538	
1974	1,025,520	109,314	5,553	258	
1975	1,020,000	86,803	4,869	103	
1976	1,090,000	73,750	2,549	480	1,520
1977	1,100,000	75,000	3,573	360	1,450
1978	1,224,924*	668,700	3,718	502	1,380
1979	1,192,000*	55,080	4,532	233	1,400
1980	1,221,000	62,676	3,814	580	1,400
1981	1,010,000	48,000	2,934	522	1,800
1982	1,022,000	47,000	2,900	1,850	1,800
1983	1,035,000	60,000	2,460	1,400	
1984	1,037,000	45,000	1,565	767	2,655
1985	977,000	49,000	1,520	2,241	4,700
1986	957,000	56,000	1,775	2,201	8,400 (est.)
1987	886,000	40,000	1,745	698	
1988	989,000	52,000	1,570	1,621	
1989	944,000	48,000	1,911	1,789	
1990	1,137,000	61,000	1,592	254	10,400
1991	918,563	68,000	1,309		15,000 (est.)

*Cubic meters

Sources: Okoume & Ozigo, 1960–1966 [723]; 1967–1974 [1412]; 1975–1991 [1308, 1364,
1365]; Cocoa, Coffee, and Palm Oil, 1960–1966 [723], 1967–1975 [929, 1412]; 1976–
1991 [1308, 1364, 1365]. (Bracketed numbers refer to the Bibliography.)

TABLE 5.   GABON: AREA AND POPULATION OF THE NINE
PROVINCES (1960 & 1970 CENSUSES)

Province	Area in km^2	-1960-		-1970-	
		Population	Density per km^2	Population	Density per km^2
Estuary	20,740	60,600	2.9	194,976	9.4
Ogooué-Maritime	22,890	41,600	1.8	120,371	5.2
Woleu-N'Tem	38,465	78,000	2.0	148,287	3.8
N'Gounié	37,750	79,100	2.1	129,859	3.4
Haut-Ogooué	36,547	43,000	1.2	127,133	3.4
Nyanga	21,285	37,700	1.8	66,517	3.1
Moyen-Ogooué	18,535	34,100	1.8	51,551	2.7
Ogooué-Lolo	25,380	36,800	1.4	51,523	2.0
Ogooué-Ivindo	46,075	35,800	0.8	59,792	1.2
TOTAL	267,667	448,564	1.7	950,009	3.5

Source: [929]. (Bracketed number refers to the Bibliography.)

TABLE 6.   GABON: POPULATION OF THE NINE PROVINCES
(1980 CENSUS & ESTIMATES)

Province	1980 Census	1980 Administrative Estimates	1980 Health Officials' Estimates
Estuary	229,600	200,000	173,350
Ogooué-Maritime	142,240	75,000	108,500
Woleu-N'Tem	174,720	116,000	99,000
N'Gounié	154,560	82,000	89,700
Haut-Ogooué	150,080	74,300	68,100
Nyanga	78,400	39,400	37,200
Moyen-Ogooué	60,480	32,600	31,000
Ogooué-Lolo	59,360	38,800	33,650
Ogooué-Ivindo	70,560	41,000	39,500
TOTAL	1,120,000	699,100	680,000

Source: [940]. (Bracketed number refers to the Bibliography.)

INTRODUCTION

Location

Gabon is located in western Equatorial Africa. It lies astride the equator between 2°30′ North latitude and 4° South latitude and between 9° and 14° West longitude. The average distance from north to south is 550 km. and from east to west, 600 km. On the western side the Atlantic Ocean stretches along 800 km. of frequently indented coast. To the northwest lies Equatorial Guinea; to the north, Cameroon; and to the east and south, the Congo (the capital of which is Brazzaville). The boundaries between Gabon and these three states separate the sources of several important rivers from their outlets along the Atlantic as well as divide ethnic groups, for they were drawn by France, Germany, and Spain in the late nineteenth century without much knowledge of the geography and peoples of the interior.

Area

European competition gave Gabon an area of 267,667 sq. km., or 103,000 sq. mi., that is, about half the size of France or equivalent to the American state of Colorado. Gabon is three-fifths the size of Cameroon and three-quarters the size of the Congo Republic, but it has nine times the area of Equatorial Guinea. Thus it is one of the smaller central African countries but by no means the smallest.

Climate

Gabon possesses an equatorial climate with uniformly high temperatures (averaging 26°C or 78°F), high relative humidities, and mean annual rainfalls from 150 to 300 cm. It has two rainy seasons (from mid-February to mid-May and from mid-September to mid-December) and two dry seasons (from mid-May to mid-September and from mid-December to mid-February).

Physical Features

Like the other western and equatorial African countries that border the Atlantic, Gabon is watered by systems of rivers and streams that empty into the ocean. Supreme among them is the Ogooué River, which with its many tributaries drains close to four-fifths of the country (220,000 sq. km.). Its largest southern tributary is the N'Gounié River, which joins it 150 km. upstream, and its largest northern tributary is the Ivindo, which enters much farther east at a point 350 km. from the coast. The two other river systems of most significance are the Como, or Gabon, River to the north of the Ogooué, whose broad mouth has been known historically as "the Estuary," and the Nyanga River to the south. The far north is drained by the Woleu and N'Tem rivers, which rise within Gabon but reach the Atlantic through Equatorial Guinea and Cameroon, respectively, and streams such as the Noya and the Temboni, which form the Rio Muni or Muni Estuary between Gabon and Equatorial Guinea. South of the several mouths or estuary of the Ogooué lie several small rivers (the Rembo N'komi, Rembo N'gove, and the N'dogo), which empty into the lagoons of Fernan Vaz, Iguéla, and N'dogo, or Setté-Cama, respectively. Only a very small portion of the southeast is drained by streams flowing into the northern tributaries of the Congo River system. Though Gabon has many waterways, most of them are cut at various points by falls and rapids, which make large portions of them unnavigable. For example, the Ogooué though 1,200 km. in length, is navigable without interruption only one-third of this distance, that is, from the estuary to the island of N'Djolé.

These rivers flow through a terrain whose relief can be separated into three regions of unequal area: plains, plateaux, and mountains. First of all, there is a low-lying coastal plain 30 to 200 km. in width that nowhere exceeds 300 meters in elevation. This plain is narrowest in the far south and broadest in the estuaries of the Como (Gabon) and Ogooué rivers. Plains also extend toward the interior through the valleys of the Nyanga, N'Gounié, and Ogooué, in the last case to within 100 km. of the frontier with the Congo Republic. Plateaux at altitudes from 300 to 800 meters cover most of the remainder of the country, in particular the north and east. Out of them rise two mountain chains, the Monts de Cristal in the north and the Massif du Chaillu in the south, separated by the Ogooué river valley. The highest point in Gabon is Mount Iboundji (1,575 meters) in the Massif du Chaillu, and Mount Tembo near Oyem in the Monts de Cristal has 1,300 meters. In the extreme southwest parallel to the coast and flanking the Nyanga River is the less elevated Mayombe chain, the bulk of which extends into the Congo Republic. The mountains are covered with dense tropical rainforest as is nearly three-fourths of the country. Grasslands, or savannas, cover one-fifth, mainly the upper Ogooué around Franceville, the upper N'Gounié above Mouila, and in the middle Nyanga river valley—especially beyond Tchibanga. Along the coast north of the Nyanga River stretches a narrow zone of marshes and mangrove trees.

Beneath the coastal plains and offshore lie cretaceous sedimentary rocks, which south of Port Gentil have yielded petroleum and natural gas at shallow depth. Gabon's other important minerals (manganese, iron, uranium, gold) derive from the interior areas of Precambrian rocks. The heavy rains and high relative humidities have tended to leach the soil in most parts of the country, which has led to the practice of shifting cultivation.

Population

The total population of Gabon is a matter of dispute. The 1960–1961 census showed 448,564 inhabitants, including several thousand Europeans and several thousand non-Gabonese Africans. The United Nations estimated the annual natural rate of increase to be .007 during the 1960s. Thus the 1970–1971 census should have revealed a population of approximately half a million. Instead it showed 950,000 inhabitants, a total that the United Nations and its agencies refused to accept. Subsequent to the 1970–1971 census Gabon experienced an economic boom, which brought many more thousands of Europeans and non-Gabonese Africans into the country. In 1978 there were approximately 30,000 Europeans, including 21,000 French; 60,000 Equatorial Guineans, most of them refugees from the Macias regime (1968–1979); and approximately 20,000 other non-Gabonese Africans. Some western observers, who consider that the methodology of the 1960–1961 census overlooked many thousands of persons, especially in the lumbering camps, estimated the population at 750,000 to 800,000 in 1978. The UN estimate of 650,000 was considerably lower. Then, in 1980 a government census produced the figures of 1,120,000 Gabonese and 112,000 foreigners, for a total of 1,232,000. The government never published the results of this census nor released the data that might have allowed specialists to study the findings. Some believe that the government inflated the results of both the 1970–1971 and 1980 censuses in order to permit Gabon to continue to qualify for various kinds of international assistance that would have been lost if it had been shown to have a higher per capita income. Others suspect that tens of thousands of Gabonese were counted both in their districts of origin and in the new urban locations where they resided most of the year. The French geographer Roland Pourtier, after the most complete study yet undertaken of available data, estimated the population in 1987 at 800,000 Africans, including a fluctuating number of non-Gabonese whom other sources estimated at 100,000, but not the 30,000 Europeans. Estimates of foreign governments, international agencies, and French Africanists have varied from 800,000 to 1,100,000. In 1991 the conservative Parisian weekly *Marchés Tropicaux et Méditerranéens* estimated the population at slightly over 1 million, including foreigners.

The rapid development of Gabon's mineral resources since the late 1950s has contributed to an even more rapid urbanization. Between 1960–1961 and 1991 Libreville grew from 44,598 to an estimated 300,000 or more, of whom one-third are foreigners (including approximately 20,000 French). In those same decades Port-Gentil increased from 21,000 to an estimated 60,000, including approximately 2,500 Europeans, mostly French, and several thousand non-Gabonese Africans. Most of the country's Europeans and non-Gabonese Africans live in these two urban areas and to a lesser extent in the vicinity of Franceville and Lambaréné. Approximately 40,000 persons are employed by the government, including in education. Larger numbers of salaried persons are involved in forestry, mining, industry, and commerce. Approximately one-half of the active population, including many women, are employed in agriculture, which is still mainly subsistence. They produce the staples of the traditional Gabonese diet—manioc, plantains, bananas, and other fruits and vegetables. *See* DEMOGRAPHY.

Peoples

Among the indigenous inhabitants there are a few thousand Pygmies, or Negrillos, who are thought to be the descendants of the oldest known inhabitants. It is possible that the various pygmoid groups may have undergone some mixing with Negroid peoples in recent centuries. The remaining 99.5 percent of the indigenous population has Negroid racial origins and has been differentiated through many centuries if not millennia into 40 or more distinct peoples (a "people" being a group linked by heredity, culture—including language—and historical experience). All of these peoples speak languages belonging to the Bantu group, the large group to which most of the inhabitants of central and southern Africa belong. These peoples vary in size from a few hundred to tens of thousands. Ethnologists have been able to distribute them among 10 groups, mainly on the basis of linguistic similarities. But there is evidence of genetic, cultural, and historical ties among certain groups as well so that in this sense the term "Bantu" has a wider sense than just language. To complicate matters, in the course of the past century there is evidence of peoples who have abandoned their original language and adopted or adapted the languages of other peoples with whom they had contacts. Several of Gabon's smallest peoples are in the process of disappearing, with the remnants assimilating to neighbors, who are sometimes but not always of the same group.

Largest numerically of the 10 groups (on the basis of the 1960–1961 census) is the Fang with 31 percent of the population, followed by the Mbédé with 25 percent and the Eshira with 22 percent. The remaining 22 percent are distributed among the other seven groups, of which two (the Vili and the Téké) have the majority of their kin in the neighboring Congo. Numerical size is not the same as historical importance, however, for the coastal

Myènè group with only 5 percent has played a larger role in the development of the country than several more numerous groups from the interior.

Sources for Gabon's History and the State of Historical Knowledge

Our knowledge of Gabon's history has been shaped by the sources available and the use to which they have been put. The indigenous peoples are non-literate and their historical traditions transmitted orally. In the process these traditions have been frequently revised or transformed in the light of changing conditions. They thus reflect the interests and values of subsequent generations rather than the events themselves. Much of what has been transmitted concerns the lineage and the clan but rarely the peoples that the clans formed. Common to all of these traditions are accounts of migrations or movements and the accompanying conflicts within and among lineages, clans, and peoples. The traditions also involve genealogies, for marriages took place outside the clan and were forbidden among persons related more closely than several generations. Some genealogies extend to 15 or 20 generations, as is the case with the Fang. But the majority, like the Bakota, go back only from five to eight generations. Oral traditions came to be recorded from time to time when literate European travellers visited the coasts and later entered the interior. But it was only from the 1840s onward when Christian missionaries from the United States and France actually lived among the Gabonese that we find very many detailed and reliable records being made. It was only after the First World War that missionaries or French administrators lived in all nine provinces and were therefore in a position to record local traditions.

It should also be recalled that the bulk of the records left by the missionaries, explorers, naval and military officers, and administrators were written for their own purposes and not too often to tell us about the history of the Gabonese. What we get in most cases is indirect evidence and much of it reflecting the interests and ethno-cultural biases of the authors. Thus most of what is known about the history of Gabon is what non-Gabonese have to tell us.

The first real historian of the indigenous peoples of Gabon was the Rev. André Raponda Walker (1871–1968), who gathered materials in the course of his long career as a Catholic priest in different parts of the country. Born in Gabon of an Mpongwe mother and a British father, Monsignor Walker knew a dozen Gabonese languages. Over many decades he assembled the histories of the peoples of the Estuary, the coasts, and the N'Gounié river valley. His sources were interviews and oral traditions supplemented by the church archives, and printed materials. Most of the results of Walker's investigations were published only in 1960 after editing by the French ethnologist Marcel Soret. By that time Hubert Deschamps (1900–1979) was undertaking the first project to record systematically the traditions of all of Gabon's peoples with the aid of local interpreters and informants. Marcel Soret continued this work in more depth and detail for the peoples adjacent to the Congo Republic a decade later as did Louis Perrois for the Bakota group and Henry Hale Bucher, Jr., for the Mpongwe.

Historical studies based primarily upon archives but using available oral data began to appear in the 1960s and increased in numbers during the 1970s. Nearly all of such studies have concerned the nineteenth century and/or earlier periods for which records were available and open to researchers. The largest collections of archival materials are located in France and the United States, with less extensive ones in Britain, Holland, Portugal, Senegal, and Gabon itself. The national archives of Gabon, which were organized in the early 1970s, are most extensive for the twentieth century. Unfortunately, the works by French scholars and Africans working in France, with the exception of François Gaulme's study of the Nkomi, have not used the full range of archival resources. In particular, they have neglected the American missionary and consular records for the period 1842–1913, British official records, and printed works in English. It is only the half dozen scholars from the United States working during the 1970s who have utilized the various archival materials on three continents and the published sources in French, English, and other languages. The work by a Gabonese scholar that suffers least from the lack of non-French sources is Nicolas Métégué N'Nah's pioneering study of resistance by the Gabonese to the impositions and exactions of colonial rule prior to 1914.

As yet, no one has incorporated the results of the various published studies and doctoral dissertations into a history. A mimeographed outline prepared by Frédéric Meyo-Bibang for use in the secondary schools in the early 1970s has some very useful material on resistance to French penetration and the abuses of the colonial regime. But its sections on elite anti-colonialism during the 1920s and 1930s and on the country's evolution after the Second World War omit essential data and thereby contribute to erroneous impressions. A more recent history by Ange Ratanga-Atoz (1985), like Meyo-Bibang's work, utilizes only published sources in French to outline the history of Gabon through 1945. Its sections on the era between the two world wars are extremely sketchy and the entire work ignores English-language scholarship.

Main Periods in the History of Gabon

The history of Gabon has been shaped by the interaction of both Africans and Europeans and by the interplay of both internal and external influences and events. On the basis of these factors, one can outline four general periods of unequal length, which can be designated by adjectives reflecting the dominant characteristics:

(1) From ancient times to A.D. 1471 (Bantu Gabon)
(2) From A.D. 1471 to 1843 (Atlantic Gabon)
(3) From A.D. 1843 to 1960 (French Gabon)
(4) Since A.D. 1960 (Independent Gabon)

Bantu Gabon

Many centuries before European peoples came along the Atlantic coasts, peoples of Negroid stock called the Bantu began their migrations into the forests that cover most of Gabon. It is believed that all of Gabon was once forest, but portions were turned into grassland by human activities through the centuries. These Bantu peoples found small numbers of peoples of an older pygmoid stock living at various points in the forest. The Bantu peoples came from the north, south, and east, and though probably all of one stock and even of one proto-Bantu language, they became differentiated in the course of their travels. It was during these centuries, both before and after their arrival in Gabon, that they developed the foundations of their societies, in which roles were assigned on the basis of sex, generations within the sexes, and kinship, as well as the material culture for survival in the forest. They were peoples of the New Stone Age, who lived from hunting, fishing and subsistence agriculture, though the manioc and some of the varieties of bananas and plantains that would subsequently become the staples of the Gabonese diet had not yet been introduced from the New World. In this period we have called Bantu Gabon the extended family, the lineage, and the clan formed the basic social units and governance seldom extended beyond them. Only on the Loango coast, centered in the Congo Republic but extending north into Gabon, were institutions developing on a larger scale.

Atlantic Gabon

The first Europeans who came along the coasts in the 1470s and 1480s were the Portuguese. They found the Mpongwe already living along the river, or estuary, to which they gave the name *gabão,* meaning hood or sleeve. they also made contact with the Orungu at Cape Lopez and the Vili along the Loango coast. Indigenous trading networks that already extended from the interior down waterways to the ocean and along the coasts gradually acquired a new overseas dimension throughout the sixteenth and seventeenth centuries as Dutch and French traders joined the Portuguese. But the networks came to be focused upon the Atlantic coasts probably only in the late eighteenth and early nineteenth centuries as the slave trade reached its height and British industrial manufactures gained a predominance. In the meantime migrations and movements of Bantu peoples continued throughout the interior. Frequently the stronger provoked the movement of the weaker and set off a veritable chain reaction of migrations. The largest in scope would be the southward and coastward movement of the Fang in the late eighteenth century and a large part of the nineteenth century whose impact would be felt throughout most of northern Gabon. Ultimately the Fang sought to make direct contact with European traders, a goal shared by other interior peoples who were moving toward the southern coasts in these same eras. The period of Atlantic Gabon also saw the sway of the Loango kingdom extend northward into Gabon at least as far as Setté-Cama and then decline in the nineteenth century.

French Gabon

France under King Louis Philippe founded a post in the Estuary in 1843 to promote commerce and to combat the slave trade. Though the French made efforts to end the slave trade, frequently as a result of British prodding, it continued clandestinely on a reduced scale until the 1860s. On the whole, the French exhibited much greater zeal in securing recognition of their sovereignty through treaties with the clan heads of the indigenous peoples as a first step in competing with the dominant British, American, and German traders. French agents resorted to deception, threats, and finally force in 1845 to gain the submission of the Mpongwe clan head at Glass, who, unlike the other clan heads, refused to consent freely to the French establishment. During the next four decades the French made treaties with all of the coastal peoples from Loango to the Rio Muni (as well as with some farther north and offshore who would eventually be assigned to Spain). In the late 1860s they penetrated the lower Ogooué river valley. Their thrust into the middle and upper reaches of the river would take place between 1874 and 1885 under the leadership of Savorgnan de Brazza as part of France's competition with Leopold II, king of the Belgians, for control of the Congo. France in 1885 and 1894 partitioned the northern and northeastern hinterlands with Germany. Then in 1900 it divided the disputed areas of the northern coasts with Spain. France would administer the Loango coast as part of Gabon until 1918, at which time most of it was transferred to the neighboring French colony of the Middle Congo.

The boundaries drawn by the colonial powers in the north and northwest divided the Fang people among Gabon, Cameroon, and Spanish Guinea as well as from the larger Pahouin group (Fang-Boulou-Beti), whose greatest numbers are located in Cameroon. The boundaries with the Middle Congo left small numbers of Vili and Téké within Gabon and split the Bakota, Bapounou, and Mbédé groups (including the Nzabi). But the fact that France controlled the Middle Congo and, after 1916, the adjacent areas of Cameroon, helped to prevent irredentist, or unification, movements. The inland boundaries with Spanish Guinea (Rio Muni) posed few barriers to the movement of either peoples or goods during the colonial period.

Between 1843 and 1886 Gabon was always administered by French naval officers jointly with French West African territories. France instituted customs duties on foreign trade to help pay the expenses of its establishment. The French used force when necessary to protect European merchants seeking to bypass the coastal traders and to deal directly with the interior peoples as well as to punish Gabonese peoples who abused or attacked European traders. One of the ironies of this situation was that France was able to interest few of its own citizens to engage in commerce in Gabon. It therefore ended up providing protection for those very British, American, and German traders with whom it had hoped the French merchants would compete. In one instance in the late 1840s in which a French entrepreneur, Le Cour, attempted to establish a commercial plantation in the Estuary, neither the Naval Ministry nor the local administration would give subsidies nor aid in labor recruitment. Later on, in the 1860s, the administration aided a private company, Victor Régis of Marseilles, to recruit so-called "free emigrants" for plantation labor in the French West Indies. The scheme deprived sparsely populated Gabon of several thousand workers who might have assisted in its own development. The French government helped Roman Catholic missionaries to establish in the Estuary in 1844 in the expectation that they would promote French cultural and political influence. Deaths and illnesses in the missionary ranks prevented them from evangelizing beyond the Mpongwe and Benga peoples or educating more than a few hundred persons at any time during their first 35 years. As far as the French government was concerned, however, the missionaries served the important purpose of providing competition to the American Protestant missionaries who had started work in the Estuary in 1842 and who entered the middle Ogooué in 1874.

In the 1880s French rule began to acquire a more typically colonialist character both in relation to the Gabonese and to other westerners. The French instituted a tax upon able-bodied persons of both sexes over ten years old and required unpaid labor for a certain number of days a year for projects deemed of public utility. In 1883 the administration closed the American Protestant schools, which had been teaching in English as well as local languages. It allowed them to reopen only after they had secured French-speaking teachers from Europe. After the Americans transferred their work to French Protestants and moved north into Cameroon, the administration showed much less zeal in enforcing the prohibition on the use of local languages for academic instruction but still vigorously encouraged the teaching of French. During the exploration and occupation of the interior, roughly from the mid-1870s through the First World War, the administration required various villages to provide foodstuffs to its posts and military units. The French paid for these provisions but generally at prices that were unattractive to both producers and transporters. The French instituted forced labor for portage and construction when free recruitment failed to yield the necessary manpower.

French colonialism saw its worst abuses and injustices as a result of the concessionary regime installed throughout the French Congo (of which Gabon formed part) in 1898–1899 and not completely terminated everywhere until 1930. The regime effectively denied the land rights of the indigenous peoples. The companies systematically emptied the country of all its available resources, backed up in many cases by French-officered Senegalese militiamen. These exactions, taken together with the demands outlined above and a doubling of the head tax, caused the flight of tens of thousands of Africans in the Ogooué and N'Gounié valleys and the abandonment of food crops, with subsequent famines and epidemics. The companies and their supporters in the growing administrative machine nearly destroyed the existing commercial networks and sent the economy into a slump from which it did not begin to recover until the large-scale production of okoumé after the First World War. Concurrent with this devastation was the institution of the *indigénat* in 1910, at the time of the organization of the federation of French Equatorial Africa to which Gabon's interests would henceforth be subordinated, and the conscious abandonment of the cultural assimilation of the educated elite, which had been official practice since the French arrival. From the institution of the federation, French educational policy aimed to create only subordinates and auxiliaries in a colonial situation where Frenchmen and French interests would be dominant for the foreseeable future.

Is it therefore surprising in these circumstances to find an anti-colonialist reaction among the educated elite? Paradoxically, their numbers had increased significantly during the first two decades of the twentieth century as a result of the coming of the Brothers of Saint-Gabriel to Libreville and Lambaréné in 1900 and the establishment of public schools in the capital and other towns in 1907 and after. This agitation by educated elements from the Myènè and Fang peoples sought to curb the abuses of colonialism, which deprived them of the basic rights of liberty and property in the land of their birth, and to achieve legal and social equality with French citizens. The demands reflected elite interests almost entirely, for though the elite possessed close ties with the masses, the latter were too much in disarray and demographic decline, not to mention different in outlook, for meaningful political links to be established in this period. Members of the educated elite failed in their main objectives. But they were successful in securing appointments as chiefs among the Estuary peoples (including by this time the Fang) and as representatives in the consultative bodies established in the wake of the Popular Front regime in France (1936–1937). Much of the post-war political leadership would come from these elements, plus a handful of educated Gabonese working at Brazzaville who rallied to Free France and gained advancement in the circle of Governor-General Félix Eboué between 1940 and 1944.

The Second World War generated decolonizing trends throughout the colonial empires that France tried to contain through a policy of assimilation, that is, by promoting the advancement of its Black African territories within a French Republic and Union dominated by Frenchmen. This policy, together with those of maintaining the federation of French Equatorial Africa and of treating all Black African territories alike, had the result of creating four different levels for Gabonese political activity (Gabon, FEA, all Black Africa, and the French Republic and Union). At the same time it projected some of the diverse interests and cleavages within French and Black African politics into Gabon. In addition to the opportunities for political participation, the Fourth French Republic (1946–1958) saw the end of the worst abuses of colonialism and the granting of basic rights to the Gabonese. Public as well as private French investment improved and expanded the ports and roads with a view to promoting the expansion of wood production and later in the 1950s the exploitation of the mineral resources—manganese, uranium, iron and petroleum. Primary education in French was extended to the bulk of the school-age population. Much smaller numbers benefited from technical, secondary, and higher education. Only in the mid-1950s were a few persons receiving secondary diplomas in Gabon itself and completing university programs in France. With just a few exceptions, political life would be dominated by those educated within Gabon prior to 1945. Most influential among them were three men with similar education backgrounds and personal ties: Jean-Hilaire Aubame (1912–1989), Gabon's deputy in the French National Assembly (1946–1958); Léon Mba (1902–1967), the first Gabonese mayor of Libreville in 1956 and the top African official in the first executive council in 1957; and Paul Gondjout (1912–1990), member of the French Senate (1949–1958) and the leading figure in the Territorial Assembly. Though both Aubame and Mba were Fang, they drew their support from different elements within that people and had different Gabonese and European allies. Gondjout, who came from the Myènè peoples, used his considerable political talents to promote his own career, but from 1954 on allied with Mba against Aubame. On the whole, Gabonese politics were influenced by personal, regional, and ethnic interests rather than by issues or ideologies. To complicate matters, independents held the balance of power between the two political parties that formed around Aubame, on the one hand, and Gondjout and Mba, on the other. In addition, the training of Gabonese for the highest levels of territorial administration began only in 1956.

Independent Gabon

Gabon arrived at political independence on August 13, 1960, as a result of decolonizing forces elsewhere in the French Union that had contributed firstly to the collapse of the Fourth Republic in May 1958 and then to the demise of De Gaulle's French Community, which had limited the African territories to autonomy or self-government. At independence Gabon possessed neither the resources nor the personnel to operate its administration and economy, much less to develop them, without continued outside aid and assistance. Much of this support was forthcoming from France and was institutionalized in the 15 *coopération* agreements signed a month before independence. At the same time, private investors from France, other Common Market countries, and the United States continued to develop the country's mineral resources. The early 1960s saw the first significant exports of manganese and uranium as well as the successful prospecting and construction of facilities that would lead to the exploitation of petroleum in the late 1960s and early 1970s.

In the meantime, within three years after independence, the political institutions modelled upon the Fifth French Republic had broken down, a victim of the rivalries of the politicians and parties. Central in the collapse was the determination of President Mba to provide a strongly authoritarian leadership, taken with the increasingly repressive measures necessary for him to do so. His actions provoked a military coup against his regime in February 1964. French military intervention, which restored Mba to office, allowed him to eliminate the restraints on his power represented by a multi-party National Assembly and to establish an authoritarian regime. It enabled him to transfer his power intact to his handpicked successor, Albert-Bernard (later Omar) Bongo (b. 1935), whose selection involved agents from De Gaulle's office. Bongo would face the difficult task of maintaining political stability while trying to establish a less repressive and more broadly based regime.

For this task Bongo possessed a number of assets. As a member of the numerically small Téké people of the far interior, he stood outside the ethnic rivalries (Myènè vs. Fang, intra-Fang) that had plagued political life for two decades. Though young, he possessed a good education in business administration and a decade of governmental experience, including several years in the president's office. Yet he had not been personally involved in the rivalries or repression of the Mba presidency. Responding to the wishes expressed in the National Assembly, which by that time included only BDG deputies, Bongo between 1968 and 1972 released those involved in the coup and the members of the provisional government of 1964. Many of them reentered government service while the remaining ones returned to private life in Gabon or abroad. Bongo took advantage of the BDG's control of the National Assembly to dissolve all existing parties, and on March 12, 1968, announced the formation of a single party, the Parti Démocratique Gabonais (PDG). Bongo's main justification for such a course was his contention that the existing parties represented conflicting ethnic and regional interests that hindered effective government and national unity. Bongo recognized the strength of such interests in his appointments to the cabinet and civil service, where the desire to balance them often took precedence over professional qualifications. Bongo intended that the PDG would undertake a *rénovation* of national political life through greater participation and by means of *dialogue*. Henceforth all political discussion, debate, and criticism could legitimately take place only within the framework of the PDG. During the early years of the Bongo presidency, a good deal of dialogue seems to have occurred within the regime with the chief executive ultimately making the important decisions himself.

The single-party system gave Gabon a new stability. But not surprisingly, it also provided the means to the president and ruling class for perpetuating themselves in power without regard to the wishes of the people. Those in power held the key positions in the party and influenced the selection of candidates for office, who ran unopposed. Revolt would have been futile because France was prepared to intervene militarily under the defense cooperation agreement to support Bongo. Jacques Foccart, De Gaulle's adviser on African affairs, aided Bongo in constructing a security apparatus that relied on Frenchmen and other foreigners to protect those in power.

In April 1969 Bongo moved to curb the independence of the organized workers by requiring them to join a single labor federation, COSYGA, which in 1973 became a special organ of the PDG. Through these means the government sought to secure the workers' conformity with its policies and to control their relations with employers. Illegal strikes, work stoppages, and slowdowns periodically attested to the workers' dissatisfaction with arrangements that denied them effective representation but that they could not alter.

To a much greater extent than Mba, Bongo sought to secure

Gabonese control of natural resources and greater benefits to the Gabonese from their exploitation. Thus came the requirements for greater Gabonese participation in the ownership and management of commercial and industrial enterprises. Given the paucity of private capital and its preference for investment in real estate and banks instead of industry or large-scale commerce, the state became the leading Gabonese participant. Gabonization advanced slowly as a result of the scarcity of Gabonese with advanced technical and managerial skills willing to work in industry instead of the civil service.

Bongo's accession to the presidency coincided with the beginning of a period of economic expansion based primarily on petroleum but also on manganese, uranium, and timber that multiplied the revenues hitherto available to the government. Between 1973 and 1985 revenues mainly from an increased petroleum production at higher prices multiplied 18-fold. On the assumption that the existing oil reserves would last only to the end of the 1980s (later additional reserves would be discovered), the government decided to use the bulk of the additional funds to promote the kind of development that would ultimately decrease dependence on petroleum and would create a much more diversified economy. To this end, it invested its own resources and sought foreign grants and loans to construct an infrastructure that would allow tapping of the minerals and timber of the interior. The cornerstone of this infrastructure was the Transgabonais Railway from the Estuary to the middle and upper Ogooué River valleys.

From the early 1970s the Bongo government pursued a more active foreign policy, primarily to get more aid for development and from greater numbers and kinds of sources. While establishing relations with additional western nations, it inaugurated relations with numerous Arab and Communist states. While becoming more independent of France in terms of policy formation, as reflected in the revised *coopération* agreements of February 1974, Gabon grew even more dependent in terms of personnel and capital investment. During the last half of the 1970s and the first half of the 1980s, several thousand additional European technicians and managers along with even larger numbers of non-Gabonese African laborers and employees entered Gabon to carry out the various development programs. Additional

Lebanese, Cameroonians, Senegalese, and Malians arrived to participate in the growing commercial sector.

By the time a major part of the first section of the Transgabonais opened to Ndjolé in September 1978, heavy charges on foreign loans and less than anticipated petroleum revenues were forcing cutbacks and slowdowns in the development programs. Also contributing to the financial woes were expenditures that *Africa Contemporary Record* estimated at as much as $900 million for a lavish new presidential palace, beautification of the capital, and luxury hotels for the 1977 OAU meeting. But by the early 1980s, with the aid of international institutions, the government was able to stabilize the country's finances and to reduce its debt. At the same time additional petroleum and uranium reserves were discovered.

The financial difficulties also contributed to a political malaise, which came into the open at the Second Extraordinary Congress of the PDG in January 1979. In unprecedented criticisms of the regime, the congress called upon the government to tackle the related problems of inefficiency and multiple office holding, which led to neglect of duties. One resolution lambasted the economic management of the country, which it stated led to "unbridled capitalism" instead of "rational exploitation of our perennial resources" and called for agriculture to be made a top priority. The Congress failed to reelect a number of top officials of the Central Committee and urged a democratization of the process for selecting party officials and National Assembly members. President Bongo responded by reshuffling his government and announcing several measures designed to satisfy the demands of the critics. In November 1979 an ordinary party congress renominated him and on December 30, 1979, he was popularly reelected to another seven-year term. It thus appeared that he had received mandates both to continue in office and to institute reforms that might deal with the nation's ills. Following two-stage parliamentary elections in February 1980, Bongo reorganized the government as a step toward dealing with the current problems.

The previous month, the Paris semi-monthly *Afrique-Asie* had brought to public attention the underside of the Bongo regime. It alleged that misuse of public funds and corruption were a major source of Gabon's financial difficulties. It claimed that President Bongo, his wife Joséphine, and her brother Jean-Boniface Assélé, director of the national police and Minister of Public Works, had acquired vast real estate holdings as well as majority interests in a score of companies involved in industry, construction, air transport, insurance, and banking. The same magazine accused the regime of using violence to intimidate or to silence its critics.

The coming to power of a Socialist government in France in May 1981 made possible the publication of a work of investigative journalism that probably would not have survived the censor during the Gaullist and Giscardian eras. In the exposé *Affaires africaines* (1983), Pierre Péan, who had worked in the administration in Libreville for several years, made serious accusations concerning use of public funds for private purposes and of public office for private gain, political violence, and personal misconduct by the presidential couple. Péan alleged that Gabon was ruled by a *clan des Gabonais,* a coterie of Gabonese and Frenchmen who were enriching themselves while purportedly serving the interests of their respective countries. Though as a result of the ensuing furor the Socialist government ultimately had to conciliate Bongo in order to protect its economic and strategic interests in Gabon, his regime had acquired an unsavory reputation in France. Even the conservative *Figaro Magazine* (Dec. 14, 1985) would thereafter comment: "His country is a sort of equatorial emirate. It has for a long time been at the heart of numerous intrigues."

In Gabon itself, the general prosperity of the late 1970s and early 1980s tended to mute popular criticism of the regime. When the Socialist-Communist victory in France encouraged the emergence of an opposition party, the Mouvement de Redressement National (MORENA), in Libreville in November 1981, it gained little popular support and was quickly crushed by the government. MORENA represented Fang and Bapounou elements who sought a more equitable distribution of wealth among provinces and individuals, a restoration of multi-party democracy, and a curb on abuses and corruption in government. After the leaders in Gabon were given harsh sentences, MORENA-in-exile continued in Paris among Gabonese intellectuals. They were led by a mild-mannered Spiritan priest, the Reverend Paul Mba-Abessolé, who emphasized that the group would work peacefully and through dialogue with those in power to achieve its goals.

The years of MORENA's challenge had seen unprecedented

new levels of public income from petroleum because of higher prices and the appreciation of the dollar, the currency in which it was exchanged. Taxes derived from this source permitted the national budget to increase from close to 40 billion francs CFA in 1973 to 328 billion in 1979 and more than 669 billion in 1986. (The value of the franc CFA fluctuated from 200 to 250 per U.S. dollar in these years.)

During the 1970s and 1980s the Bongo regime continued to neglect agriculture and the maintenance of the road network that brought both foodstuffs and export crops to market. Government inaction thus helped further to empty the countryside of its vital elements. The government had created a number of largely state-owned companies to provide food for the urban areas. Despite these efforts, Gabon was importing 85 percent of its food. At the same time, these agro-businesses tended to create a rural proletariat rather than to revitalize the peasantry. On the whole, government policies helped to transfer tens of thousands of rural populations into the urban areas, particularly into Libreville (the administrative and commercial center) and Port-Gentil (the center for mining, timber, and industry). Into these centers also came the bulk of Europeans, non-Gabonese Africans, and 60,000 Equatorial Guinean refugees from the two Nguema regimes. While some of the latter did agricultural work, including for the agro-businesses, the majority chose to settle in Libreville. Thus by the late 1980s an estimated 45 percent of Gabon's population, including the foreigners, were living in urban areas.

Within this urban population were great disparities in income. *Le Monde* (March 20, 1990) reported that during the 1970s and 1980s only 2 percent of Gabon's population received 80 percent of all personal income. Thus the ruling class enjoyed a standard of living comparable to the most privileged in western nations. At the same time the rest of the 40,000 government employees and 80,000 salaried workers in private enterprises shared to a lesser extent in the prosperity. Their families came to occupy decent housing with running water and electricity, and to have the convenience of a motor vehicle, an electric refrigerator, and a television set. Many families obtained better health care, and more of their children gained access to secondary, technical, and higher education. Not so fortunate were the thousands of day laborers occupying makeshift housing without amenities and subsisting precariously from irregular employment and help from their extended families. Although the government devoted the bulk of its expenditures for social services to the urban areas, it could never keep up with the needs of this burgeoning population for housing, health care, and education. While some of the non-Gabonese Africans held rather secure employment, most of them had uncertain incomes whose levels were linked to the health of the economy. A portion of them were small-scale independent retailers. Others, along with some of the Lebanese traders, risked the wrath of the government through their activities in the informal sector of the economy. The non-Gabonese Africans frequently lived in an unfriendly and sometimes insecure atmosphere. They were resented by many Gabonese, who saw them as necessary to the functioning of the economy in good times but as competitors to be sent away in bad times. Because the government required employers to compensate Gabonese workers nearly 25 percent more than foreigners, employers preferred to hire the non-Gabonese Africans, and to lay off the Gabonese first in times of downturn.

Such conditions arrived in Gabon in the course of 1986 and persisted throughout the rest of the decade. Falling prices for oil in the world market and the weakness of the dollar drastically reduced the government's revenues. Whereas before 1985 oil had provided 65 percent of the budget resources and 85 percent of export receipts, in 1988 oil generated only 30 percent and 18 percent, respectively. During the late 1980s income from manganese, timber, uranium, cocoa, coffee, and palm oil barely remained stable or declined slightly. Thus in 1987 and 1988 the national budgets were only half those of 1984 to 1986. Development projects in particular were cut back severely. Whereas the investment budget had totalled 400 billion francs CFA in 1985 (8 billion FF), it fell to 60 billion francs CFA in 1988. At the same time higher interest rates increased the expenses of the government. In these circumstances unemployment grew to the point that domestic consumption dropped one-third. Schools lacked books and supplies, hospitals were deficient in medicines and equipment, while the roads deteriorated further. In mid-1989 the secretary-general of Cosgya announced that 50,000 workers had lost their jobs since 1985, one-third of them in the private sector. Altogether, 200 companies had closed down. The public sector had been hard hit since completion of work on the Transgabonais in 1987.

A series of austerity measures that the government introduced between 1987 and 1989 in order to qualify for international loans reduced the income of employees in both the public and private sectors. During 1989 the ordinary people had reason to hope for the return of good times as the onshore oilfields at Rabi-Kounga began to produce, though the increased revenues would not become available to the government until 1990. As 1989 wore on, it became evident that the austerity measures were hitting hardest the portion of the population least capable of supporting them while allowing the ruling class to maintain its affluent life-style at only a slightly reduced scale.

At this point it was learned that during the 1980s approximately one-fourth of the national revenues had been diverted into private hands. During a decade in which the annual salaries of all 40,000 government employees totalled two billion FF, top officials had transferred some 28 billion FF to foreign bank accounts. This was a sum nearly double the national debt of 1990 which the country was struggling to repay. *Le Monde* (Feb. 25, 1989) reported that President Bongo and his associates had amassed personal fortunes that collectively totalled 30 billion FF. Bongo's alone was estimated at 500 million FF, making him one of the wealthiest men in the world. In the wake of these revelations, MORENA tracts circulated in Libreville identifying the president as the "Gabonese evil," a term previously employed by Aristote Assam in his exposé, *Omar Bongo ou la racine du mal gabonais* (1985). News of events in Europe, relayed into Gabon by international radio and television, also had an impact. The celebration of the 200th anniversary of the French Revolution throughout 1989 drew attention to a historic popular revolt against privilege. Focus on the rights of man and the citizen served to remind the Gabonese of the restraints on the exercise of such rights under the Bongo regime. The disintegration of the repressive communist regimes throughout Eastern Europe encouraged the dissatisfied to think of the possibility of replacing long-entrenched regimes and rather quickly. Bongo himself recognized these latter influences several months later as they began to affect several formerly French states in West Africa when he observed: "The winds from the East are shaking the coconut trees." To help defuse popular discontent,

Bongo encouraged a week-long visit in May 1989 by Father Mba, whose proposals for change he promised to consider. Mba was treated more like a visiting dignitary than the leader of a suppressed political party, much to the consternation of some of the PDG's less flexible leaders.

In September and October 1989, the government announced that it had discovered and suppressed two related plots to assassinate the president and to overthrow the government. They were led by Bapounou elements that included civil servants and military men in league with foreign business interests and a religious sect led by a Malian trader. In mid-December, after new austerities provoked a strike by electricity and water workers that brought industry and commerce to a standstill, Bongo observed that the austerity measures had reached the limits of the supportable.

Then on January 16 began the wave of strikes and demonstrations that shook the foundations of the Bongo regime. On that date students at the Omar Bongo University who had been boycotting classes went on strike over the shortage of professors and library works, which diminished the quality of the education they were receiving. The students, most of whom were dependent upon the government for financial support, also showed concern about the impact of the austerities, which were eroding their purchasing power and limiting the expansion of educational facilities. The following day, the police forcibly evicted students from the economics and law faculty who were occupying the campus. On January 18, high school students took to the streets to demonstrate their solidarity. They were joined by adults who were not students and who the government claimed were mainly non-Gabonese Africans; these latter elements were blamed for the rioting that involved looting of Lebanese properties in the popular quarters and other criminal damage. Police firing at the feet of demonstrators killed five persons and injured at least 70. Two hundred and fifty arrests took place. Bongo met with student representatives on January 22 to air their grievances and to defuse their discontent.

Following the riots of January 18, and despite government measures to curb protest, demonstrations intensified in Libreville and strikes spread to workers in both public and private sectors, bringing the capital almost to a standstill. Demands focused upon higher wages, fairer distribution of the country's wealth, and democratic reforms. Neither Bongo's concessions to particular groups between February 14 and 24 nor his banning of all strikes and demonstrations on February 22 failed immediately to halt the protests. The crisis peaked on February 26 when airport personnel, telecommunication workers, and gas station attendants joined teachers and physicians striking for better pay and working conditions. Workers also demanded the creation of free trade unions not under government control and Gabonization of jobs. By the end of the month most strikers had returned to work after obtaining presidential promises to establish committees to consider their grievances and demands.

By that time, the events were pressuring the government to undertake changes in the political system away from the one-party regime. From a commission on democracy created in January came the recommendation to dissolve the PDG in order to pave the way for a new political grouping, the Rassemblement Social et Démocratique Gabonais (RSDG), that would be open to various currents of opinion. The commission intended that the RSDG would provide an apprenticeship for political pluralism over a five-year period. For Bongo the RSDG was a means of permitting wider participation while maintaining his control over the nation's political forces. He summoned a national conference to begin on March 23 to discuss the new arrangements.

Then on February 26 Bongo announced a new provisional government replacing the one of August 1989. While he brought into office several younger and highly qualified ministers with well educated or experienced advisers, he retained most of the previous ministers who had held key posts. Among them as prime minister was Léon Mébiame, known to have little sympathy for democratic reform.

On March 21, amid continuing popular economic and social unrest, the government granted legal recognition to 74 political associations so that they might participate in the national conference that the president had summoned to discuss reforms. Although Bongo would have preferred to keep all parties under his control in the RSDG, the opposition rejected such incorporation. Though the opposition was splintered into many groups, there were broadly two tendencies among them. MORENA under Father Mba-Abessolé represented Christian democracy with a strong populist bent. MORENA had strong support from both

Catholic and Protestant elements, including some troubled by the influences of Masonry and Islam in the Bongo regime. It was most extensively implanted in the north and among the Fang people. The secular and socialist tendency was represented by the Parti Gabonais du Progrès (PGP), which had its strongest support among workers and in the coastal regions. Its leaders were respected professionals of aristocratic background, mainly Nkomi and Orungu from Port-Gentil, who included professors at the university who had been imprisoned during the 1970s for an alleged Marxist plot against the government. Among them were Joseph Rendjambe, professor of economics and a successful businessman, and his relative Pierre-Louis Agondjo-Okawe, former dean of the economics and law faculty at the university and currently head of the bar in Gabon. Because the PDG also included reformist elements, led by the president's son Ali Bongo, among others, forces favoring reform had a majority in the national conference.

The national conference asked Omar Bongo to serve out the rest of his term as president (until December 1993) but to resign as head of the PDG and to put himself above parties. It also called for the return of a multi-party political system, which was reestablished on May 22. A new government had been formed on April 27 under a respected technocrat, Casimir Oyé-Mba, in which minor posts were given to some opposition party members. Elections for a new National Assembly, which had been postponed pending the outcome of the national conference, were scheduled for September 1990.

In the meantime, also on May 22, the death of PGP leader Rendjambe in suspicious circumstances in a Libreville hotel owned by Bongo set off an explosion of violence in the main cities and towns the following day. The inability of the government to control the violence and destruction at Port-Gentil, which threatened French lives and property, led on May 24 to a French military intervention to restore order. Intervention had the effect of propping up the regime until it could regain control in Port-Gentil.

The circumstances of the assembly elections in September and October, which involved many irregularities, intimidation, and fraud, allowed the PDG to retain a slight majority of the seats. It held 62 out of 120 with 27 going to the two factions of MORENA,

19 to the PGP, and 12 to other, mainly socialist, parties. Casimir Oyé-Mba gave minor cabinet posts to some opposition deputies in the new PDG-dominated government, which he headed. On March 5, 1991, the National Assembly unanimously adopted a new constitution that restored multi-partyism and contained guarantees concerning civil liberties. The constitution provided for a strong president but strengthened the powers of the prime minister.

While the upheaval of 1990 restored multi-partyism and a freer exercise of speech, press, and assembly, it left President Bongo and his associates of the PDG in control of all branches of government. Their actions are, however, now open to public scrutiny in the National Assembly and in the media. The regime has a strong political base only in the president's own Haut-Ogooué Province and among PDG officeholders in the other provinces and the capital who have benefited from arrangements that gave them both power and wealth. If the seats in the National Assembly had been distributed more strictly according to population, the PDG would not have retained its majority in that body or control of the government. At the same time the two markedly different broad tendencies within the opposition might make a coalition government among them difficult.

The increased revenues from the Rabi-Kounga oil field during the early 1990s permitted the Bongo regime to secure the international loans to keep the government afloat. But its unwillingness or inability to institute a financial discipline that would lessen the privileges of the ruling class has delayed needed economic restructuring and the restoration of adequate levels of services in education and health care. As a result, chronic unrest has continued among the urban population, evidenced by periodic strikes, work stoppages, and demonstrations by both public- and private-sector employees. Whether leadership will emerge that can deal with these problems remains to be seen as the country awaits the presidential elections of 1993.

Conclusion

At the start of this historical section it was stated that the history of Gabon has been shaped by the interaction of both Africans and

Europeans and the interplay of both internal and external influences and events. The summaries of the four periods indicate that Gabon came into being with its present frontiers as a result of European expansion and competition during the last half of the nineteenth century. Gabon became independent in 1960 as a result of decolonizing trends elsewhere in the colonial world, for while the country had developed anti-colonialism among its elite, it had not yet developed what one might call a nationalist movement. Ethnic diversity and rivalry, the geographic barriers to establishment of linkages between the political elite and the masses dispersed throughout the interior, the absence of economic development, except for the timber industry, together with the devastation wrought by the concessionary companies, the small numbers with an education beyond the early primary grades—all these factors inhibited the rise of a nationalist movement that might have mobilized popular energies for securing freedom from foreign rule, creation of national unity, and the modernization of the economy and society. Independence arrived with the vast majority of the population remaining politically unaware while retaining patterns of subsistence activity and social relations not terribly different from the previous centuries.

The development since independence with the most far-reaching consequences has been the vastly extended exploitation of the country's natural resources under arrangements that, during the Bongo regime, have benefited Gabonese at least as much as foreigners. This exploitation from the late 1960s multiplied the revenues available to the government, thereby presenting unprecedented opportunities to reshape the economy and society and thus to improve national life. Unfortunately the French military intervention of 1964 permitted Bongo and his associates to institute a single-party political system that transferred the bulk of this new wealth to a tiny ruling class that no longer had to be responsible to the people. Until the socialist victory in France in May 1981, the threat of renewed intervention on behalf of a regime that served French economic and strategic interests made opposition within Gabon both dangerous and futile. Although the regime was able quickly to suppress MORENA within Gabon in late 1981 and early 1982, it could not stifle its emergence in Paris. Nor was it able to prevent the exposure in the French press of its financial misdeeds and political intrigues involving French partners. Much less could it forestall the economic downturn, linked to world market conditions, that began in 1986 and continued into the early 1990s.

The reluctance of Omar Bongo and his associates to alter policies and practices that might diminish their personal advantage and political support prevented effective action to deal with the prolonged crisis. The regime's attempts to reduce the salaries and benefits of ordinary government employees and workers without putting its own house in order contributed to a malaise in the late 1980s that turned into an upheaval in 1990 in the wake of student demonstrations. While that upheaval revealed widespread popular dissatisfaction with the regime throughout the coastal regions and the north and forced it to restore multi-partyism, it left the president and his associates in power. Though they now have to face public criticism from opposition parties and to account for their actions, they still control the government.

During the events of 1990, President Bongo showed a remarkable capacity to adjust to the rapidly changing conditions that led to the restoration of multi-partyism and an atmosphere of free expression. Encouraged by the reformist elements within the PDG (including his son Ali), he dropped from the cabinet longtime ministers who opposed changes or showed little real competence. He replaced his figurehead prime minister with a respected and talented technocrat.

But what Bongo and his associates have not shown is a willingness or an ability to eliminate the financial indiscipline and other practices that stand in the way of finding meaningful long-term solutions to the country's problems. Most critical among them are two: the revival of agriculture and the rural road network in order to supply food to a population that is now close to half urban; the provision of adequate health care and education to all of the people. The leaders appear to be temporizing, resorting to short-term expedients and half-measures in the hope that the international economic situation will improve sufficiently to allow them to avoid reforms. In the meantime the recurrent socioeconomic strife and the criticism of the opposition bear witness to the persistence of the problems and the failure of the regime to deal effectively with them. The general strike of 1991 organized by the opposition parties was able to force the regime to form a new government in conformity with the constitution of

March 1991. But only the leadership of the president, whose term of office extends until the end of 1993, and a change in the habits of the ruling class can create the conditions for securing freedom and justice for all of Gabon's growing population.

THE DICTIONARY

ABESSOLO, JEAN-BAPTISTE NGUEMA (1932–   ). Educator and author. Born at Oyem on February 15, 1932, Abessolo received his early education at the regional school there and at the upper primary school of Libreville. He prepared for a career in educational administration at the École des Cadres Supérieurs at Brazzaville and then at the École Normale Supérieure at Mouyondzi, Congo. Between 1952 and 1982 he served as a school administrator and primary-school inspector, except for a year in 1960–61 at the École Normale Supérieure in Paris. In December 1982, he was named director-general of the International Center of Bantu Civilizations at Libreville. His stories have been published both in Gabon and France. [1141, 1167]

ADAM, JEAN-JÉRÔME (1904–1981). Last French archbishop of Libreville and linguist. Monsignor Adam was born on June 8, 1904, at Wittenheim, Alsace. He was educated in the seminaries of the Holy Ghost Fathers. Arriving in Gabon on September 29, 1929, he spent 18 years as a missionary in the Haut-Ogooué Province where he prepared a grammar of Mbédé, Ndumu, and Duma. After serving as the bishop (1947–1955) and then archbishop of Libreville (1955–1969), he returned to Franceville, where he died on July 11, 1981. [1311]

ADMINISTRATIVE HISTORY. France established its sovereignty in Gabon on the basis of treaties concluded with the representatives of indigenous peoples between 1839 and 1885. In the treaties the Gabonese leaders are usually identified as chiefs but they were in most cases clan heads, for only the Orungu and the Vili (and the Nkomi for a time in the nineteenth century) had chiefs who ruled an entire people. Specifically, French naval officers made treaties with the Mpongwe clan heads of the Estuary (1839–1849); the Benga of Cape Esterias (1852); the Orungu in the vicinity of Cape Lopez (1862); various peoples at the Mondah River and the Rio Muni (1845–1885); various peoples of the lower Ogooué and with the Enenga, Okandé, Apindji, Bakota, and Adouma farther upstream (1867–1885); the Nkomi of Fernan-Vaz, the Ngowe of Iguéla Lagoon, Loumbou of Setté-Cama, and the Vili of Loango (1867–1885). (Between 1842 and 1885 the French also made treaties with peoples along the coast of Equatorial Guinea and the Cameroons in areas eventually assigned by negotiations to Spain and Germany.) Recognition of French sovereignty was generally accompanied by the cession of a plot of ground for a French post. The first French post was Fort d'Aumale established on the northern shore of the Estuary in 1843. While the French Navy patrolled the coasts, rivers, and streams of the areas under French sovereignty, the establishment of permanent posts was a slower and later process. French occupation of much of the interior took place only in the late nineteenth and early twentieth centuries, either as a result of competition with other colonial powers or in the wake of boundary agreements with them. Thus France made agreements with Portugal and the Congo Free State of King Leopold II concerning the southern boundaries (areas that in 1918 were transferred to the Middle Congo) and with Spain and Germany defining the northern ones. In 1911 as a result of a Franco-German agreement giving France a free hand in Morocco, Germany was ceded portions of northern Gabon extending south of Equatorial Guinea, which was consequently bordered on the three land sides by German territory. France reoccupied these areas in 1914 and regained them formally through the Treaty of Versailles of 1919.

Throughout nearly all of the period of French colonial rule, Gabon was attached administratively to other French territories—between 1843 and 1886 to various possessions in West Africa, and from 1886 to 1958 to others in Equatorial Africa. The administrators from 1843 to 1886 were naval officers under the authority of the Ministry of the Navy in

Paris. The *commandant-supérieur,* who had responsibility for various West African settlements in addition to Gabon, also headed a Naval Division—up to 1860 covering the area from Senegal to Gabon and after that from the Gulf of Guinea to Gabon. Under the *commandant-supérieur* was a *commandant-particulier* charged with the administration of Gabon.

In the wake of French expansion into the interior, in February 1883 the explorer Savorgnan de Brazza (q.v.) was named government commissioner for the upper Ogooué and the Congo. In 1886 the colonies of Gabon and Congo were placed under Brazza as commissioner-general with a lieutenant governor under his authority having charge of Gabon. These territories would be known collectively as the French Congo, a name formally adopted in 1891. Further French expansion produced several reorganizations and ultimately the formation in 1910 of the federation of French Equatorial Africa (q.v.). Gabon was headed by a lieutenant governor under the authority of the governor-general, who from 1903 resided at Brazzaville. (The name French Congo would henceforth be restricted to the French colony next to the Congo Free State or Belgian Congo; after 1903 the colony was formally called the Middle Congo and is today's People's Republic of Congo.)

In the meantime responsibility for the French colonies had passed in March 1894 from the Ministry of the Navy to a separate Ministry of the Colonies. Between 1882 and 1894 there had been an under secretary of State for the Colonies, a position held by a civilian politician drawn from the Chamber of Deputies. Within the Ministry of the Colonies a single bureau handled matters concerning both French West Africa and French Equatorial Africa, which encouraged the already present tendency to consider the latter as a less populated and poorer version of the former. In the mid-1930s the Popular Front changed the name of the Ministry of the Colonies to the Ministry of Overseas France.

After the Second World War the lieutenant governor of Gabon was retitled governor, a designation that would be retained throughout the Fourth French Republic. Within Gabon from the 1880s the lieutenant governor or governor was assisted by territorial administrators, who at first were often naval or military officers and later, after organization of the Colonial School in Paris, professionally trained civilians. Gabon was divided into a number of regions (also called *circonscriptions* in the early period and *préfectures* later), which were subdivided into districts. The boundaries within Gabon and between Gabon and the Middle Congo were frequently redrawn between the 1880s and 1946. For example, the Loango coast formed part of Gabon between 1883 and 1918 while the Upper Ogooué Region was attached to the Middle Congo between 1925 and 1946. Gabon acquired its present international boundaries and nine regions only in 1946.

In 1975 Gabon began an administrative reorganization. The regions were retitled provinces and the districts prefectures. (This usage of prefecture differs from the usage above where the prefecture was the equivalent of a region.) Subsequently the prefectures were retitled departments. The number of provinces has remained constant at nine, but by 1987 the number of departments had increased from 37 to 44. Governors appointed by the president head the provinces while prefects direct the departments. Some departments are subdivided into districts headed by a subprefect. The districts are further subdivided into cantons placed under the authority of canton chiefs; each canton regroups a number of villages. In 1987 there were 10 districts, 119 cantons, and a multitude of villages. The departments also contain the *communes de plein exercice,* cities with elected mayors and municipal councils. The officials of these cities are responsible to the prefects of the departments of which they form part. In 1975 there were eight communes (Libreville, Port-Gentil, Oyem, Bitam, Mouila, Lambaréné, Moanda, and Franceville) and in 1987 there were 12.

See GOVERNORS. [394, 191, 118, 69, 325, 479, 1]

ADOUMA. A people of the Mbédé-speaking group who occupy the left bank of the upper Ogooué in the area of Lastoursville. Expert canoemen, they played an important role at the time of Brazza (q.v.). According to their traditions, they arrived from the east or southeast, travelling down the Sébé River to the Ogooué and then down it to the Doumé rapids where they encountered Pygmies. They made canoes of okoumé. They sold slaves to the Okandé (q.v.) for transmission down the Ogooué. In exchange they received salt, guns and powder, fabrics, matches, and copper utensils. Lastoursville was an Adouma village before De Lastours established a French post there. The SHO (q.v.) opened a factory there and purchased rubber, ivory, and ebony. The Adouma traders purchased various products (mats, raphia thread, gourd seeds, groundnuts, palm oil) and went to sell them at Lambaréné. In the past two decades many Adouma have been settling downriver toward Port-Gentil (q.v.). [284, 266]

ADYUMBA. The Adyumba people are part of the Myènè (q.v.) linguistic group of the Bantu. They were originally an Mpongwe (q.v.) clan that inhabited the banks of Nazareth Bay near the mouth of the Ogooué River. Their activities included canoe making and weaving but their speciality was ceramics. After initially friendly relations with the Ombéké or Orungu (q.v.) immigrants to their region, misunderstandings developed in the late eighteenth century, which expanded into war. An Adyumba remnant, including Chief Repéké, fled to the region of Lake Azingo, where they became by the 1810s an important link in the trading network between the Agulamba clan of the Mpongwe on the lower Remboué River and the Lambaréné sector of the Ogooué River. [394, 362]

AFFAIRES AFRICAINES Affaires africaines (1983), an exposé by Pierre Péan on the inner workings of the Bongo regime and its links with France. Péan, a free-lance journalist, served as an attaché in the Ministry of Finances in Libreville during the 1960s. The title of the work may have several meanings: simply African affairs; the unsavory sense that the word ''affairs'' has acquired in both French and English; the office within the presidency of the Fifth Republic established by De Gaulle to handle relations with the former French states. Headed by Jacques Foccart (1917–   ) under presidents De Gaulle (1958–1969) and Pompidou (1969–1974), and under President Giscard d'Estaing (1974–1981) by René Journiac until his death on February 6, 1980, it promoted and protected France's interests through personal relations, special services, and covert actions.

The work has importance for at least two reasons. Despite the author's failure to control his sources on some matters, it provides generally accurate accounts of French involvement in the affairs of Gabon during the Fifth Republic and the inner workings of the Bongo regime. Its publication caused a severe rift in the already troubled relations between the Bongo regime and the French Socialist government under President François Mitterrand (1981–). The work popularized the expression *Clan des Gabonais,* which refers to the coterie of Frenchmen and Gabonese, including the extended families of the presidential couple, Omar and Joséphine Bongo, who exercised power and influence while enriching themselves and their associates. Prominent members of the clan included Maurice Robert (q.v.), Maurice Delauney (q.v.), Pierre Debizet (q.v.), Georges Rawiri (q.v.), Jean-Boniface Assélé (Joséphine's brother) (q.v.), Jérôme Okinda, and Alex Mbouzi.

Péan alleges that members of the clan were responsible for the deaths and attempted assassinations of presidential rivals and critics of the regime. The case that caused the greatest sensation in France was the assassination of a Vietnamese housepainter in southern France on October 27, 1979, for allegedly persisting in his relationship with Joséphine Bongo. Incidents relating to this affair were expunged from French police blotters, and the assassins were never apprehended or brought to justice by the officials of the Giscard regime.

Affaires africaines also indicates that France used the Bongo regime to aid secessionist Biafra, and to trade with the breakaway settler regime in Rhodesia and the Afrikaner nationalist government in the Republic of South Africa. Gabon was used as the base for mercenary forces against the regimes of Ali Solih in the Comoros and Mathieu Kérékou in Bénin. [603]

AGONDJO-OKAWE, PIERRE-LOUIS (1936–). Attorney and opposition leader. Agondjo-Okawe was born on December 30, 1936, at Omboué in the Ogooué-Maritime Province into a prominent Nkomi family. His half brother is Jean Ping, a PDG stalwart and officeholder, and the late Joseph Rendjambe was a close relative. After schooling in Gabon, Agondjo-Okawe pursued legal studies at the universities of Lille and Paris, receiving his doctorate in 1967. Between 1966 and 1968, he was an assistant (equivalent to an American assistant professor) at the law faculty of the University of Paris. From 1968 to 1970 he taught law at the interstate university in Brazzaville. With the organization of a separate university for Gabon, he returned to Libreville as professor of law in 1970. Accused of clandestine activities against the Bongo regime in the so-called professors' plot (q.v.), along with fellow professor Rendjambe and others, he was held in prison for a long period before being tried and convicted. After his release, he returned to the university where in October 1976 he became dean of the faculty of law. Thereafter, he developed an important private legal practice and became head of the bar in Gabon. He refused offers from the Bongo regime of positions in the government, which would have required him to become a member of the PDG. On at least two occasions he represented clients accused of plotting against the government.

During the upheaval of 1990 Agondjo-Okawe emerged as one of the two most important leaders of a new party based at Port-Gentil, the Parti Gabonais du Progrès. After the death of the PGP's general secretary, Joseph Rendjambe, in suspicious circumstances in late May 1990, Agondjo-Okawe became the head of the party. He led it to victory in the coastal areas during the elections of September–October 1990, during which he was elected to the National Assembly from Port-Gentil. He helped to organize the successful general strike of opposition groups in June 1991 to put pressure on President Bongo and the PDG government to accelerate implementation of the new constitution of March 1991. This pressure contributed to formation of a new council of ministers at the end of that month. Though having close relations with Bongo, to whom he is related by marriage, Agondjo-Okawe has urged the president's resignation as a necessary step toward solving Gabon's problems.

See PARTI DU PROGRÈS GABONAIS; PROFESSORS'
PLOT; POLITICS.

AGRICULTURE. Over half of Gabon's active population works
at agriculture, most of it for subsistence and the rest for local
markets. Women play the largest role in raising food crops.
Many farmers still use traditional methods and hand tools.
Manioc (cassava) and plantains are the two most important
staples, supplemented by yams, sweet potatoes, taro, maize,
groundnuts, sugarcane, pineapples, and cucumbers. Mountain rice is grown only in the southwest savannas around
N'Dendé and Tchibanga. Fruit trees such as the mandarin,
orange, mango, papaya, and *atangatier* are the most common
in the northern half of the country. Dairy products, meat,
wheat, various fresh fruits and vegetables, the taste for which
has grown since independence in the wake of urbanization,
have to be imported. By 1990 Gabon was importing 85
percent of its food.

Only one-half of one percent of Gabon's area is under
cultivation, given the poor quality of the soils, the rapid
leaching when tilled, and the difficulty of transporting
produce to markets. After independence, the government
failed to maintain the system of roads that enabled producers
of foodstuffs around the country to supply the provincial
towns and coastal cities with regularity, and the farmers of
the Woleu-N'Tem Province to market their cocoa and coffee.
By the early 1990s half of the cocoa and coffee plantations,
whose renewal had been neglected, were more than 40 years
old and the average age of the commercial farmers was more
than fifty years. A great many of the younger people had
joined the rural exodus toward the towns and cities. The
government was able to diversify the locations in which
coffee was grown and to increase output by the early 1980s
to satisfy the needs of the domestic market and to undertake
some exporting. But cocoa exporting remained in the dol-
drums.

As a result of governmental policy, agriculture's share of
the gross domestic product, which had been 16 percent in
1964, declined to 2.8 percent in 1974, but then rose of 4.5
percent in 1984. The slight increase reflected public invest-

ment in industrial agriculture rather than the revival of
peasant production. The funds devoted to agriculture in the
various national development plans were as follows:

	Millions of francs CFA	% of total investments
1966–1970	1,130	1.25
1971–1975	1,795	1.20
1976–1980	38,820	4.50
1980–1982	37,900	10.00
1984–1988	122,000	9.70

The bulk of these funds were assigned to parastatals that
produced rubber, palm oil, sugarcane, beef cattle, and meat
chickens mainly for the domestic market (except in the case
of the rubber). (Efforts in the late 1970s to produce rice and
plantains failed.) For the most part, European technical and
managerial personnel have charge of these enterprises while,
given the scarcity of Gabonese labor, non-Gabonese Africans provide a portion of the workers. The parastatals so far
have served to proletarianize the Gabonese drawn from rural
areas rather than revive peasant farming or stem the rural
exodus. While the government in the late 1980s finally began
to give serious attention to repair of the roads, programs to
rehabilitate cocoa and coffee production remained unfunded.
[940, 754, 706, 744, 11, 929]

AKENDENGUE, PIERRE (1943–   ). Musician and composer.
Akendengué was born on the island of Awuta off the coast
from Port-Gentil. His experiences with Awuta's forested
environment, creatures, and people have inspired many of
the songs that he has composed during the last three decades.
After studies at Port-Gentil, during the 1960s he pursued
degrees in psychology at the University of Caen in France.
While there, he met the popular singer Mireille, who encouraged him to pursue a career in music. His first recording,
made privately, presented his own compositions in Nkomi
and French, which he sang to his own guitar accompaniment.
Thereafter he set to music poems about everyday life by
fellow countryman, P. E. Mondjegou, including "Le Chant
du Coupeur d'Okoumé" ("The Song of the Okoumé Cut-

ter''). Back in Gabon for a time, he studied solfeggio and plainchant with the priests of a Catholic college. At the same time he sought to utilize traditional Gabonese musical forms involving choruses, vocal soloists, instrumentalists, and dancers. During the late 1970s and early 1980s he presented spectacles at Lagos and Paris featuring his compositions for these ensembles. In the same years, he made professional recordings of some of his works. This discography includes *Naudifro, Africa Obota, Eseringila, Owendo, Meugo, Awana' Africa,* and *Mando.* Music for Akendengué came to be an assertion of the dignity of the African, the revaluation of his cultural patrimony, and the cornerstone of the affirmation of his identity. After further study at the University of Paris, in 1986 he completed a doctorate with the thesis concerning religion and traditional education among the Nkomi. Since then, he has lost his vision. [1281]

ALAR AYONG. *Alar ayong* in Fang means "to unite the clans." It was a movement among the Fang of the northern Woleu-N'Tem in the late 1940s and early 1950s to revitalize their traditional structures and values by a regrouping of the 150 or so Fang clans. Alar Ayong originated among the Ntumu and Boulou recipients of American Presbyterian mission education in southern Cameroons in the late 1930s and early 1940s. These peoples, like the Fang, belonged to the Pahouin group of peoples. Their researches into the Pahouin past as contained in clan genealogies, legends, and myths revealed an unexpected degree of organization in the clan relationships of the peoples under colonial rule, which had heretofore thought to have been extremely scattered and disorganized. Their findings encouraged the Fang to find similar linkages, which they did, and on the basis of which they undertook a regrouping of their clans. While the French administration favored a regrouping of the populations for convenience in providing services and securing revenues, it was suspicious of any movement with links to the trust territory and American missionaries. It also feared that the Alar Ayong leaders might try to displace the chiefs recognized by the French. In these circumstances the movement did more to restore Fang self-esteem by affirming the relevance of the ancestors and of the clans than it did to modernize society along western lines. [795, 827]

ALIHANGA, MARTIN (1930–   ). Catholic priest and thinker. The Rev. Martin Alihanga was born at Franceville on August 30, 1930. Seven years earlier, his father, Obamba, chief of the village of Eyouga 35 km. from Franceville, and his father's brothers had founded a new quarter in that town. From 1940 to 1946 the young Martin studied at the Catholic primary school where his paternal uncle, a graduate of the École Montfort, was teaching. In 1947 he entered the minor seminary at Libreville, and in 1952 the major seminary at Brazzaville. After ordination in 1960, for six years he held various posts in teaching and administration in southern Gabon. From 1966 he pursued graduate studies in philosophy and social sciences at the St. Thomas Aquinas Pontifical University in Rome, where he received his doctorate in sociology in 1975. Alihanga derived the adjective *altogovéen* from Latin to describe the precolonial civilization of the Upper Ogooué. In his doctoral thesis, he advocated what he calls "communitarianism," a social philosophy rooted in the traditional structures and values of the Altogovean peoples, updated in the light of Christianity and contemporary needs, as the best way to promote a development that is morally and materially sound.

Since 1976 Father Alihanga has been teaching sociology at the graduate levels at the Omar Bongo University. He has served concurrently as secretary-general of the Gabonese National Commission for UNESCO. In 1978 he became dean of the Faculty of Letters and Human Sciences and technical adviser for higher education in the Ministry of Higher Education and Scientific Research. In these roles he helped to organize CICIBA. [890]

ALLISON, FRANCIS. Allison was the first bookbinder in Gabon. A Grebo from Cape Palmas, he learned bookbinding in New York City and served the ABCFM mission in Gabon as binder and teacher from 1843 to 1846 and from 1848 to 1856. [1031]

AMBOUROUE-AVARO, JOSEPH (1934–1978). Historian and educator. Joseph Ambouroué-Avaro was born at Port-Gentil on August 17, 1934, among the Orungu people. Following secondary studies at the Collège Bessieux in Libreville, he earned a doctorate in history from the University of Paris in 1969. After his scholarship was suppressed for political reasons, he taught history and geography in French lycées from 1967 to 1969. In 1969 he returned to Libreville where he taught successively at the Lycée Léon Mba, the National School of Administration, and in the Faculty of Letters and Human Sciences at the university. In 1972 and 1974 he was arrested and inquisited by the police concerning political activities and issues. Between 1975 and 1978 he served as dean of the Faculty of Letters and Human Sciences. But he was dropped from that position following a strike of students over conditions in which he showed sympathy for their grievances. Ambouroué-Avaro died on November 17, 1978, in the crash of a private plane he had rented to fly from Libreville to Port-Gentil. Ambouroué-Avaro belonged to the first generation of African scholars who as students in western universities sought to reconstruct and to reinterpret the precolonial and early colonial history of their own peoples. He urged a revival of traditional Orungu values, adapted to new circumstances, as a means of dealing with contemporary life. [229]

AMOGHO, EUGENE (1918–   ). Politician. Amogho was born at Franceville on June 17, 1918. A civil servant, he was elected to the Territorial Assembly from the Haut-Ogooué Province in March 1952 and reelected in March 1957. He served as one of Gabon's councillors in the Grand Council of French Equatorial Africa from 1957 to 1959. Amogho entered the first Gabonese executive in March 1957 and subsequently held various ministerial posts while serving in the Territorial and then National Assembly. He was a member of the short-lived provisional government of February 1964. In January 1969 he became president of the Caisse Gabonaise de Prévoyance Sociale. [1380, 1310, 1373, 1367]

ANGUILE, ANDRE-FERDINAND (1922–1991). Monsignor Anguilé was the first Gabonese to be named Roman Catholic Archbishop of Libreville in July 1969. A relative of the Mpongwe clan head, King Quaben (q.v.), and a member of a prominent *métis* family, Anguilé was ordained a priest in July 1950 and became pastor of the main church in Libreville, St. Peter's, in October 1956. From 1963 to 1969 he served as director of the Catholic schools in the archdiocese. The archbishop resides in a magnificent villa originally constructed by the government near the cathedral for the visit of Pope John-Paul II. [987, 988, 1021]

ANGUILE, ANDRE GUSTAVE (1920–   ). Civil servant. Anguilé was born at Libreville on March 3, 1920, into a prominent *métis* family. His father was the wealthy lumberman, Augustin Anguilé. André-Gustave was one of the three Gabonese who obtained a baccalaureate in France between the two world wars. After secondary studies at Bordeaux and Sens, he specialized in forestry engineering in Paris, where he was active in African politics. On his return to Libreville, he directed a forest exploitation from 1946 to 1952. With Léon Mba (q.v.) and Paul Gondjout (q.v.) he was involved in the Bloc Démocratique Gabonais (q.v.). From 1952 to 1957 he served as secretary-general of the Territorial Assembly. Between 1957 and 1964 he held various ministerial posts concerned with the economy, and particularly industrialization. He was involved with the formation of UDEAC (q.v.) in 1964. With Jacques David, a French customs expert, he published *L'Afrique Sans Frontières* (1965) on the background and functioning of the UDEAC and questions of industrial development in Equatorial Africa. In June 1973 he became director-general of the Société Nationale des Bois du Gabon (until October 1975 called Office des Bois). Anguilé was regarded as one of Gabon's most talented and able administrators. [1367, 1380]

ANTCHOUEY, LAURENT (1897–1926). Mpongwe critic of colonialism and defender of elite interests. Antchouey and his cousin Louis Bigmann (q.v.) graduated from the Ecole Montfort (q.v.) at Libreville. They served as noncommissioned officers in a Gabonese regiment of the French army that fought in the Cameroons against the Germans during the First World War. In 1920 they became clerks for a shipping company in Dakar. There, with the protection of the French law that existed in the four communes of Senegal and with financial backing from the Mpongwe and Vili elites and the Ligue des Droits de l'Homme, Antchouey in 1922 founded a monthly newspaper, *L'Echo Gabonais: Organe d'Union et de Défense des Intérêts Généraux de l'A.E.F.* After three issues and until his death he edited the paper from Nice, France. His articles, based on steady correspondence with Mpongwe at Libreville and Brazzaville, made sophisticated attacks on the colonial administration at both territorial and federal levels. In addition to criticizing the *indigénat,* (q.v.), native courts, forced labor, and various forms of discrimination, Antchouey accused European merchants and the SHO (q.v.), Gabon's largest trading company, of attempting to instill a feudal regime. Antchouey and his paper sought reforms, above all, that would benefit the Estuary peoples and those assimilated to European culture. He sought the assimilation of these elements into the French nation as a means of political and social advancement. He was sympathetic to Pan-Africanism, hostile to Marcus Garvey's Back-to-Africa movement, and opposed to ties with the Communist Party. By including news of all French territories in *L'Echo,* he enlarged the horizons of the Estuary elite. Through his work in the Nice chapter of the Ligue and his contacts with leading French politicians and colonial ministry officials, he provided Gabon with a spokesman in the metropole. In April 1925 Antchouey returned to Gabon and encouraged the formation of a cooperative among African foresters, the Association Organisatrice du Progrès Economique du Gabon. The association gained recognition from the administration, which favored such economic activity, but confined its activities to a defense of African lumbering rights. Antchouey accidentally drowned on October 26, 1926, shortly before the Libreville branch of the Ligue gained official recognition. [550]

ANTINI, SISTER HYACINTHE (1878–1952). The first Gabonese to become a Catholic sister. The explorer Savorgnan de Brazza (q.v.) found her as an eight-year-old Ndoumou orphan on the upper Ogooué in 1896. He placed her with the Immaculate Conception Sisters at Libreville where she became a novice under the direction of Mother Louise Raynaud. She took vows on May 15, 1890, in the presence of Brazza. Sister Hyacinthe served at Donguila between 1894 and 1919, and thereafter at Fernan-Vaz until her death on July 16, 1952. President Mba dedicated the social center of Nomb-Akèlè to her memory. [1049]

APINDJI. People of the east side of the middle N'Gounié River north of Mouila belonging to the Okandé linguistic group. Essentially a river people, they were excellent navigators and freshwater sailors. They provided expert canoers, which facilitated the expeditions of Brazza (q.v.). It is believed that they came originally from the banks of the upper Ogooué River and were a numerous people at one time. Their ranks were decimated by the epidemics of 1877 and the famine of 1922. In addition to making iron goods and canoes, they produced a raphia cloth of high quality, which was their main export toward the coast. They sold palm oil to the Eshira (q.v.) and later to the SHO (q.v.) when it acquired a concession over their lands. It is their religious cult, Bwiti (q.v.), that was taken over and adapted by the Fang during the twentieth century. A Roman Catholic mission located among them in June 1900. By the time of independence few Apindji still inhabited their home region, most of them having resettled at Lambaréné, Sindara, and Fougamou. [394, 203, 266, 284, 981]

ART. The traditional art of several of Gabon's peoples has been sufficiently studied to relate them to broader artistic traditions. The art of the Mpongwe (q.v.) belongs to a geographic area extending northward along the West African coast into Yorubaland (Nigeria) while the art of the Vili (q.v.) reflects, in addition, influences from the Congo Basin. At the same time the art of both the Fang (q.v.) and the Bakota (q.v.) adheres to traditions developed in the grasslands farther north and northeast. All four of these peoples have created objects of wood, stone, and metals that form an intimate part of their religious and social lives. Masks are used in traditional religious ceremonies and statuary serves as the tombs and tomb decorations of the ancestors. At the same time other decorated objects from these same materials are employed in everyday life.

Among the most notable artistic creations in Gabon for ritual use are the Mpongwe polychromed, soft-wood masks; the Fang dark-lacquered hardwood and metal statuettes; and the Bakota sculptured faces of wood covered with brass and copper. The traditional art of the Vili was a sumptuary art analogous to that of the Benin kingdom of western Nigeria in its great variety of richly decorated objects for both ritual and daily use. Several peoples of the southern Gabon interior (e.g. the Mitsogo [q.v.]) developed dyed raphia cloth of high quality as well as great beauty. [1392, 1324, 1279, 1252, 1245]

ASSELE, JEAN-BONIFACE (1939–). The brother of Joséphine Kama, Omar Bongo's wife from 1959 to 1988, was born at Akiéné in the Haut-Ogooué Province on February 9, 1919. He undertook primary studies in the public schools of Franceville and Brazzaville, graduating in 1954. Thereafter, he pursued secondary education at the Normal College of Dolisie, Congo, at the Lycée Savorgnan de Brazza in Brazzaville, and the Collège Bessieux in Libreville, earning the *brevet élémentaire* and the first part of the baccalaureate by 1958. Thereafter he taught from 1958 to 1960 in the regional school of Franceville. From 1960 to 1962 he specialized in political studies at the Institute of Advanced Overseas Studies in Paris. He also graduated from the Advanced International Police School at Dakar. From 1965 to 1970 he served in various intelligence units of the police before being named director-general of the Sûreté Nationale. When the latter was transformed into the national police in 1977, Assélé was named commander-in-chief and promoted to general. Concurrently he held several cabinet posts: Minister of Youth (1975–1976), Minister of National Education (1976–1983), Minister of Public Works (1983–1990). In

1989 Assélé was removed from his position as head of the national police force, allegedly because he failed to prevent the entry of MORENA tracts into the country and their distribution. In February 1990 he was transferred from the Ministry of Public Works to the Ministry of Water, Forests, and National Parks. In April 1990 he was dropped from the cabinet entirely. [1321]

ASSOCIATION GENERALE DES ETUDIANTS DU GABON (AGEG). An organization of Gabonese university students in France, important in the 1950s and 1960s. The first Gabonese scholarship holders arriving in France in 1949 organized the AGEG to promote and defend the interests of Gabonese students in higher education. The AGEG was modelled after the general African students' organization, the Fédération des Etudiants d'Afrique Noire en France (FEANF), with which it was affiliated. The FEANF was usually Marxist and militant in its support of anti-colonialist and left-wing political causes, but the AGEG tended to limit its activities more to student matters. Until 1960 it received a subsidy from the government. Politically active Gabonese students formed a separate organization, the Mouvement Gabonais d'Action Populaire, which published irregularly a newspaper, *La Cognée* (*The Hatchet*), and political tracts. While its members pursued their activities in relative freedom under the Fourth Republic, they ran into trouble after Gabon acquired its own government, which moved against its student critics. The activities of the Mouvement led to the suppression of the scholarships of some of its leaders and legal actions against them in 1960. Though the movement continued to exist until 1967, it was in 1960 that the AGEG became more active politically. For the next decade it would provide a permanent external opposition to the government in power. In January 1961, its president Xavier Onde-Ndzé, and a member of its executive bureau, N'Dong-Obiang, were arrested at the Cité Universitaire of the University of Paris and expelled from France at the request of the Gabonese government. Subsequently the AGEG strongly criticized the French military intervention of February 1964 and called for revolutionary action to bring down the Mba government. Its monthly newspaper, *L'Etudiant du Gabon,* was thereafter banned in Gabon. In 1965 its president, Marc Mba-N'Dong, was expelled from France. Continued criticisms and policies of the Bongo government led to legal restrictions on their activities. On July 18, 1971, the Gabonese Council of Ministers dissolved all corporative associations of Gabonese students both at home and abroad. It authorized the students of the national university to create a representative movement that alone would have the right to speak and act in their name. Every student receiving financial aid must belong to this movement. Action was taken among the governments of overseas countries that receive Gabonese students, especially the French government, to ensure execution of these requirements. Thus weakened, the AGEG for all practical purposes ceased to operate. [599, 547, 965]

ASSOCIATION PROFESSIONNELLE DES AGENTS INDI-GENES DES CADRES LOCAUX DU GROUPE DE L'AFRIQUE EQUATORIALE FRANCAISE. With the bureaucratization of the colonial administration in the late nineteenth century and the growth of discrimination against Africans, the civil service was divided into a European cadre and a "local" one. Only Africans who held the baccalaureate were henceforth admitted to the European cadre (one Gabonese received the bac at Rennes in the 1890s and three others at Nice and Bordeaux in the 1930s) and the local cadres received considerably lower salaries than their metropolitan equivalents and fewer fringe benefits. After the First World War, higher Myènè and West African civil servants at Libreville, who shunned activity in the Ligue des Droits de l'Homme for fear of reprisals by the administration, formed the Association to ensure their representation on a commission sitting at Brazzaville to determine salaries. They delegated a Gabonese working there to represent them and spurred formation of branches at Brazzaville and Bangui. The Association gained satisfaction on some issues because of their moderation and fear by the government-general of loss of trained functionaries to the Belgian Congo, which often raided the cadres at Libreville. After a dormant period, the Association revived in the late 1930s in the more favorable climate of the Popular Front. At that time the Gabonese elite at Brazzaville maintained an Association des Fonctionnaires, which was dominated by three young civil servants who had studied together at the Catholic seminary—Jean-Hilaire Aubame (q.v.), René-Paul Sousatte (q.v.), and Jean-Rémy Ayouné (q.v.). In June 1940, after the fall of France, the Association's leaders told Governor-General Pierre Boisson that they supported continued resistance to the Germans. They later established close links in August 1940 with the Free French. After the Second World War the Association Professionnelle itself was transformed into an Association des Fonctionnaires with branches at the federal capital and in each of the four territories of French Equatorial Africa. [550]

AUBAME, JEAN-HILAIRE (1912–1989). Gabonese politician (1946–1964) and French deputy (1946–1958). Aubame was born into a Fang family near Libreville on November 10, 1912. Left an orphan at an early age, he came under the care of the Abbé Jean Obame (d. 1934), who arranged for his education in a Catholic primary school and at the minor seminary. When Aubame left the major seminary, Father Obame's brother, Léon Mba (q.v.), helped him to obtain a position in the customs service. Transferred to Brazzaville in 1936, he founded a branch of the Mutuelle Gabonaise in cooperation with a brother of Louis Bigmann (q.v.). He became involved along with Jean-Rémy Ayouné (q.v.) and René Sousatte (q.v.) in various Catholic and *évolué* organizations and activities. He was among those who rallied to the Free French movement (q.v.) and was therefore sent by its leadership in November 1940 to Libreville to win over the Fang to the Free French cause. Back in Brazzaville, in February 1942 he became a protégé of Governor-General Félix Eboué (q.v.) and his main informant on African affairs. In February 1943 Eboué promoted him, along with several other Africans, into the European section of the civil service. In 1944 Eboué named Aubame as president of the new municipal commission of the Poto Poto section of the capital, to which he also named three other Gabonese. Aubame was among the *évolués* who helped to prepare position papers for the Brazzaville Conference of January–February 1944. After Eboué's death, Aubame became an adviser to Socialist Governor-General André Bayardelle and to his secretary-general, André Soucadoux. With their encouragement and support, he returned to Gabon to seek election as the second electoral college's deputy to the French National Assembly. Within Gabon he had the support of the administration and the missions. Aubame was elected in November 1946 and then reelected in June 1951 and January 1956. He thus served until the end of the Fourth French Republic in September 1958. In Paris he affiliated at first with the Socialists but then with an African parliamentary group, the Indépendants d'Outre-Mer, which was led by Léopold Sédar Senghor of Senegal and Dr. Louis-Paul Aujoulat of Cameroon. Aubame played an important role in several Assembly committees dealing with overseas matters. He purchased a home in Paris and established his family there to facilitate the education of his many children. At the same time he made annual tours of all the provinces of Gabon.

In Gabon itself Aubame was active right after the war in the efforts to revitalize the Fang and was influential in the movement to regroup the clans (the *alar ayong*) (q.v.) to this end. In 1947 he organized the Union Démocratique et Sociale Gabonaise (q.v.), a party centered upon regional notables throughout the interior but drawing its leadership from the Fang of the Woleu-N'Tem Province. In March 1952 Aubame was elected to the Territorial Assembly from the Woleu N'Tem and was reelected in March 1957. Though his party received 60 percent of the votes cast in that election, it won only 18 of the 40 seats. The Bloc Démocratique Gabonais (q.v.) and independents, backed by some of the wealthy Europeans in the Assembly, selected Léon Mba by a vote of 21–19 as the vice president of the first government council. Aubame's party accepted four of the 12 ministerial posts, but Aubame himself did not enter the government. After independence Aubame cooperated with President Mba by accepting nomination on a single slate of candidates for the National Assembly selected by the latter. Elected to the National Assembly in February 1961 from the Moyen-Ogooué Province, he thereafter joined a coalition government as Minister of Foreign Affairs. He served until May 1962 when, as a result of conflicts with the president, he was demoted to Minister of State for Foreign Affairs. Early in 1963 he was dropped from the cabinet after his refusal to join a single party headed by Mba. Mba thereupon appointed him president of the Supreme Court in the expectation that he would have to abandon his Assembly seat and thereby lose his parliamentary immunity. But on January 10, 1964, Aubame resigned instead from the court. When Mba dissolved the National Assembly and announced new elections with arrangements that favored the BDG, Aubame and his party declared their intention to abstain from participation. Soon thereafter occurred the coup of February 1964 against Mba by elements of the army and gendarmerie and their establishment of a provisional government, to which they called Aubame its head. After the intervention of French troops and the restoration of Mba, Aubame was arrested. Though not considered by most observers to have been a party to the organization of the coup or to have had foreknowledge of it, he was placed on trial at Lambaréné in August 1964. On September 10 he was condemned to 10 years hard labor and 10 years banishment. On Independence Day 1972 President Bongo released him. Thereafter he lived in Paris and was no longer active in politics. During a visit to Libreville in the fall of 1981, Aubame accepted the largely honorary appointment as special adviser to President Bongo. He disappointed the supporters of MORENA by his refusal to take up their cause. Extremists who nevertheless believed him sympathetic to that movement bombed his home on December 12, 1984, on the eve of a press conference by MORENA-in-exile. Aubame and his family barely escaped harm. Aubame died in 1989. *See* COUP OF FEBRUARY 17–20, 1964; POLITICS. [65, 550, 599, 593, 569, 1380]

AVARO, PIERRE (1911–date of death unknown). Politician. Avaro was born on March 15, 1911, at Port-Gentil among the Orungu (q.v.) people. He was one of the handful of Gabonese to earn the higher primary diploma before the Second World War. Keenly interested in education, he organized the Association of Parents of Pupils and Students of Gabon (Association des Parents d'Elèves et d'Etudiants du Gabon). (*Elèves* is the term for the primary level, *étudiants* for the secondary.) Avaro gained eminence as the president of the labor union which grouped the workers on Gabon's plantations and forest enterprises. He himself headed the administration of a national forestry enterprise dealing in okoumé. From 1960 to 1963 Avaro served as secretary-general of the BDG (q.v.), which earlier he had helped to organize. He sat in the National Assembly from February 1961 and headed six different ministries at various periods between November 1960 and December 1966. [1380]

AWANDJI. The Awandji are an Mbédé-speaking people south of Lastoursville in the upper Ogooué and are closely related to the Adouma (q.v.). Traditionally they exchanged their meat for the Adouma's fish. In 1928–1929 they revolted against the exactions of the colonial administration.

The revolt resulted from the increasing demands of the French administration upon a population already victimized for three decades by the commercial monopoly of the SHO (q.v.). The French instituted a *capitation,* or head tax, among the Awandji in 1923 and *prestation,* or unpaid required labor, in 1926. In December 1927 they demanded that the Awandji bring provisions regularly to the market at Lastoursville for the benefit of the French post. Not only were the prices paid unattractive but appearance at market made the Awandji more liable for enforcement of the capitation and prestation, not to mention recruitment for construction of the Congo-Ocean Railroad (1921–1934). Starting in January 1928, Chief Wongo led 12 other chiefs and about 1,500 villagers in resisting French demands for bringing foodstuffs to Lastoursville. French attempts at repression encountered a guerrilla warfare, which was not suppressed until May 1929. At the Awandji surrender the African militia (*tirailleurs*) executed scores of resisters and took 150 prisoners. Chief Wongo and another leader, Chief Lessibi, died three months later aboard a steamer in transit to Bangui for trial. [283, 266, 313, 319]

AYOUNE, JEAN-REMY (1914–   ). Civil servant and intellectual. Ayouné was born in an Nkomi (q.v.) area, at Assewe
near Fernan-Vaz in the Ogooué-Maritime Province on June
5, 1914. He received his early education in the Catholic
school at Lambaréné. His studies for the priesthood at the
Catholic seminaries of Libreville (1927–1931) and Brazzaville (1931–1933) made him one of the best educated
Gabonese of his day. Ayouné joined the federal civil service
in 1934 at Libreville. There with François-de-Paul Vane
(q.v.), he founded the Mutuelle Gabonaise (q.v.) of which he
served as secretary. Thereafter in July 1937 he was assigned
to Brazzaville, where he held senior posts in the financial and
personnel departments of the government-general.

In February 1942 he became the secretary-general of the
Union Educative et Mutuelle de la Jeunesse de Brazzaville,
an organization led by young educated Gabonese. In 1943
Governor-General Félix Eboué (q.v.) promoted him, along
with other Gabonese, into the European cadres of the civil
service, provoking lawsuits by European co-workers and
strikes by Congolese employees. In January 1944 Eboué
named him to the municipal commission of the Poto-Poto
district of Brazzaville. At the same time, a paper he prepared
for the Brazzaville Conference on the respective roles of
African and western cultures in an evolving Africa revealed
him as a talented social philosopher. The essay,
''Occidentalisme et Africanisme,'' was later published in
Renaissances (1944). Between 1946 and 1960 Ayouné held
various positions in the civil service at Libreville, except for
1956–1957 when he served in the Délégation de l'AEF in
Paris. In September 1957, he was named an administrator of
Overseas France, that is, a member of the top-level of the
civil service, heretofore occupied by Europeans. With the
arrival of independence, he held several ambassadorial posts
(1960–1964) and high administrative positions (secretary-
general of the government, 1964–1966; Minister of the Civil
Service, 1966–1968; Minister of Foreign Affairs & Cooperation, July 1968 to June 1971; Minister of Justice, June
1971–September 1972). In July 1976 Ayouné became presi-

dent of the Chamber of Commerce, Agriculture, Industry, and Mines. [1205, 135, 550, 1367, 4, 5]

- B -

BABUISSI. A people who are linguistically part of the Eshira group. They live inland in the upper Nyanga River Basin. Part of them inhabit the Congo Republic. [283]

BAKELE. The Bakèlè were important hunters, especially of elephant tusks, and traders over large areas in northern Gabon during the nineteenth century. They are better known historically under the Myènè name, Bakèlè or Akèlè, than by their own name, Bongom or Bougom. Bakèlè traditions indicate their presence many centuries ago throughout vast areas of the forests and savannas from Booué on the middle Ogooué River west to the lower Como, and from the Monts de Cristal to the lower N'Gounié and to the various lakes on both sides of the lower Ogooué to the northwest and southwest. At their arrival they found only Pygmies, with whom they sometimes lived in symbiosis. Though they established farming villages, their hunters continued to range far and wide in search of elephants and other game. In the process they came into conflict with other peoples who were entering these areas. By the early nineteenth century they had become parts of the trading networks that fanned out from the Estuary and Ogooué River delta. On the upper Como and Bokoué (a Como tributary) rivers, from the Fang they obtained ivory, which they exchanged along with their own ivory, with the Séké on the lower Como, who exchanged it with the Mpongwe of the Estuary. On the Ogooué and N'Gounié rivers they were involved in a more linear type of network in which they controlled sections of the rivers and therefore all trade going either upstream or downstream. In the wake of the increased demand for slaves between the 1760s and 1860s the Bakèlè became more active in slave raiding. They were the only Gabonese people, in fact, to indulge in large-scale slave raiding of their neighbors in addition to purchasing slaves and to selling some of their own people. In the middle third of the nineteenth century the Bakèlè were believed to number at least 25,000 persons, a total double that of the largest Myènè (q.v.) people. They were nowhere so numerous, however, as the Fang peoples whose southward and westward migrations began to force them to move down the Como and the Bokoué toward the Estuary and ultimately to disperse for the first time into the upper Ogooué and Ivindo rivers and their eastern tributaries where several thousands of Bakèlè still live. Though the Bakèlè were fierce warriors, they were sent into retreat by the equally intrepid Fang (q.v.), who were better organized for warfare.

During the 1870s the Bakèlè on the middle Ogooué were almost the sole suppliers of rubber to the European traders who were penetrating the region. From these locations they also continued to export dyewood and ebony.

Some Bakèlè chiefs on the Como River along with some Séké chiefs made a treaty on December 2, 1846, recognizing French sovereignty, but the absence of central authority, the wide dispersion, and the semi-nomadic life of many Bakèlè made it impossible for the French to deal with most of them. It also hindered American Protestant missionary efforts among them. The ABCFM of Boston, which had its headquarters at Baraka east of Libreville, in 1849 established a mission 25 miles to the east and 12 miles up the Ikoi Creek at Olandebenk, among the Bakèlè. Missionaries transcribed Dikèlè into the Latin alphabet, prepared some school booklets and tracts, and translated portions of the Scriptures. Unsettled conditions in the area, resulting from conflicts among the Bakèlè between them and other peoples, forced the closing of the post by the end of the 1850s. Later the ABCFM ministered to the Bakèlè from the island of Nengenenge, where the Bokoué flows north into the Como River, a work assumed by the American Presbyterians in 1870. At Nengenenge the first Mpongwe Presbyterian pastor, the Reverend Ntâkâ Truman, and his wife, Emma, ran a boarding school for Bakèlè children until 1881. The American Presbyterian missionary, Robert Hamill Nassau, M.D., in 1882 opened a station among the Bakèlè at Talagouga on the middle Ogooué. This station would be transferred to the French Protestants in 1892.

Independence in 1960 would find the Bakèlè the most widely dispersed of any people in Gabon and numbering around 10,000. Though now absent from the Como and Remboué rivers as a result of Fang pressures, they have settled in the Lambaréné department and in 10 other departments from the Atlantic to the eastern frontiers. Those in the extreme east live among the Bakota (q.v.) to whom they are gradually assimilating. [394, 261, 362, 252, 234, 1028]

BAKOTA (or KOTA). The Bakota of northeastern Gabon are one of the country's most numerous peoples. Other thousands of them inhabit adjacent regions of the Congo Republic. According to their traditions the Bakota came from the upper Ivindo region along the Singoué and Nona rivers (its western tributaries) in the nineteenth century to their present locations farther south and east in the face of Bakouélé invasions. These invasions were known as the War of Poupou after a ferocious cannibalistic Bakouélé warrior. The Bakouélé (q.v.) themselves were being forced south and east by Fang (q.v.) invaders. En route the Bakota encountered the Chiwa (q.v.) with whom they established friendly relations and who were also heading downriver. On the southward trip some Bakota headed westward where they eventually became the Benga. Others descended to the junction of the Ogooué where they were attacked by another Bakouélé warrior, Mékomba, following Poupou's death. Finally, some of the Bakota were able to defeat the Bakouélé and kill Mékomba. They assimilated the Bakouélé remnants. Other Bakota settled on the eastern tributaries of the Ivindo River and along the upper Ogooué toward Lastoursville. Arrival of the Fang around Booué forced the Bakota there to move east beyond the Ivindo. Those who settled around Mékambo used the iron of the vicinity to make high-quality weapons and tools. These traditions suggest that the present Bakota are quite a mixture of peoples swept together by the various Bakouélé and Fang invasions. The presence of some of the same clans among the Bakota and other peoples of the east and even among the Fang gives further evidence of this mingling.

The SHO (q.v.) concession in the 1890s encompassed the

Bakota areas. The Bakota exchanged ivory, rubber, goats, and chickens for guns, axes, matches, knives, and fabrics. With the arrival of the French military Booué became a commercial center for the Bakota areas, and porters were required to a greater extent. Companies based in the Congo basin such as the Tréchot Brothers and the Compagnie Ngoko-Sangha also traded in the Bakota regions. [365, 885, 283]

BAKOUELE. The Bakouélé people occupy the upper Ivindo River as far as Makokou as well as adjacent areas of the Middle Congo and Cameroon. They also have several villages north of Mékambo. Their traditions relate that they migrated to these areas from the sources of the Ivindo under pressures from the Fang (q.v.). At the arrival of the French, they had advanced along the Ivindo as far as Mipemba but thereafter regrouped above the French post at Makokou. From there they exchanged ivory and rubber for various manufactures and salt. [894, 284]

BANKING. The organization of the country's banking reflects its French colonial past and continuing ties with France and other capitalist countries. The largest bank, the Banque Gabonaise de Développement (BGD) has a capital of 4 billion CFA francs of which 54.5 percent represent the participation of the state. It was organized as a public institution in 1960 as the successor to the Société Gabonaise de Crédit to provide both financial and technical assistance for economic development. It undertakes operations on its own account and on behalf of the government and public institutions. It can make loans of up to 10 years to private enterprises and subscribe capital to them for the same maximum period. There are several commercial banks, including such important foreign ones as the Banque de Paris et des Pays-Bas (the Paribas), Barclay's Bank International, and Citibank. Some Brazilian and Arab banks also have branches in Libreville. [723, 440, 1364, 1365]

BANTU SETTLEMENT. All of the 40 or so peoples native to Gabon, other than the Pygmies, belong to the Bantu group.

Bantu peoples today inhabit the southern half of the African continent. The origins and movements of the Bantu have been sources of much investigation and speculation during recent decades. It is believed that at a distant time, perhaps several thousand years ago, there was a single Bantu people defined by its common heredity, culture, and language. During movement that covered many hundreds of years, the original people divided and subdivided and became differentiated culturally and linguistically. At the same time various Bantu absorbed and incorporated elements from non-Bantu groups while some non-Bantu groups adopted elements of Bantu culture and language. As a result of these several processes, the term Bantu has come to refer primarily to language and only secondarily to culture and heredity.

Research by German scholars has produced evidence for the possibility of Bantu speakers, particularly of the Myènè (q.v.) group, in the Estuary as long as 2,000 years ago. More certain is that the movements of Bantu peoples into Gabon occurred throughout many centuries and that once within Gabon they transferred to new locations as a result of pressures from or conflicts with other peoples. The oral traditions of practically all the Bantu peoples tell of such developments as well as of encounters with groups of Pygmies (q.v.), who often served them as guides and who moved farther into the dense forests to pursue their own way of life. When the Portuguese arrived along the northern coasts and the Estuary in the late fifteenth and sixteenth centuries, they encountered groups that well may have been the ancestors of the Mpongwe, Séké, and Nkomi (qq.v.). The populations they found south of Fernan-Vaz as far as Loango (q.v.) may have been the ancestors of the Vili (q.v.). Of other peoples, it is difficult to speak with certainty about much more than the general directions from which they came. Thus it is believed that the Bakèlè, Benga, Bakota, and Okandé group (Mitsogo, Shimba, Pove [qq.v.]) came from the north and northeast; the Eshira, Bapounou, and Loumbou (qq.v.) from the south and southeast; the Téké and Mbédé group (Obamba, Ndoumou, Awandji, Adouma [qq.v.]) from the east.

In the late eighteenth century and early nineteenth century, the Fang (q.v.) left the north and northeast and moved toward the south and southwest, generating new movements among most of the peoples they encountered and leading to a new wave of conflicts. The Fang eventually spread out over the northern half of the country, except for the extreme northeast, and into the southern coastal regions as far south as Setté-Cama. The Fang were seeking to make direct contact with European traders along the coasts and rivers, which is the same reason that had moved other peoples in a coastal direction in the previous three centuries. [394, 284, 102]

BAPOUNOU (or POUNOU). The Bapounou are numerically one of the most important peoples. They inhabit inland areas of southwestern Gabon in the mountains and grasslands in the upper N'Gounié and Nyanga River systems. In earlier periods, the name Bayaka, which they consider to have a pejorative sense, was applied to them. Other Bapounou inhabit the adjacent Divénié and Mossendjo districts as well as Kibangou District north of the buckle of the Niari River in the Congo Republic. Until 1925 Divénié District formed part of Gabon. Bapounou traditions indicate a migration in the wake of wars to their present areas prior to the nineteenth century from the south, from regions as far away perhaps as the Congo or as close as the Niari-Kwilou Rivers. During the nineteenth century the Bapounou sent slaves from their own ranks or acquired from inland peoples to Loango and Fernan Vaz. They also gathered rubber for export. Like the neighboring Eshira (q.v.), to whom they are linguistically related, they produce a fine cloth of palm fibers as well as arrowheads, spears, and sabers of high-quality iron. [834, 852, 856, 888, 284, 384, 834]

BATSANGUI (or TSANGUI). An Mbédé-speaking people, closely related to the Nzabi. They inhabit an enclave within Nzabi lands in the southeast. Other Batsangui live in the Congo Republic.

BENGA. The Benga people of Cape Esterias on the northern coast are fishermen who accepted French rule in 1852. Part of the Benga inhabit Corisco Island and the coast of Equatorial Guinea.

Benga traditions suggest distant origins in the grasslands

of Cameroon north of the rain forests from which they began to migrate as a result of pressures from other peoples, quite possibly in the eighteenth century. The migrants travelled southward along rivers until, at the Ivindo River, they separated into several groups. One group remained there and became the Bakota (q.v.). Other groups, which became the Benga, followed the rivers and streams that enter the Atlantic north of the Estuary in Gabon, Equatorial Guinea, and Cameroon. These latter groups located near the mouths of these rivers and adjacent coasts and on offshore islands. By 1800 they had become important middlemen in the ivory and redwood trade north of the Estuary. Thus in the late 1840s at the arrival of Christian missionaries the Benga were inhabiting Cape Esterias, Corisco, and the Elobey Islands, as well as Cape San Juan (St. Jean). They lived mainly from fishing, agriculture, and trading. Corisco and the portions of the mainland where the American Presbyterians evangelized from 1850 later became part of Spanish Guinea or Rio Muni (the mainland portion of today's Equatorial Guinea). The French Catholic mission at Cape Esterias came under French sovereignty in 1852 as a result of a treaty with several Benga clan heads. In 1855 the French navy had to intervene to rescue the Holy Ghost Fathers (q.v.) and some of their converts whom traditionalists had captured and threatened with death, and to evacuate the Sisters of the Immaculate Conception (q.v.). In 1859 the Catholic missionaries decided to withdraw completely when disputes with the traditionalists again threatened their safety and that of the Christian community, which by this time numbered several hundred persons. Some Benga children continued to pursue their education in the Catholic schools of Libreville. The missionaries returned between 1878 and 1904, at which time they withdrew definitively because the population they served had dwindled to only 200. During the twentieth century some Benga moved into the Libreville area where they assimilated with the Mpongwe (q.v.). Among the most notable Benga in public life was François-de-Paul Vané (q.v.), who played an important role in politics in the 1920s and 1930s. He was a descendant of Chief Vané of Venje, one of the early Catholic converts, who had moved his family to Libreville in 1859.

On the Protestant side, the first Presbyterian convert on Corisco, Ibea J. Ikenga (q.v.), was later ordained a pastor in 1870. Rev. Ibea's influence for several decades extended to some of his fellow Benga on the mainland in French territory. [283, 394]

BESSIEUX, JEAN-REMY (1803–1876). Founder of French Roman Catholic mission in Gabon and first bishop. Monsignor Bessieux was born on December 24, 1803, at Villieux in the Montpellier diocese. He served as a parish priest and minor seminary teacher before entering the Holy Heart of Mary Congregation in August 1842, which François Libermann had founded to evangelize the black race. (In 1848 it merged with the older Holy Ghost Fathers [q.v.] and retained that name.) Bessieux arrived in Gabon in September 1844 in the company of Brother Grégoire Say. He founded a post at Okolo in the territories of the Agekaza-Quaben clan of the Mpongwe people not far from the French fort. Bessieux learned Mpongwe well enough to publish a grammar (1847). He founded a boys' school and St. Mary's Church and arranged for the arrival of the Immaculate Conception Sisters of Castres (1849). His attempts to found other posts in the Estuary in the early 1850s proved unsuccessful. Except for brief visits to Europe to restore his health, he labored in Gabon, after December 1848 as bishop, until his death on April 30, 1876. Bessieux's experiences in Gabon influenced the missionary doctrine of his congregation, which in its comparative lack of ethnocentrism was far ahead of its time. Bessieux's determination to remain in Gabon even without official support if necessary, on several occasions when the government was thinking of withdrawing, quite likely influenced the French decisions to remain. [1016, 1029, 1001, 1002, 1068, 305, 236]

BIFFOT, LAURENT-MARIE (1925–). Sociologist. Born at Nkovié in the Moyen-Ogooué Province on February 25, 1925, into a prominent Mpongwe (q.v.) family, Biffot was sent to the Ecole Montfort (q.v.) in Libreville for his early studies and thereafter entered a Catholic seminary for several years. He completed his secondary education at Rennes,

France, where he later received a doctorate in sociology. In December 1957 he became a researcher for the Office de la Recherche Scientifique et Technique d'Outre-Mer (q.v.) in Paris and then after December 1959 in Libreville. He has made important studies of the rural populations, youth, and labor. After the opening of the university at Libreville in 1970, Biffot became a professor there as well as dean of letters and social sciences. From 1973 to 1975 he served as vice rector and in 1975–1976 rector of the university. Since then he has held a variety of posts in the PDG and the government. [1205, 1367]

BIGMANN, LOUIS (1897–ca. 1988). Journalist and politician. Bigmann was born at Libreville on October 18, 1897, into a prominent Mpongwe (q.v.) family. His family name is a translation of the Mpongwe name *Onom'mpolo* or "big man" given to an Agwempónó clan ancestor who was a highly successful trader. Bigmann is also descended from Toko (q.v.), the leading trader at Glass in the mid-nineteenth century and is a nephew of the wealthy lumberman, Paulin Auleley. After studies at the Ecole Montfort (q.v.), Bigmann served as a non-commissioned officer, along with his cousin, Laurent Antchouey (q.v.), in the Cameroons campaign, 1916–1919. After the war the two became active in the Ligue des Droits de l'Homme. Together they went in 1921 to work as shipping clerks at Dakar where they founded the anti-colonialist paper *L'Echo Gabonais,* which Antchouey thereafter edited at Nice, France. Bigmann served in the French army again during the Second World War, this time on the western front, where he was wounded and taken prisoner in the battle of the Somme at the same time his colleague Captain Charles N'Tchoréré (q.v.) was assassinated by a German officer. After release in 1942 Bigmann joined the resistance. In October 1944 he founded the journal *l'Empire.* Repatriated to Gabon in May 1946, he thereafter worked as a journalist and was frequently an unsuccessful candidate for office, between 1948 and 1953 as representative of the Gaullist movement, the Rassemblement du Peuple Français. From 1953 to 1955 Bigmann headed the association of war veterans. As an ally of Léon Mba (q.v.), he became administrative secretary of the BDG (q.v.) and editor of its paper, *L'Union Gabonaise*. In February 1961 he became president of the National Assembly and later in 1966 president of the Supreme Court. [252, 550, 663]

BLOC DEMOCRATIQUE GABONAIS. The BDG was a political party founded by Senator Paul Gondjout (q.v.) in April 1954 to oppose the UDSG (q.v.) of Deputy Jean-Hilaire Aubame (q.v.). Aubame had succeeded in replacing René-Paul Sousatte (q.v.) with Jean-Jacques Boucavel (q.v.) in 1953 when the Territorial Assembly elected its representative to the Assembly of the French Union. Gondjout feared that he would not be reelected to the Senate if he did not organize Aubame's opponents. Gondjout served as secretary-general of the BDG, and Léon Mba (q.v.) became its Secretary. Between June 1954 and 1961 the BDG edited a paper, the *Union Gabonaise*. Though the UDSG won a majority of the popular votes in the April 1957 Assembly elections, the BDG with the aid of Independents and French allies was able to name the first government under the Loi-Cadre reforms. The party thereafter controlled the legislative and executive branches of the government. After independence, Mba quarreled with Gondjout over the form of the government with Gondjout favoring a parliamentary regime and Mba wishing a presidential one. Mba jailed Gondjout and replaced him as secretary-general of the BDG. After Mba's death in November 1967, President Bongo dissolved the BDG and other parties on March 12, 1968, and replaced them with a single party, the PDG. [550, 551, 617]

BONGO, ALI (1959–). Politician. The son of President Omar Bongo was born on February 9, 1959. Following his father's conversion to Islam in 1973, he also became a Muslim and changed his name from Alain to Ali Bongo. After receiving a doctorate in law from the University of Paris, Ali in March 1984 became the personal representative of the president. From August 1989 to June 1991, he served as Minister of Foreign Affairs, a post he had to relinquish because of the new constitutional requirement that ministers must be at least thirty-five years old. Ali Bongo was among the younger and better-educated elements within the Central Committee of the PDG who sought democratic reforms without further delay in 1989–1990. In September 1990 he was elected to the National Assembly from the Haut-Ogooué Province. He is married to a daughter of former prime minister Léon Mébiame and is a friend of Jean-Christophe Mitterrand, the French president's son.

BONGO, MARTIN (1940–   ). Politician. The relative of Omar Bongo was born at Lekei in the Leconi district of the Haut-Ogooué Province on July 4, 1940. After primary education at Franceville, he prepared for a career in primary education at the Normal School in Mitzic, followed by *stages* at the Advanced Normal Schools of Brazzaville and Abidjan, where he earned the Certificat d'aptitude à l'Inspection de l'Enseignement Primaire. Thereafter he was named an inspector of primary education in the Haut-Ogooué Province. In 1966 he left teaching to become the *directeur de cabinet* for the vice president. After a year as head of primary education during 1972–1973, from October 1973 until April 1975 he served as Minister of National Education and Scientific Research. In August 1976 he became Minister of Foreign Affairs, a post he held until succeeded by Ali Bongo in August 1989. [1321]

BONGO, OMAR (1935–   ). President since November 1967; reelected in 1973, 1979, and 1986. Bongo, who had the first names of Albert-Bernard until 1973, was born on December 30, 1935, at Lewai, the Lekoni Prefecture, Haut-Ogooué Province, among the Téké (q.v.) people. He was the youngest of nine children, and his father died when he was seven. The Haut-Ogooué formed part of the Middle Congo at that time, so young Albert was sent to a public school in the Bacongo section of Brazzaville where relatives lived. He completed secondary studies in commerce at the technical lycée in the capital, and in 1958 entered the posts and telegraphic services of the administration. During this period Bongo was encouraged by Chief Postal Inspector Naudy, a militant socialist, to pursue a career in administration. As a member of the socialist union, the C.G.T.-Force Ouvrière, he acquired familiarity with socialist doctrines. Between July 1958 and October 1960, he served as a second lieutenant in the French Army of the Air, with postings in Chad, the Central African Republic, and the Congo. At Ndjaména he was able to study philosophy and, as an independent candidate, pass the examinations for the baccalaureate. While still serving as a lieutenant, he was assigned to the Ministry of Foreign Affairs of Gabon (1960–1962). Between 1962 and 1965 he served as assistant director and then director of the president's cabinet, that is, top assistant to President Mba (q.v.). At the same time he had responsibility for information and tourism (February 1963–April 1964), and then for national defense (April 1964–September 1965) in the wake of the February 1964 coup. In September 1965 he became minister-delegate of the presidency responsible for national defense and coordination. In November 1966 Mba named him vice president of the government responsible for defense, the plan, information, and tourism. By that time Mba was aware of his own serious illness and the necessity of providing for a succession. He thus advanced the date of the presidential election and established the position of vice president of the republic. In a national election on March 19, 1967, Bongo was elected vice president and Mba reelected president. At Mba's death on November 28 of that year, Bongo became president.

Upon his succession, Bongo responded to the urgings of the National Assembly for a policy of reconciliation with the opponents of Mba but without altering the authoritarian regime with its strong presidency. Thus between 1968 and 1972, he released or reduced the sentences of the coup makers and the members of the provisional government sentenced at the Lambaréné trial in 1964. The capable and cooperative among them were reintegrated into the civil service, and, in several cases, given ministries or lower cabinet positions. The exception was Jean-Hilaire Aubame (q.v.), whom Bongo criticized in 1968 as "having brought the country to the brink of catastrophe through his reckless ambition." Bongo released Aubame from solitary confinement on the Ile des Perroquets in August 1972 and permitted him to leave the country.

As a part of reconciliation under authoritarian rule, President Bongo dissolved all existing parties and on March 12, 1968, created a single party, the Parti Démocratique Gabonais (q.v.), of which he is the secretary-general. He urged a *rénovation* or renewal that would invigorate national life through greater participation and zeal and that would involve greater *dialogue*. This would take place within the PDG, which was the only legal forum for political discussion and criticism.

In addition to being president and party head, until August 1981 Bongo also headed the government (the prime minister was the vice president of the government) and several ministries. Among them were defense, information, planning and development (1969–1981), territorial management (1972–1981), national guidance (1974–1981), and postal services and telecommunications (1975–1981). At times he was also minister of foreign affairs. In 1981, in response to criticism within the party, Bongo transferred the headship of the government to the prime minister. But in practice Prime Minister Léon Mébiame (q.v.) was allowed very little initiative. Bongo at the same time formally relinquished his ministries. But he controlled the ministries of foreign affairs and defense by appointing members of his family and close relatives to head them. As foreign affairs minister, he selected Martin Bongo (q.v.) (1981–1989), Ali Bongo (q.v.) (1989–1991), and Pascaline Bongo (June 1991–   ). Bongo reshuffled some of the more than 40 cabinet posts (ministers and secretaries of state) three to four times a year to secure greater efficiency and continued loyalty. He required members of the government to take a loyalty oath to him as head of state and party. Until 1990 all male members of the cabinet were required to belong to the Masonic lodge in Libreville that Bongo heads and that gives him valuable contacts in France. Bongo personally took charge of the civic service and specialized organisms of the party.

In his life-style the president followed a policy of grandeur involving considerable extravagance. He reportedly spent as much as $300 million for the new presidential palace, which contains his residence and the executive offices. Sparing no expense to hasten construction, he had Carrara marble flown in from Italy. The palace was built on the site of two historic buildings, the colonial governor's residence and St. Peter's Catholic Church, both of which were razed to secure a large enough space. The president also maintains other residences at Libreville, Port-Gentil, Franceville, and abroad. Bongo is believed to have spent vast sums to host the 1977 meeting of the Organization of African Unity, some of them for hotel construction of permanent use, and on the beautification of the capital. In 1986, when Gabon had already entered an economic downturn, Bongo added $70 million to the costs of the Transgabonais by hastening completion of construction in time for his fifty-first birthday.

After his marriage to Joséphine Kama in 1959, Bongo showed an interest in the Catholic religion of his wife but did not become a Christian. In September 1973 he announced his conversion to Islam, which he stated was a personal decision, and took the name of Omar, later calling himself El Hadj Omar after a pilgrimage to Mecca. Bongo's son, Ali Bongo, also became a Muslim as did a handful of politicians with the encouragement of the president. In this period Bongo undertook increased contacts with Arab countries in North Africa, some of which, as in the case of Libya, did not produce the expected results in terms of development aid. But the ties with the Morocco of Hassan II knotted at this time proved to be more durable. Scores of Moroccans would later serve in the Presidential Guard, which has responsibility for the president's safety.

In the area of foreign relations, Bongo, in 1973, announced a policy of nonalignment, which was followed by the establishment of diplomatic relations with the Arab and Communist nations as well as additional western ones. At the same time, while remaining closely linked with France, Bongo secured an adaptation of the cooperation agreements of 1960, which governed their relations, to permit greater Gabonese independence in policy-making and use of resources as well as less overt dependence on France.

Bongo's accession coincided with a wave of economic expansion based primarily on petroleum but also on manganese, uranium, and woods. To a much greater extent than Mba, he sought to secure Gabonese control over natural resources and greater benefits to the Gabonese from them. This led to the requirement for greater state participation in the ownership of enterprises and Gabonization of their senior personnel. State participation was necessary in view of the paucity of private capital. Gabonization advanced slowly because of the scarcity of Gabonese with advanced technical and managerial training. To promote the long-term development of the country, the president sought to use the increased revenues to construct an infrastructure that would decrease the dependence on petroleum products and would create a more diversified economy. To this end Bongo undertook the construction of the Transgabonais Railroad between Owendo on the Estuary and Franceville between 1974 and 1986 at a cost of at least $3 billion. By September 1978, when the first section between the Estuary and N'Djolé on the middle Ogooué opened for use, Gabon's economy was facing serious difficulties. Heavy charges on foreign loans for development and less than anticipated petroleum revenues were forcing cutbacks and slowdowns in the development programs.

The government's success in stabilizing the country's finances and reducing its debt during 1978 did not head off criticism of its policies at the Second Extraordinary Congress of the PDG in January 1979. The unprecedented criticism of the leader of the sole party by the delegates revealed a serious erosion in his authority. Nevertheless in November 1979 an ordinary party congress renominated him for another term as president to which he was popularly elected on December 30, 1979. Thereafter Bongo made changes in the electoral procedures that gave the local sections of the PDG a greater voice in selecting the candidates for public and party offices.

In January 1980 the Paris semi-monthly *Afrique-Asie* alleged that misuse of funds and corruption were a major source of Gabon's financial difficulties. It claimed that the president, his wife, and her brother, Jean-Boniface Assélé (q.v.), director of the national police and Minister of Public Works, had acquired vast real estate holdings as well as major interest in a score of companies involved in industry, construction, air transport, insurance, and banking. As the 1980s unfolded, it would be learned that Bongo and his associates were diverting one-quarter of the national budget for their personal use. Bongo himself has amassed wealth estimated at $100 million. No amount of wealth could enable Bongo to prevent the publication in October 1983 of *Affaires africaines* (q.v.), an exposé of his misdeeds and political intrigues involving French interests. Though the Mitterrand regime had to placate him in order to end the ensuing crisis, his reputation had suffered, even in conservative circles.

In the meantime, favorable world-market conditions during the first half of the 1980s had brought Gabon unprecedented revenues from petroleum, which could be used for development and social services. The Gabonese state expanded its role in the economy through several dozen parastatals, including some in agro-business. Bongo and his associates grew still richer. His regime, though concerned by the appearance of MORENA (q.v.), easily suppressed the new opposition, which had little popular support.

But the prolonged economic downturn that began in 1986 ultimately created sufficient popular discontent to bring about an upheaval during the first half of 1990. Though Bongo had to permit the restoration of multi-partyism and such freedoms as speech, press, and assembly, he was able to remain in office and to perpetuate his control of the government. At the same time the recurrent socioeconomic strife bore witness to his inability or unwillingness to reform his regime sufficiently so that it could undertake meaningful solutions to Gabon's long-term problems.

On a personal level, President Bongo's marriage to Joséphine Kama ended in divorce in 1988. As first lady she had devoted efforts to improving health care for women and children while pursuing her own literary interests. In early January 1990, Bongo married Edith Sassou-Nguesso, age twenty-seven, a recent graduate in medicine of the Marien Ngouabi University in Brazzaville. She is the daughter of Denis Sassou-Nguesso, former president of the Congo Republic. A daughter was born to the presidential couple in Paris in July 1991 and a son in August 1992. Bongo has three older children: Pascaline Bongo, Ali Bongo (q.v.), and Albertine Philiberte Bongo (d. 1993). *See* DECOLONIZATION; FOREIGN RELATIONS; POLITICS; INTRODUCTION. [1321, 603, 1, 65, 568, 601, 599, 418, 546]

BONGO, PASCALINE. Minister of Foreign Affairs. The eldest daughter of President Omar Bongo received part of her higher education in business administration during the early 1980s at the University of California at Los Angeles. Upon her return to Gabon, she served in the Ministry of Finances. When her brother Ali Bongo (q.v.) became ineligible for further service as Minister of Foreign Affairs under the terms of the constitution of March 1991 because he was under thirty-five years of age, she was appointed to succeed him. The father of Pascaline Bongo's child and her longtime companion is Jean Ping, Minister of Mines and Energy since August 1991. A PDG stalwart and former minister who has served as a presidential adviser, Ping is widely recognized for his expertise on economic and financial matters related to the petroleum industry.

BOUCAVEL, JEAN-JACQUES (né Boukakad; 1923–date of death unknown). Politician. Boucavel was born on February 21, 1923, into a Bapounou (q.v.) family at Kibangou, Congo Republic, just across the frontier from southern Gabon. He was educated to be a primary-school teacher at the Ecole Renard in Brazzaville and thereafter taught at Mouila. He was active in politics throughout the Fourth Republic. He allied with the Union Démocratique et Sociale Gabonaise (q.v.) of Jean-Hilaire Aubame (q.v.) at that time. He served in the Territorial Assembly from 1952 to 1957, in the Grand Council of the federation during the same period, and in the Assembly of the French Union from 1953 to 1958. In August 1958, he allied with René Sousatte (q.v.) in organizing a new party, PUNGA (q.v.), to represent southern peoples and to campaign against Gabon's joining the French Community in the September 1958 referendum. Subsequently he held various posts in the administration. Between September 1964 and February 1980, he was president of the Economic and Social Council. Thereafter, he served as a *haut conseiller d'État*. [1310, 550]

BOUET-WILLAUMEZ, EDOUARD (1808–1871). As a young naval officer from Brittany and then governor of Senegal, Bouët played a significant role from 1838 on in securing and implementing the policy that led to the establishment of a French post on the Estuary in June 1843. Bouët personally negotiated treaties with King Denis (q.v.) (February 9, 1839) and King Louis (q.v.) (March 18, 1841) that provided the legal bases for the French installation. The French decision of December 1842 to establish a naval station and trading post (*comptoir*) implemented a policy of the Orleanist regime to compete more actively in the commercial sphere in the Gulf of Guinea with the British, the dominant traders who seemed to be on the verge of further expansion. Bouët campaigned against the slave trade in both France and Great Britain. In this connection he wrote an important work, *Commerce et traite des noirs aux côtes occidentales d'Afrique* (1848). Bouët also was involved in the establishment of the settlement of freed slaves at Libreville in 1849. Born at Brest on April 24, 1808, he died in France on September 10, 1871. [283, 382, 332, 256]

BOUMAH, AUGUSTIN (1927–   ). Career civil servant. Boumah was born at Libreville on November 7, 1927. He received a secondary education there at the Collège Moderne (1942–1945) and professional training at the Ecole des Cadres Supérieurs in Brazzaville (1945–1948). He later attended the Ecole Nationale de la France d'Outre-Mer, the Paris school that trained the highest level of overseas administrators. As a career civil servant from 1949, he held important posts under the French and several high offices since independence. Among them have been head of the National School of Administration (1963–1967), president of the Supreme Court (1975–1980), and president of the National Assembly (Feb. 1980–June 1990). Boumah was a close relative of Léon Mba, who aided his political career, and he has been a confidant of Omar Bongo. [1367, 1321]

BOURDES-OGOULIGUENDE, JULES (1938–   ). Politician. Bourdès-Ogouliguendé was born on February 28, 1938, at Libreville. He studied at the Ecole Montfort there, then at the Ecole Saint-Louis of Port-Gentil, and the Collège Bessieux in Libreville. He did advanced studies in law at the universities of Lille, Montpellier, and Paris, receiving his doctorate from the last institution in 1972. Upon his return to Gabon, he held posts as magistrate before entering the government in March 1976 as Minister of the Civil Service and Administrative Reform to which was added the function of Minister of Justice in February 1978. In August 1981, he was made Minister of State for Labor and Employment. Then from 1983 to January 1990 he served as Minister of State for Higher Education and Scientific Research, a position from which he was ousted following a student strike at the Omar Bongo University. Thereafter he became Minister of Commerce, Industry, and Parliamentary Relations in the transitional government of April 1990. He was the only PDG candidate to gain election from the Ogooué-Maritime Province in the elections of September–October 1990 for the National Assembly. In November 1990, he was elected president of that body. [1321]

BRAZZA, PIERRE SAVORGNAN DE (1852–1905). Explorer and creator of the French Congo. An Italian-born aristocrat, Brazza became a French citizen in August 1874 while serving as a career officer in the French navy in Equatorial Africa. During his three expeditions under Naval Ministry auspices (1875–1878, 1880–1882, 1883–1885) he founded the French post at Franceville in June 1880, made a treaty with the *makoko* of the Téké (Tyo) at the Stanley Pool on September 10, 1880, and played a role in securing a treaty with the Maloango on March 12, 1883. His explorations helped to establish the bases for French sovereignty in the middle and upper Ogooué River system, on the Loango coast and the Kwilou-Niari River, and in the Congo River system north of the Pool. Brazza brought into being the colony of French Congo in 1886 of which an enlarged Gabon and Middle Congo formed the components. Further additions to territory, including some by him, would lead to the reorganization of the French Congo as the federation of French Equatorial Africa in 1910. Thus his activities had the effect of linking the evolution of Gabon to the three other territories (Middle Congo, Oubangi-Chari, Chad). Most Gabonese consider that this connection ultimately drew away their revenues and hindered their development.

Brazza's explorations added significant geographic information. He showed that the Ogooué River was not part of the Congo River system and there was no direct water route from Gabon into the Congo interior. At the same time he found out that the headwaters of the M'Passa River, an Ogooué River tributary, rose only a few miles from the headwaters of the Alima River, a northwestern tributary of the Congo.

Brazza served as commissioner-general of the French Congo from 1886 to 1897. He spent much of his energies in extending French control and claims, especially in relation to Germany. In 1905 Brazza was summoned from retirement to head an inquiry into the abuses of the concessionary regime, which the French government had installed in 1899 to promote economic development by private companies. He was overwhelmed by the injustices and brutalities of the system, to which his exaggerations about the riches of Equatorial Africa had inadvertently helped to give support. Though his report was never published and colonialist elements tried to discredit him, his inquiry resulted in the mitigation of some of the worst abuses and scaling down of many of the concessions. Moreover, Brazza retained his reputation among the peoples of the Ogooué and Congo as a peaceful explorer and friend. Brazza died at Dakar en route to France in September 1905. [394, 243, 265, 116]

BROTHERS OF SAINT GABRIEL. The Brothers of Saint Gabriel are a French congregation of professionally trained primary-school teachers founded by St. Louis Grignion de Montfort (1673–1717) and reorganized in the nineteenth century by Gabriel Deshayes. Brothers arrived in Gabon on October 7, 1990, to assume direction of the boys' schools at Libreville and Lambaréné. They withdrew from Lambaréné in October 1910 for financial reasons and from Libreville in July 1918 for lack of staff but returned in November 1924. At their Ecole Montfort (q.v.) in Libreville they provided an education of high quality to a large portion of the Gabonese elite during the first half of the century. Perhaps the best-known member of the congregation is Brother Macaire Clémenceau (1905–1980), who headed the Ecole Montfort from 1936 to 1963 and who sat in the Territorial Assembly.

He is the author of many primary-level texts used throughout Equatorial Africa and Cameroon. Today the Brothers of Saint Gabriel direct primary schools for boys at Libreville, Lambaréné, Port-Gentil, and Oyem. [1030, 1021, 1058, 987]

BUSHNELL, ALBERT (1818–1879). American missionary in Gabon, 1844–1879. The Rev. Albert Bushnell was born in Rome, New York, on February 9, 1818, and educated at Lane Theological Seminary in Cincinnati, Ohio. After ordination as a Presbyterian minister, he was sent as an ABCFM missionary to Gabon; after 1870 he served under the Presbyterian Board for Foreign Missions. He became an expert in Mpongwe and translated portions of the Scriptures. But his major work was a ministry to young men who were former pupils of the Baraka boys' school for whom he maintained a Bible class. With his second wife, Lucina Boughton (1834–1887), he also directed the girls' boarding school there. Bushnell died in Sierra Leone on December 2, 1879. [1028, 1031, 1008]

BWITI. Originally a masculine secret society of the Mitsogo and Apindji, now a syncretic cult of the Fang (q.v.). Practically all Gabon's peoples traditionally had secret societies of both men and women that sought protection and benefits from the spirits of the ancestors and natural forces. These societies also served to strengthen and enforce group solidarity. Bwiti, a masculine secret society of peoples along the N'Gounié River, was spread to various non-Myènè peoples on the middle Ogooué and to the coasts from the Estuary to Setté-Cama as a result of the slave trade, in particular. The Fang, who arrived in new locations throughout northern Gabon in the last half of the nineteenth century, were by the early twentieth century finding Bwiti attractive. Its rituals and beliefs were much more elaborate and dramatic than those of the *bieri* and other traditional Fang secret societies. The Fang used various elements from the original Bwiti to fashion a new cult that reinterpreted traditional Fang rituals and beliefs in the wake of the new situations arising from their migrations and contacts with Europeans. Bwiti ceremonies involved the use of *iboga*, a hallucinatory plant, to communicate with the ancestors, among other things. Between the late 1930s and the early 1950s, Fang Bwiti further incorporated Christian elements into its rituals and beliefs in response to missionary advances among them. The creator God of the Bantu peoples, formerly considered to be aloof, now was regarded as concerned with the affairs of human beings. A female deity, who blends the qualities of St. Mary in Catholicism with the female river spirit Mboumba characteristic of African religions south of the Ogooué, has an importance equal to her brother, the creator God. Men and women hold equal importance in the cult, a departure from the separate societies of the past and male dominance. Taken as a whole, Fang Bwiti can be seen as an attempt to adjust to the situations emanating from their migrations and acculturation. Léon Mba in the Estuary in the 1920s sought to spread Bwiti as a means of restoring solidarity among the fractionated clans there. At independence there were five different branches of Bwiti, which had constructed 100 cult chapels to which an estimated 8 percent of the Fang belonged (perhaps 20,000 persons). But the influence of Bwiti extended well beyond formal membership, often with attendance by Christians who were not particularly fervent or devoted. Given the equalitarian character and loose social organization of Fang society, Bwiti has never developed into a Messianic movement, that is, one led by a single influential leader who elaborated rituals and beliefs. Rather there have been several figures, all of only local importance. [1027, 827, 617, 1005, 1076, 1033, 1039, 1052, 1081]

- C -

CAISSE CENTRALE DE COOPERATION ECONOMIQUE (CCCE). The official agency through which the government of the French Fifth Republic has since 1958 channeled, banked, and administered its aid to Francophone Africa. It also handles the funds dispersed by the European Economic Community's Economic Development Fund. The CCCE succeeded the Caisse Centrale de la France d'Outre-Mer

(CCFOM) of the Fourth Republic (1946–1958), which administered the aid of FIDES. The CCCE handled the grants from the Fonds d'Aide et de Coopération (FAC) and also carried out credit operations on its own account. Thus it extends medium- and long-term loans to African governments, public corporations, and private concerns. But it has sought, whenever possible, to work through the development banks of the African states such as the Banque Gabonaise de Développement (BGD), which was established in 1960 as the successor to the Société Gabonaise de Crédit. [723, 444]

CATHOLICISM. Between 1766 and 1776 French priests based at Loango reached the southern coasts of Gabon. Though numerous deaths and illnesses forced their withdrawal, some of their influence persisted. When Admiral Linois visited Mayumba in 1802, he found Africans who knew French and elements of the Roman Catholic religion. In 1777 Italian Capuchins based on São Tomé and Príncipe briefly operated a mission at the mouth of the Gabon Estuary. But they had to withdraw when the Portuguese authorities of the islands refused to permit foreign missionaries to be based there or to offer hospitality to members of their congregation working on the mainland.

Roman Catholicism was permanently introduced into the Estuary region in September 1844 by French missionaries who belonged to the congregation of the Holy Heart of Mary. The order had been founded only a few years before by F. M. X. Libermann (1802–1852) to minister to black people. The Holy Heart of Mary group merged in 1848 with the older congregation of the Holy Ghost (Spiritans) (q.v.) whose name was retained for the unified organization. In July 1849 Sisters of Our Lady of the Immaculate Conception (q.v.) or Blue Sisters of Castres, France, arrived to work with women and girls. After the failure of early attempts at expansion, the Catholics limited their work until 1878 to the Mpongwe communities of the northern shore of the Estuary, except for a brief mission (1849–1858) among the Benga at nearby Cape Esterias. In the late 1870s, concurrent with a new wave of French expansion into the interior of Gabon linked with the expeditions of

Savorgnan de Brazza (q.v.), the Holy Ghost Fathers made new efforts to reach other peoples of Gabon. In 1878 they resumed their work among the Benga and established a post among the Estuary Fang at Donguila. In 1881 they sought to compete with the American Presbyterians in the Lambaréné area among the Galoa, Bakèlè, and Fang. Between 1881 and 1897 they extended their work successively to the Vili of Loango, the Adouma of Lastoursville, the Séké near the Rio Muni, the Nkomi at Fernan Vaz, the Loumbou at Mayumba and Setté-Cama, the Eshira of the southwest interior, and to various peoples of the middle and upper Ogooué and N'Gounié rivers. But they arrived at Port-Gentil only in 1927 and established posts in the Fang areas of the far north only between 1929 and 1935. The sisters located in many of these places and the Brothers of Saint-Gabriel (q.v.) arrived in 1900 to operate primary schools for boys.

Throughout the nineteenth century the Catholic missions received aid from the French government, which hoped that the missionaries would spread French culture and promote French influence. The missionaries preferred to evangelize in the indigenous languages and prepared catechisms and other materials in 15 of them. They taught French above all in order to enjoy official support. The missionaries made little headway among adult Africans for several decades because of their opposition to polygamy, which was an important aspect of African economic and social structures. Most of the missionaries' early converts came from the boarding pupils in their schools. Catholics began to make numerous converts among the general population from the 1880s when they were able to train catechists who lived in the interior villages among peoples less involved in overseas trade. The Catholic population of Gabon has grown as follows:

1870: 1,105
1900: 12,500
1930: 29,234
1960: 186,607 plus 27,828 catechumens
1977: 399,453 plus 16,632 catechumens
1987: 614,618 plus 17,300 catechumens.

From the earliest days the Catholic mission sought to prepare an indigenous clergy and for most of the time after 1856 operated a minor seminary where Latin was taught. But the first Gabonese priest, André Raponda-Walker (q.v.), was ordained in 1899 and the next three in 1919. Between 1895 and 1963, Catholics in northern Gabon ordained 39 priests and professed 32 brothers. Between 1879 and 1938, the Mayumba seminary, which served the Loango coast as well as southern Gabon, ordained 15 priests. The first African brothers were Dominique Fara (1876–1922) (q.v.) and Jean-Marie Ogwaruwé (1874–1955), both professed in 1895. At first the brothers were auxiliaries to the Holy Ghost Fathers. In 1952 they were organized as the Brothers of St. Joseph. Their novitiate from 1959 was placed under the direction of the Frères Auxiliaires du Clergé. The first African sisters including Hyacinthe Antini (1878–1952) (q.v.) made professions in 1890 as auxiliaries of the Blue Sisters. In 1911 a separate congregation for them was organized, the Sisters of St. Mary of Gabon, which in 1987 had 34 professed members in eight convents. Implementing the Vatican's policy of Africanization, the first Gabonese bishop was appointed in 1960. Today the archbishop of Libreville and the bishops of Oyem, Mouila, and Franceville are all Gabonese. They direct a church that has 28 Gabonese and 76 foreign priests; 10 Gabonese and 24 foreign brothers; and 36 Gabonese and 132 foreign sisters. While a large part of the foreign clergy is Spiritans (q.v.), there are also 10 Salesian priests and two brothers, and four Claretan priests. The scarcity of new vocations among Gabonese men suggests that the Gabonese church will be dependent upon foreign clergy for a long time to come. In 1987 there were 95 young men in the minor seminary (secondary level), eight from the dioceses in philosophy studies, and 11 in theology studies (seven from the dioceses and four from the Spiritans). Church authorities in September 1988 publicly expressed concern over the small amount of religious practice, especially in the urban centers, and among the educated elite and young people. Catholic schools, which receive government aid, at the end of 1987 enrolled 2,297 in kindergarten; 53,613 at the primary level; and 7,741 at the secondary level. Sisters direct many of these schools and operate catechetical centers for public-school children and adults. Sisters are also involved in health care and social work, fields in which they pioneered from the middle of the nineteenth century. *See* ROMAN CATHOLIC BISHOPS. [987, 988, 1029, 1045, 1049, 1001, 1016, 1021, 1030, 1094]

CENTRE INTERNATIONAL DE CIVILISATIONS BANTU (CICIBA). Centre International de Civilisations Bantu (CICIBA) was organized at President Bongo's initiative at Libreville in January 1983 to preserve and promote the authentic values of Bantu civilization, the cultural patrimony of a majority of Africa's peoples. Angola, the Central African Republic, the Comoros, Congo, Equatorial Guinea, Rwanda, São Tomé and Príncipe, Zaire, and Zambia joined Gabon in this enterprise, but Gabon provides 65 percent of the budget. Headquartered in Libreville, the center contains a documentation center and hopes to construct a museum. The center publishes the multi-disciplinary, multi-lingual review *Muntu*. The first president of the center's administrative council was the Gabonese physicist, François Owono Nguema, and its first director-general, the Congolese historian Théophile Obenga. [1311, 1]

CHAMBER OF COMMERCE, AGRICULTURE, INDUSTRY AND MINES. A semi-official body of representatives from the private sector of the economy that advises the government. During the colonial period it was the organism through which French interests formally had access to the territorial administration and brought influence to bear upon it. Since independence it has continued to represent all individuals and companies, whether Gabonese or foreign, conducting business in Gabon.

CHIWA (or BICHIWA). These people are celebrated in the history of exploration under the Okandé name of Osyéba, that is, the people who blocked the passage of Marche and Compiègne up the Ogooué because they were guided by the

Okandé (q.v.). The Europeans called them the Fang Makina. Today the remnants of the Chiwa inhabit several villages on the Ogooué downstream from Booué. Linguistically the experts classify Chiwa as a Fang dialect. Some of the Chiwa state that their language most closely resembles that of the Ngumba of the Kribi Region of Cameroon, and after that, the Bakouelé, and only then the Fang.

Chiwa traditions declare a common origin with the Ngumba in an unknown area to the north from which they reached Gabon by descending the Ivindo River. Some settled along the lower Ivindo near the junction of the Ogooué and others along the Ogooué downstream toward Booué. Thereafter the Danbomo and the Shaké arrived in these same areas. At the granting of the SHO (q.v.) concession, the French administration forced the relocation of the Chiwa villages at the Ivindo-Ogooué junction in order to use the land for the company. [284, 199]

CINEMA. As early as 1936 French companies began to make films, mainly documentaries, in Gabon. After independence, Gabon's first professionally trained actor, Philippe Mory (or Maury) (b. 1932), who had won acclaim for his role in Parisian films, organized the Compagnie Cinématographique du Gabon (1962). In collaboration with a French company, he wrote and produced *La Cage,* which earned much praise at the Cannes Film Festival in 1963. During the following years, Mory, Pierre-Marie Ndong, Louis Mébalé, and Simon Augé produced films privately, including some for local television after 1963. Ndong's television drama *Carrefour humain* (1969) dealt with the problem of the social integration of persons of mixed race (*métis*). President Bongo installed a cinema seating 400 persons in his new palace, and in 1975 established the Centre National du Cinéma with Mory as director, a position he held until 1985. Bongo, however, devoted far more resources to Les Films Gabonais, a company that he founded. It produced two films based on plays on social themes by his wife Joséphine, *Obali* (1976) and *Ayouma* (1977), as well as a third written by the president himself, *Demain, un jour nouveau* (1978). Ga-

bonese filmmaking thus tended to become an enterprise
supported and supervised by the Bongo couple.

COMITE MIXTE GABONAIS (CMG). A political party organized by Léon Mba (q.v.) early in 1947 in the wake of the
disintegration of the PDA (q.v.) from personal rivalries and
administration pressure on its members who were also active
in the GEC (q.v.). It included some members from the
Estuary elite who were not Fang, but the majority came from
the Comité Fang, which had been organized by Mba's
supporter, Edouard N'Guéma in 1944 to promote Fang
interests. The main Fang members were Mba's nephew, Paul
N'Guéma, Jean-Baptiste Obiang, and N'Dong-Mebale at
Libreville and two primary-school teachers, François Meye
(q.v.) and Philippe Ndong (q.v.) at Oyem. The "Mixte" in
the name referred to the goal of surmounting tribalism and of
including all peoples of Gabon. At a later time the CMG
became known also as the Comité Mixte Franco-Gabonais in
order to emphasize that it was anti-colonialist but not
anti-French. The two names seem to have been used inter-
changeably after 1949. The CMG replaced the PDA as the
local branch of the inter-territorial RDA (q.v.), which until
1949 had ties with the French Communist Party and the
Communist-dominated labor confederation, the CGT. In the
course of 1947, the administration transferred from Libreville all those civil servants who had been active in the
GEC and thus removed an important segment of the CMG
from the capital. After François Meye was transferred to
Libreville in June 1949, he became the CMG's secretary and
contributed most of the group's articles to the Brazzaville
RDA paper, *AEF Nouvelle*. The CMG also became a focus
for opposition to the Fang deputy, Jean-Hilaire Aubame
(q.v.) and his UDSG (q.v.), which had the support of the
Christian missions and, until 1956, the sympathy of the
administration. Further it became a vehicle for the political
career of Léon Mba after Senator Paul Gondjout (q.v.) helped
him to secure the restoration of full civil rights, including the
right to seek office, of which his conviction on a criminal
charge in 1933 had deprived him. In 1954 most of the CMG

membership followed Mba into Gondjout's BDG (q.v.), which replaced the CMG as the main opponent of the UDSG and became the local affiliate of the RDA. [550]

COMITE MPONGWE. Founded officially in January 1936 after two years of informal activity by Mpongwe leaders to defend and to regain their traditional rights, especially land rights in the Estuary. The Comité was led by Amaka-Dassy, Frédéric Moreau, and François-de-Paul Vané (q.v.), the last named of Benga ancestry but assimilated to Mpongwe society. The Comité sought the creation of a single superior chief, a position that they wished vested in a member of the educated elite. The Comité successfully supported Vané for election as Gabon's delegate to the governor-general's council of administration in October 1937. Vané was instrumental in securing a ministerial decree of February 10, 1938, recognizing traditional land rights, previously weakened by the concessionary regime and other legislation, and providing a more equitable basis for compensation. The Comité secured the nomination of its candidates for *chefs de groupes de quartier* in the Libreville sections of Louis and Glass, and its president, Amaka-Dassy, as *chef de groupe* of Glass. Vané and Prince Félix Adandé (q.v.) from the Comité became the first African members named to the Libreville municipal commission. These measures strengthened the Mpongwe people in relation to other peoples and the Europeans as well as the younger educated elements within the Mpongwe clans in relation to the rest.

The Comité unsuccessfully supported Mpongwe candidates for the French Constituent and National Assemblies in 1945–1946 and saw two Fang elected to represent Libreville in the Territorial Assembly in December 1946. During 1946–1947 Governor Roland Pré attempted to settle the Mpongwe problems. He made a settlement with the leaders of the Comité Mpongwe that provided for election of an Mpongwe chief and council. The council was to control most of the land in the quartiers of Louis & Glass and to decide judicial disputes among Mpongwe. But the governor-general at Brazzaville vetoed the agreement. In 1950 the administration gave the Comité the task of dividing 20 million CFA francs to indemnify Mpongwe landholders (roughly $80,000 U.S. at that time). In 1955 a delegation to Paris composed of Princes Félix Adandé and Louis Berre (q.v.), Vané, and Louis Bigmann (q.v.) failed to get a second grant for this purpose. [550]

CONCESSIONARY COMPANIES. In the aftermath of the European scramble to partition Africa, France sought ways to exploit and to develop its vast territories in French Equatorial Africa (q.v.), including Gabon, with as little expense to the French taxpayer as possible. It turned over economic control of most of the equatorial areas in 1899 to more than 40 chartered companies that were given monopolistic privileges in trade and/or exploitation of natural resources other than minerals for 30 years. The government, imitating the policy of Leopold II in the neighboring Congo Free State, hoped that the companies would make the investments in infrastructure (roads, ports, telecommunications) that the French state was unable or unwilling to make. France also hoped that the concessionary system would transfer the trade of its territories from English and German merchants in the case of Gabon, and Dutch and Belgian ones in the case of the Middle Congo, to French ones. But matters did not work out as planned. Most of the concessionary companies were family enterprises that lacked the capital and technical skill to undertake the huge tasks assigned them and who sought quick return on short-term commercial investments. The companies encountered a lack of manpower and many barriers to transportation and communication in the vast, sparsely populated equatorial regions. These situations contributed to an often brutal exploitation of the population and to many abuses. The European merchants of the previous trading system, which was long established in the Estuary and the Loango coast and more recently (the 1870s) on the Ogooué and Congo rivers, resisted and protested, the British ones with the support of their Foreign Office. Following an official inquiry by Savorgnan de Brazza (q.v.) in 1905, the half dozen companies in Gabon other than the SHO (q.v.)

abandoned their vast concessions in exchange for outright title to thousands of hectares (two acres = one hectare) of rich and accessible forestlands or the right to cut trees over even larger areas. These new arrangements provided the basis for profitable European development of okoumé (q.v.) and other woods during the 1920s and after. In general, the concessionary companies during the years of their functioning contributed to the displacement of African populations and the disorganization of agricultural production with disastrous consequences throughout subsequent decades. They helped to keep Gabon's total population stationary at 389,000 from 1921 to 1955 and to create patterns of underdevelopment that are being altered only in our own times. [264, 266, 81, 212]

CONSTITUTION. The constitution of March 26, 1991 shows the commitment of the Gabonese people to liberal democracy and particularly to a multi-party system and the exercise of civil liberties. Some of the provisions reflect their dissatisfaction with authoritarian rule from 1964, and a single-party system from 1968 as well as a desire to prevent abuses of power. The constitution was drafted by a committee of 20 members representing different political parties and appointed in the aftermath of the national conference in March-April 1990. Approved by the council of ministers on December 21, 1990, it was adopted unanimously on March 5, 1991, by a new multi-party National Assembly elected the previous September and October.

The constitution more closely resembles the presidential form of government of the Fifth French Republic than did the earlier constitution of February 21, 1961. It provides for a strong chief executive and a National Assembly with legislative powers. The president as head of state nominates the prime minister, who as head of the government selects the members of the Council of Ministers. The ministers are in practice largely drawn from among deputies in the 120-member National Assembly. The Assembly confirms the Council of Ministers and, following western European parliamentary practice, may oust the government through a vote of no confidence after a certain period; the prime minister also may choose to dissolve the National Assembly under certain conditions before the end of its five-year term.

The constitution gives the prime minister, as head of the government, more extensive powers, including some previously held by the president as head of state than did the constitution of 1961. The president continues to be popularly elected. But he now has a five-year term that is renewable only once instead of a seven-year term that was renewable without limitation.

The constitution contains other important changes or innovations. It provides for an upper house called the Senate, which "assures the balance and regulation of powers while the National Assembly continues to exercise its traditional competences." It establishes a Supreme Court as the highest institution in a judicial branch that is now unequivocally coequal with the executive and legislative branches. The former administrative chamber of the court becomes a court of appeal in administrative matters. The constitution further provides for a Constitutional Council, which decides the constitutionality of laws, interprets the constitution in cases of doubt to its meaning, and has the responsibility for organizing and administering elections. There is also a National Council of Communication, which assures balanced treatment of information by the organs of the state and in general safeguards the freedom of the media. The constitution perpetuates the Economic and Social Council as an advisory body composed of representatives of socioprofessional organizations. But it renders it more independent of the government by allowing it to elect its own officers. (The new institutions are to be organized during the first year of the constitution's operation.) Finally, the constitution provides strong guarantees for both individual and public liberties. A Charter of Parties voted at the same time as the constitution defines the role of political parties in a multiparty democracy.

The composition of the new Council of Ministers, which was named by the president and confirmed by the National Assembly on June 28, 1991, reflected the provisions of

Article 31. That article requires all ministers to be at least thirty-five years of age and makes unsuccessful candidates for public office during the preceding 18 months ineligible for appointment. Thus leading PDG reformers Ali Bongo and André Mba Obame, who were underage, and Jean Ping, Minister of Mines, who failed to win election as deputy from Port-Gentil in September-October 1990, were forced to relinquish the ministries they had held in the previous council.

Earlier, between 1946 and 1961, Gabon was governed by the provisions of two French constitutions and two short-lived ones of its own. As an Overseas Territory of the Fourth French Republic from October 1946 to September 1958, Gabon came under the provisions of its constitution of October 13, 1946. With the establishment of the Fifth French Republic in September 1958, Gabon became an autonomous republic within the French Community. Its place in the community was regulated by the French constitution of September 1958 and it acquired its own constitution of February 19, 1959, for internal matters. That constitution established a basically parliamentary system. With the trans-formation of the Community, Gabon became an independent republic with a new constitution of November 14, 1960, that perpetuated the parliamentary system. By the end of 1961, most of the provisions concerning the Community were no longer operational, but Gabon remained a member.

In the meantime, through the constitution of February 21, 1961, Gabon adopted a presidential form of government in which the executive branch had far greater powers than the legislative or judicial branches. As in the American system, the president headed both the state and the government. He appointed the members of the Council of Ministers or Cabinet; but unlike the American practice, he did not have to seek confirmation of his appointments from the legislative branch. Nor did he have to do so in making appointments to the judicial branch.

The constitution of 1961 underwent a number of important amendments that reflected the political evolution of the country. At the start, there was a vice president of the government, the post to which President Mba appointed Bongo on November 11, 1966. Then as a result of the need to provide for an orderly succession to the presidency in light of Mba's terminal illness with cancer, the law of February 16, 1967, established the position of vice president of the republic. Bongo, who was elected to the post on March 19, 1967, therefore became president at Mba's death on November 28, 1967. Thereafter Bongo, through the law of December 13, 1967, abolished the position of vice president of the republic. Though he appointed Léon Mébiame as vice president of the government on January 30, 1968, he formally reinstituted that position months later through the law of November 9, 1968. Then on April 15, 1975, a constitutional revision suppressed the post of vice president of the government while establishing a prime minister and deputy prime minister of the government. Yet the president himself remained head of the government until the constitutional revision of August 22, 1981, made the prime minister the head. That change came about as a result of criticism during the Second Extraordinary Congress of the PDG in 1979 about the enormous amount of executive power concentrated in the presidency. (Prior to August 22, 1981, Bongo also held a number of key ministries. Though he formally relinquished them, he maintained control of the ministries of Foreign Affairs and National Defense by appointing members of his immediate family and close relatives to these posts.) Under the revision, the prime minister and his government remained responsible to the president but became responsible as well to the National Assembly and the Central Committee of the PDG.

Since 1968 the PDG had exercised an institutional role in the constitutional system. The law of March 12, 1968, which established the PDG as the country's only legal party, gave that organization, its central committee, and political bureau roles in the executive and legislative processes not found in the constitution. Only years later, through the laws of July 29, 1972 and April 15, 1975, was the constitution amended to reflect these roles and to elaborate further upon them. An additional amendment of March 1983, in reaction to the challenge of MORENA, put into the constitution the terms of the law of March 12, 1968, making the PDG the only party.

Other amendments to the constitution through the years increased the number of deputies from 70 to 89 (1980) and then to 120 (1985) with the president himself selecting nine of them. In 1980 the terms of deputies were reduced from seven to five years, but the presidential term remained at seven years.

On May 22, 1990, in the aftermath of the national conference called to discuss reforms, the National Assembly revised the constitution of 1961 so as to remove the PDG from an institutional role in government and to permit the restoration of multi-partyism prior to the legislative elections of September and October. [636, 602, 656, 622, 623, 9]

COUP OF FEBRUARY 17–20, 1964. The account of the coup in the first edition of this book was based primarily on the works of U.S. Ambassador Charles Darlington and his wife Alice [569], who observed many but not all of the events, and of Jean-François N'Toutoume [598], a Gabonese graduate student who interviewed participants and observers soon after the event. In this revision some additions from François Gaulme [65], editor-in-chief of *Marché Tropicaux et Méditerranéens,* who interviewed many years later some of the Gaullist officials involved in the French decision to intervene militarily, are incorporated. Gaulme's account also corrects some details concerning the times of day and length of the fighting.

The coup reflected dissatisfaction by young Gabonese officers, trained at St. Cyr, with the regime of President Léon Mba (q.v.). The coup took place in the wake of conflicts between Mba and opponents in the National Assembly, which had led Mba to dissolve that body on January 21, 1964, and to call for new elections on February 23. The opposition refused to participate because the revised arrangements discriminated against them. On the night of February 17–18, 1964, 150 soldiers led by Lt. Valère Essone and Lt. Jacques Mombo seized the presidential palace and other government buildings. They captured Mba and Louis Bigmann (q.v.), president of the National Assembly, and thereafter arrested all the cabinet except the respected technician André-Gustave Anguile (q.v.). A committee of six junior officers, including Lt. Essone and Second Lt. Ndo Edou of the First Army; Lt. Jacques Mombo and Second Lt. Daniel Mbene of the National Police (*gendarmerie*), announced that the revolution was taking place to prevent disturbances during the elections. After cancelling the elections, declaring martial law, and forcing Mba to broadcast a resignation and an apology for authoritarian rule, the committee handed power to a 10-member provisional government. The government, which was headed by Jean-Hilaire Aubame (q.v.), included two other prominent UDSG politicians, Jean-Marc Ekoh (q.v.) and Eugène Amogho (q.v.), leading opponents of Mba within the BDG such as Paul Gondjout (q.v.) and Philippe Ndong (q.v.), the editor of *Réalités Africaines;* Eloi Chambrier, M.D., Gabon's only physician; and Philippe Maury, the country's only actor. The provisional government announced it would respect Gabon's treaties and other obligations. The overthrow of the Mba regime produced no popular reactions or manifestations in its defense.

In the meantime the French response to the coup was taking shape. As early as 1 A.M. on the 18th, Albert-Bernard Bongo, Mba's cabinet director, who was working late in the palace, alerted the French commander of the gendarmerie of unusual activities by the troops. The commander, after ascertaining that the rebels had taken over the military camp at Baraka, notified the French embassy. By 2 A.M. in Paris, Jacques Foccart, secretary-general for African and Malagasy Affairs, initiated preparations for a military intervention, discussing details with the army minister, Pierre Messmer. At 7 A.M., President de Gaulle gave his approval for the intervention. He dictated a note indicating that France was acting under the terms of its agreements with Gabon in order to ensure the safety of President Mba and to free him from the rebels.

The rebels had not attempted to take over the airport, which was under control of French troops stationed in Gabon. Thus it was possible for French General Kergaravat and paratroopers from Brazzaville to land while awaiting reinforcements from Dakar. On the 19th, delayed by a pre-dawn tornado, the 600 French troops attacked the Baraka camp later in the morning, destroying rebel resistance within two hours. Twenty-five Gabonese rebels, including Lt. Edou, and two French soldiers, were known to be killed. The Darlingtons report seeing French planes firing on the rebels. They attribute civilian injuries and possible deaths to the actions of these craft, which official French sources claim were only conducting reconnaissance for ground forces. A rebel garrison at the presidential palace surrendered to the French at 4 P.M. on the 19th. President Mba was located at Lambaréné, where the rebels had taken him, and was returned to the palace. The French intervention provoked popular outbursts and daily protests against the regime at Libreville in the following three weeks, including some countermanifestations by Mba supporters.

On February 26, the French Minister of Information announced that the intervention had resulted from an appeal by the legitimate authorities for help against the coup makers.

Gaulme's sources indicate that French forces based at Port-Gentil were able to locate Vice President Paul-Marie Yembit, who was touring the N'Gounié Province and was out of contact with the capital, late on the 18th. He thus was able to authorize an appeal for French military intervention under the terms of the cooperation agreements prior to the attack on the Baraka military camp. The Darlingtons contend that the intervention took place before he could be reached.

The De Gaulle government may have intervened out of friendship for Léon Mba, as is suggested in the general's writings. But it definitely acted to protect French interests, particularly the uranium, which was essential for securing an independent nuclear force, and investments in petroleum, manganese, iron, woods, and commerce. It may have been concerned about the future of the French troops stationed outside Libreville. The De Gaulle regime incorrectly regarded Aubame as less friendly to French involvement in Gabon and more favorable to increased American involvement, a claim that Aubame denied. In this same vein, elements in the French government and among the settlers in Gabon sought to make the United States the scapegoat for the coup. They refused to recognize that some Gabonese by themselves had sufficient grievances and initiative to undertake a revolt against the regime. It appears that the coup makers were concerned about the state of the country under Mba and the luxury living of the ruling class. Some of them may have harbored personal grievances against the regime.

In the aftermath of the coup, Mba promised vengeance for his opponents, but Ambassador Cousseran privately urged him to be more conciliatory and apparently persuaded him to hold the Assembly elections on April 12 under fairer arrangements than contemplated for February 23. Cousseran also influenced the decision to establish a special commission of inquiry to investigate the coup. For his pains Mba had him recalled. Unfortunately, Mba prevented the commission from undertaking anything resembling an unbiased inquiry. Mba's arrest of the members of the provisional government and 150 other opponents and critics contributed, along with the French intervention and continued hostility to his regime, to a wave of demonstrations in several regions. A demonstration by several hundred Mba supporters on February 23 at Libreville led to a counterdemonstration on March 1 by 500 workers and students and 1,000 others shouting for "an end to dictatorship." A similar manifestation the following day was accompanied by a strike of *lycéens*. Government repression of the demonstrations involved brutality and many arrests. The demonstrations spread to the lycées of Port-Gentil and N'Dendé. At the latter town national police fired on the students, killing one and leading to the death of a gendarme.

The elimination of the opposition leaders from the electoral campaigns, along with numerous irregularities, prevented fair elections. Even then, Mba's party only narrowly won the populous Estuary and N'Gounié Provinces, possibly by falsifying the results in the latter case, and lost the Woleu-N'Tem to the opposition. With only 50.38 percent of the popular vote, it still acquired two-thirds of the assembly seats. Announcement of the results brought a nationwide strike by opponents on April 16. Additional student disorders led to the early closing of the schools for annual vacation. After police operations in July eliminated open manifestations of opposition, the government proceeded with the trials of the military rebels and provisional government under strict security at Lambaréné in August. The special court condemned Aubame to 10 years at hard labor and 10 years banishment, and lieutenants Essone and Mbene to 20 years at hard labor. It confirmed the internment of Gaston Boukat, Marcel Rahandi, Dr. Eloi Chambrier, Philippe Maury, and Philippe Ndong. But it released Lt. Mombo and acquitted Paul Gondjout. It appears that despite Aubame's conviction, he had no foreknowledge of the coup. Rather, he seized the opportunity offered to him by the rebels to assume power. There are indications that other civilians, including Aubame's nephew Pierre Eyeguet, who received a sentence of 20 years at hard labor, had some foreknowledge of the coup or were in contact with the plotters.

President Bongo (q.v.), in order to promote national reconciliation, beginning in 1968 pardoned or reduced the sentences of the civilians sentenced at Lambaréné and gave many of them positions in his government. The last to be released was Jean-Hilaire Aubame, who in August 1972 left his solitary confinement on the Ile des Perroquets in the Estuary.

The long-term significance of the coup is that it led to the French military intervention, which in turn enabled Léon Mba to install the authoritarian regime that held sway without serious challenge until 1990. That regime allowed a tiny ruling class that represented no more than 2 percent of the population, in alliance with French interests, to rule undemocratically and to appropriate 80 percent of the national income for themselves while repressing opponents and critics. [565, 567, 569, 598, 65]

CURRENCY. The currency is the franc of the Communauté Financière Africaine (CFA). The CFA franc is equal to 0.02 French francs so that 50 CFA francs equal one French franc.

In the aftermath of the Second World War, France established a colonial franc for its Black African territories, the CFA franc. (CFA at that time stood for Colonies Françaises Africaines; in 1962 it was renamed the Communauté Financière Africaine.) The colonial franc was tied to the French franc. For the four Equatorial countries and Cameroon, France established the Institut d'Emission de l'Afrique Equatoriale Française with a capital of 250 million CFA francs, which issued a single currency in both notes and coins for all five countries. At independence the five states remained in the franc zone and continued their monetary union with the Banque Centrale des Etats de l'Afrique Equatoriale et du Cameroun issuing a common currency but with separate notes for Cameroon and distinctive serial numbers for each state. This central bank was reorganized in November 1964 as a multinational institution.

The broad principles governing the functioning of the monetary system are contained in the five states' cooperation agreements with one another and France. France guarantees the convertibility of the CFA franc into French francs and is represented on the board of directors of the central bank. These agreements also provide for coordination of commercial and financial policies vis-à-vis countries outside the franc zone.

In 1977 the headquarters of the central bank, now called the Banque des Etats de l'Afrique Centrale, were transferred from Paris to Yaoundé, Cameroon, paralleling the move of the bank for the West African states to Dakar several years earlier. On April 3, 1978, a Gabonese, Casimir Oyé-Mba, became its first African director-general, or governor, all the previous heads having been French. In 1991 a branch of BEAC opened in Libreville. [8, 723, 1364, 1365]

- D -

DAMAS, GEORGES ALEKA (1902–1982). Public figure and composer of the national anthem, *La Concorde*. Damas was born at Libreville on November 18, 1902, and was educated at the Ecole Montfort (q.v.). He served as a bank clerk from 1924 to 1939 and then as head bookkeeper for the Compagnie Maritime des Chargeurs Réunis from 1939 to 1959. As a young Mpongwe working at Brazzaville in 1934, he wrote a series of letters to the *Etoile de l'AEF* attacking the creation of special rights for *métis*. The Free French appointed him to represent Gabon on the governor-general's council of administration between 1943 and 1946. He also served as an adviser to the governor of Gabon from 1948 to 1954 and as a member of the governor's council of administration. He was active after the Second World War in the formation of labor unions affiliated with the French Socialist confederation, the CGT-Force Ouvrière, and in territorial politics. From November 1956 to 1963 he served on the municipal commission of Libreville, his first elective post. In 1959 he represented Gabon on the Economic and Social Council of the French Community. Between 1961 and 1964 he served as ambassador to the Common Market and the Benelux countries and later to West Germany. In April 1964 he was elected to the National Assembly, which selected him as its president, a post he held until 1975. On May 29, 1968, he was named president of the Bureau of the Parti Démocratique Gabonais (q.v.), the country's new single party. He later served as the party's treasurer-general for several years. Between April 1975 and his retirement in February 1977 he acted as an adviser to President Bongo. Damas died at Libreville on May 4, 1982. [1367, 1205, 550]

D'ARBOUSSIER, GABRIEL (1908–1976). Civil servant and RDA leader. Gabriel d'Arboussier was born on January 14, 1908, at Djenne, French Sudan (now Mali), son of the French governor, Henri d'Arboussier, and an African mother. He graduated in law from the University of Paris and from the Colonial School for overseas administrators. He was assigned to Brazzaville late in 1944, where he served as interim director of political affairs and *chef de cabinet* for Secretary-General André Soucadaux in the administration of Governor-General Charles-André Bayardelle. Bayardelle encouraged and supported his successful candidacy for the first college (European) deputy to the First Constituent Assembly in October 1945 from Gabon and Middle Congo. In that assembly he allied with the nine African deputies in Lamine Guèye's Bloc Africain and developed a close working relationship with the Communists, which antagonized his European electors and led to his defeat in the elections of June 1946 for the Second Constituent Assembly. He stayed on in Paris to coordinate the work of the Rassamblement Démocratique Africain, a movement in which all the territories of Black Africa were represented. In Gabon the local RDA branch was at first the Parti Démocratique Africain (q.v.) and then the Comité Mixte Gabonais (q.v.) (1947) and later the Bloc Démocratique Gabonais (q.v.) (1954). D'Arboussier published the monthly newspaper *AEF Nouvelle* at Brazzaville, which contained party and political news from Gabon and the rest of the federation. In 1947 he was elected a councillor of the Assembly of the French Union from the Ivory Coast. The RDA's branch in Gabon in 1951 opposed D'Arboussier's position on maintaining ties with the Communists in the face of administrative pressures and repression. They sided with Félix Houphouet-Boigny in abandoning these ties and seeking an accommodation that might allow them to come to power. D'Arboussier, who died in 1976, is remembered as one of the finest political orators of his day. [550]

DARLINGTON, CHARLES FRANCIS (1904–1986). First full-time American ambassador to Gabon. Darlington was born in New York City on September 13, 1904. After receiving an A.B. from Harvard University, he studied economics at the universities of Oxford and Geneva. Thereafter, he served in the League of Nations (1929–1931), in international banking at Basle, and in the U.S. Department of State (1935–1939). In 1945 he participated in the San Francisco Conference that organized the United Nations. Between 1946 and 1961 he was a director of the Socony Vacuum Oil Company. President John F. Kennedy named him ambassador to Libreville where he served from October 1961 to July 26, 1964. The account of Gabon's political evolution, which he coauthored with his wife, Alice Nelson Benning, is critical of President Mba. The Darlingtons contend that De Gaulle betrayed the Gabonese people by his intervention on behalf of Mba and his support of Mba's repressive policies. Ambassador Darlington died at Mt. Kisco, N.Y., on April 11, 1986. [Source: *Who's Who in America*]

DEBIZET, PIERRE (1922–). Born on December 20, 1922, Debizet became active in the Resistance during the Second World War. Thereafter he served in the Rassemblement du Peuple Français's forces of order and played a role in General De Gaulle's return to power in June 1958. Later he broke with the Gaullists over the issue of Algeria, which he wished France to retain. He later became, nevertheless, a close associate of Jacques Foccart, who arranged his appointment as head of the Service d'Action Civique. From 1968, Debizet served as a technical adviser to Omar Bongo, assigned to problems of security. In this capacity he created the Service de Contre-Ingérences, a counterespionage service involved in surveillance over those who are responsible for Bongo's security. He had to withdraw from Gabon because of a scandal at Marseilles involving the SAC. [603, 65]

DECOLONIZATION. Decolonization may be defined as the process by which Africans and Asians have achieved emancipation from western control. In a narrow sense it refers to the political aspects that led to self-government and/or independence. In a broad sense it refers to the elimination of all forms of external control—economic, cultural, psychological, as well as political.

Between the mid-nineteenth century and the Second World War Gabon was a French colony and its indigenous inhabitants subjects of the French Empire. The Second World War undermined the ideological and political foundations of western colonial rule in Asia and Africa. France, which did not wish to relinquish control of its overseas possessions for fear of losing its rank as a great nation, nevertheless realized that it had to reform the colonial system to permit the advancement of the Africans and Asians. In the case of Black Africa, the Free French government sponsored the Brazzaville Conference of colonial administrators and officials in January-February 1944 to plan post-war reforms. The Conference, while reasserting the attachment of the African territories to France, advocated representation of the Africans in decision making as well as publicly funded programs to promote economic, social, and educational advancement. The French provisional government headed by General De Gaulle (1944–1946) and the two Constituent Assemblies (1945–1946) abolished many of the oppressive aspects of colonial rule such as forced labor, the *prestation* (labor tax), travel controls, and the *indigénat* (q.v.) (administrative justice). Whereas the draft constitution defeated by the French electorate in the spring 1946 would have permitted the Black African territories the long-range possibilities of self-government or independence within the French Empire (now called the French Union), the constitution finally adopted in October 1946 denied them these options. It offered them only a greater degree of participation in their own administration under the continued domination of metropolitan France. Thus the constitution made Gabon and the other territories of French Equatorial Africa (q.v.) and French West Africa overseas territories of the Fourth French Republic. As such, Gabon and the others each acquired a territorial assembly comparable to a general council (*conseil général*) of a metropolitan department, which treated many local matters in cooperation with French administrators. While the constitution gave the Africans the protection of the French law and most of the same rights as the citizens in Europe, it left the important matters of representation and voting to legislation. Voting at first was restricted to a tiny fraction of the African population (e.g., primary-school graduates, notables, war veterans), nearly all of whom were men. A system of two electoral colleges was established that gave the Europeans living in the African territories about one-third of the representation.

Thus in the case of Gabon, a few thousand Frenchmen held one-third of the seats in the Territorial Assembly at

Libreville and 400,000 Africans two thirds. Gabon's delegation to the French National Assembly, Council of the Republic (Senate), and Assembly of the French Union in Paris contained a similar proportion. While these arrangements had the effect of overrepresenting French interests, they also provided the Gabonese with a valuable political education. Many of them quickly became adept questioners during the discussions of the territorial budget and the implementation of the various five-year development plans under FIDES (q.v.). Gabonese representatives in Paris established ties with the representatives from other African territories. At Brazzaville, where Gabon had five representatives in the Grand Council of the federation of French Equatorial Africa, they acquired an understanding of the problems of the three other territories and Gabon's place in the federation.

While the Gabonese thus obtained some political representation in institutions dominated by Frenchmen, they were unrepresented until the late 1950s in the administrative corps that ran Gabon. Not until the mid-1950s did any Gabonese enter the Ecole Nationale de la France d'Outre-Mer in Paris, which trained the top overseas officials such as heads of the nine regions and 37 districts. By that time a few Gabonese were graduating from French universities and could be assigned to technical and supervisory positions in the bureaus of the central administration in Libreville.

Between 1946 and 1956 France, in response to African pressures, extended the suffrage in stages to include all adults of both sexes and even the illiterate. In 1956 it abolished the special representation of the French residents, some of whom would subsequently be elected on lists with Africans, and it established municipal government in the larger towns. Although these reforms represented an advancement in terms of African participation, it did not alter the basic constitutional and political arrangements that centralized the government of the entire republic in Paris and placed legislative and executive power in metropolitan hands. Responding to African demands for the transfer of decision making to the territorial level, France under the Loi-Cadre, or Enabling Act of June 23, 1956, and the decrees of April 1957 implementing it, created a legislative assembly and an executive council in each territory. These changes, which resulted from developments in Indo-China and North Africa at least as much as in Black Africa, were quickly superseded as a result of the collapse of the Fourth Republic in the wake of the revolution at Algiers on May 13, 1958.

Under the constitutional arrangements of the Fifth Republic, the African territories became self-governing, but not completely independent states. No longer part of the French Republic, they became in March 1959 autonomous republics within the French Community in which metropolitan France still had the final word on matters of foreign policy, defense, higher education, and monetary arrangements. Given the decolonizing currents emanating from the other African countries, including the British and Belgian ones and the former French trusteeship territories of Togo and Cameroon, General De Gaulle permitted the revision of the constitution to allow the African states to accede to independence and yet remain in the Community. Gabon, like the other French African states, opted for independence on August 13, 1960. By the end of 1961 the Community had ceased to function. Gabon's relationship with France would be governed by the cooperation agreements negotiated in 1960 and then revised in 1974.

Decolonization in the economic sphere occurred in the 1970s as Gabon took steps to gain greater control over its natural resources and a greater share of the benefits from them. In the cultural sphere, Gabon has voluntarily decided to retain French as its national language and medium of instruction. These policies were reaffirmed by the First Extraordinary Congress of the PDG (q.v.) in 1973. [593, 617, 331, 551, 966, 552, 136, 96]

DEFENSE AND SECURITY FORCES. The organization and functioning of Gabon's defense and security forces follow French models. As chief of state the president has authority over all defense and security forces, but most of them are administered by the Ministry of National Defense. (Between November 1967 and August 1981 President Bongo also served as the Minister of National Defense. Since that time others have exercised these functions.) At independence the army, navy, and air force were placed under the defense ministry. In 1967 the gendarmerie was placed under that ministry as was the national police (formerly called the Sûreté Nationale) in 1977. The gendarmerie has charge of surveillance and security at a national level. Its forces can be dispatched to any point in order to maintain or establish order. The national police are stationed at posts within the 44 departments of the nine provinces where they protect persons and property, maintain law and order, and direct traffic. The Mobile Security Units, which were created in 1986 to deal with increasing clandestine immigration and the mass protests in the urban areas arising from the economic downturn, also function under the ministry. By contrast, the Presidential Guard, which succeeded the Republican Guard in 1970, is under the administration of the president whose safety it must protect. The guard is organized as an army battalion group; it contains one reconnaissance armored company, three infantry companies, artillery, and an antiaircraft battery. Whereas all other defense and security forces are commanded by Gabonese advised by Frenchmen according to the terms of the military cooperation agreement of August 17, 1960, the Presidential Guard is commanded by French and Moroccan officers recruited outside the framework of that agreement. In May 1990 Bongo used the Presidential Guard to restore order in Port-Gentil among the African population following the disorders there, and the French military intervention to protect French nationals and property.

Under the military cooperation agreement, France helps to train Gabon's defense and security forces. In 1990 there were 125 French officers and enlisted men seconded to the Gabonese forces for this purpose. Three hundred Gabonese underwent military training in France. France has a force of 650 paratroopers stationed near Libreville that can intervene at the request of the president of Gabon. In May 1990 France used some of these troops in its military intervention at Port-Gentil. It acted unilaterally, apparently without prior consultation with the government of Gabon. For its part the

Gabonese government did not seek French intervention to deal with the disorders, which broke out after the death in suspicious circumstances of an opposition leader.

France had intervened in February 1964 to suppress the military coup against President Léon Mba under the terms of the agreement, though it is questionable whether French authorities obtained the formal consent of Vice President Yembit prior to intervention. In 1981 the Socialist government in Paris made clear that it would no longer intervene militarily to protect African regimes from purely domestic opponents. The indecisiveness of that government in dealing with the Libyan invasion of Chad, with which it had a similar agreement, made Libreville wonder whether it could count on French help in an attack from the exterior.

The uncertainty of French assistance during a decade in which political opposition surfaced and plots were discovered against the regime may explain the quadrupling of Gabon's defense and security forces between 1978 and 1988, as well as the creation of the new Mobile Security Units. In 1978 the army had numbered 950, the navy 100, and the air force 200, a total of 1,250 in the defense forces. In 1988 the army had grown to 3,343, the navy to 600, and air force 1,026, plus 300 firemen, a total of 5,269. An oversized officer corps contained 83 generals. Several top generals had been incorporated into the Central Committee of the PDG and had been named to posts in the cabinet.

In 1978 the gendarmerie and the national police had 2,000 members. In 1988 the gendarmerie had 2,655, the police 2,400, and the Presidential Guard (previously numbered within the army) 1,900, a total of nearly 7,000. The numbers in the new mobile security units have not been made public. There is also a Coast Guard with 2,800 members. All of these forces possess the latest weapons and up-to-date training.

From 1970 to 1989, President Bongo's brother-in-law, Major-General Jean-Boniface Assélé, directed the national police. In March 1988 Bongo's nephew, Major-General André Oyini, became chief of the General Staff, replacing General Louis Martin, who was appointed special adviser to the president on security matters.

Since the 1980s, the African Institute of Strategic Studies has been located at Libreville. It is headed by Léon Augé (1929–), a career civil servant and magistrate who until early 1990 also held high positions in the PDG. [662, 668]

DELAUNEY, MAURICE (Ca. 1918–). French administrator and diplomat, close associate of Omar Bongo. Trained as a career overseas administrator at the École Nationale de la France d'Outre-Mer in Paris, Delauney spent three years of the Second World War as a prisoner of war in Germany. Thereafter, he was involved in the Resistance and the army that liberated western France. As an administrator in the Cameroons for eight years, he had charge of the repression of the U.P.C. rebellion in the Bamiléké areas around Dschang. As French ambassador to Libreville from 1965 to 1972, Delauney looked after French interests and the security of the Gabonese regime. He was involved in the selection of Omar Bongo as Léon Mba's vice president and eventual successor. From 1975 to 1979, he returned to Libreville as ambassador, thereafter becoming the president of the Compagnie des Mines d'Uranium de Franceville, which handles Gabon's uranium production. Delauney had to withdraw as ambassador in the wake of a scandal involving the Service d'Action Civique at Marseilles. Delauney describes some of his experiences in Gabonese public life in his autobiography, of which there are two editions, *De la casquette à la jaquette, ou de l'administration coloniale à la diplomatie africaine* (1982) and *Kala, Kala* (1986). [603, 65]

DEMOGRAPHY. Westerners in Gabon from the 1840s on noted the small size and low density of the population. They attributed the low density to the thick rain forests, which hindered concentrations of population, and the small size to a variety of natural and human factors. They observed a decline in the numbers of the coastal populations, which they attributed in part to contact with Europe. Traders from the West had introduced alcoholic beverages, new venereal diseases, and smallpox. Their commercial activities and those of their African agents helped to spread sleeping sickness (trypanosomiasis) and other diseases over larger areas of the country. Smallpox epidemics between 1845 and 1870 reduced the population of the Mpongwe by one-third to one-half. Westerners noted a high level of infertility among the women of the Estuary and the practice of abortion, generally linked with prostitution. They also observed the dislocation and decimation of the Séké and the Bakèlè in the Estuary as well as the Bakèlè and other peoples in the middle Ogooué River as a result of the oceanward movements of the more numerous Fang.

During the late nineteenth and early twentieth centuries the exactions of the colonial regime and the concessionary companies contributed to the dislocation of settled life throughout the country, the separation of men from their families, and a diminution of the population. Requisitions and recruitments imposed upon the Gabonese in the course of the First World War diminished food production in ways that increased the tolls of epidemics and famines for a decade thereafter. The conscription of forced labor for the construction of the Congo-Ocean Railroad between 1918 and 1924 contributed to food shortages, particularly in the Fang areas of the North during the 1920s. Sleeping sickness and the ensuing permanent exodus of adult males from the Haut-Ogooué Province between 1908 and 1930, but particularly from 1923 to 1930, caused a permanent decline there.

Few Gabonese had access to western medicine prior to the 1930s. The American Protestant mission between 1842 and 1906 included several physicians (Drs. Henry Ford [q.v.], Robert H. Nassau [q.v.], George W. Taylor, and Henry M. Bachelor), but medical practice was incidental to their work of evangelism. Only with the establishment of Dr. Albert Schweitzer (q.v.) under SME auspices in 1913 did the indigenous peoples acquire a full-time missionary physician. French Holy Ghost Brothers (q.v.) and Immaculate Conception Sisters (q.v.), who cared for the sick at Libreville, possessed mainly practical training. The French navy and administration brought in physicians to look after the health of their employees. These doctors also treated the general population in their vicinity. But only after the completion of the construction of the Congo-Ocean Railroad did the administration undertake to provide health care for the population at large. During the 1930s it was able to eradicate sleeping sickness. Bilharzia (schistosomiasis) and malaria continued to afflict large portions of the population; malaria and its complications remained the most common cause of death.

Colonial censuses indicate that Gabon's population remained basically stagnant during the four decades between the First World War and independence. The census of 1921 showed 389,000, and that of 1959, 416,000. The censuses and other administrative inquiries provide evidence of rising infertility under colonial rule. Malaria may have contributed to infertility by causing miscarriages that led to sterilizing infections. Almost all ethnic groups suffered from high sterility rates during these decades. The direct medical cause of sterility among women who were examined by French physicians was blockages in the fallopian tubes due to scarring and lesion from infection usually suspected to be gonorrhea. The poverty of rainforest diets may also have played a role in sterility.

Censuses between the two world wars found that 20 percent of Gabonese women born before 1890 had never produced a living child compared with 13 to 14 percent in the Middle Congo and Ubangi-Shari. The percentage of sterile women increased during this era as did secondary sterility, the inability of mothers to bear additional children. In addition to the environmental factors, social and economic conditions favored the diffusion of venereal disease. Timber workers between the two world wars were separated from their families. They returned home with not only the bride wealth to acquire a second wife but also venereal disease. Some women left alone in the villages became involved in prostitution in order to pay their taxes or to buy cloth. The African auxiliaries of the administration, most of whom had venereal disease, spread it so extensively that in the early 1920s women near administrative posts had a sterility rate 50 percent greater than the average for the country. Despite the administration's concern about venereal diseases, its own agents and policies did more to spread them than its health service did to eradicate them.

The censuses between 1921 and 1959–1960 indicated that children (under fifteen) formed only 20 percent of the population of Gabon, a percentage that was lower than in the Middle Congo and Ubangi-Shari. Despite administrative efforts to improve health care for mothers and children, the percentage of children did not increase between 1929 and independence. This situation reflected a high rate not only of sterility but also of infant mortality. The census of 1959–1960 showed an infant mortality rate of 229 per thousand. Inquiries revealed that 38.43 percent of the children born to the women surveyed were no longer alive at the time of the census. Early deaths came to infants from digestive and respiratory problems. Malaria, which normally appeared toward the sixth month, may have accounted for one-fifth of the deaths. Intestinal parasites acquired by crawling infants contributed to malnutrition and gastrointestinal problems. Heavy work demands on women, including the raising of food crops, placed infants in situations that menaced their health.

The absence of reliable census data after 1960–1961 hinders the analysis of population trends since independence. (It is believed that the Bongo regime inflated the results of the 1970–1971 and 1980 census in order to retain a per capita average income that would continue to make Gabon eligible for various kinds of international assistance.) But administrative surveys and studies by international organizations indicate that the rate of population growth has increased during the past three decades. Between 1960 and 1970 the birth rate remained the same, 35 per thousand, while the death rate fell from 30 to 20 per thousand. Thus the rate of natural increase tripled from .5 percent to 1.5 percent. During the first half of the 1980s the birth rate averaged 34 per thousand while the death rate declined further to 18 per thousand. Then during the last half of the 1980s the average annual birth rate rose to 39 per thousand while the death rate fell to 16 per thousand. A World Bank study (1985) found that the average annual rate of growth had been 1.4 percent between 1973 and 1983, and 2.6 percent since 1983. The larger figure in 1983 may reflect an increased immigration as well as natural growth. Between 1960–1961 and 1991 the infant mortality rate (death in the first year) had declined from 229 to 106 per thousand. Whereas in 1960 one-third of all children died before the end of their fifth year, by 1991 only one-sixth were dying in that period. Life expectancy in 1960–1961 for males had been estimated at twenty-five years and for females forty-five years. In 1991 life expectancy for males had doubled to fifty years, and for females it had increased to fifty-three years. *African Recovery* (no. 3, 1991) gave the annual natural increase rate of Gabon's population as 3.5 percent and the fertility rate as 5.0 percent. UN agencies at the end of the 1980s gave the following distribution of the population by age categories: 34.6 percent under fifteen; 24.4 percent for fifteen to twenty-nine; 18.3 percent for thirty to forty-four; 13.3 percent for forty-five to fifty-nine; 7.6 percent for sixty to seventy-four; 1.8 percent seventy-five and older. These various statistics suggest that while the birth rate began to increase only during the 1980s, the mortality rate declined in the course of three decades to half of its previous levels, among children in general and particularly among adult males.

The explanations for the growth of Gabon's population, other than through immigration, are linked to the improved standard of living, particularly for the increasing percentage that lived in urban areas. In 1960 one-third of all children died before reaching the age of five years. This situation reflected the living conditions of a population that was 80 percent rural and lacked access to medical facilities. It also showed the lack of sanitation and the deficiencies in rural diets. Very real efforts by the government to provide medical services for all provinces, including care programs for mothers and children, and to control communicable diseases, have significantly reduced the rates of sterility and infant mortality. The government also tackled the problem of infertility at the CIRMF opened at Franceville in 1979.

The urbanization of the country connected with the development of its mineral resources and the neglect of agriculture have placed nearly half of the population in the cities and larger towns where they enjoy better hygiene, better nutrition, improved health care, and a higher standard of living in general. A further factor concerning health is that as many as 90 percent of the country's medical personnel are now concentrated in the vicinity of Libreville, Port-Gentil, and Franceville.

A further question is the size of the population growth since independence. It is generally agreed that the census of 1960–1961 was accurate in general but may have under-counted the people in timber and mining camps. On the basis of the most complete data available, the geographer Roland Pourtier estimated the population in 1987 at 800,000. This figure included the up to 100,000 non-Gabonese Africans but not the 30,000 Europeans. Estimates by foreign governments and international agencies have varied from that figure to 1,100,000. [916, 940]

DENIS, KING or ANTCHOUWE KOWE RAPONTCHOMBO (c. 1780–1876). Most eminent of the nineteenth-century Mpongwe clan heads, first to accept French sovereignty and to promote French influence in Gabon. Antchouwé Kowe was known to the French as King Denis and to the British as King William. Denis headed the Asiga clan of the Mpongwe (q.v.) from 1810 to 1876. The Asiga occupied the peninsula at the extreme western tip of the Estuary and along the Atlantic. There, in the last third of the 1700s and first half of the 1800s, they actively engaged as middlemen in a slave trade with the interior and Cape Lopez to the south. Denis personally profited from the trade. He himself possessed 300 to 400 domestic slaves and 40 to 50 wives. Though non-literate, Denis could speak English, French, Spanish, and Portuguese as well as several African languages. He impressed European and American visitors to his court by his keen intelligence and cultivation. He acquired a reputation for wisdom and honesty and enjoyed great respect and influence. His assistance to European seamen and traders on many occasions led to a medal from Queen Victoria in 1839. The same year he was named a Chevalier of the Legion of Honor and later received a medal from Pope Gregory XVI for his aid to the Roman Catholic mission. Throughout his lifetime he continued to serve as an intermediary in conflicts between European and African traders and in disputes among the Gabonese.

Denis's actions in regard to the establishment and extension of French rule, however, contain inconsistencies and contradictions that lend themselves to different interpretations. Denis was the first Mpongwe clan head to make a treaty recognizing French sovereignty and ceding a site for a French establishment (February 9, 1839). He encouraged other clan heads to make similar treaties and served as an intermediary between the French and them to this end. Yet he successfully maneuvered to prevent the French from establishing their post on his lands as he had agreed. He prevented European traders from residence in his lands and withdrew active support from the Holy Ghost Fathers (q.v.) mission (St. Thomas), which he had allowed to be established in 1851. It failed and was closed in 1853, in part also because of a lack of personnel and resources. At the same time, Denis sent several of his children, including his son and successor Louis Félix-Adandé (q.v.), to the Catholic mission schools at Libreville and maintained cordial relations with the French priests. As a polygamist, Denis could not receive baptism without renouncing all but one of his wives, so his entrance into the Catholic Church was postponed until just before his death on March 9, 1876.

Given the fact that Denis's relationships with Europeans were essentially commercial, he may have thought of the treaty with France as formalizing this situation. He may have hoped that acceptance of French sovereignty and the cession of a plot would lead to the establishment of a commercial post that would promote trade in commodities other than slaves without interfering in the latter. The post would give him advantages over his Agekaza rivals on the northern shore who were allied with English and American traders, for the treaty made no mention of the slave trade or its suppression. When Denis became aware of French intentions to establish a degree of political control and to suppress the slave trade, he used diplomacy to prevent a post on his lands. He took measures in cooperation with the Spanish traders who operated barracoons at his capital to protect the slaving operations from French surveillance. Having failed to interest his subjects in commercial alternatives to the slave trade, he may have sought to perpetuate and profit from the nefarious business as long as he could. At the same time he maintained good relations with the French authorities, who were far more interested in the 1840s–1860s in establishing and extending French control and in gaining commercial supremacy over British rivals than in suppressing the slave trade. In 1862 he helped the French to secure treaties with the Orungu chiefs of the Cape Lopez area. Throughout his lifetime he refused to permit American Protestant missionaries to operate schools or preaching stations on his territories. It is his clear preference for the French, above all, at a period in which, despite their treaties, their commercial and cultural influence was very much secondary to the British, American, and later the Germans that has endeared him to them. Denis is more responsible than any other Mpongwe ruler, including King Louis (q.v.), for attaching Gabon to France and promoting French influence. [252, 362, 394, 332, 335]

DEPENAUD, NDOUNA (1937–1977). Educator and writer. Ndouna Depenaud is the pen name of Dieudonné Pascal Ndouna-Okogo, who was born at Akiéné in the Haut-Ogooué Province on July 7, 1937. He received his secondary education at Libreville, and his higher education at Brazzaville and Abidjan (the École Normale Supérieure). He served as a school director, professor, and Inspector of National Education. Depenaud was married to Marie-Josephine Kama prior to her marriage to Albert-Bernard Bongo. Depenaud was assassinated in Libreville in 1977, according to Pierre Péan, by Moroccans in the Presidential Guard. His assassins were never brought to justice. His literary works include poems, *Rêves à l'aube, Passages,* and a four-act play, *La Plaie.* [1205, 603]

DORSEY, JOSIAH (d. 1860). Dorsey was an Afro-American from Baltimore, Maryland, who taught in the schools of the ABCFM mission at Cape Palmas (1838–1842) and in Gabon (1842–1855). He learned Mpongwe well and taught in it as well as in English. In 1846 Dorsey married Mary Clealand, a Grebo, whose uncle was King Freeman of Cape Palmas. Their son, William, or Guillaume Dorsey (1849–1869), became a Catholic seminarian and studied at Ngazobil, Senegal, prior to his death. Their daughter, Sarah (b. 1851), became a prominent member of the Baraka church. She married William Lewis (Owondo), an Mpongwe trader who became one of the first elders of the American Presbyterian church at Baraka in January 1874. After Dorsey's death, his widow married a Scottish trader, Kirkwood, at Glass. [1031, 1028]

DU CHAILLU, PAUL (1831–1903). Nineteenth-century Franco-American explorer and author. Du Chaillu was born on July 31, 1831, possibly in Paris but more likely on Reunion to a French father and a mulatto mother. While living in Gabon from 1848 to 1852 with his trader father, he resided with the American missionary John Leighton Wilson (q.v.) and attended the school of the Holy Ghost Fathers (q.v.). He learned several Gabonese languages in the course of his journeys with his father. Between 1852 and 1855 he studied natural history in Philadelphia, where he may have become an American citizen. He returned to Gabon in 1855 with modest support from the museums of Philadelphia and Boston to explore and to collect fauna and flora. During the next four years he was the first European and literate observer to explore many parts of Gabon. He went inland 100 miles from the Rio Muni through Séké (q.v.) country to Fang (q.v.) areas at the edge of the Monts de Cristal. With Nkomi (q.v.) help, he went up the Rembo Nkomi as far as the Ofoubou River among the Bakèlè and thereafter visited the Eshira (q.v.) and Apindji (q.v.) peoples en route to the N'Gounié River. During a second voyage between 1863 and 1865, he collected museum specimens, including the gorilla. He travelled east from the N'Gounié into the Massif du Chaillu, which still bears his name, through the territories of the Bapounou, Mitsogo, and Obongo Pygmies of so-called Ashango land (Massango) (q.v.) as far as Mouaou Kombo, a bit east of modern M'Bigou.

Despite exaggerations in his first book and some sensationalism, his works are valuable sources for the life and customs of various peoples of Gabon at this time. They have more value for the coastal peoples than the ones of the interior, but in both cases Du Chaillu was a keen and sympathetic observer. [361, 393, 397, 249]

DURAND-REVILLE, LUC (1904–). Longtime director of the most important concessionary company, the Société du Haut-Ogooué (q.v.), Luc Durand-Reville was born to French parents in Cairo on April 12, 1904. He studied law and commerce at the University of Paris before going to Gabon. There in 1942 he became president of the SHO. Durand-Reville represented Gabon in the French Senate from 1947 to 1958, and in the Senate of the French Community from 1959 on. In the French Senate he affiliated with the Rassemblement des Gauches Républicains and maintained friendly relations with the Gaullists of the Rassemblement du Peuple Français. He ably represented European lumbering and commercial interests and promoted the economic development of Gabon. [550, *Who's Who in France*]

- E -

EBOUE, FELIX (1884–1944). Black French colonial governor and Free French leader. Born in French Guyana and a graduate of the Colonial School for career administrators in Paris, Eboué served mainly in Oubangui-Shari before becoming governor of Chad in January 1939. In that position he was instrumental in rallying Chad to the Free French movement in late August 1940, which in turn aided the Gaullists to gain control of the other territories of French Equatorial Africa (q.v.), including Gabon. As Free-French governor-general (1940–1944) Eboué granted a special status of *notable évolué* to 200 educated Africans, which freed them from some of the burdens of the ordinary colonial subject (e.g., the *prestation,* or labor tax). Eboué integrated several Gabonese civil servants into the European cadres and did not retreat when there was a furor among some whites and Congolese. He encouraged the formation of discussion and cultural groups among the *évolués* and civil servants. He took a personal interest in the careers of some Gabonese civil servants at Brazzaville; among them were the future deputy (1946–1958) Jean-Hilaire Aubame (q.v.), the future foreign affairs minister Jean-Remy Ayouné (q.v.), and future councillor of the Assembly of the French Union René-Paul Sousatte (q.v.). In 1944 Eboué named Aubame president of the new municipal commission of the Poto Poto commune of Brazzaville, which he had established to permit greater African participation.

Despite the problems of wartime, Eboué tripled expenditures for education, including important subsidies to the Catholic and Protestant mission schools, which had previously been receiving only token amounts. Though himself a socialist and freemason, Eboué was determined to enlist all available forces to promote educational progress. The government of the Fourth French Republic would make Eboué's practice a policy, thus enabling the mission schools to continue to play a major role in education in the post-war period (and since then in Gabon). In 1942 Eboué opened an *école supérieure* (grades seven to ten) in each territory, including one at Libreville. This school provided the first secondary education in Gabon outside the missions' seminary and Bible schools. Together with the increased primary enrollments, it permitted the expansion of the numbers of Gabonese in middle-level positions in the administration and upper-primary teaching.

Eboué favored the promotion of the French language and culture but advocated the revitalization of traditional African institutions in his circular *La Nouvelle Politique Indigène* (*The New Native Policy*) of November 8, 1941. He played an important role in organizing a conference of French administrators at Brazzaville in January-February 1944 to plan the postwar reform of the colonial empire. [381, 292, 992]

ECOLE MONTFORT. The Ecole Montfort refers to the boys' primary school at Libreville directed by the Brothers of Saint

Gabriel (q.v.), which played a vital role in educating the elite, especially between 1900 and the end of the Second World War. The Holy Ghost Fathers (q.v.) operated schools for boys from their arrival in the Estuary in 1844. But they were not a teaching order and in 1900 gained the assistance of the Brothers of Saint Gabriel, a congregation of professional teachers, to upgrade the instruction in some of their schools. The first brothers arrived on October 7, 1900. Led by Brother Fulgent Boisdron (1853–1903), they assumed direction of the school near St. Peter's Church at the center of Libreville to which the boarding pupils at St. Mary's Church two miles away also came daily. The brothers were aided by African monitors and seminarians. They were able to provide several hundred boys an education of higher quality and more advanced level than hitherto had been available. Specifically, they gave their most advanced pupils instruction in French equivalent to the French *brevet élémentaire,* that is, several years beyond the *certificat d'études primaires indigènes* that was granted locally after approximately six years of study. The brothers also took direction of the boys' school at Lambaréné between December 1901 and October 1910 where the Catholics were facing strong competition from the Protestants who had preceded them into the area. The termination of state subsidies in 1907 in the wake of the separation of church and state in France contributed to their withdrawal from Lambaréné. Immediately after the First World War those at Libreville went on leave and were not replaced. Their departure brought forth a strong reaction from the Gabonese elements who had been benefiting from their instruction. The brothers had drawn their pupils from all over Gabon and a few from other territories of French Equatorial Africa. Their former students were holding important positions in the administration, commerce, education, and religion in Gabon and throughout West and Equatorial Africa and the Belgian Congo. The elite elements accused the administration of eliminating the means for their entrance into the higher levels of the civil service and commercial management and for the achievement of equality with Europeans. The departure of the brothers indeed meant that Gabon could no longer produce enough personnel locally and had to recruit African staff from Senegal, Dahomey, Togo, Cameroon, and even Nigeria. From being an exporter of educated staff, Gabon was transformed once more into an importer. In November 1924 the Brothers of Saint Gabriel returned to Libreville at the request of the French Spiritan bishop and resumed direction of the boys' school. But apparently they no longer attempted to provide instruction beyond the local primary certificate. In 1927 a new Ecole Montfort in central Libreville was once more giving an education to 700 boys. It thus provided instruction for a large segment of the educated elite throughout the rest of the interwar period during which public education was little developed. The graduates of the Ecole Montfort would form an important part of Gabon's politicians and civil servants during the Fourth French Republic and the 1960s. [1013, 1030, 550]

ECONOMY. The economy of Gabon has always contained both subsistence and market sectors. From prehistoric times the inhabitants of the equatorial forests, savannas, and coastal marshes hunted, fished, gathered fruits and nuts, and raised foodstuffs and livestock. The presence of the tsetse fly in most regions usually made herding all but impossible. The poor soils, which leached rapidly under rainstorms, led to shifting cultivation and gradual but regular population movements. The introduction of new food staples from the Americas in the sixteenth and seventeenth centuries, particularly manioc (cassava), new varieties of plantains, bananas, yams, and the sweet potato, made the forests much more viable homes for the various peoples entering them from the neighboring savannas. Iron deposits in both the northeast and southwest made possible the manufacture of tools and weapons. In the southwest, palm fibers, including raphia, were woven into cloth and mats of often high quality.

The salt of the Loango (q.v.) coast, including from Mayumba and Setté-Cama, which was evaporated from seawater, was especially desired by the peoples in areas of heavier rainfall and damper climate. The salt was being sent inland and north along the coasts as far as the Bight of Benin even before Europeans first appeared on the coasts late in the 1400s.

The coming of the Europeans led to the establishment of additional coastal markets, especially at the mouths of the rivers, which gave access to the interior, for water transportation was a necessity in a sparsely populated country like Gabon. Porterage was an expensive supplement ordinarily employed to circumvent the sandbars at river mouths as well as the falls and rapids upstream. In these circumstances, much of Gabon's foreign trade centered upon the Estuary or Gabon River (now considered part of the Como River) and the Ogooué River, whose watershed encompassed nearly four-fifths of the country. Trade with the Europeans included such items as dyewood (*padouk*), beeswax, gum copal, palm oil, ivory, and, by the nineteenth century, rubber. The fine-quality palm cloth and matting of southern Gabon were much sought after until gradually replaced in the nineteenth century by inexpensive mass-produced British textiles. Copper reached the Loango coast from the inland area around Mindouli in today's Congo Republic. From Europe and North America traders brought such items as cloth strips, rum and other strong alcoholic beverages, firearms, gunpowder, knives, and iron bars. Trade in goods was frequently accompanied by trade in slaves, but the slave trade did not achieve importance until the late eighteenth century and trade in goods never ceased even during its height between 1760 and 1860.

Between the sixteenth and mid-nineteenth centuries, coastal peoples served as commercial middlemen between European and American traders and inland peoples. Trading routes and networks developed that were tiered or layered, as in the Estuary, or basically linear, as in the Ogooué where each people controlled a portion of the river and all traffic both upstream and downstream. Each people involved in the network thus profited from the transmission of goods.

Trade in northern Gabon up to about 1840 depended upon informal understandings between a clan head or chief trader and an individual captain or supercargo, on the one hand, and between the coastal leader and the network of inland chiefs, on the other. In the aftermath of the French establishment on the Estuary and northern coasts, European trading companies founded permanent posts and under French protection penetrated inland and eliminated the various middlemen. These processes transformed the former middlemen into European agents and employees and transferred a greater share of the profits to the companies. Prior to 1860 most of the traders and trading firms in northern Gabon were British, American, and German rather than French. Ninety-five percent of the commercial shipping was either British or American. Most of the expansion into the Ogooué in the late 1860s and 1870s, first at Fernan-Vaz and then at Lambaréné, was undertaken by British and German firms. In 1900, out of 224 trading posts in Gabon (of which 80 were in the Estuary, 9 at Cape Lopez, 15 at Fernan-Vaz and 120 up the Ogooué), Hatton & Cookson of Liverpool (in Gabon since 1851) had 78; John Holt of Manchester 59 and Adolph Woermann of Hamburg 20. The only major French company was the recently organized SHO (1893), which had been given a commercial monopoly over vast areas of the upper Ogooué.

Though the steamboat came into use in the 1870s, it could not be employed farther than 80 miles up the Como River or beyond N'Djolé on the Ogooué. The SHO (q.v.), whose territories lay above N'Djolé, was obliged to depend on local canoers and porters for much of its transport of rubber and other commodities. It encountered somewhat the same kind of labor shortage that had doomed French attempts at commercial plantations in the Estuary in the 1840s.

In the late 1890s the administration of the French Congo of which Gabon had become a part sought to develop its natural resources through the kind of concessionary regime previously installed in the neighboring Congo Free State. The regime installed by these monopolistic companies, which extended to all of Gabon except the Estuary, disrupted the existing trading networks without replacing them with viable alternatives. In the face of growing abuses and injustices, the companies were phased out by the time of the First World War except on the upper Ogooué where the commercial monopoly of the SHO persisted until 1930.

From the 1890s Gabon began to export okoumé (q.v.) used for plywood, and various hardwoods, first to German and Dutch markets, and in the twentieth century to French ones. French industrial firms became dominant in logging after the First World War. The woods were obtained from an area that extended from Spanish Guinea south to Setté-Cama and that encompassed the Estuary, the lower and middle Ogooué, and the lower N'Gounié. The absence of roads limited the exploitation of timber to areas near waterways down which the logs could be floated to the coast. Woods would remain Gabon's leading export until the late 1960s when petroleum (q.v.) surpassed them in value.

During the 1920s and 1930s, the colonial administration sponsored commercial agriculture, in particular in the Woleu-N'Tem Province where peasants produced cocoa and coffee for export. Roads were constructed to permit transportation of these commodities to waterways and coastal ports. Though the administration became more active in promoting economic development, imports and much of the exports were handled by such large European firms as the Compagnie Française de l'Afrique Occidentale, the Société Commerciale de l'Ouest Africain, Hollando, and Hatton & Cookson. These companies imported the bulk of such consumer goods as food and beverages, textiles and clothing, and household items. They controlled the wholesale and much of the retail operations as well as the transport of goods. The role of these enterprises in the commercial sector would persist with little change until the late 1970s when the Gabonese government began to intervene in these activities through creation of parastatals. By that time more Lebanese merchants had become involved in retailing and more non-Gabonese Africans in small-scale trading.

After the Second World War the administration implemented a number of programs of economic development through FIDES (q.v.) to expand exploitation of timber and production of cocoa and coffee. But it did little to introduce modern agricultural methods that might have ensured the country an adequate supply of foodstuffs while stabilizing a more prosperous rural population. During the mid-1950s France abandoned its traditional policy of excluding foreign capital from the industrial and mining sectors in its overseas territories in order to permit a more extensive and rapid development of their natural resources. Thus, during the late 1950s, while reserving the exploitation of uranium for itself, France began to develop manganese and petroleum production and to plan for the exploitation of iron and other metals and minerals in cooperation with American, British, and Dutch investors.

With the arrival of independence in 1960, the Gabonese government gained control over the country's natural resources and a greater share of the revenues from them. By investing some of these revenues in transportation facilities and parastatals, it was able to promote further development of natural resources, processing industries, and manufacturing. At the same time, it remained dependent upon foreign capital and expertise for this economic expansion. Because of the country's small population, it also needed the assistance of foreign labor, both unskilled and skilled, to develop the economy further.

The resource whose exploitation since the 1960s has had the most far-reaching consequences is petroleum. Whereas the production of manganese, uranium, and timber continued to provide the country steady income, exploitation of petroleum multiplied the revenues available to the state many times over. Given the expectation that the oil reserves would last only until the end of the 1980s, the government embarked upon the building of the Transgabonais Railroad in order to reach additional resources in the interior, including the iron ore deposits in the northeast and additional timber. Between 1974 and 1986 the railroad was constructed from Libreville to Franceville, but world market conditions did not permit its extension into the area of the iron ore. At the same time the $3 billion enterprise was running at an annual deficit of $20 to $30 million at the start of the 1990s. In the meantime, in 1985 in southern Gabon at Rabi-Kounga, oil deposits were discovered that doubled the country's known reserves to 130 million tons and extended the possibility of production well into the twenty-first century. Other small deposits continued to be located both offshore and onshore as extensive prospecting was renewed. Unfortunately, world market conditions and international finances both in the late 1970s and again much more extensively from 1986 on diminished the revenues from petroleum compared with earlier boom times. Because world demand for manganese, uranium, and timber remained stable or declined slightly from the 1980s, these commodities could not compensate for the downturn in the petroleum sector.

During the period of the oil boom the government neglected the production of agricultural exports, for which world demand was unsteady, while allowing the system of roads that carried these crops to the ports to deteriorate. At the same time it neglected even more the production of food crops, for which there was increasing demand in the burgeoning coastal cities. It became involved in commercial agriculture through the organization of parastatals to feed the cities, but peasant agriculture languished, contributing further to the rural exodus. By the end of the 1980s Gabon was importing 85 percent of its food.

The oil boom, which led to the creation of additional secondary industries, many of them also parastatals, helped to transfer larger portions of Gabon's population into the cities, so that by the early 1990s close to half resided in the urban areas. While many among the urban masses benefited from regular employment and improved social services (particularly education and health care), the ruling class that formed 2 percent of the population kept 80 percent of the national income for itself. The inequitable distribution of income, the corruption involved in perpetuating the process, and the deficits of the poorly managed parastatals all contributed to the upheavals of 1990.

Three decades after independence, Gabon continues to have the bulk of its trade and to secure most of its investment capital from western nations. It maintains strong ties with France, which is still its main trading partner and source of financing and expertise. It has important links with other members of the European Community, the United States, and Japan. It has little trade with neighboring countries, except for Cameroon, from which it receives foodstuffs, or with the rest of Africa. Its economy thus remains an enclave within Equatorial Africa that is highly vulnerable to world market conditions. *See* AGRICULTURE; FORESTRY; GOLD; IRON; LABOR UNIONS; MANGANESE; OK-OUME; PETROLEUM; PHOSPHATES & RARE ELEMENTS; TRANSPORTATION; URANIUM. [940, 1, 232, 65, 378, 777, 11, 129, 326, 261, 266, 929]

EDUCATION. Education among the indigenous peoples of Gabon, who were nonliterate, was always informal. Formal education was introduced by Christian missionaries in the mid-nineteenth century. Congregational and Presbyterian missionaries sponsored by the ABCFM of Boston opened the first schools in the Estuary region in 1842. They taught religion, reading, writing, arithmetic, other elementary subjects, and the domestic arts (the latter only to girls), using both Mpongwe and English as the media of instruction. The missionaries sought to prepare teachers, Bible readers, catechists, and preachers as well as Bible-reading laymen. In early 1845 members of the Congregation of the Holy Ghost (Spiritans) (q.v.) from France started a similar kind of instruction for boys in the vicinity of present-day Libreville employing French and Mpongwe. The Sisters of Our Lady of Immaculate Conception (q.v.) of Castres, France (Blue Sisters), who arrived in 1849, taught domestic and literacy skills to girls. The Spiritans by 1856 were teaching Latin to the most talented boys in an attempt to prepare an indigenous clergy as well as catechists and teachers. They also began apprenticeship programs in gardening, agriculture, woodworking, masonry, and other skilled trades. The pupils of the schools included orphans, recaptives, and *rachétés* (slaves whose freedom the missionaries purchased) from the entire Gabon and Congo areas and the Portuguese islands of São Tomé and Príncipe in addition to the Mpongwe in the Estuary. In the 1850s the Protestants opened schools among the Bakèlè and the Catholics among the Benga. Presbyterian missionaries sponsored by the PBFM of New York, based on Corisco Island since 1850, also educated some mainland Benga north of Cape Esterias. In the 1870s, these Presbyterians, having assumed the work of the ABCFM, undertook instruction of the Fang farther up the Estuary and of the Fang, Galoa, and Bakèlè on the middle Ogooué River at Lambaréné and N'Djolé. During the decades in which the American Protestants operated schools, several hundred boys and several scores of girls learned to read and write in English and in Mpongwe, Dikèlè, Benga, or Fang. Many of the young men became employees of the British, American, and German trading firms that dominated the export trade until late in the 1800s.

The French government, which subsidized the educational work of the Catholic missions but did not regulate it, became increasingly nationalistic in the aftermath of the Franco-Prussian War (1870–1871). In April 1883 it instituted a primary-school curriculum based on Jules Ferry's recent metropolitan one in which at least half of the program involved teaching the French language and culture. It forbade the teaching of other languages, including indigenous ones. The American Protestants secured French-language teachers from France and Switzerland but then transferred their work on the Ogooué in 1892–1893 to French Protestants sponsored by the SME of Paris. The SME missionaries added instruction in various trades and established separate programs to prepare catechists and preachers. After the departure of the Americans, the government still pushed for the teaching of French but tolerated religious instruction in local languages. It granted small subsidies to the French Protestant schools. In the wake of the anti-clerical legislation and the separation of church and state in France (1905), the government withdrew all support from the mission schools and used the funds to open a public school at Libreville in 1907 to compete with the École Montfort (q.v.), established seven years earlier there by the Brothers of Saint Gabriel (q.v.). In 1922 the federation of French Equatorial Africa resumed the granting of small subsidies to mission schools teaching the official programs, but reserved the bulk of expenditures for the handful of public schools it had founded in the main towns. Between the two world wars the government devoted less than 1 percent of its budget to education. During the Second World War, the Free French administration under Governor-General Félix Eboué (q.v.) increased educational spending to 4.75 percent of the budget and granted important subsidies to the mission schools, which the war had cut off from their French supporters.

Until after the Second World War, the numbers who attended school were always tiny. For example, in 1882 the American Presbyterians taught 90 boys and 55 girls, and the French Catholics taught 216 boys and 79 girls, all of them in the Estuary or along the Ogooué. In 1898 the Catholics had 1,118 pupils and the American and French Protestants had 430, now including the upper Ogooué, the N'Gounié, and the southern coasts. During 1929–1930, the Catholics had 2,100 primary pupils, the Protestants had 680, and the public schools had 457, for a total of 3,237. During the interwar period, the school programs were adapted to emphasize practical skills and more material on Africa was added. Only local diplomas were given, which inhibited further education abroad for even those whose parents might be able to afford it. In these circumstances the only Gabonese who earned the baccalaureate in France during the 1930s were three sons of wealthy lumbermen. In Gabon itself the only education beyond the six primary grades was in the seminaries and Bible schools of the missions. In 1935 the government opened a higher primary school and a one-year teaching training course at Brazzaville to which several Gabonese were sent.

Prior to 1945 only a minority of those who entered school stayed long enough to achieve literacy or to learn a skilled trade. Yet it was this small group that permitted the colonial institutions to function. Its members served as the employees of the administration and commerce and as teachers, pastors, and priests. Some of them later would sit in the territorial and federal assemblies created in 1945–1946 and in the representative institutions of the French Fourth Republic. It is they who would be most responsible for transferring the metropolitan programs into Gabon after 1945, thus giving Gabon an educational system more closely modelled after the French in both form and content than at any previous period and permitting Gabonese to continue their education in France. The educated Gabonese saw education identical with that of France, not one adapted to Gabon, as the only effective means of securing equality and advancement.

Gabon as an Overseas Territory of the Fourth Republic received aid under FIDES (q.v.) for construction and equipment of schools and assistance in staffing the newly opened secondary schools. Primary enrollments increased from 9,082 in 1945–1946 to 50,545 in 1959–1960, but most pupils were enrolled in the early grades and remained only two to three years. The consequences of the situation were illustrated by a survey taken in mid-1963. It indicated that 48.6 percent of all Gabonese over fifteen years of age could speak French but that only 12.3 percent could read or write it. Much larger percentages of men than women knew French. In 1959–1960 the secondary schools enrolled 2,036 students, double the number only two years earlier. Small numbers of Gabonese received government scholarships for secondary programs not available in the federation and for higher education in France. In 1957–1958, 87 Gabonese were studying in French universities, 60 of them on scholarships. But on the eve of independence in August 1960, only a handful of Gabonese had completed the full secondary program or programs in higher education. This situation meant that independent Gabon continued to depend upon French personnel to staff the higher levels of the bureaucracy and economy. At the same time, Gabon, with French aid, undertook an expansion of enrollments at all levels of the existing system.

Today the educational system of Gabon still closely resembles that of France. Material about Gabon and Africa is included in the courses in geography, history, literature, and science, but the heavy emphasis on the French language and culture remains. The primary level has six grades, one more than in France, to enable the children to spend their first year adjusting to instruction in French. The possibility of the introduction of indigenous languages as the instructional media in the early primary grades, as has been undertaken in other Francophone states, seems remote. Secondary education has both general and technical programs with long cycles of seven years leading to the baccalaureate and short cycles of four years leading to the *brevet d'études du premier cycle* (BEPC). Holders of the baccalaureate are eligible for the university, while BEPC holders may enter programs for primary and lower secondary teachers, middle-level positions in national administration, and a variety of professional and paraprofessional positions such as medical-social assistant, nurse, accountant, and forestry technician. Since the late 1960s, the requirements for entering various programs have been upgraded from the primary level to the BEPC level, on the one hand, and from the BEPC to baccalaureate, on the other. The government since the mid-1970s has devoted even greater attention to technical education than previously with the aim of preparing increased numbers of Gabonese for technical and managerial careers. Traditionally such careers have proved less attractive than those in public administration, law, and education.

Gabon continues to subsidize the schools of the Catholic and Protestant churches in which European and American missionaries form a portion of the staff at the secondary level. The government pays most of the operating expenses of the church schools and the salaries of the African staff, including the Gabonese sisters in the Catholic schools. The church schools frequently offer a more extensive program in domestic sciences than the public schools. Religion is taught in addition to the official programs. The percentage of pupils in the church schools declined during the 1980s. Whereas in 1979 the church schools taught close to half of all primary pupils and one-third of the secondary ones, by 1987 they enrolled only one-third at the primary level and one-fifth at the secondary. In 1987 the Catholic schools had 53,613 primary pupils and 7,741 secondary.

In recent years school enrollments have been increasing at a more rapid rate than general population growth. Whereas in 1975 there were 128,552 primary pupils, in 1987 there were 195,049. While in 1975 there were 22,542 at the secondary level (19,721 in general education, 2,450 in vocational, and 371 in teaching training), in 1987 there were 48,274 (32,922 in general education, 9,967 in vocational, and 5,385 in teacher training). Girls formed 49 percent of the primary pupils throughout the period, but their percentage at the secondary level increased from 35 percent to 43 percent.

Most of the teaching staff at the primary level is Gabonese, but non-Gabonese, particularly French teachers provided through cooperation agreements, form an important part of the staff for the last three years of general education, technical education, and teacher training at the secondary level. The percentage of women among the primary teachers increased from 25 percent to 37 percent between 1979 and 1987. Women in 1987 still formed only 19 percent of the teaching staff at the secondary level.

School enrollment is obligatory for all children ages six to sixteen. Instruction is free. A UNESCO study in the mid-1980s indicated that while nearly all children enroll in school at some time in their lives, only three-quarters were actually attending at that time. There are several reasons for this situation. The increased urbanization of Gabon's population during the 1980s worsened the shortages of classrooms, equipment, and instructional materials in the schools of the Libreville area, in particular, but also in other cities. The economic downturn from 1986 on further diminished the ability of the government to deal with the deficiencies. The shortages, together with the inadequate preparation of many teachers in the early grades where overcrowding is greatest, and the sole use of French as the medium of instruction, have contributed to a high rate of repeating and dropout. In 1987 31 percent of the pupils at the primary level were repeating, with the highest percentages in the first grade (39 percent) and the sixth or final grade (36 percent). Twenty-five percent of the pupils at the secondary level were repeating, with the highest percentage in the final year (32 percent). The average child stays in school five to six years but completes only the first four grades in that time. A majority of children never graduate from the primary level, while fewer than one-quarter reach the secondary level. At the secondary level in 1987, 53 percent were in the first two years and only 11 percent in the last two. In 1989 only 897 of the 2,696 Gabonese candidates for the baccalaureate, that is, one-third, were successful. Among them were 616 men and 281 women. Nearly all of the *bacheliers* continued into higher education.

Higher education in Gabon has recent origins. After more than a century of primary education in the French language, Gabon in the late 1940s acquired its first secondary schools.

Their graduates had to go abroad for further study until the organization of the Fondation de l'Enseignement Supérieur en Afrique Centrale (FESAC) in 1961 by the four Equatorial states and France. Gabonese students attended three- to four-year programs in law and economic sciences and mathematics, and secondary teaching at Brazzaville, Congo Republic; agronomy at Mbaïki, the Central African Republic; animal husbandry at Ndjamena, Chad; and polytechnics in Libreville. Students in other programs and advanced students continued to go to France. The growth of the number of secondary-school graduates, political tensions in the Congo Republic, interstate rivalries, and Gabon's desire to educate its future leaders at home all contributed to the dissolution of FESAC in April 1971. Earlier in August 1970, Gabon with French support and encouragement created its own national university at Libreville, which during 1970–1971 enrolled 168 holders of the baccalaureate.

In January 1990 the Omar Bongo University at Libreville enrolled 2,568 students, of whom 2,361 were Gabonese and 207 foreigners. The University of Sciences and Technology at Masuku, which opened in 1987 near Franceville, had 499 students, including 29 foreigners. Specialized institutes enrolled 1,018 students, including 202 foreigners. Eight hundred and thirty Gabonese students were studying abroad on scholarships, of whom 480 were in France, 50 in Italy, 47 in the Soviet Union, 32 in China, and 27 in Canada. Thus Gabon had a total of 4,477 students in higher education, among whom were 1,330 women (29.7 percent). In September 1979 there had been 1,120 Gabonese studying within the country, and in 1976–1977, 1,366 studying abroad on scholarships. The expansion of facilities and the development of programs during the 1980s had made it possible for a majority of the students to remain in Gabon for their higher studies. Whereas in 1980 higher education offered only the first- and second-year programs leading to the university diploma and the third-year to the license (*licence*), by 1990 there was a fourth year in many fields, the first year of the master's (*maîtrise*). Only in the health sciences were fifth- and sixth-year programs available leading to the second year of the master's and the first year of the doctorate.

The Omar Bongo University has faculties of law and economic sciences, and of letters and human sciences as well as a center for health sciences. Masuku has a faculty of sciences and a polytechnic school. Among the 3,067 students enrolled in the two universities in 1990, 62 percent held the baccalaureate in economics or letters and 33 percent in the physical or natural sciences. The specialized institutes include such fields as management, information science, administration, teacher education, and advanced secretarial studies.

The rate of failure and repeating in higher education resembles the situation in other Francophone countries. In the examinations at the end of the 1988–1989 school year, only 48.8 percent passed; 35.3 percent repeated or were reoriented to other programs during 1989–1990; 15.9 percent quit. Of 956 seeking university diplomas 606 were successful in their examinations in 1988–1989.

Whereas during the 1970s a majority of the teachers in the university were French, in 1990, 201 of the 356 in the two universities were Gabonese, though two-thirds of those at Masuku were French.

The structure and programs in higher education remain nearly identical to those adopted in France in implementation of the law of November 12, 1968. They contain the modifications made during the late 1960s by the 14 Francophone states (excluding Guinea, but including Madagascar) of Black Africa jointly with French assistance, which added African content. Gabonese diplomas are valid in these 14 Francophone countries of Africa, France, Belgium, and Canada.

During demonstrations and strikes between December 20, 1989 and January 20, 1990, students of the Omar Bongo University expressed concern over the deterioration of educational conditions that was causing a decline in the quality of instruction. Many were worried that they would not be qualified to undertake further studies abroad, particularly in France. President Bongo was surprised to learn that the library of the university that bears his name lacked even the most elementary texts, that practical work and directed review could not be undertaken for want of teaching assistants, and that unsanitary conditions existed in many school buildings. In a mass meeting with 1,500 students on January 22, 1990, and later with their leaders, he promised to correct these deficiencies. He personally donated 600 new books to the university library.

Gabon greatly increased the percentage of its revenues devoted to education between the 1970s and 1980s. Whereas in 1975 it spent 8,902 million francs CFA (2.1 percent of GNP), in 1987 it spent 53,372 million francs CFA (5.9 percent of GNP). During the 1980s, it regularly spent a minimum of 20 percent of its functioning budget for education as well as additional funds for facilities and equipment. During the mid-Eighties, capital items accounted for one-fourth to one-third of total expenditure.

About one-fifth of the total educational expenditure is devoted to higher education. A portion of the students within the country receive grants for room, board, and incidentals that give them an income higher than someone working at minimum wage. Gabon also provided in 1990 665 of the 830 scholarships for those going abroad for advanced or specialized studies. Seventy-four of these scholarships came from the French Ministry of Cooperation, 50 from the Soviet Union, and 32 from China.

In addition to the formal system of education, Gabon has programs of adult education and professional formation, the latter for students eighteen years of age and over. The Agence Nationale de Formation et de Perfectionnement helps to supplement the education of job seekers through further training for particular employment opportunities.

The results of Gabon's considerable efforts in education in recent decades have been disappointing. The system is wasteful of national resources as evidenced by the rates of failure, repeating, and dropout. In 1990 only an estimated three-fifths of the population over fifteen were literate, including three-fourths of the males and close to half of the females. The country had to import Europeans for administrative and technical positions in the government and the economy, and teachers for the sciences and engineering, in particular. Given the very real financial and political obstacles to introducing meaningful changes, educational reform has remained largely at the level of rhetoric. The recommendation of the Estates General on Education, summoned by President Bongo in 1983, to use indigenous languages in the early stages of primary instruction as a step toward retention of more pupils is an example of a much needed reform that has not been implemented. President Bongo later spoke of using one African language, without specifying which one it might be—as well he might, given the very real ethnic tensions in the country. Subsequently, Paulette Moussavou Missambo, Minister of National Education since April 1990 and a specialist in Bantu languages, renewed the discussion on the necessity of introducing mother tongue instruction in the beginning grades of primary school. But the financial problems of the government and the continued social unrest that resulted in the interruption of classes at all levels of education for weeks and months at a time prevented action on her proposals. Thus the ill-adapted French-derived system persists with the unhappy results that have been noted.

In January 1993 *Jeune Afrique Economie* reported that in 1991–1992 Gabon had 225,000 pupils at the primary level with 4,782 teachers. The secondary level had 50,400 pupils, half of them in the Estuary Province, with 2,200 teachers. It is unclear whether these totals include pupils in vocational and teacher training institutions. The largest technical high school, the Lycée Omar Bongo at Owendo adjacent to Libreville, had 3,224 pupils. Three hundred and sixty new classrooms were under construction, a large part of them in the Estuary Province where recent population growth has been greatest, with the aid of funds from the African Development Bank. [961, 962, 965, 966, 967, 968, 1029, 1030, 1031, 975, 976, 979, 985]

EKOH, JEAN-MARC (1929–). Politician. Ekoh was born on November 12, 1929, at Bitam in the Woleu-N'tem Province into a family prominent in the French Protestant mission. He was one of the first Gabonese after the Second World War to receive a secondary education and to attend French universities. He became active in the Union Démocratique et Sociale Gabonaise and its youth movement from 1947. In March 1957 he was elected to the Legislative Assembly from the

Woleu N'Tem and later to the National Assembly. He held ministerial posts from the first government council in March 1957 through the end of the government of national union in 1963, including the post of Minister of National Education after independence. As a member of the short-lived provisional government in February 1964, Ekoh was arrested and sentenced to detention. He was later pardoned by President Bongo and rejoined the cabinet in 1968. Then in September 1970 he was accused of masterminding the kidnapping of a civil servant, Bernard Eyi (q.v.), and his wife. He was sentenced to 10 years in prison and 10 more under house arrest. Released early, he then taught in a Protestant secondary school in his home area. On March 3, 1982, during a church synod, Ekoh was arrested and charged with belonging to a group aimed at overthrowing the government (MORENA), acting against the security of the state, and committing outrages against the president. Though Ekoh denied the charges and the government produced no evidence to substantiate them, he was nevertheless among those convicted in November. He was among 13 sentenced to forced labor for 20 years with loss of civil rights thereafter. Publicity by Amnesty International and intervention by the French government influenced Bongo's decisions in 1983 and 1984 to reduce Ekoh's sentence. He was released in 1985. [1366, 598, 591, 593, 612, 544]

EMANE TOLE (1840 to 1850–1912 to 1914). Emané Tolé was a village chief among Fang clans that during the 1880s were monopolizing commerce on a stretch of the Ogooué River upstream from N'Djolé Island. He first clashed with French colonial troops in 1886 when they intervened on the side of the Bakota in a dispute that his people were having with the latter. In 1895 he abused an agent of the SHO who tried to trade directly with the Adouma of Lastoursville but survived a French reprisal that destroyed his home village. He organized 13 Fang clans in the N'Djolé area between February 1901 and September 1902 to resist the policies of the SHO (q.v.), a chartered company that had been given a commercial monopoly by the French government in 1897. The SHO sought to lower the prices paid for Gabonese products, to raise sharply the prices on European manufactures, and to impose a head tax (*capitation*) that would offset their administrative costs. The Fang clans were able to block the river for many months, but ultimately a reinforced colonial militia broke the resistance. The French deported Emané Tolé and his son Tolé Emané to Grand Bassam in the Ivory Coast. After Emané Tolé's death, his son was allowed to return to the Ogooué. [266, 348, 377, 340]

ENENGA. The remnants of the Enenga, a Myènè-speaking (q.v.) people, today inhabit the area around Lake Zilé, a widening of the middle Ogooué River between Lambaréné Island and the junction with the N'Gounié River. According to their traditions, the Enenga came to this area from the upper Ogooué and later ceded some of their new territory to the Galoa (q.v.) after the latter's arrival. The Enenga gradually became Myènè speakers to the point that by 1900 only the older people knew their original language, which belonged to the Okandé group. In the nineteenth-century the Enenga controlled trade on portions of the middle Ogooué and N'Gounié rivers. They purchased slaves from the Adouma (q.v.) and Okandé (q.v.) for transfer downstream to the barracoons of Cape Lopez. King Ranokè, who was one of three blind co-rulers—along with queens Evindo and Mbumba—from the 1860s to the 1880s, himself possessed many slaves. When R. B. N. Walker, founder and first director of the British firm Hatton and Cookson attempted to advance up the N'Gounié without Ranokè's permission, the chief detained him for six months. But on May 17, 1867, Lt. Antoine Aymès gained Ranokè's signature on a treaty recognizing French sovereignty by taking two of his sons hostage and by putting him in irons aboard the *Pioneer*. In 1873–1874 Ranokè aided the Marquis de Compiègne and Alfred Marche, and Brazza in 1875 and after, to obtain the expert canoemen that allowed them to pass the various rapids and heavy currents of the middle and upper Ogooué. Queen Evindo ceded the plot at Lambaréné that became the site of the Roman Catholic mission in 1881. [394, 340, 261]

ESHIRA. The Eshira people appear to have migrated into the grasslands and gallery forests south of the Ogooué River, west of the lower N'Gounié River, and on both banks of the Rembo Nkomi in the mid- or late eighteenth century in the wake of wars with the Bakèlè (q.v.) or others. In the nineteenth century they exchanged slaves from the interior with the Nkomi (q.v.) of Fernan Vaz. They raised a popular tobacco and produced a fine cloth of raphia that was much sought after by other Africans. Though they still ranked as an important people in numbers, their ranks were decimated by smallpox epidemics in 1865 and 1898. The Holy Ghost Fathers (q.v.) established a mission among them in 1895 and transcribed their language in the Latin alphabet.

When the explorer Paul du Chaillu (q.v.) passed through Eshira areas in 1858 and 1864, each clan controlled its own affairs. The most important chief, Mulenda of the Kamba clan, possessed 300 to 400 slaves. He died of smallpox in 1885. At du Chaillu's visit, the raphia textiles were losing ground to inexpensive British fabrics, which ultimately destroyed the local industry. [284, 294, 394]

EVEIA. The Evéia people are part of the Okandé linguistic group. They inhabit the middle N'Gounié River in the vicinity of Fougamou. According to their traditions, they came from the sea, where they had Mpongwe (q.v.) neighbors and spoke a Myènè (q.v.) language. They moved inland to escape slave raiders and traders. It is likely that they relocated because of Orungu (q.v.) control of the main mouths of the Ogooué, which dislocated their economy. During the nineteenth century, they moved into the Ogooué valley near Lambaréné to escape pressures of the Bakèlè and Fang (qq.v.); from there they migrated up the N'Gounié River. On the right bank of the N'Gounié where they settled, they were divided into river clans and mountain clans. In 1866 British firms established trading posts among them, including at their main village of Bwali. At the time the French established their post at Sindara in 1899, their main village was Mokandé [284, 807]

EXPLORATION. Various explorations between the 1470s and the early 1900s made the geographical features and peoples of Gabon known to the western world and, often, to the Gabonese themselves. In the 1470s and 1480s, Portuguese navigators came along the coasts of Gabon in their search for the routes to India, China, and the Indies. To various geographical features they gave the names that are still in use today, including the name of Gabon itself. In 1471 Vasconcellos discovered the island of São Tomé (St. Thomas) off the coast. The following year, the Portuguese discovered the Estuary or Gabon River to which they gave the name *gabão* (hooded cloak). Late in 1472, Lopo Gonçalves (called Lopez Gonzalves in Spanish) reached the cape to which he gave his name, Cape Lopez. In 1475 Ruy de Sequiera reached Cape St. Catherine 100 miles to the south. In 1480 Fernan Vaz attained the coast near the lagoon that still bears his name. Two years later Diogo Cão (Diego Cam in Spanish) reached the mouth of the Zaire River, which he named the Congo for the Kongo people on its banks.

While a number of later travellers and merchant adventurers have left useful accounts of the coastal peoples (particularly the Dutchman Willem Bosman in 1705 and the Englishman T. Edward Bowdich in 1815), increased knowledge of the interior peoples would have to await the second period of exploration between the 1840s and the early 1900s. Though these explorations would involve missionaries, merchants, and adventurers from France, Britain, the United States, Germany, and Spain, French naval officers and officials tended to predominate as did the desire to reach the heart of central Africa and the French wish to extend their control and influence.

Between 1844 and 1860 a number of expeditions by various French naval officers collectively revealed that the Estuary or Gabon River was really a bay into which flowed the Como River and its tributaries from the east-northeast and other rivers such as the Remboué from the east/ southeast. Specifically, in 1844 Lt. Rodolphe Darricau de Traverse (1807–1877) explored up the Como as far as Cobangoi; in 1846 Lt. Jean Pigeard (1818–1885) and Engineer Deschamps reached Kango; and later the same year Lt. Eugène Mecquet (1812–1887) arrived at the junction of the Bokoué. The Como was explored farther upstream in 1857 by Rev. G. du Mesnil (1834–1865) and between 1857 and 1859 by Lt. Jules-Édouard Brazouëc. In 1860, Dr. Gaston Roullet (1846–1871) and Lts. Touchard and Louis Genoyer identified the sources of the Como.

In 1856 the Franco-American adventurer, Paul du Chaillu (q.v.), who claimed that he had been commissioned by the National Academy of Sciences in Philadelphia, Pennsylvania, to explore and collect fauna and flora, explored the Rio Muni inland to the Monts de Cristal. There he made contact with the Fang and saw a live baby gorilla. Between 1857 and 1859, French lieutenants Brazouëc and Genoyer reconnoitered in the Rio Muni and the Mondah River. Taken as a whole, these explorations indicated that the Rio Muni and the Mondah River did not lead into the heart of the continent. Later in 1873, an expedition sponsored by the Geographical Society of Berlin and headed by Dr. Oscar Lenz (1848–1925) further explored the region of the Rio Muni and the Temboni River.

In 1854 two American Protestant missionaries, the Reverends Ira Preston (q.v.) and William Walker (q.v.), made a pioneering exploration up the Nazareth mouth of the Ogooué River halfway to the site of Lambaréné. In two expeditions, 1855–1859 and 1863–1865, du Chaillu explored inland at various points from Sangatanga, north of Cape Lopez, south as far as Cape St. Catherine. He was the first European to travel up the Mpoulounié mouth of the Ogooué and near Lake Anengué. After extensive explorations in the area of Fernan-Vaz, he went up the Rembo Nkomi and overland to the N'Gounié River without realizing it was a tributary of the Ogooué. East of the N'Gounié River he reached the mountainous terrain that still bears his name, the Massif du Chaillu. His descriptions of the various peoples he encountered were the first accurate and detailed accounts to reach the western world. In June 1862, after the signing of a treaty with the Orungu chiefs who controlled the known mouths of the Ogooué River, two French naval officers, Lt. Paul Augustin Serval (1832–1886) and the surgeon Dr. Marie-Théophile Griffon du Bellay (1829–1908), attempted to ascend the river. But they were forced to turn back by other Orungu upstream. In December 1862 they sought to reach the Ogooué by travelling southeast up the Remboué and then overland. Though illness forced Serval to abandon the trip midway, Dr. Griffon du Bellay reached the Enenga village of Orongo, not far from Lambaréné. In 1865–1866 Robert Bruce Walker, English agent for the Hatton & Cookson firm, took the Remboué route to Enenga territory and, after being delayed for six months by chiefs ReMpolé and Ranokè, finally advanced upriver into Okandé territory at the junction of the Lopé River in July 1866. In 1867 Lt. Antoine Aymès (1836–1910) travelled up the Ogooué itself to Enenga territory, and in 1871 the German merchant Schultz followed the same route to the Lopé River junction. In 1873–1874 Victor du Pont, the Marquis de Compiègne (1846–1877), and Alfred Marche (1844–1898) ascended the Ogooué as far as the junction of the Ivindo, its chief northern tributary where in June 1874 the hostility of the Osyéba (possibly a Fang clan) and the Okandé forced them to turn back. In 1876 Dr. Lenz, with aid from Marche and Brazza, reached the junction of the Sébé River, where ill health forced his return.

By this time, exploration of the Gabon interior had become part of the European competition and scramble to control and eventually to partition and to occupy Africa. Within this context took place the three expeditions of Pierre Savorgnan de Brazza (q.v.) (1875–1878, 1880–1882, 1883–1885), under the auspices of the French Navy. His first expedition proved that the Ogooué River system was distinct from the Congo River system. At the same time he found out that the headwaters of the M'Passa River, an Ogooué tributary, rose only a few miles from the headwaters of the Alima River, a northwestern tributary of the Congo. Unfortunately, the hostility of the Apfourou people prevented his descent down the Alima. During his second expedition he founded the post of Franceville at the junction of the M'Passa and Ogooué in June 1880. Thereafter he crossed overland and followed the course of the Lefini River down to the Congo River. The following year he explored the Kouilou-Niari River valley, which linked the area of the Stanley Pool with the Loango coast. Brazza's third expedition served more to establish French authority on the upper Ogooué than to explore new territory.

In October 1884 Manuel Iradier and Amado Ossorio, M.D., as part of the efforts of Madrid's Society of Africanists to retain the Rio Muni in the face of growing French involvement in the region, travelled up the Noya River to Masai. From Pamué chiefs the Spaniards secured treaties recognizing Spanish sovereignty and promises not to interfere with European traders. In August 1885 an associate of the two, José Montes de Oca, undertook an expedition farther up the river to Desamaijon for the same purpose. He explored territory later conceded by Spain to France in the Treaty of Paris of 1900. In January 1886, Ossorio made treaties with chiefs in areas south of the N'Tem River that a Franco-German agreement of December 12, 1885, had assigned to France and that France would retain under its later treaty with Spain.

The portions of northern Gabon between the Como and Ivindo Rivers were explored in the wake of agreements between France and Germany, on the one hand, and France and Spain, on the other, delimiting the frontiers of Gabon, the Cameroons, and Spanish Guinea (Rio Muni). Paul Crampel and Alfred Fourneau (1860–1930) in 1888–1889, Dr. Cureau in 1900 to 1903, Captain Cottes in 1905 to 1907 all explored in these areas as part of the process of delimitation. [394, 1299, 15, 397, 299, 306a, 293a, 892]

EYI AFFAIR OF 1970. A dispute between a high-ranking civil servant, Jean Bernard Eyi, and Monsignor Camille Nziboe, vicar-general of the archdiocese of Libreville, had repercussions in both the Catholic and Evangelical Protestant churches and in the government. Details on some aspects of the affair are lacking despite the government's issuance of a White Paper. But it appears that after Eyi accused Monsignor Nziboe, who belonged to the same Fang clan as his wife, of employing her without his permission and maintaining a personal relationship with her, three clansmen of the Monsignor on August 10, 1970, kidnapped Eyi and his wife and beat Eyi. He was detained in the residence of Nziboe with the prelate's knowledge. In the police investigation that followed upon Eyi's complaint, a noted cabinet minister, Jean-Marc Ekoh (q.v.), was adjudged as an accomplice and the brains behind the kidnapping. Ekoh was a brilliant Fang intellectual from the Woleu N'Tem province who had held high government office in the late 1950s and early 1960s. He was also a person of high standing in the Evangelical Protestant Church. He had only recently been restored to a cabinet post by President Bongo after being pardoned for his role in the provisional government of February 1964. Ekoh was removed from office as a result of the trial of the five accused. He received a sentence of 10 years in prison and 10 more in forced residence. Monsignor Nziboe was sentenced to eight years in prison and five in residence. One of the three kidnappers received a sentence identical to Ekoh, and two received sentences of six years in prison and three of residence. Collectively the five were required to pay damages of 1 million CFA francs (about $5,000 at the time) to the Eyis. The official White Paper gives no real information on Ekoh's alleged motives or role in the affair so that the matter is still clouded with mystery. Ekoh and Nziboe were released from prison early and were allowed to assume positions in secondary teaching and the parish ministry, respectively, in the Woleu N'Tem Province. [591]

- F -

FANG. The Fang today form nearly one-third of the population of Gabon. The Fang are part of a larger group, called the Pahouin by French scholars, that includes the Beti and Boulou in southern Cameroon. Nearly as many Fang live in Cameroon and in eastern Equatorial Guinea as in northern Gabon.

The geographical origins of the Fang and their movements into and within Gabon have evoked a good deal of interest among scholars in recent decades. It appears that the Fang originated in savanna regions from which at unknown times in the past they began to move into the equatorial forests. Linguistic evidence suggests that they may have been in northern Gabon and neighboring Equatorial Guinea for much longer than once imagined, perhaps even for centuries. In any case, they made a successful adaptation to the new environment of the forests. It is possible that Pygmies may have taught them to survive and to thrive by hunting, especially for the elephant. The Fang gradually became involved in the trading networks that sent ivory from the hinterland to the coastal markets. The Fang brought with them a superior technology for iron working. While learning how to raise such forest crops as cassava, bananas, plantains, and oil palms, they retained cultivation of such savanna crops as peanuts, gourds, and tobacco. Once in the forest, the dynamic of further migration was the exhaustion of the elephant herds and the soil around their villages. Villages seemed to uproot themselves quite regularly every 10 to 15 years and to relocate in the sparsely populated country beyond the last Fang settlement. In the northern Gabon forests east of the Monts de Cristal, the Fang by the 1840s encountered the semi-nomadic Bakèlè (q.v.) hunters with whom they exchanged their ivory. When the Fang learned that their ivory was being sold to European traders on the Estuary for 10 times the price they received as a result of its transmission through a network of Bakèlè, Séké, and Mpongwe (qq.v.) middlemen, some of them accelerated their efforts to contact the Europeans directly. While many Fang remained in the forests of the Woleu-N'Tem Province, others began migrations that carried them into the upper Como River by 1846, the Estuary in the early 1860s, the Ogooué in the late 1860s, and the northern coasts by the 1870s. Dispersing or absorbing the peoples in their path, by 1900 they had become the most numerous people in northern Gabon. Fang success derived from their superior social organization, which reduced internal fighting among the Fang and mobilized large numbers of villagers for warfare against the clans of other peoples.

During these movements, leadership tended to be based more on prowess and wealth than on kinship, which enabled the Fang clans to benefit from the best talent among them in the task of expansion. Most of the peoples upon whom the Fang encroached fled. The remnants were usually absorbed into Fang ranks, the children by adoption, the women by marriage, and the men by consent or by slavery. The Fang ordinarily did not possess slaves and did not sell any until the

1860s, that is, during the last gasp of the trade in the Estuary and on the Ogooué.

The first Fang who made contact with European traders and their representatives on the Como River began to seize European merchandise, attack the ships of European firms, and take prisoners for ransom. French efforts at repression were largely unsuccessful because the Fang fled into the forest. Eventually the French succeeded in capturing and hanging a few Fang chiefs and notables and taking some hostage to ensure the good behavior of their kin. Gradually, under missionary influence, the Fang in the Estuary abandoned their violence. The first Fang boys entered the Catholic schools at Libreville in the 1860s, all of them at first in the apprenticeship programs rather than in the academic ones. In 1879 the Holy Ghost Fathers (q.v.) opened their first mission among the Fang on the Estuary at Donguila. The American Presbyterians, who were already working with other Fang at Bokoué in the Estuary, in the mid-1870s established posts just above Lambaréné and farther upstream among the Fang and other peoples. French Protestants and Catholics entered the Woleu-N'Tem mainly after the First World War. By the mid-twentieth century a large majority of the Fang had become Christian, though a minority retained their ancestral religion or adopted the syncretist cult Bwiti. It was also among the northern Fang that the Great Revival of 1935 had its greatest impact, leading to the organization of the Pentecostal churches (Assemblies of God).

In the meantime various Fang had migrated throughout northern Gabon and had penetrated the southern coastal regions as far as Setté-Cama. In the process there were renewed conflicts with other Gabonese peoples, European traders, and the French administration. Among the most notable examples were Fang blocking of the middle and upper Ogooué River for nearly a decade, beginning in 1865, to other traders and European explorers, and the resistance led by Chief Emané Tolé (q.v.) in 1901–1902 to the SHO's attempts to dominate the rubber trade around N'Djolé.

French troops undertook the military penetration of the Woleu-N'Tem in the course of delimiting the frontier with the German Cameroons during the first decade of the twentieth century. In several instances the Fang resisted but were overpowered by the superior French weaponry. The installation of colonial rule on the eve of the First World War would have disastrous consequences for large parts of the population.

The recruitment of troops and porters for the war effort, along with higher taxes paid in produce that was undervalued, exhausted the population and led to the neglect of food crops. The undernourished and weakened population succumbed by the thousands to the Spanish flu (influenza) in 1918 and after a while famine stalked the land. Labor recruitment for forestry work on the Ogooué and N'Gounié rivers during the 1920s removed one-third to one-half of the young men. Hundreds of others were taken away to construct the Congo-Ocean Railroad between 1921 and 1934. Other administrative exactions, including the forced cultivation of cocoa, also contributed to the shortage of farm labor for food crops, which gave rise to the famines of the mid-1920s. These circumstances contributed to the deaths of additional thousands of Fang during the smallpox epidemics of the period. Thus the populations of the Woleu-N'Tem and Okano *circonscriptions* (the administrative units of that period equivalent to today's provinces) fell from 142,000 in 1911 to 65,000 in 1933. At the same time the Fang of the Woleu-N'Tem began to accept the cultivation of cocoa, and later coffee, as cash crops. Many of them were transformed into genuine peasants working individually owned plots in family groups.

During the 1940s, among the northern Fang there took place a movement to revitalize the clans by regrouping them. The *alar ayong* (q.v.) movement, as it was called, had its origins across the frontier among the Boulou of the French trusteeship territory. The alar ayong did a good deal to restore Fang self-esteem, particularly among those who remained in the northern rural areas. At the same time the French administration sought to address Fang problems through the Fang or Pahouin Congress held at Mitzic in February 1947. Under the leadership of the Fang deputy in the French National Assembly, Jean-Hilaire Aubame (q.v.), whose parents had come from the Woleu-N'Tem, there was an administrative regroupment of populations, as much as possible on the basis of clan ties, in order to permit increased social services (schools, dispensaries, sports facilities, meeting places). Aubame, and a leader of the Estuary Fang, Léon Mba (q.v.), became two of the three most important political figures during the era of decolonization and independence (the other being Paul Gondjout [q.v.], a Myènè).

It is commonly believed that a terminally ill President Mba, having accepted the recommendations of French officials that Albert-Bernard Bongo should become his vice president and successor, insisted that a Fang should occupy the number two position in the regime. Thus in January 1968, Bongo selected Léon Mébiame (q.v.) as vice president of the government, and after the abolition of that position in 1975, as prime minister. Casimir Oyé-Mba (q.v.), who succeeded Mébiame as prime minister in April 1990, is also a Fang. *See* BWITI; CHIWA; MADEMOISELLE. [830, 259, 260, 392, 186, 187, 188, 795, 788, 392, 603]

FARA, BROTHER DOMINIQUE (1876–1922). The first African in Gabon to become a Catholic brother, in 1895. Of Congolese origin, he assisted Father Théophile Klaine (q.v.) in the school at St. Mary's near Libreville and taught the beginning class at the Ecole Montfort (q.v.). He died of sleeping sickness on June 21, 1922. [1049, 1098]

FELIX-ADANDE RAPONTCHOMBO, KING (1847–1911). Also called King Félix-Denis and King Louis-Félix. First Mpongwe (q.v.) clan head who was Christian and western educated, he headed the Asiga clan from 1876 to 1911. Louis Félix-Adandé was the son of King Denis (q.v.), who chose him as successor. Félix-Adandé was educated at the primary school and minor seminary of the Holy Ghost Fathers (q.v.) at Libreville. Thereafter he served as an accountant in the French naval administration where he had European subordinates. In 1867 he married Elisa Antchondie Bobié (1850–1883) whose father Henri Oréniga was one of the first Catholic converts in Quaben village and whose brother Rémi Remombe (q.v.) (1852–1873) became a seminarian. Elisa was a pupil of the Immaculate Conception Sisters' school at

Libreville. Félix and Elisa had six children; their eldest son, Jean-Félix Rapontchombo (q.v.) (1872–1903), was the first Gabonese to earn a baccalaureate (French secondary diploma), and their second son, Jean-Rémi Onanga, was the father of Prince Félix Adandé (q.v.), head of the Mpongwe collectivity of Glass at Libreville in the 1950s. (The Prince's mother belonged to the ruling lineage of the Agekaza-Glass.)

Félix-Adandé accepted French rule and western civilization. He personally encouraged and advanced western education and Roman Catholicism among his subjects. At the same time he expected the colonial administration to respect his authority as clan head, to live up to the terms of the treaties France had made with his father, and to allow him and his subjects the protection of French law and the enjoyment of the same basic rights as Frenchmen. In an age of increasing colonialism and rising French nationalism, Félix-Adandé clashed almost immediately with the local French commandants, who were intensely concerned about their own authority in a colony where British and German traders and Anglo-American cultural influence remained preponderant. There is also some evidence that Félix-Adandé may have been involved in the clandestine slave trade between Cape Lopez and São Tomé, which the French had failed entirely to suppress. In 1878 he was imprisoned for organizing a successful boycott against the French merchant Caron whose business practices the Asiga considered to be unjust. In 1880–1881 he used his good offices at the request of Commandant Hanet-Cléry to settle a commercial dispute between French merchants and the Nkomi (q.v.) of Fernan-Vaz. Hanet-Cléry recommended him for the Legion of Honor, but it was awarded only many years later, shortly before his death. Late in 1882 Félix-Adandé was unable to pay a debt to a French commercial house because Commandant Edouard Masson had halved his government pension, which embroiled him in a legal dispute with the authorities for the next decade. Then in October 1884 Commandant Cornut-Gentille accused him of enslaving some escaped slaves from São Tomé and had him put in chains aboard a ship for trial in West Africa. He escaped with the aid of Mpongwe relatives and Bishop Pierre Le Berre (q.v.) and was ultimately acquitted. The French later accused him of capturing and retaining some slaves fleeing Cape Lopez. Félix-Adandé eventually won his case with the French commercial house in the court at Gorée, Senegal, but was unable to collect the damages awarded to him as a result of local officials' abuses of authority. Though protesting his continued loyalty to France, he refused to make the kind of abject submission demanded by the local authorities.

Félix-Adandé failed in his attempts to revitalize agriculture among the Asiga to replace the revenues lost through the suppression of the slave trade. He spent his last years seeing many of his subjects transferring to the north shore to engage in commerce in Glass Town (Libreville). There they became assimilated to the Agekaza clan to such an extent that after 1938 the Asiga no longer possessed their own clan head. [384, 377]

FELIX-DENIS ADANDE RAPONTCHOMBO, PRINCE or **DENIS-MARIE ADANDE** (1899–). The great-grandson of King Denis (q.v.) was born at Fubu in June 1899. He graduated from the Ecole Montfort and taught there. In 1921 he went to work as an accountant at Kinshasa in the Belgian Congo. After his return to Libreville, perhaps a decade later, he worked in the same profession and became active in the movements among the Mpongwe (q.v.) to assert their traditional rights, especially rights to lands in the Estuary, in the face of administration and Fang encroachments. The Comité Mpongwe (q.v.) advanced his candidacy for head chief of the Mpongwe of Libreville. They succeeded in the late 1930s in having him named *chef de groupe de quartier* for the Glass section of Libreville, from whose nineteenth-century rulers he was descended through his mother. The French also named him as one of the first Africans on the Libreville municipal commission. He remained active in Mpongwe affairs throughout the Fourth Republic and at one point headed a delegation to Paris to secure further indemnification for lands. After independence, he directed the National Tourist Office (1962–November 1966) and served as president of the Supreme Court (November 1966 to November 1968). [1367, 550]

FIDES. During the Fourth French Republic (1946–1958), France promoted the economic, social, and educational development of its African territories through public programs under the Fonds d'Investissements pour le Développement Economique et Social (FIDES), the initials of which form the Latin word for faith. FIDES involved grants from the metropolitan taxpayers and long-term, low-interest loans through the Caisse Centrale de la France d'Outre-Mer. Most of these loans were ultimately cancelled at independence or thereafter. The African territories also made budgetary contributions to the various projects. What was new about FIDES was both the overall planning and the outright grants, for prior to the Second World War all development was supposed to be funded by the territories themselves. FIDES funded public projects and contributed to private ones. In French Equatorial Africa as a whole FIDES invested 59 billion francs CFA and private interests invested 51 billion, that is, more than $400 million U.S.

Gabon, which had one-twelfth of the population of the federation, received roughly the same fraction of the investments, that is, approximately $25 million. The bulk of this amount went for development of the economic infrastructure in order to permit the expansion of production, especially timber. The largest single project, which cost $11 million, was construction of the road from Libreville to Lambaréné. Other important sums modernized the ports and airfields of Libreville and Port-Gentil and built an okoumé factory at the latter town. Lesser sums went for the construction and equipment of schools, a hospital, and dispensaries. [59]

FIRST WORLD WAR. The First World War placed new burdens on the peoples of Gabon without bringing them benefits. During the conflict, France used the resources of its colonies in French Equatorial Africa (F.E.A.), in cooperation with Britain, to defeat the Germans in the Cameroons and then to aid its war effort in Europe. At the outbreak of the war in August 1914, throughout all of F.E.A., France had only 950 European and 6,440 African troops. Three-quarters of these black troops (*tirailleurs*) came from French West Africa. The administration immediately recruited another 2,196 black volunteers for the duration of the war from among able-bodied men eighteen years of age and older. Among them were some non-commissioned officers, including Charles N'Tchórérè (q.v.), Louis Bigmann (q.v.), and Laurent Antchouey (q.v.).

In the course of the campaign in the Cameroons during the next 18 months 1,500 more volunteers were recruited from Gabon. The largest part of them came from the Estuary. Recruits earned 40 francs a day plus a premium of 0.50 franc and meals. The troops from Gabon were organized into a column that reoccupied the 40,569 square kilometers (12 percent of Gabon's area) containing a population estimated at 62,000 (15.8 percent of the total) conceded to Germany in the Convention of November 4, 1911. They then invaded Cameroons, where the Germans were finally defeated in January 1916, and occupied the South. The heavily forested terrain of northern Gabon and the southern Cameroons, together with the absence of roads usable by motor vehicles, necessitated a large force of porters to carry supplies for the column. Gabon's administration employed 4,085 permanent porters of the 14,414 in F.E.A. and 56,000 temporary ones. Porters were paid 20 francs a day and given their meals. The largest numbers came from the coastal regions, particularly along the lower Ogooué. The recruitment of 5 percent to 20 percent of the able-bodied male population of some regions for war service created huge tensions involving uprisings, desertions from villages, flights during transfer, and self-inflicted injuries to secure medical excuses. Victory in January 1916 came at a time when each new period of recruitment was bringing fewer men.

Earlier, in December 1915, the French had begun recruitment of volunteers for Europe, offering a bonus of 200 francs in addition to the daily amounts cited above. The governor-general of F.E.A. fixed Gabon's quota as 500 troops out of the 3,350 sought in the federation. Out of 566 accepted, 412 (73 percent) were found physically fit for military service. But because French officers during the Cameroons campaign had noted a lack of aptitude among many of the new recruits, the new ones were used to relieve the Senegalese troops in the occupation of the Cameroons and the recovered territories.

During the war, the metropole drastically reduced the subventions that it had been providing to the budget of F.E.A. In 1914 it had provided 1,200,000 FF out of a territorial budget of 2,200,000 FF. Therefore, the administration in August 1914 raised the annual rate of the head tax (*capitation*) from three to five francs. Then at the end of 1915 it increased the rate further to 10 francs at Libreville, 7 to 10 francs in economically developed regions, and 5 to 7 francs in remote regions. Very few Gabonese in this period were involved in the money economy. Therefore, they were forced by the fiscal agents of the administration to pay in products such as rubber, palm kernels, palm oil, ivory, wood, millet, and livestock for which they were undercompensated. The average Gabonese spent four to five times as many hours as before the war in working to pay the head tax. In the Estuary the average person who brought in palm kernels had to spend 22 days a year to gather and transport enough of them to make 10 francs. Food crops were neglected to the point that there were serious shortages by 1916. There was flight from the villages when the administration used force to collect these sums, and sometimes permanent abandonment of crops. The colonial administration made the task of the Gabonese cultivators more difficult by refusing them access to modern guns and powder for use against the elephants and other animals that were devastating their plantations. Nor could Gabonese hunters legally have such weapons; the administration feared that dissatisfied elements might use them to resist its exactions. During 1917 and 1918, in order to aid the war effort in France itself and to obtain greater revenues, the administration lowered even further the prices for products given to the tax collectors. Thus the capitation produced 80 to 90 percent of the budget compared with only 50 percent as before the war.

In January 1918, Prime Minister Georges Clemenceau ordered a draft of 10,000 troops from F.E.A., including 1,500 from Gabon. A first levy was conscripted from the Estuary in January and a second from the rest of the country in March. The principal military camp was located at Baraka near Libreville. Originally it was intended that the volunteers from F.E.A. would relieve the Senegalese troops in Chad, the Cameroons, and French West Africa. But when the military situation in Europe worsened, they were destined to the western front. Of the 2,065 Gabonese who volunteered, 1,700 were accepted (82.3 percent), among whom the Fang were found to be the most robust. One-quarter of the volunteers became sick and died, either at Camp Baraka while awaiting transport to Europe, en route, or while training at Fréjus in southern France. Few actually saw service. In the meantime, Gabon developed shortages of transport for the increased palm production, leading to spoilage.

At war's end, F.E.A. was on the verge of famine. The situation worsened as a result of requisitions to feed troops and porters. These demands proved especially disastrous for the Fang areas, where a real crisis in food production between 1918 and 1920 contributed to famines during the 1920s in which thousands died. Other thousands, weakened by malnutrition, succumbed to the epidemics of Spanish flu in 1918 and after. [288, 289, 357, 247a]

FORD, HENRY A., M.D. (1818–1858). American missionary and specialist in tropical fevers. A New Yorker, Dr. Ford served under the ABCFM in Gabon from 1850 until his death on February 2, 1858. He is buried in the Baraka cemetery. Dr. Ford's study *Observations on the Fevers of the West Coast of Africa* was published in New York City in 1856. [1031]

FOREIGN RELATIONS. Gabon achieved political independence on August 17, 1960, without possessing the technical and administrative personnel to operate its government and economy. It lacked the expertise and capital to promote further economic development. In these circumstances it turned primarily to France, in whose Community it had retained membership, for continued aid and assistance. The framework for French support was provided in the *coopéra-tion* agreements, or accords, signed at independence or shortly thereafter. These 15 agreements included several key policy areas (foreign policy, defense and strategic materials, education and culture, monetary policy and currency); economic, financial, and technical assistance; and such matters as fishing, civil aviation, and the merchant marine.

Gabon became an associate member of the European Economic Community, to which its French mentor belonged, and thereby expanded its economic relations with these states, particularly with the Federal German Republic, and received development assistance from the EEC's Development Fund and Investment Bank. These arrangements perpetuated the association of Gabon with the EEC, which had begun under the terms of Article 131 of the Treaty of Rome of 1957 while Gabon was still an overseas territory of the Fourth French Republic. Later on, Gabon adhered to the first Yaoundé Convention (operational June 1964 to May 1969) between the Common Market nations and their African associates. It provided for a common market and free monetary exchange as well as gradual suppression of the bilateral preferences between France and its former territories.

Under President Léon Mba (q.v.), Gabon followed a liberal economic policy. It therefore sought to secure aid and assistance from western governments to develop its infrastructure and private investments from these same nations to develop its natural resources, particularly its minerals and forests. During the 1950s France had brought in American and West German investors to participate in the development of manganese and iron while keeping uranium and forests entirely as its own preserve. The Mba government retained this policy in seeking investments from the United States, West Germany, and other Common Market countries to develop its oil and natural gas. Gabon derived revenue from these activities primarily through taxation at the time of export.

It was the desire of Gabon to retain the revenues derived from its own resources that had caused it to oppose the maintenance of the federation of French Equatorial Africa (q.v.) in 1957 and after. During the period of the federation (1910–1957) it had seen its customs revenues, particularly from wood exports, go to develop the other territories, especially the Congo and the federal capital at Brazzaville.

Gabon thus in May 1960 refused membership in a political federation, the Union des Républiques de l'Afrique Centrale (URAC), which would have acceded to independence as a single state within the French Community. But Gabon was perfectly willing to cooperate with the other Equatorial states and Cameroon in a number of economic and financial matters. Soon after the formation of the Community, the four Equatorial states worked out the principles for a customs union, the Union Douanière Equatoriale (1959) to which Cameroon adhered a year after its independence (1961). The five states arranged to maintain the franc CFA as their common currency issued by a central bank. The Equatorial states established common agencies for transportation facilities such as ports and railroads and for posts and telecommunications. A Conférence des Chefs d'Etats d'Afrique Equatoriale organized on June 24, 1959, met at least twice a year to decide policies and to discuss other matters of mutual interest. In December 1964 the Equatorial states and Cameroon formed the Union Douanière et Economique de l'Afrique Centrale (UDEAC) (q.v.) and organized a Banque des Etats de l'Afrique Centrale (BEAC). UDEAC established a common market and sought to promote economic development, including industrialization, by harmonizing customs, fiscal, and investment policies. The arrangements for UDEAC granted a preferential status to the countries of the EEC (including France, of course) and to the members of the Organisation Africaine et Malgache pour la Coopération Economique (OAMCE); it thereby disadvantaged other industrial nations such as the United Kingdom, the United States, and Japan.

Between 1959 and 1971 under French auspices Gabon cooperated with the other three Equatorial African states in the field of higher education. With France the four countries formed the Fondation de l'Enseignement Supérieur en Afrique Centrale (FESAC) to share students and facilities. This form of cooperation, which was always uneasy because of the problem of the distribution of facilities among the four states, after August 1963 became acute as a result of the coming to power of Marxist elements in Brazzaville where the liberal arts, law, and education divisions were located.

Cooperation in higher education broke down completely by the late 1960s and was officially terminated in 1971. FESAC was replaced by national institutions in Gabon and elsewhere.

During mid-September 1962 troubles broke out in Brazzaville between a visiting Gabonese football team and local Congolese, which produced brutal retaliatiory attacks on the Congolese populations of Libreville and other centers on September 18–20 and their abrupt official expulsion. Congo responded by expelling the tiny numbers of Gabonese in its territories. Ultimately the heads of state, Mba and Fulbert Youlou, met in November 1962 under Cameroonian auspices, to restore peace and agreed to indemnify the victims.

Gabon thereafter sought to maintain good relations with all of its neighbors but especially with the Congo, through whose territory ran the *téléférique* and railroad that evacuated Gabon's manganese and uranium to the coast. Even after the building of the Transgabonais and a mineral port at Owendo on the Estuary, roughly half of the manganese was still evacuated via the Congo.

Under President Mba, Gabon established links with the other former French states that had joined the Community. Thus it joined the Union Africaine et Malgache in 1961, which was subsequently replaced by the Organisation Commune Africaine et Malgache (OCAM) in 1964. OCAM involved a good deal of consultation and functional cooperation in such enterprises as an inter-state airline, Air Afrique. Gabon joined the Organization of African Unity in June 1963, but not the African Development Bank organized in September 1964. Though it joined the United Nations in late 1960, it played a very minor role there, and its delegates were often absent from the sessions prior to 1968.

The Mba government maintained only a dozen embassies abroad, including six in non-African countries (France, Spain, West Germany, the United States, Israel, Taiwan). The ambassadors in these countries handled relations with a number of other states. Gabon chose to play a modest role in keeping with its size and resources at the time. It maintained very close relations amounting to a dependency upon France from whom came the bulk of its aid and assistance. It had relations with Spain, which until 1968 controlled its neighbor, the Rio Muni, or Spanish Guinea, which after independence together with Fernando Po would be known as Equatorial Guinea. It received technical aid and assistance from the other four states, for forestry from Israel and for rice culture from Taiwan. From the United States, beginning in 1962, it received Peace Corps volunteers, who were active in secondary education and school construction in all nine provinces.

The military coup and French intervention of February 1964 to restore President Mba to power focused the latter's attention upon domestic concerns for much of the remainder of his life. Serious health problems and a long illness in a Paris hospital further precluded any real changes in foreign policy during the last two years of his regime. Albert-Bernard Bongo (q.v.) as vice president exercised day-to-day supervision of foreign relations during the last year of Mba's life. At Bongo's accession to the presidency in November 1967 he turned his attention inward to healing the wounds left by the political struggles of the previous decade. Some of those whom he released from prison or detention abandoned politics, and a few of them left the country. But the majority of Mba's opponents were willing to accept Bongo's leadership in the development of the country and were therefore incorporated into the regime. Once he had established a firmer political base, Bongo was free to proceed to economic development and to the changes in foreign relations that might facilitate it. His accession to power had taken place simultaneously with the first important output from the country's petroleum resources. This new situation presented Gabon with vastly increased revenues to use to raise standards of living while promoting further development of its other resources. At the same time it offered possibilities for decreasing some aspects of the country's dependence upon France, particularly in the areas of policy-making and control of resources.

From 1968 on, Gabon gradually undertook new orientations in foreign policy, which were most clearly articulated by President Bongo only in 1973. The changes involved the abandonment of the isolation or very limited role in world affairs established by President Mba, a loosening of the kind of ties with France that amounted to a close dependency, and a search for worldwide support and cooperation to escape underdevelopment and to promote development. In 1973 Bongo enunciated the main lines of the new orientations under the slogans "Gabon First" (*Gabon d'abord*) and "realism." He expressed the desire to establish relations with all nations that would respect Gabon's sovereignty and role as a free arbiter (*libre arbitre*) and that would cooperate in its development.

As part of the new orientations, between 1968 and 1973 Gabon established commercial and/or diplomatic relations with three groups of nations: additional western nations (Switzerland, Italy, United Kingdom, Netherlands, Canada, Japan); Eastern European Communist nations (Bulgaria, Czechoslovakia, Romania, Yugoslavia, the Soviet Union); and Arab states, particularly those of North Africa (Mauritania, Morocco, Egypt, Libya, Algeria, and Sudan). From all three groups Gabon hoped for profitable commercial exchanges plus aid and assistance for development. In the case of the Communist nations, Gabon had feared that diplomatic relations would bring the dangers of subversion through liaisons with local Marxists. In 1970 Bongo said that he did not like the countries of the East. But in 1972 he spoke of an open door for Gabon's products toward the East as well as the West. In the case of the Arab nations, Gabon was propelled in their direction by the general movement of Black African countries toward them after the 1973 Arab-Israeli war. This movement involved a loosening or abandonment of ties with Israel. Gabon acquired additional contacts and common interests with the Arab oil producers as an oil producer and OPEC member (1973).

Gabon's relations with the Arab countries entered a new phase in late 1973 and 1974 in the course of the search for funds with which to construct the Transgabonais Railroad. By the early 1970s the railroad had come to be seen as the necessary means to all further development—in order to tap the iron and woods of interior regions and to open them to world markets as well as better to exploit the manganese and uranium. Long negotiations with the World Bank, which was to be the chief supplier through loans for the first stage of

$200 million from Owendo to Booué, finally resulted in a negative decision during 1972. After this failure, President Bongo stated Gabon's readiness to look anywhere in the world for the necessary support.

Gabon had enjoyed commercial relations with Israel since 1962 and had established an embassy in Jerusalem in 1965. It received Israeli aid in forestry development. But it became obvious that Gabon could not develop close relations with the Arab nations, much less obtain development aid from their oil producers, if it maintained relations with Israel. In September 1973 Gabon, which had not attended the first summit of nonaligned nations at Cairo in September 1964, sent a delegation to the second summit at Algiers in September 1973. It is believed that there Gabonese leaders made contact with Libya, which promised aid if Gabon broke relations with Israel, an action that an important portion of the cabinet opposed. On October 30, 1973, Gabon broke relations when Israel refused to heed the United Nations resolution on peace negotiations in the wake of the war with the Arab states earlier that month. After a visit to Libya and conferences with its president Khaddafi, Bongo, who professed no religion but had previously shown some interest in the Roman Catholicism of his wife, announced his conversion to Islam. After a pilgrimage to Mecca he took the name and title of El Hadj Omar Bongo. In April 1974 he went to the U.N. in the company of the Arab oil producers. Unfortunately for Gabon's development plans, the promised aid from Libya for the Transgabonais, which was to result from their cooperation treaty, was not forthcoming and the treaty itself was abrogated in June 1974.

The imperatives for building the Transgabonais caused Bongo to reestablish good relations with the United States. Relations had been tense with the U.S. since the 1964 coup, for some French residents had convinced President Mba that the Americans supported his opponents. These same Frenchmen, of course, feared that the United States wished to replace French interests in Gabon. In 1968 Bongo had sent away the Peace Corps on the grounds that he did not like large numbers of foreigners whom the government could not control working at the grass roots throughout the country.

But he arranged for the return of the Peace Corps in 1972 and secured American help for the financing of the Transgabonais. American investors were encouraged to play a greater role in prospecting and marketing Gabonese oil, the bulk of which was going to France.

As for France itself, Gabon secured changes in the cooperation agreements on February 12, 1974, as the bulk of the former French states had already done or were doing. Bongo chose to call the changes an "adaptation" rather than a revision. Taken as a whole, they rendered Gabon more independent in policy-making areas in the control of its resources but perpetuated its dependence upon French aid and assistance. Gabon no longer coordinated its foreign policy and monetary policy with France's, though it remained within the franc zone. France no longer had the right of preemption of primary materials, and its access to strategic materials such as uranium was no longer tied to the question of defense. The French agreed to pay more for the uranium and to compete for other products. Frenchmen could no longer possess Gabonese nationality; the double nationality provision, which was terminated by De Gaulle's regime for Gabonese and other Black Africans in France in the early 1960s, thus ended for the French in Gabon. Therefore they could no longer vote or play a formal role in the country's internal affairs. (Later, however, on occasion Bongo extended the right to vote in presidential elections—in which he was the sole candidate—to foreigners resident in Gabon for at least three years, but not in all local elections.) The one aspect of cooperation that remained unchanged was the defense agreement, which permits Gabon to call upon France for both internal and external threats. Even by the time of the Giscard presidency, there was no assurance that such a request would be answered positively. Gabon also signed a new civil-aviation agreement with France in 1977 following its withdrawal from Air Afrique.

France also showed a willingness to continue aid and assistance on these changed terms as it did elsewhere in its former territories, nearly all of which renegotiated their cooperation agreements during the first half of the 1970s. In 1978 there were 725 French functionaries detached for service in Gabon, of which 435 were in education, almost entirely at the secondary and higher levels. Although the period of independence saw many more Gabonese university graduates, the number of positions also increased, and few Gabonese entered such technical fields as engineering and business administration. In 1977 France gave Gabon 226 million French francs in aid (roughly $55 million) and through the European Development Fund (EDF) of the EEC additional assistance. During the late 1970s France remained Gabon's single most important source of financial aid. It was also Gabon's most important trading partner, supplying 69 percent of its imports and taking 42 percent of its exports (1976). Other EC countries supplied 13 percent of the imports and took 19 percent of the exports.

Gabon adhered to the second Yaoundé convention of the African states with the EEC in 1969. It also adhered to the Lomé Convention of February 28, 1975, and seven protocols between the EEC states and countries of Africa, the Caribbean, and the Pacific. It continues to receive aid through the EEC's EDF and Investment Bank.

In June 1972 Gabon required all companies doing business in the country to turn over without compensation 10 percent of their capital to the state. In February 1976 it required that a representative of the government sit on the administrative council of each firm. In March 1977, while declaring that economic liberalism would be maintained, it decreed that all future enterprises installed in Gabon would have a minimum of 49 percent participation by the state. At present the state's participation varies from 10 to 60 percent. In 1974 Gabon had increased its participation in many enterprises, including French banks (40 percent); petroleum distribution (51 percent); 30 percent in Sogara; 60 percent in cables; 60 percent in Somifer (which previously since 1963 had been 50 percent Bethlehem Steel, 34 percent French, and 10 percent German).

Concerning Gabon's relations with other Black African states, including its neighbors, Gabon followed De Gaulle's lead in recognizing the secessionist state of Biafra. It was one of four African states to do so—Ivory Coast, Tanzania, and Zambia being the others. Gabon gave sanctuary to 4,500

Biafran refugee children who returned home only after January 1973 when relations with the federal government of Nigeria were restored.

In 1968 Zaire attempted to destroy UDEAC by taking away some of its members into a new Central African union under its leadership, the Union des Etats de l'Afrique Centrale. Chad left UDEAC, which it did not reenter until 1984, but the Central African Republic returned after a time, and the seat of UDEAC is located in Bangui. Equatorial Guinea joined UDEAC in 1984 and the franc zone in January 1985. Gabon sought to provide leadership for cooperation toward industrialization in the UDEAC states. In this connection it helped to organize an oil refinery in June 1966 that would serve their needs. It would do so until Cameroon and Congo developed their own refineries in the early 1980s. At the meeting of the heads of UDEAC states in Bangui in December 1989 President Bongo tried once more to secure cooperation in industrialization. On May 3, 1976, UDEAC formed the Development Bank of the Central African States (BDEAC) with its headquarters at Brazzaville.

On August 23, 1972, Gabon, in an effort to establish ownership of the possible offshore oil deposits, unilaterally extended its territorial waters to 170 miles. It was immediately accused by Equatorial Guinea of invading several of its tiny islands, really sandbanks (Congo, Mbanié, and Cocotiers), which were located 18 km. offshore from Gabon but 35 km. from Equatorial Guinea. In September 1972, when Guineans fired upon Gabonese fishermen in the disputed areas, Gabon sent two ships and 40 gendarmes into the zone. Congo and Zaire offered their good offices to settle the dispute. It was agreed to let a four-nation commission from the Organization of African Unity fix the maritime frontier between the two states, which was apparently done. In early 1974 there was renewed trouble over Mbanié Island, which seems also to have been settled quickly.

The oppression of the Macias Nguema regime (1968–1979) caused up to 60,000 Equatorial Guineans to take refuge within Gabon. Some farmed in the Woleu-N'Tem Province or worked for agro-businesses. But the majority located in Libreville where they put further strain on housing and social services. In February 1978 a police check of Equatorial Guinean refugees in the capital led to attacks upon them by Gabonese and to the looting of their homes. Gabon cooperated with U.N. refugee officials in relief efforts for the victims. Most of the refugees chose to remain in Gabon in the light of the troubled conditions of the Obiang Nguema regime (1979–). After Equatorial Guinea joined the franc zone, it was easier for the more prosperous ones to send remittances to their kin back home.

In May 1977, Colonel Mathieu Kérékou of Benin (formerly Dahomey) accused high Gabonese officials of involvement in the unsuccessful invasion plot of mid-January that tried to oust him as president. Kérékou and the heads of other African states, influenced by the report of a multi-national commission that investigated the affair, tried unsuccessfully to prevent the OAU from meeting in Libreville in July. In reaction, Gabonese mobs attacked hundreds of Béninois immigrants, pillaging and looting their properties. The Gabonese police then arrested the victims. Gabon denied any connection with the attempted coup. After Kérékou reiterated his charges at the Khartoum meeting of the OAU in July 1978, Bongo sent home all of the approximately 11,000 Béninois who were not working under government contract. These thousands included some who had been residing and working in Gabon for many years, particularly in food retailing and clerical tasks. During the expulsion, a considerable number were treated brutally, some were wounded, and at least one killed. Relations between Gabon and Bénin were not restored until February 1989.

Late in 1979 problems arose involving members of the Lebanese community, who have been working in retail trade in Gabon since the period of the French mandate over their country between the two world wars. There was considerable dissatisfaction with them in general because they repatriated a large part of their earnings (often to support their families back home) and invested little permanently in the country. In addition to the involvement of a number of Lebanese retailers in a scheme to defraud the telephone company, others participated in a far more extensive customs' fraud that had deprived the government of an estimated 60 billion francs

CFA over a five-year period. Arrests involved 23 Gabonese customs collectors, eight Lebanese merchants, and two French importers. Twenty Lebanese in all were imprisoned for "economic sabotage," and all 479 living in Gabon were forbidden to leave the country pending completion of the official investigations.

Earlier, in September 1976 Bongo had pulled Gabon out of OCAM, which he felt no longer served its interests and was expensive. He withdrew Gabon from Air Afrique as of June 1977. As of November 1978 OCAM had only nine members left: Benin, the Central African Republic, Ivory Coast, Upper Volta, Mauritius, Niger, Senegal, Togo, and Rwanda.

While some African countries became active against the minority regimes in Rhodesia (Zimbabwe) and South Africa, Gabon did not. It followed a wait-and-see policy (*attentisme*). Though not maintaining formal relations with these states, Gabon nevertheless received regular flights of vegetables, fruits, and meats from them unofficially. Soon after the World Bank rejected loans for the Transgabonais Railroad, Pretoria reportedly offered 5 billion francs CFA (roughly $20 million U.S.) in loans. Though President Bongo had publicly stated that he would make a pact with the devil if necessary to get the funds to build the railroad, it appears that he did not ultimately accept the South African offer, which would have endangered his relations with other African states.

Gabon joined the OAU's Development Bank during its search for funds to build the Transgabonais. It gave 250 million francs CFA annually to the OAU's Sahel Fund during the late 1970s.

It is difficult to secure accurate statistics concerning the amounts of foreign aid and assistance African countries have received. A French scholar, Michel Cathala, indicates that between 1959 and 1972 non-French sources gave Gabon 14,164,500,000 francs CFA in aid, nearly all of it for economic development. Brigitte Masquet reports that between 1975 and 1980 the EC gave Gabon 761,600,000 French francs in aid. *Africa South of the Sahara, 1978–1979* noted that the French Fonds d'Aide et de Coopération (FAC) gave grants of 12,800,000,000 francs CFA between 1959 and 1970; between 1971 and 1975 it gave approximately two-thirds of the 95 billion francs CFA, the rest coming from the European Development Fund, West Germany, the United Nations agencies, and the United States. The Gabonese scholar Pierre-Claver Maganga-Moussavou reported that between 1960 and 1978 the FAC gave Gabon grants of 262,629,975 French francs (13,131,000,000 francs CFA). Of this total, 140 million French francs went for infrastructure; 41 million for mines, industry, and energy; 34 million for education; and 25 million for rural development. Between 1966 and 1978 the Caisse Centrale de Coopération Economique (CCCE) loaned 178,908,000 French francs, the largest portions of which, some 81 million, went for energy, water, and electricity; 35 million for infrastructure; 33 million for housing and hotels. Between 1960 and 1978 the number of technical assistants rose from 360 to 709 with an average of 492. France in 1978 supplied 28,972,274 French francs to support these agents. *Europe-France-Outre-Mer* reported that annually during the late 1970s France was providing Gabon $50 to $60 million U.S. in aid. Gabon was also receiving millions from other western sources, including Canada and Japan, for construction of infrastructure and development of its natural resources.

The coming to power of a Socialist president and government in Paris in May 1981 after 23 years of Gaullist and Giscardian rule had important consequences for Gabon's relations with France. The Socialist Party and its Communist Party allies had long criticized various aspects of their country's policies toward the former French possessions in sub-Saharan Africa. In particular, they condemned the promotion of French strategic, economic, and cultural interests at the price of supporting authoritarian regimes tainted by injustice and corruption. The appointment of Jean-Pierre Cot as Minister of State for Cooperation under the authority of the Minister of Foreign Affairs symbolized the new government's commitment to the promotion of human rights and social justice in Africa.

The election of François Mitterrand, which had been enthusiastically followed in some circles in Libreville on national television, gave rise to the hope that the new government would aid them in restoring multi-partyism, reforming abuses, and securing a more equitable distribution of income. Some of them viewed Jean-Hilaire Aubame, who as deputy during the Fourth Republic had affiliated with Mitterrand's party (the Union démocratique et sociale de la Résistance), and thereafter had maintained personal ties with the Socialist leader, as the person best qualified to lead a movement to bring about these changes. During Aubame's visit to Libreville in the autumn of 1981, antigovernment elements distributed tracts and scribbled slogans hostile to the Bongo regime on the walls of the main post office. But Aubame, now old and ailing, declined to become the leader of or spokesman for this opposition. After accepting the largely ceremonial position of special adviser to the president, he flew back to Paris.

Then on December 1, 1981, a new group calling itself the Mouvement de Redressement National (MORENA) distributed tracts at the main bus terminal and edited a White Book setting forth its program. MORENA criticized Bongo for personal extravagance, corruption, nepotism, and tribalism, among other things. France gave no encouragement or support to the MORENA members and followers. The Gabonese authorities quickly suppressed demonstrations among university and secondary students on behalf of the program. They arrested the rector, whom they accused of MORENA sympathies, and closed the university for a month. Twenty-nine of the 37 individuals put on trial for their part in the movement were given harsh sentences in November 1982.

While the Socialist government did not interfere in these internal matters, it angered the Bongo regime by allowing French radio and television to comment critically upon the events and permitting Gabonese living in France (some 3,000 reside there permanently) to proclaim openly their adherence to MORENA-in-exile in early 1982. The Gaullist and Giscardian governments had previously suppressed criticism of the Bongo regime in the publicly owned radio and television, and to a certain extent in the press. These governments had also curbed the activities of African dissidents in France. MORENA-in-exile, which was headed by a Spiritan priest, the Reverend Paul Mba, sought to work peacefully to restore multi-party democracy, to curb the abuses of those in power, to end corruption, and to work toward a more equitable participation in government by all peoples and regions with a fairer distribution of national wealth among them. MORENA's leaders gained access to the French media, further angering Gabon's government. But the movement itself soon was weakened by internal rivalries and disagreements about strategies.

Bongo was further vexed during 1982 because the Mitterrand regime would not suppress press articles about the Robert Luong affair, whose handling reflected badly on its predecessor. Luong, a Vietnamese housepainter working in Gabon, was kidnapped by persons believed to be members of a clandestine rightist organization, the Service d'Action Civique; he was taken to France in order to prevent him from continuing his relationship with Joséphine Bongo, the president's wife. After Mrs. Bongo resumed the relationship with Luong in Paris, he was assassinated. The Giscard government suspiciously abandoned the investigation and suppressed the evidence.

While the removal of Jean-Pierre Cot in December 1982 signalled France's waning commitment to reform overseas, the publication of *Affaires africaines* in 1983 by a free-lance journalist, Pierre Péan, brought the Luong affair, along with other intrigues, once again to the attention of the French public. The Bongo regime sought in various ways to prevent the publication of this exposé, which was so damaging to its reputation. Despite lawsuits by several of the French figures whose activities were described in the book challenging the accuracy of the accounts, the French courts permitted publication. They required, however, the addition of statements that the accuracy was disputed. The French executive's refusal to interfere in order to spare the feelings of the Bongo regime led to a very real crisis in Franco-Gabonese relations. In October 1983 Bongo instituted a blackout of all news concerning France throughout Gabon. He lifted it only after important conciliatory measures by Paris, which had to back down in consideration of the important French interests in Gabon, including the 26,000 French residents and the considerable investments in petroleum, manganese, and uranium. These measures included a crackdown in France on the activities of MORENA-in-exile, which no longer had access to the television and radio networks, and which was not allowed to hold public meetings and press conferences. The French media curbed their criticisms of the Bongo regime. But at the same time, Mitterrand continued to urge clemency for the MORENA members condemned in 1982. The French also agreed to build a nuclear power plant in Gabon, a project that proved financially unviable.

Despite these concessions and a visit by Prime Minister Pierre Mauroy to Libreville in January 1984, this episode further weakened Gabon's close relationship with France. It influenced Gabon to diversify and to strengthen its ties with other states. Earlier, as soon as the Socialists had come to power, Bongo had doubted whether he could still rely on French military intervention under the defense agreement to resist domestic challenges to his regime. He had thus begun to build up the Presidential Guard. The guard, which was trained and directed by French and Moroccan mercenary officers headed by General Louis ''Loulou'' Martin, became more powerful than the regular army, which was under Gabonese command. The president's bodyguards within the Presidential Guard were composed of Moroccans. Bongo also sought to strengthen the security services of his regime, which had originally been organized with the aid of De Gaulle's special adviser on African affairs, Jacques Foccart, and directed within Gabon by trusted French agents.

At the same time, Bongo had sought to develop Gabon's relationship with the United States, which had $250 million of investments in petroleum and manganese and had become a major purchaser of Gabon's oil. Bongo aimed to use the threat of a closer relationship with the United States to pressure France to follow policies that better served the interests of his regime. While the Reagan administration declined to replace France as the protector of the security of the Bongo regime, it proved eager to expand economic relations with Gabon.

During 1981 and 1982, in the aftermath of Bongo's visits to Washington, American purchases of oil greatly increased, while investments, mainly in petroleum, rose to $700 million during the course of the 1980s. Bongo's visits also led to the establishment of a branch of a major American bank in Libreville and to the selection of an American firm as Gabon's international banking advisers. The failure of French-planned investment strategies, as well as a desire to show Gabon's independence of French interests, influenced the selection of the Bechtel Corporation to formulate the plan of 1984–1988. Gabon was influenced in this direction by the success of the IMF Stabilization Plan of 1980–1982, which, though internationally ordained, had been American in-spired. It was the first time that officials of the French Ministry of Cooperation were not involved in such planning. The appointment of Pierre-Claver Maganga-Moussavou as presidential adviser for economic affairs reflected an official questioning of earlier French-planned strategies for develop-ment as well as a readiness to rethink the entire economic relationship with France. As a result of his study of French public aid to Gabon, Maganga-Moussavou questioned whether the existing arrangements really benefited Gabon as much as they might. He argued for a diversification of trade and investment, especially involving the United States. While advocating that Gabon remain in the franc zone, he wished to limit the transfer of funds to France and to reduce the French presence in government.

During 1984 Gabon arranged with France for a reduction in the number of technical *coopérants* by about 100 over a two-year period. (In 1983 there had been 820 such personnel, 440 of them in education.) France agreed to pay a slightly larger portion of their salaries and expenses, roughly half in total. Such a reduction reflected also the growing pressure for Gabonization. Unfortunately, the portion of well-educated Gabonese who possessed the particular professional and technical expertise to replace the departing Frenchmen dis-liked daily office work. They preferred to serve as advisers to ministries or as party officials.

On August 12, 1985, following defections of two promi-nent members of MORENA-in-exile to take important posi-tions in the government in Libreville, MORENA announced the formation of a government-in-exile in Paris. Bombings of the homes of several MORENA leaders as well as Aubame's

followed thereafter. Bongo, having understood that a government in exile would not be permitted, reacted bitterly. He
nevertheless defused the situation by pardoning and releas-
ing the last of the 29 MORENA members sentenced in 1982
by August 1986.

As a result of the French elections of March 1986, a
Gaullist-Giscardian coalition regained control of the Parliament. Prime Minister Jacques Chirac, accompanied by his
special adviser on African affairs, Jacques Foccart, represented France at the inauguration of the second stage of the
Transgabonais in late December 1986. By that time the
Socialist regime had largely abandoned the idealism of its
African policy in favor of a realism that closely resembled
the much criticized policies of its predecessors. One result of
this shift was that Bongo, during the presidential and
parliamentary election campaigns of 1988, contributed not
only to the candidates of the Gaullist and Giscardian parties
and to Jean Le Pen's National Front but also to François
Mitterrand and the socialists.

The severe economic crisis of 1986 further served to
restore closer ties with France throughout the following
years even though the Left regained control of Parliament in
1988. In the last half of the 1980s, Gabon sent approximately
one-third of its exports to France, including important quantities of oil, and received roughly one-half of its imports from
there. Total French aid, including both grants and low-
interest loans, in 1987 totalled 110 billion francs CFA
(project aid, budgetary aid, technical aid, and debt rescheduling). Gabon's debt to France totalled 440 million FF.
Between 1985 and 1988, according to OECD sources, France
provided 80 percent of the bilateral aid to Gabon. In this
period multi-lateral aid, including that of the EEC in which
France was a participant, formed only 11 percent of all aid
(e.g., slightly under 10 million dollars in both 1985 and
1988). France was instrumental in rescheduling Gabon's
external debt in cooperation with other EEC states, the
United States, and Japan. In 1989 France seconded eight
financial experts to Gabon to handle the structural adjust-
ment program required by the IMF, though the American
firms of Shearson Lehman and Hutton and Warburg contin-

ued to advise the treasury. In the previous year, France provided Gabon with military assistance of 65 million FF, which was used to support 110 French officers and NCOs seconded to the Gabonese armed forces and to provide matériel. Two hundred Gabonese were receiving military training in France itself. Stationed near Libreville were 520 French troops, members of the forces of rapid intervention.

Troops were dispatched from this base on May 24, 1990, to Port-Gentil to protect the lives and property of Frenchmen during violent demonstrations against the Bongo regime in the wake of the suspicious death of an opposition leader at Libreville. After demonstrators took hostage the French consul and several oil company personnel and threatened the security and property of other French citizens, the troops occupied the airport, communications facilities, and oil installations. Eighteen hundred of the 2,500 French residents, including 180 out of 220 on the staff of Elf-Gabon, chose to depart by airlift, and Elf suspended operations for five days. The military intervention, which took place at France's initiative and not at Gabon's, did not aim to restore the authority of the Bongo regime. Yet it had that effect indirectly while showing a lack of confidence in Bongo's ability to control the situation. That the Elf officials suspended operations, which cost Gabon $50 million a day in revenues, in order to embarrass Bongo and even to force him to leave office, as some charged, is possible. Bongo himself later attributed their action to a lack of sangfroid. At the time, he ordered Elf to resume production or lose its licenses, an order with which it complied. In any case, both aspects of the crisis—the intervention and the suspension—raised suspicions in Gabon about the French government's motives. At the same time, French officials played an important role in reestablishing communication between the Bongo regime and the leadership of the PGP and to calming the tense situation. France urged Bongo to proceed with reforms that would enable the opposition parties to compete fairly in the coming elections for the Legislative Assembly. Concurrently, it worked closely with him to deal with Gabon's economic difficulties, including lower rates of interest on some outstanding loans. France's task was made more difficult in the early months of 1991 by the failure of the Bongo regime to establish a financial discipline that would enable it to live up to previous agreements for financing the national debt, which grew from seven billion FF in 1987 to sixteen billion FF by early 1992.

Gabon hosted the Franco-African summit at Libreville October 5–7, 1992, which was attended by only 12 of the 28 African heads of state. The emphasis of the conference was upon the crisis in the international economy in contrast to the summit of 1990 at La Baule which had focused on democratization. Prime Minister Bérégovoy announced that France was establishing a fund to convert some of the debt of so-called middle-income countries such as Gabon, Congo, and Cameroon into development projects. Since 1990 these states had been pressing France to cancel their debts in order to aid their recovery. On November 29 Bongo began an official visit in Paris where he conferred with President Mitterrand whose preoccupation with the referendum on the Maastrict accords and failing health had prevented him from coming to Libreville.

During the events of 1990, President Bongo received a letter from 46 of the 100 members of the U.S. Senate, both Republicans and Democrats, praising his efforts at democratization and recalling his sincere friendship for the United States. The United States continued to provide Gabon with a small amount of military aid annually. Bongo also served as an intermediary between President Eduardo dos Santos of Angola and the American government in settling the rebellion of UNITA. Gabon itself undertook cooperation in air transport with the Luanda regime in an effort to lessen the deficit of Air Gabon.

Throughout the 1980s President Bongo acted as a mediator in the conflict in Chad by trying to resolve the differences between competing factions. He strongly criticized France for failing to live up to what he considered its responsibilities to prevent Libya from taking control. After Libya agreed to a cease-fire in September 1987, he chaired a committee of the OAU concerning the disputed Aouzou strip.

Gabon's relations with the Libya of Colonel Khaddafi had not led in the late 1970s to the desired financial assistance in building the Transgabonais. Relations soured over Gabon's role in helping France to establish a regime at Ndjamena that would be free from Libyan control. Libya gave as the reason for closing its embassy in Libreville the extensive French military maneuvers at Franceville in August 1980. Gabon thereafter closed its embassy in Tripoli.

What remained from the Libyan connection was the cluster of relations that Gabon had established in the mid-1970s with Arab states in the Maghrib and the Nile Valley. To this group it would add relations with Saudi Arabia, Kuwait, the United Arab Emirates, and Khomeini's Iran. Through these links Gabon would receive loans from the Arab Bank for Economic Development and the Islamic Development Bank for various projects (e.g., $14 million from the latter in 1990 for telecommunications). Receipt of such loans made it impossible to seriously consider resuming ties with Israel, as was accomplished by the Ivory Coast, Cameroon, and Zaire during the late 1980s. Despite the absence of diplomatic relations, Israel continued to purchase important quantities of Gabonese timber.

Though President Bongo stated that his conversion to Islam was a personal matter, his attachment to that faith led to close relations with Morocco, support for Morocco's position on the Western Sahara, the use of Moroccans within the Presidential Guard, and Hassan II's gift in 1983 of a large mosque opposite the presidential palace in Libreville. The mosque cost 2 billion francs CFA.

Saudi Arabia, Kuwait, and the United Arab Emirates have all donated funds for building mosques in Gabon. In 1988 Iran donated a mosque and classrooms to propagate Islam among the residents of Libreville. In May 1986 President Bongo, following a visit by Yasir Arafat, recognized the Palestinian Liberation Organization. Arafat made a second visit to Libreville in December 1990.

Gabon's relations with its resident community of 600 Lebanese, many of whom specialize in the sale of cloth, electrical appliances, and food products, entered a new period of troubles in January 1985. After President Bongo made a strong attack on foreigners involved in the economy, particularly "the Lebanese, who rob us" by their illegal importing, mobs looted Lebanese shops. The rest of the Lebanese merchants closed their establishments for fear of similar troubles. Bongo thereafter appealed for calm and urged the Lebanese to resume their activities.

During the popular demonstrations in 1990, mobs again pillaged Lebanese shops on several occasions in both Libreville and Port-Gentil. Bongo scoffed at the demand of the Lebanese ambassador for compensation of 6 billion francs CFA even though observers estimated the damages as high as 10 billion. While some of the attacks on the Lebanese reflected a breakdown in law and order during a crisis, others show Gabonese concern over lack of national control of the economy during a prolonged period of downturn.

Gabon broke relations with Taiwan in 1974 at the time that it established them with the People's Republic of China. Taiwan nevertheless buys oil and timber from Gabon. In the late 1980s Gabon discussed with China the possibility of constructing the third stage of the Transgabonais from Booué to Belinga to reach the iron deposits of the northeast. China had acquired considerable experience in railroad construction across Tanzania. In exchange for assistance to Gabon, China would receive iron ore and timber. World market conditions forced an indefinite postponement of these plans.

At present China provides Gabon modest financial and technical assistance in health and agriculture. China's neighbor, Japan, has invested in petroleum and purchases oil and manganese while selling the majority of new cars in Gabon.

During the early 1980s, Gabon began to sell a larger portion of its oil to the Caribbean and Latin America, particularly Curaçao, Brazil, and Argentina. By 1983 Brazil was the third largest importer, after France and the United States. In 1981 Gabon arranged to purchase armored cars and, in 1984, amphibian tanks and training aircraft from Brazil through loans made available by its government. Brazilian banks opened branches in Libreville. Gabon undertook discussions with Argentina on nuclear technology.

On May 20, 1981, an unhappy incident occurred in Gabon's relations with Cameroon, the most important trading partner among its neighbors. A disputed soccer match in Douala, which led to spectator assaults on Gabon's team, shown on Gabonese television, led to violent reprisals the following week at Libreville and Port-Gentil against hundreds of the 20,000 Cameroonians in the country. Some Cameroonians were holding positions in the middle levels of the civil service while others were involved in trade and transport. After many Cameroonians were injured and their properties wrecked or pillaged, the Cameroonian government on May 24 began an airlift of 10,000 people. France loaned planes to aid in the rescue. Most of the refugees had to leave the bulk of their possessions behind. This incident soured relations with Cameroon while depriving Gabon of an industrious portion of its service sector whose jobs could not be filled by qualified Gabonese. It interfered with the commercial food supply from Cameroon to Libreville and Port-Gentil as well as air traffic between the two states. In the aftermath of the incident, Gabon tightened restrictions on immigrants. It created a position of Minister of Public Security to undertake surveillance in these matters.

In July 1992 a soccer match in Libreville in which a Zairian team ended the Gabonese team's hopes for advancing to the play-offs resulted in riots in which two persons were killed and several dozens hospitalized. In December Gabon renewed its dispute with Equatorial Guinea over ownership of several tiny islands in the Rio Muni Estuary, which are believed to contain petroleum.

During the late 1980s, during the prolonged economic downturn, Gabon took steps to repatriate some of the immigrants who no longer had employment. It arranged late in 1989 to airlift to Senegal some of the 10,300 Senegalese, many of whom had arrived in the early 1970s. In October 1991 the government of Mali agreed to cooperate in the repatriation of illegal or unemployed immigrants among the estimated 35,000 Malians in Gabon. In October 1992 Gabon expelled more than 10,000 illegal immigrants from Nigeria following a police swoop through urban areas. Seven thousand of them were returned to Lagos by cargo ship, which resulted in some complaints of mistreatment.

In September 1991 an accident took place on the Congo-Ocean Railroad that had serious repercussions for Gabon's relations with the Congo Republic. Following a collision on

September 5 between a passenger train and a COMILOG train carrying manganese from Gabon that killed more than 100 Congolese and injured many others, the Congolese Minister of Transport blamed the COMILOG train for the disaster. Gabon thereupon suspended use of the railroad; negotiations to resume the traffic ended in failure. The Transgabonais has the capacity to transport the manganese and uranium carried by the COMILOG trains, which can be evacuated through the port of Owendo. The stoppage idled 900 mainly Congolese COMILOG employees at an annual loss of 733 million francs CFA to the Congolese economy. The defeat of Congo's President Denis Sassou-Nguesso, who is the father-in-law of Omar Bongo, for reelection in August 1992 may have diminished Gabon's incentives for resumption of negotiations.

On October 17, 1983, at Libreville the Communauté Économique des États de l'Afrique Centrale (CEEAC) was formed of 10 states (Cameroon, the Central African Republic, Chad, Congo, Equatorial Guinea, Gabon, Zaire, Rwanda, Burundi, and São Tomé and Príncipe). Angola declined to join for the time being. The community embodied a long-standing project of the U.N. Economic Commission for Africa as further developed in the Lagos Plan. It laid plans for establishing a common market over an eight-year period and other forms of cooperation. Whether the CEEAC will have greater success in promoting mutual well-being than the smaller UDEAC remains to be seen. The provision in the agreement for the free circulation of persons, goods, services, and capital will require Gabon to adopt an equitable and consistent policy on immigrants, whose treatment has heretofore not infrequently been unjust and inhumane. Its opposition to the inclusion of such provisions does not augur well for its compliance with them.

Gabon was the moving spirit in the creation in January 1983 at Libreville of the Centre International des Civilisations Bantu (CICIBA) (q.v.). Members include Angola, the Central African Republic, the Comoros, Congo, Equatorial Guinea, Gabon, Rwanda, São Tomé and Príncipe, Zaire, and Zambia.

In February 1981 the opening of a shortwave radio station

that could be heard from Senegal to Zaire, Africa No. 1, put Gabon in the position of propagating the use of French over much of West and Central Africa. The station is largely staffed by French personnel, who broadcast locally produced programs 12 hours a day. The station also rents transmission time to Radio France Internationale, for six hours daily and to Radio Suisse Internationale. The station is thus an important instrument for maintaining and expanding the influence of France, its language, and its culture.

Gabon's most consistent trading partners during the 1980s after France and the United States were the other states of the EEC. The United Kingdom, West Germany, and Italy were all involved in the construction of the Transgabonais. Spain, in November 1981, loaned Gabon $120 million as part of a maritime transport agreement. In February 1988, Spanish and French fishing interests under the auspices of the EEC obtained fishing rights in Gabon's territorial waters for three years at $3,500,000 per year, license fees based upon catches (mainly tuna), and $745,000 for scientific research.

Gabon continued to maintain its relationship with the European Community. It had adhered to the second Yaoundé convention of African states with the EEC in 1969. Thereafter it adhered to the Lomé Convention through the agreements of 1975, 1979, and 1984, which ran through the end of 1990. The Convention, between the EEC and 66 African, Caribbean, and Pacific states (the ACP), including 45 African states, guaranteed duty-free entry to the EEC for certain commodities produced by the ACP. The third agreement in 1984 lowered more trade barriers and simplified considerably the rules of origin. Other innovations provided for cultural and social cooperation, preservation of the environment, encouragement of European private investment in Africa, further cooperation in fisheries and shipping, and a human rights clause.

Gabon has received aid through the Community's European Development Fund (EDF) and European Investment Bank (EIB). The stabilization of export earnings scheme (Stabex) was established to cover losses of earnings caused by a drop in prices or production of the main ACP agricultural exports (48 at present). Sysmin, a special financing fund for minerals, including manganese, aims to contribute to the creation of a more solid basis for the development of ACP states whose economies are dependent upon the mining sector.

Discussions for a Fourth Lomé Convention revealed the European Community's desire to attach conditions on aid from the EDF along the lines required by the International Monetary Fund while leaving the rest of the convention relatively unchanged. Opposition from the ACP states delayed completion of the agreement. It was signed on December 1989 and ratified by the European Parliament in May 1990. The convention will run for 10 years. Lomé IV introduces the question of environmental protection into development strategies, a feature that Gabon has already included in its plans for many years. As of October 1990, not all of the funds from Lomé III had been dispensed, much less spent.

After the Republic of South Africa released Nelson Mandela from prison in February 1990 and continued the dismantling of apartheid, President Bongo urged that international sanctions against that country's government be lifted. South Africa Airways thereafter was officially granted landing rights in Gabon, possibly to promote tourism in addition to greater importation of foodstuffs. [418, 565, 425, 464, 523, 97, 65, 603, 605, 445, 500, 405, 490, 491, 1365]

FORESTRY. Various kinds of forests cover 225,000 sq. km. out of 267,000 sq. km., that is, more than 80 percent of Gabon. Dyewood or redwood from the southern coast around Mayumba was exchanged perhaps even before the arrival of Europeans on the coast. It became an important export in the seventeenth century and after. In the 1880s okoumé (q.v.), a softwood used in the manufacture of plywood, began to be exported to Germany and Holland, and after the First World War to France. By 1903 Gabon had become the leading African producer of tropical woods, a position it ceded to the Ivory Coast only in the 1970s. Mahogany, ebony, and walnut came to be exploited by French firms during the 1920s in important quantities, though they never achieved the significance of okoumé. The economy of Gabon depended heavily upon the timber industry until the start of mineral exploitation in the early 1960s.

In 1963 timber formed 80 percent of the country's exports, but by the late 1970s only 10 percent. Whereas in 1972 woods still constituted 8.6 percent of the gross domestic product, they formed only 1.3 percent in 1983 and 1.9 percent in 1988. In 1990 timber exports, two-thirds of which were okoumé, were valued at $202 million (compared with petroleum at $1,994,000,000 and manganese at $198 million). Gabon remained Africa's chief exporter of plywood and its fourth most important producer of tropical woods.

Timber exploitation is carried on by mechanized French and Gabonese firms and by non-mechanized Gabonese family groups, the so-called *coupes familiales*. Government policy encouraging and favoring Gabonese involvement resulted by the early 1970s in reducing production by French firms to a slight majority of the total. But thereafter the necessity of large capital investments to reach the woods of the interior restored the lead to the French companies. In the wake of the depletion of forests in the coastal areas—the so-called first zone—where evacuation by water routes was generally possible, exploitation has increased in the second zone, which covers the central portions of the country from north to south. In this zone rapids and waterfalls preclude water transportation for much of the export route so that construction of a road network has been necessary. These projects were begun in the 1970s along with reforestation schemes in the first zone. Construction of the Transgabonais Railroad connecting Owendo on the Estuary with Franceville on the upper Ogooué River has aided in the evacuation of logs from the second zone. The railroad reached N'Djolé in 1978, Booué in 1983, and Franceville in late 1986. The deepwater port completed at Owendo in 1979 is equipped to handle up to 1,500,000 cubic meters of timber annually. The timber of the third zone in the eastern center of the country remains largely unexploited for lack of transportation facilities.

The sawmills of the timber industry are located at Port-Gentil, Libreville, and Mayumba. Port-Gentil contains an important plywood factory. But in the early 1990s, only 20 percent of the logs were being processed into sawn lumber, plywood, and veneer before export, a percentage the government was seeking to increase.

Though production of timber has remained in private hands, marketing is the monopoly of a state organism, since October 1975 a parastatal called the Société Nationale des Bois du Gabon (SNBG). The SNBG regularly operated at a deficit that reached $10 million in 1987. It added costs to sale prices that in the opinion of the loggers weakened their competitiveness in world markets. The situation became acute from 1984 on because of increased competition from cheaper Southeast Asian woods and the weakness of the dollar at a time of lessened demand. In 1989 the SNBG renounced its monopoly over the export of all but the two main woods, okoumé and ozigo, in order to meet some of the criticism and encourage diversification of output. Other species, which had represented one-quarter of the total volume in 1983, totalled only one-sixth in 1988. At that time France was still purchasing close to 40 percent of Gabon's woods, with Israel, Greece, Spain, Morocco, and Taiwan the other leading customers. [940, 1, 929, 738, 1105]

FRANC ZONE. The franc zone is a monetary transaction association first organized by France in the aftermath of the Second World War and including its Black African territories. It was reorganized after the independence of these countries and continues to include all of them except Guinea and Mali. National and regional currencies, including the CFA franc of the four Equatorial countries and Cameroon, are pegged to the French franc. They are freely exchangeable and transferable within the franc zone under French fiscal control. [723]

FRANCEVILLE. Third largest city and mining center. In June 1880 the explorer Brazza established a post at the junction of the M'Passa and Ogooué rivers as a part of his efforts to extend French control into the interior. The Upper Ogooué region had more extensive economic links with the Congo Basin than with the Lower Ogooué. Thus between 1925 and 1946 the French administered the region as a part of the Middle Congo. Franceville has developed in the past quarter of a century as a result of the attention given to it by President

Bongo, a native of the province. He located there a technical lycée, a university of engineering and scientific technology (Masuku), and a center for medical research. He had the Transgabonais Railroad built to promote the area's economic development, particularly its mineral resources, of which Franceville is the hub. [940, 294]

FREE EMIGRANTS SCHEME or FREE LABORERS SCHEME. In March 1857 the Régis Company of Marseilles signed a contract with the French government to provide 20,000 African workers for the French West Indies over a six-year period. The Africans were destined mainly for labor on the sugar plantations in the aftermath of the abolition of slavery in 1848, which had freed 74,000 slaves on Martinique and 93,000 on Guadeloupe. The Régis firm, already known for its promotion of French commerce and of French political control in West Africa, established its headquarters for this enterprise at the Congo mouth and in Angola. By 1862 Régis had signed up 15,000 Africans from regions between Gabon and Angola. An unknown number of them came from southern Gabon. In 1857 the Vidal Company of Nantes, which had a factory in Gabon, began recruiting under terms similar to those of Régis. Many of the workers became ill while waiting for ships from the unaccustomed diet and from crowded conditions. Seventy-four of the 340 emigrants from northern Gabon died en route to Martinique and French Guyana, each of which Vidal had contracted to supply with 500 workers. At the same time, the Chevalier Company obtained emigrants by paying the ransom of persons enslaved through debt. In 1857, 32 of the 279 taken aboard ship died en route to a transfer point in West Africa. The desire of the company to fulfill its contract to supply 1,500 workers influenced its decision in 1859 to purchase many in ill health or of very young age. Forty-eight died before two ships arrived to take them to the New World, and 31 more died en route. Thirty-six of the 573 who arrived in Guyana had to be hospitalized immediately on arrival. Of the roughly 1,200 recruited in the Estuary between 1857 and 1859, none ever returned at the end of their seven-year contracts.

The African "volunteers" were called "free laborers" in

Britain and free emigrants (*émigrants libres*) or free enlistees (*engagés libres*) in France. Their terms of employment resembled those of indentured servants in the British North American colonies during the seventeenth and eighteenth centuries. But the conditions under which they were recruited and were kept at the coastal factories and onboard ship closely resembled the slave trade. Growing British criticism of these aspects of the scheme, of which French officials in the Estuary had become aware by 1859, resulted in an Anglo-French agreement of July 1, 1861, to end the program after one year. [252, 235, 110, 248]

FREE FRENCH MOVEMENT (1940–1944). On June 18, 1940, the government of the Third French Republic made an armistice with Nazi Germany. The Germans occupied the northern three-fifths of France, including the Atlantic coasts, and a French state at Vichy headed by Marshal Philippe Pétain controlled the remainder. On the same day in London General Charles de Gaulle, a longtime critic of France's inadequate defenses, issued a call for formation of the Free French movement to keep Frenchmen in the war on the Allied side. De Gaulle hoped to use the resources of the vast French empire, still in French hands, to liberate the mother country. Whereas the French communities in North Africa and West Africa rejected de Gaulle's appeals and gave allegiance to Vichy, those in the Cameroons and French Equatorial Africa rallied to his side between August 26 and 30, 1940.

But in Gabon complications immediately arose. On the 30th, after consultation with French notables, including the influential Chamber of Commerce president Henri Seignon (q.v.), the colonial governor, Pierre Masson, took Gabon into the Free French camp. On September 1st he reversed his decision. He was apparently influenced by the criticism of the Catholic bishop of Libreville, Monsignor Louis Tardy, and the prominent businessman René Labat, as well as by the arrival of two Vichy gunboats on the coast and high Vichy colonial appointees by air. Gabon thereafter became the scene of a civil war among the Free French, based in the Cameroons and the Middle Congo, and their French supporters in Gabon, on the one hand, and the Vichy forces and their local French supporters, on the other. Free French Colonel Parant (1897–1941) in early September took Mayumba, rallied the N'Gounié Province, and laid siege to Lambaréné, which the Vichyites abandoned only on November 5th. On the ninth, Parant's forces combined with those of Colonel Leclerc from the Cameroons, which had previously rallied the Woleu-N'Tem Province, to take Libreville from the Vichyites. After Port-Gentil surrendered to the Free French on November 11, further Vichy opposition ceased. Colonel Parant briefly headed Gabon under Governor-General Félix Eboué (q.v.) at Brazzaville.

During the war years the British purchased Gabon's exports, using the okoumé (q.v.) in the construction of Royal Air Force planes. Hundreds of Gabonese served in the Free French forces in North Africa and Europe and subsequently received pensions. These war veterans (*anciens combattants*) would be an important element in upholding close ties with France in the coming decades.

The Free French government sponsored the Brazzaville Conference of January–February 1944, which planned for postwar liberalization of the colonial regime within a French framework. The conference advocated greater participation by Africans in their own administration as well as public programs to promote economic and social advancement. [119a, 966, 315, 135, 548, 566, 336]

FREEDOM VILLAGES (VILLAGES DE LIBERTE). At the beginning of the twentieth century the French Anti-Slavery Society (Société Anti-Esclavagiste de France) sponsored the organization of three villages in the Gabonese interior for slaves whose freedom it had helped to purchase. The communities were located adjacent to the mission posts of the Holy Ghost Fathers on the lower N'Gounié River (1899), at Franceville (1902), and at Lambaréné (1903). During the previous half century the Catholic missionaries had purchased the freedom of ill-treated slaves, generally orphan children whom they subsequently raised, educated, and prepared for Christian marriage. On several occasions they had also formed villages of free converts near their posts to provide continued instruction and to protect them from the pressures of their pagan relatives. But the freedom villages, which were first initiated by the colonial administration of French West Africa, contained mostly adults of both sexes whose freedom was purchased with funds from the French Anti-Slavery Society, a body organized by Cardinal Lavigerie in 1888 with the blessings and support of the papacy. The three in Gabon were among 30 organized throughout French West and Equatorial Africa. The Holy Ghost Fathers (q.v.) formed two other villages, among the Eshira (1887) and at Fernan-Vaz (1901), without outside support. Though the freedom villages did not promote evangelization to the extent the missionaries had hoped, they did secure the permanent freedom of several hundred persons in an era when the colonial administration was not yet in a position to terminate the worst forms of domestic slavery. [241]

FRENCH EQUATORIAL AFRICA. Between 1910 and 1958 Gabon was administered as part of the federation of French Equatorial Africa. The federation was created from a model developed in French West Africa to administer the lands France had acquired in Central Africa during the nineteenth and early twentieth centuries. It included four territories: Gabon, Middle Congo, Ubangi-Shari, and Chad. Each territory was headed by a lieutenant governor (1910–1946) or governor (1946–1958) responsible to the governor-general in the federal capital at Brazzaville. The federation possessed a budget in addition to the four territorial budgets. Thus revenues raised in Gabon through customs duties and other taxes were transmitted to Brazzaville to help pay for the central services and federal functions. For example, Gabonese revenues aided construction of the Congo-Ocean Railroad (1921–1934) from which Gabon derived no benefits at a time when it needed a railroad for its own development.

The federation was changed into a ''group of territories'' in April 1957 as a result of the decrees implementing the Loi-Cadre of June 23, 1956. The federation was abolished at the end of the Fourth Republic in September 1958. Attempts by the four states to replace the federation with some sort of cooperative political structure failed. Gabon saw few advantages in having a federation with states that were poorer than itself and that it might have to continue to subsidize. It wanted to use its own considerable timber and mineral resources to develop itself. Ultimately Gabon agreed to cooperation in a number of economic areas, which led to UDEAC (q.v.), and between 1959 and 1971 in higher education. *See* GOVERNORS. [14, 129]

- G -

GALOA (or GALWA). The Galoa are a Myènè-speaking (q.v.) people who early in the nineteenth century migrated from their homes around Lakes Onagué, Ezanga, and Oguemoue to Lambaréné Island in the Ogooué and along the river downstream. The Galoa were submitted at first to the rule of the Enenga (q.v.). At the death of the Enenga king Re-Mpole in 1860, Nkombe (d. 1874), his paternal nephew, whose mother was Galoa, declared Galoa independence and became their king. Ruling from his village at Adolinanongo, he procured slaves upstream for transport to Cape Lopez and Fernan-Vaz. He aided various explorers to obtain canoers for their trips farther upstream. He encouraged British and German as well as French trading firms to establish in his territories in 1867 and after to deal directly with them and eliminate the Orungu (q.v.) and Nkomi (q.v.) middlemen on the coast. It is likely that he accepted French sovereignty in 1867, though the treaty is missing. It is in large part Nkombe's policies that resulted in Lambaréné and vicinity becoming the center for European commercial penetration and exploration of the middle and upper Ogooué system in the 1870s and 1880s. During Nkombe's reign the Fang (q.v.) began to encroach on Galoa territory. At his death he left 120 wives and several hundred slaves. The French clashed with Nkombe's successor, Magise, whom they deported to Dakar.

In 1877 American Presbyterians founded a mission at Kangwe on the north bank of the Ogooué near Lambaréné and the Holy Ghost Fathers (q.v.) located on the island itself in 1881. The Galoa flocked to the schools of both missions and there acquired the skills that permitted them to serve as the agents and auxiliaries of European firms, French exploration parties, and eventually the colonial administration. The Galoa also converted either to Protestantism (the French Protestants replaced the Presbyterians in 1893) or to Roman Catholicism.

The Rev. André Raponda Walker (q.v.) claimed that the Galoa were originally an offshoot of the Eshira (q.v.) people who adopted a Myènè language as a result of their migration to the Lambaréné area. This view has been refuted by Paul-Vincent Pounah (q.v.) on the basis of oral data he gathered from Galoa notables from the 1940s on. Pounah's research further suggests that the Galoa, together with the Orungu, in the distant past may have lived in Loango. When the two peoples in the course of migrations northward reached the Ogooué, the Orungu turned downstream toward the delta and the Galoa upstream toward Lambaréné. [394, 367, 368, 369, 881, 214]

GENTIL, ÉMILE (1866–1914). Colonial administrator. Gentil was born at Volmunster in the French department of the Moselle on April 4, 1866. After studies at Nancy, he entered the Naval School at the age of seventeen. As an ensign in 1888, he was sent to Gabon where he did hydrographic soundings along the coast between the Estuary and the mouths of the Ogooué (1890–1892). Thereafter, as a colonial administrator he was involved in the expeditions that established French control over Ubangi-Shari and Chad. On July 5, 1902, he was named lieutenant governor of the French Congo residing at Brazzaville at a time when the governor himself resided at Libreville. From 1904 to 1908, he served as commissioner-general of the French Congo, with its capital now at Brazzaville. He had to deal with major financial and administrative problems, including troubles in the N'Gounié. He cooperated with De Brazza's investigation of the abuses of the concessionary companies in 1905. In 1907 he organized the first public education in Gabon at Libreville with both primary and vocational instruction.

Gentil died at Bordeaux on March 30, 1914. The city of Port-Gentil is named for him. [1302]

GEORGES, KING or RASSONDJI (d. 1847). Georges headed the Agulamba clan of the Mpongwe (q.v.) on the southern shore of the Estuary from at least the 1810s until his death. At his village of Nghaga near the lower Remboué River, he possessed 300 to 500 slaves. He and his clan were much involved in the slave trade with the Ogooué and Cape Lopez, which was at its height during his reign. Georges allowed the ABCFM missionaries to open a school in his territories in the 1840s staffed by an Afro-American so that the boys might learn English, the leading trading language. In a treaty with Lt. Mecquet of November 4, 1846, Georges ceded the Avazé River or Georges Creek to France. At his death Georges was succeeded by his brother, the best known of the Agulamba traders, called Tom Lawson, who reigned from 1847 to 1860 under the same names, Georges and Rassondji, which has led to a good deal of confusion. To compound matters, other successors also took the name of Georges without adding numbers or other names that might have distinguished them from their predecessors. [252, 254, 362, 332, 394]

GLASS, KING or R'OGOUAROWE (d. 1848). R'Ogouarowe headed the Agekaza-Glass or Agekaza w'Olamba clan of the Mpongwe (q.v.) people on the northern shore of the Estuary from 1839 to 1848. His village of Glass was the most important trading center in the region. It was the headquarters for British and American traders and after June 1842 the site of an American Protestant mission. The territories of R'Ogouarowe were also the center of the opposition to the establishment of French rule in the 1840s. King Glass recognized French sovereignty in a treaty of March 28, 1844, which was probably obtained through deception by naval officers and their African colleagues. He thereafter sought to repudiate the agreement but could not obtain the support of the British and American governments to this end. Glass eventually served on the French commission for arbitrating trade disputes. There is confusion about the identity of the heads of the Agekaza-Glass clan because several of R'Ogouarowe's successors also used that name without further distinction. [252, 255, 362, 332, 394]

GOLD. In 1935 a Mr. Romano discovered gold that could be exploited commercially on the Mayumba coast. Two years later gold was discovered at N'Djolé on the middle Ogooué where in 1938 Raphaël Duloz (d. 1977) and Jean Duloz (d. 1983) founded the Société Minière Duloz Frères and began production. During the early 1940s the Duloz mine employed 300 to 400 Gabonese workers, mostly Fang, and 60 Europeans. The mine produced until 1964, but it was sold in 1952 to the Bureau Minier de la France d'Outre-Mer, a government company. The Bureau Minier introduced more modern technology while also buying gold from individual Gabonese prospectors. In 1962 the buying office at N'Djolé was paying 200 francs per gram. In the meantime, in 1937 Mr. Raynal, a former agent of the Compagnie de la Haute-N'Gounié, who had had experience with gold mining in the Belgian Congo, began prospecting in the areas of the Mitsogo (q.v.) people, around the villages of Etéké, Mombo, and Punga. By 1941, his company, the Société Or-Gabon, was exporting 1,686 kg. annually. Gold was subsequently located in other portions of the interior, but the sites were soon worked out. The production of gold, which is now in Gabonese hands, in the late 1960s and early 1970s averaged 400 kg. annually. But in 1985 it had declined to 50 kg., mainly from Etéké. Recent prospecting has located new important lodes northeast of Lastoursville in the Ogooué-Lolo Province. Purchase and sale of the gold is handled by the Société Gabonaise de Recherches et d'Exploitations Minières (SOGAREM). [929, 378]

GONDJOUT, PAUL INDJENJET (1912–1990). Politician. Gondjout was born on June 4, 1912, at Lambaréné of Enenga and Orungu parents. His father was an active member of the Ligue des Droits de l'Homme and a friend of Léon Mba (q.v.). Young Paul was educated at Catholic schools at Libreville, including the Ecole Montfort (q.v.). From December 1928 through 1964 he served in the administration, at first at Port-Gentil. In 1943 he founded the Cercle Amicale Mutualiste des Evolués in response to encouragement from Governor-General Félix Eboué (q.v.) for organizations that would provide leadership by the French-educated in a liberalized French empire. In November 1946 he won election to the Territorial Assembly from Port-Gentil. In 1949 that body elected him as a Senator in the French upper house, the Council of the Republic, to which he was reelected in 1952 and served until 1957. In 1954, after reelection to the Assembly in March 1952, he founded the Bloc Démocratique Gabonais (q.v.) and became its secretary-general and editor of its newspaper, the *Union Gabonaise.* The BDG sought to organize the peoples outside the Woleu-N'Tem against Jean-Hilaire Aubame (q.v.), his UDSG (q.v.), and the northern Fang. It became the local branch of the inter-territorial RDA after Léon Mba joined and became an officer. In 1958 Gondjout became president of the Legislative Assembly, a post that he continued to hold until November 1960 when President Mba jailed him for attempting a motion of censure designed to prevent Mba from transforming the government from a parliamentary to a presidential type. After his release from prison late in 1962, Mba appointed him president of the Economic and Social Council. As a member of the provisional government established in the wake of the February 1964 coup, he was arrested and tried but exonerated. President Bongo appointed him as secretary-general of the National Council of the Office des Bois in January 1968 and then president of the Supreme Court from September 1968 to April 1975. On April 16, 1975, he became president of the National Assembly. [550, 551, 593, 1366]

GOVERNORS AND GOVERNORS-GENERAL, FRENCH. [1392, 1394]

Lieutenant-Governors
of Gabon:

1886–1889	Noël Ballay
1889–1891	Charles de Chavannes
1891–1904	(directly under the French Congo)
1904–1905	Louis Ormières

	1905–1906	Alfred Fourneau
	1906–1907	Fernand Therond
	1907–1909	Alfred Martineau
	1909–1910	Léon Richaud
	1910	Joseph François
	1910–1911	Adolphe Cureau
	1911–1913	Georges Poulet
	1913–1919	Casimir Guyon
	1919–1922	Maurice Lapalud
	1922–1923	Jean Marchand
	1923	Jocelyn Robert
	1923–1924	Louis Cercus
	1924–1931	Joseph Bernard
	1931–1934	Marcel Marchessou
	1934–1935	Louis Bonvin
	1935–1936	Charles Assier de Pompignan
	1936–1937	Louis Bonvin
	1937–1938	Georges Parisot
	1938–1940	Georges Masson
	1941–1942	Victor Valentin-Smith
	1942–1943	Charles Assier de Pompignan
	1943–1944	Paul Vuillaume
	1944–1946	Numa François Sadoul
Governors of Gabon:	1946–1947	Roland Pré
	1947–1949	Numa François Sadoul
	1949–1951	Pierre Pelieu
	1951–1952	Charles Hanin
	1952–1958	Yves Digo
	1958	Louis Sanmarco
High Commissioner of Gabon:	1959–1960	Jean Risterucci
Commissioners-General of the French Congo:		
	1886–1898	Pierre Savorgnan de Brazza

1898–1901	Henri de la Mothe
1901–1904	Louis Grodet
1904–1908	Emile Gentil
1908–1910	Martial Merlin

Governors-General of French Equatorial Africa:

1910–1917	Martial Merlin
1918–1919	Gabriel Angoulvant
1920–1924	Victor Augagneur
1924–1934	Raphaël Antonetti
1934–1935	Edouard Renard
1935–1939	François Joseph Reste
1939–1940	Pierre Boisson
1940	Louis Husson
1940	René de Larminat
1940–1944	Félix Eboué
1944–1947	Charles-André Bayardelle
1947	Charles Luizet

High Commissioners of French Equatorial Africa:

1947–1951	Bernard Cornut-Gentille
1951–1958	Paul Chauvet
1958	Pierre Messmer
1958	Yvon Bourges

High Commissioner-General of French Equatorial Africa:

1959–1960	Yvon Bourges

GROUPE D'ETUDES COMMUNISTES (GEC). The GEC founded at Libreville in 1944 or 1945 was modelled upon the GECs organized throughout French West Africa in 1943 and thereafter by European administrative employees who had received appointments during the era of the Popular Front. The GECs sought to provide a political education for *évolués* that would be both Marxist and anticolonialist. The European leaders encouraged and aided the African members in the formation of territorial political parties affiliated with the Rassemblement Démocratique Africain (RDA) and labor unions linked with the Communist-influenced Confédération Générale du Travail (CGT).

In Gabon the federal administration encouraged Fernand Saller, an Antillese, and two physicians, Drs. Lucien Cordier and Eggenberger, to organize a GEC in order to keep left-wing political activity under European direction and to counter conservative and mission influences. The GEC at Libreville helped to organize labor unions of European and African civil servants and private employees affiliated with the CGT. It also aided the formation of a political party, the Parti Démocratique Africain (PDA) (q.v.), to contest elections in 1945–1946 for the French Constituent, French National, and Gabonese Territorial assemblies. The most important figures in the PDA were Emile Issembé (q.v.), Léon Mba, Georges Damas (q.v.), and Paul Gondjout (q.v.).

The PDA became the Gabonese branch of the RDA in 1946 but was not allowed by the administration to send the delegates it selected to the Bamako conference of that year. In March 1947, the administration, now under different direction and acting as part of the Africa-wide repression of the French Communists' African allies, transferred the two physicians to other areas. At that moment Léon Mba became the president of the GEC and Gérard McKenzie, an Mpongwe métis (q.v.), the secretary. Other leaders were Frédéric Moreau, the secretary of the Comité Mpongwe; Paul Taty; Jean-Pierre Tchikaya, a Vili (q.v.) and a close friend of the RDA deputy, Jean-Félix Tchicaya (q.v.); and David Cadorelle, a young Congolese schoolteacher. Moreau, Taty, and Cadorelle were very active n the CGT unions among civil servants. Under strong pressures from the administration, the GEC was forced to stop meeting by the end of 1947. Some of the members would join Léon Mba's Comité Mixte Gabonais (q.v.), which had succeeded the PDA as the local branch of the RDA. [550]

- H -

HEALTH AND SANITATION. Historically the population was plagued by endemic parasitical diseases and malnutrition.

Smallpox epidemics on the coasts in the mid-nineteenth century and in the far north in the early twentieth-century decimated various peoples. Sleeping sickness and malaria were endemic in many areas. Almost all African peoples had doctors who employed natural medicine to deal with various ailments. Western medicine arrived with the Christian missionaries and French naval physicians in the 1840s and thereafter. Under the federation of French Equatorial Africa (q.v.), health services based at Brazzaville pretty well eradicated sleeping sickness during the 1930s. In 1913 Dr. Albert Schweitzer (q.v.) established his famous hospital at Lambaréné. His use of methods of treatment adapted to local conditions brought much criticism in the West. Since January 1981 a new modern Schweitzer Hospital, which opened there financed mainly by foreign donors, functions in part with government aid. The new hospital of the Christian Alliance Church at Bongolo operates independently of the government. But the bulk of health care and preventive medicine is, in fact, provided by the government. In 1991 most of the 340 physicians were in government service, the bulk of them concentrated in the Estuary Province. In 1983 Gabon had 16 multi-purpose hospitals, 97 medical centers, 12 centers for protection of mothers and infants, and 284 rural dispensaries. There were 5,000 hospital beds, more than 800 of them recently built.

Physicians and other medical personnel are trained at the Omar Bongo University in Libreville. Many of them prepare their theses and undertake practical training at the Center for Medical Research in Franceville. The Center, financed by Elf-Gabon, opened in December 1979 to study the problems of low fertility, using the Franceville region, an area par excellence of low birth rate, as sources of data. An international staff has been investigating the physiology, pathology, and biology of reproduction; sexually transmitted diseases; parasitical diseases (e.g., malaria and filariasis *du loa-loa*), which at present infect one-third of pregnant women; infections, viral, and parasitical diseases of early childhood; and experimental pharmacology.

The government operates various programs of sanitation, disease prevention, and control. Increased urbanization in recent decades has contributed to improved diet and health care for large parts of the population. Gabon's annual growth rate, formerly among the lowest in Africa, now approximates the continent's average. [307, 1129, 916, 1134, 1137]

HOLY GHOST FATHERS (or SPIRITANS). The most important Catholic missionary congregation in Gabon since 1844. In 1841 Rev. François Libermann (1802–1852) founded the Congregation of the Holy Heart of Mary to evangelize the black race. In 1848 his group merged with the older Holy Ghost Congregation (Spiritans) of which he became the ninth superior. Libermann and his clergy were well in advance of their time in their comparative lack of ethnocentrism. They also worked from the very start to prepare an indigenous clergy and skilled tradesmen. Spiritans held the position of bishop until gradually replaced by Gabonese diocesan clergy with the coming of independence. Among the most noted Spiritans in the nineteenth century were the cofounders of the mission, Jean-Rémy Bessieux (q.v.) and Pierre-Marie Le Berre (q.v.); Alexandre Le Roy (q.v.), who with Le Berre organized the late nineteenth century expansion outside the Estuary; an amateur botanist, Théophile Klaine (q.v.); and an ethnologist, Henri Trilles (q.v.). In 1980 there were 50 French Spiritans in Gabon, and in 1990, 38. The Spiritans at Libreville have a scholasticate that prepares 17 future African priests of their congregation from several African states, including four from Gabon. [1029, 1030, 1045, 1002, 1041, 1042, 1016]

- I -

IBEA (or IBIYA), J. IKENGA (1834–1901). J. Ikenga Ibea was a Benga (q.v.) from Corisco who became the first convert of the American Presbyterian mission established among his people in 1850. After primary studies in the mission school and private theological instruction, he was ordained as the first African pastor in 1865. He practiced his ministry among the Benga on the Gabon mainland opposite Corisco as well as on his native island. When in 1875 the missionaries, in view of the unhealthy climate and the reestablishment of Spanish rule, transferred to the mainland, they left the Corisco church under Ibea's leadership. When Spanish missionaries of the Congregation of the Immaculate Heart of Jesus (Claretians) arrived in 1885, Ibea helped them to learn Benga. They in turn attracted away his pupils to the school they opened in 1888 and sought to frustrate his work. His protests to the authorities led to his being sued for writing an "insulting letter" to Lieutenant Governor Ibarra of Elobey and exiled to the island of Fernando Po.

Ibea is notable for his plans to free the African church from dependence on outside funding by the establishment of plantations and the acquisition of skilled trades among a people at that time involved mainly in fishing. Ibea published a work in Benga, *Customs of the Benga and Neighbors*. He died on February 28, 1901. [1009, 1004, 1025]

IMMACULATE CONCEPTION SISTERS (or BLUE SISTERS). The Sisters of Our Lady of the Immaculate Conception of Castres, France, have carried on educational and charitable work in Gabon since 1849. The congregation was founded by the aristocratic Emilie de Villeneuve (1811–1854) to educate poor and orphaned girls and to improve the condition of women. In response to an appeal from Monsignor Jean-Rémy Bessieux (q.v.) in 1847, the founder arranged with the Holy Ghost Fathers to send sisters to Senegal and Gabon to educate girls and to care for the sick. The first four sisters arrived near Libreville in July 1849. Among them was Sr. Constance Fontaine, who held the *agrégation* and who taught school among the Benga at Cape Esterias until her death in 1851. Among the best known of the sisters have been Mother Louis Raynaud (1818–1905), who headed the IC community at Libreville from 1849 to 1889; Sr. St. Charles Villeneuve (1834–1911), who operated an open-air dispensary that treated thousands of persons between 1860 and 1909; Mother Edouard Prat (1839–1927), who initiated educational work among Fang girls at Donguila in 1893 in order to prepare them for Christian marriage and who remained there until 1919; and Sr. Dorothée Fournié (1849–1920), who cared for the sick for 40 years at Lambaréné. In

1989 55 IC sisters were involved in education, health care, and social service in close cooperation with Gabonese Sisters of St. Mary. [1019, 1049]

INDIGENAT. The *indigénat* refers to the civil status of the native Africans as French colonial subjects between 1910 and 1946. The indigénat was a product of French colonial thinking in the wake of the large-scale territorial expansion of the late nineteenth and early twentieth centuries. The goal of assimilation was abandoned in favor of a policy of association under which only a tiny elite would be assimilated to French culture and a French life-style. This group would serve the colonial regime as auxiliaries and intermediaries with the traditionally oriented masses. While individuals from the elite group might be admitted to the status of French citizen with the accompanying rights and legal protection, most of the elite would have the same status as the *sujets indigènes* (native subjects) or masses. The latter would retain much of their traditional culture and would be administered under a special system having its historical roots in colonial Algeria. It was more authoritarian and more restrictive than the system for citizens. Thus African subjects did not possess the same rights of free expression, association, and movement as Europeans. They were required to provide unpaid labor for public purposes (*prestation*) and were liable to be conscripted for paid forced labor on projects of public utility as well as for portage. In Gabon all able-bodied persons over ten years of age had to pay an annual poll tax (*impôt*), the rate of which varied from region to region and which could sometimes be paid in produce or labor.

The indigénat gave to French administrators the right to impose penalties on subjects for violations that in some instances they themselves had previously defined without having to justify their actions before any judicial authorities. Thus heads of regions and districts could impose sentences of up to 15 days' imprisonment and fines up to 100 francs without appeal. In dealing with offenders the administrators served at one and the same time as policeman, examining magistrate, public prosecutor, judge, and executor of the sentence. The system in effect gave administrators a wide rein to control their African subjects and to enforce the policies and decisions of the government and its officials.

Arbitrariness was perhaps even more widespread in cases involving the African common or customary law, which was unwritten and therefore open to all kinds of interpretations. The administrators, who generally did not know indigenous languages and customs, were dependent upon the knowledge and integrity of African notables in obtaining the information necessary to decide cases. Their ignorance and incompetence often gave these assistants the opportunity to influence decisions in directions that served neither justice nor those judged.

The indigénat was a constant source of friction between the French administration and the Gabonese. It was a major factor in the elite's quest for French citizenship in the interwar period, a status only a handful achieved. The indigénat was dismantled piecemeal by various metropolitan laws and decrees in 1945 and 1946. Its continuance was incompatible with the Lamine Guèye Law of May 7, 1946, making African subjects French citizens, a provision incorporated into the constitution of October 13, 1946. [125, 81]

INTERNATIONAL BOUNDARIES. The international boundaries of Gabon were established between 1885 and 1946. A Franco-German Treaty of December 12, 1885, and a convention of March 15, 1894, established the northern frontier with the Cameroons. After joint delimitation on the actual terrain, slight adjustments were made to fix the frontier along the courses of rivers, formalized in the convention of April 18, 1908. Portions of northern Gabon assigned to Germany under the convention of November 4, 1911, were returned to France in the Versailles treaty of 1919.

The Franco-Spanish convention of June 27, 1900, established the frontiers between Gabon and Spanish Guinea (Rio Muni). Small adjustments took place at the completion of delimitation in 1924.

The boundary between Gabon and the neighboring French territory of the Middle Congo was fixed in its present form by a decree of October 16, 1946, as part of a general reorganization of the territories of French Equatorial Africa.

The Kwilou Region and the Divénié District of the Niari Region, which had formed parts of Gabon prior to 1918, were permanently placed in the Middle Congo. But the Haut-Ogooué Region, which had been part of the Middle Congo from 1925 to 1946, was returned to Gabon. The Haut-Ogooué is the site of Gabon's manganese (q.v.) and the home of its president since 1967, Omar Bongo (q.v.). [13, 271, 324]

IRON. The existence of iron deposits in many parts of Gabon, particularly the southwest, far north, and northeast, has been known for centuries. The peoples of these areas made iron tools and weapons, sometimes of a high quality. Prospecting during colonial times revealed important deposits in three different provinces: the Ogooué-Ivindo (at Mékambo, Belinga, Boka-Boka, and Batoala); the Nyanga Province (at Tchibanga, its capital); the Woleu-N'Tem Province (at Minkébé). The deposits at Mékambo have a very high quality (65 percent iron), and the reserves are estimated at a billion tons. Exploitation was assigned in the 1950s to a consortium in which the Bethlehem Steel Company of the United States had a 50 percent share and French and German companies most of the rest. In 1974 the Gabonese state acquired 60 percent of the firm, the Société des Mines de Fer de Mékambo (SOMIFER). It expected to start production as soon as it could extend the Transgabonais from Booué on the middle Ogooué River northeast for 230 km. to reach the deposits. But by the time the railroad reached Booué in early 1983, funding for construction was lacking and world market conditions for iron unpromising, a situation that has persisted from that time. [929, 1364]

ISLAM. Whereas in the 1970s there were only a few Gabonese Muslims, by the mid-1980s Islamic sources estimated the numbers to be 3,700. At the same time, the numbers of non-Gabonese Muslims had grown from approximately 3,000 to an estimated 30,000. Islam until recently has been a religion of foreigners, mainly of the Senegalese troops imported to sustain French colonial rule from the nineteenth century and of the Hausa traders who arrived during the twentieth century. There is no evidence that either group actively sought to spread their Islamic faith to the Gabonese. Two noted Muslims, Sheikh Ahmadou Bamba, founder of the Mouride Sufic brotherhood in Senegal, and Samori Touré, who led resistance to the establishment of French rule in present-day Guinea and the Ivory Coast, spent years of exile in Gabon. Sheikh Ahmadou Bamba stayed at Lambaréné from 1895 to 1902, and Samori Touré at N'Djolé until his death in 1900. They do not seem to have spread Islam among the Gabonese of their vicinity, for the Moyen Ogooué Province where the two lived has only 50 Gabonese Muslims today. The largest numbers are found in the Estuary (1,000), N'Gounié (1,000), Nyanga (800), and Ogooué-Maritime (500) provinces. Three-quarters of all Gabonese Muslims are men, a situation that is not easy to explain. In 1973, President Albert-Bernard Bongo, during a visit to Libya, converted to Islam and took the name Omar. Though Bongo emphasized the personal nature of his conversion, thereafter he made official visits to a number of Arab states, and Gabon broke relations with Israel. Bongo also encouraged other prominent Gabonese to convert to Islam, which some in high places have done. (More common among the high officeholders is Masonry, which Bongo leads in Gabon and which he also encourages.)

Bongo's son Alain also became a Muslim and took the name Ali Bongo (q.v.). From 1989 to 1991 he served as Minister of Foreign Affairs. An uncle of the president, Al-hadi Mamadou Léo, who in 1927 was one of the first Gabonese converts to Islam, heads the Muslim community at Franceville.

President Bongo worships at a large mosque built by Morocco near his presidential palace in Libreville. Many Moroccans serve in the Presidential Guard, which protects the president. Saudi Arabia, the United Arab Emirates, and Khomeini's Iran have also contributed to the construction of mosques and classrooms. The largest of the two dozen mosques in Gabon are located at Libreville, Franceville, Port-Gentil, and Oyem. Connected with the mosques are madrasahs, schools that provide religious instruction in the afternoons for young people who attend the public schools in the mornings, as well as for adults.

Among the non-Gabonese Muslims, mainly from Senegal and Mali, the Mouride brotherhood has the largest following with the Tijani brotherhood second in influence. [1040, 285]

ISSEMBE, ARISTIDE (1910–). Civil servant and diplomat. Issembé was born at Libreville on December 20, 1910. His father, Jean-Rémy Issembé, a wealthy Mpongwe lumberman, sent him and his brother Emile (q.v.) to a lycée in Nice, France, where Aristide received his baccalaureate in 1932. The Issembé brothers and André-Gustave Anguilé (q.v.) were the only Gabonese to earn the *bac* during the inter-war period. Aristide Issembé spent four years studying law at the University of Paris, where he was the only Equatorial African to belong to Leopold Sédar Senghor's Association des Etudiants Ouest-Africains. Though a French citizen, he was refused entrance to the Colonial School, which trained the top-level overseas administrators. Upon his return to Gabon, he nevertheless was admitted to the European section of the federal civil service. He served in the financial branch at Bangui, Fort Lamy, and Ati (Chad) where he ran unsuccessfully for the Territorial Assembly. In 1949 he accepted an administrative assignment in Gabon. From 1957 to 1959 he served the first Gabonese executive, vice president of the government council, as *attaché de cabinet*. In 1959–1960 he represented Gabon as the Secretary-General of the French Community and in 1961–1962 became his country's first ambassador to France. In August 1964 he served as government prosecutor at the Lambaréné trials of the military rebels and provisional government members. After 1969 he served in ambassadorial posts, including in Canada during the late 1970s. [1367]

ISSEMBE, EMILE. Son of the wealthy Mpongwe lumberman, Jean-Rémy Issembé, Emile Issembé studied at the Ecole Montfort (q.v.) and earned the baccalaureate at Nice in 1932 at the same time as his younger brother Aristide (q.v.). He thereafter served, partly as a result of his French citizenship, in the European section of the federal civil service in Chad. During the Second World War, he fought with the Free French forces, including for a time in Cameroon. He became widely known throughout Equatorial Africa for his newspaper articles condemning racial discrimination. Without returning to Gabon, he ran unsuccessfully for the French National Assembly in the territory in November 1945. Then in February 1946 he assumed an important position in the political affairs division of the administration at Libreville. He joined the Groupe d'Etudes Communistes (q.v.) and the Parti Démocratique Africain (q.v.), which was affiliated with the inter-territorial Rassemblement Démocratique Africain. He was the PDA's unsuccessful candidate for the National Assembly in November 1945 and November 1946. The following month he failed to win election to the Territorial Assembly as part of a list in the N'Gounié Province. In 1949 he became president of the administration's cultural center in the capital. Between 1951 and 1959 he served at his own request in the administration of Ubangi-Shari (CAR) and Chad. Issembé organized the Parti de Défense des Institutions Démocratiques (PDID) to oppose President Léon Mba's policies in the parliamentary elections of April 12, 1964. Though the PDID received nearly half of the popular vote, because of the gerrymandering of the districts, it won only 16 out of the 47 seats. Its showing nevertheless was a moral victory for the opposition and the imprisoned leaders of the provisional government such as Jean-Hilaire Aubame. [550]

- J -

JAMES, BENJAMIN VAN RENSSALAER (1814–1869). First printer in Gabon. James was born on April 21, 1814, in Elizabethtown, New York, into an Afro-American family. He served in the ABCFM mission at Cape Palmas from 1836 to 1844 and at Baraka from 1844 to 1846. He helped to print the first works in Mpongwe. Ill health forced James's departure from Gabon. He settled in the Afro-American colony at Monrovia, Liberia, where he taught English and other subjects in a high school under the auspices of the American Presbyterian mission. [1031]

JEUNES GABONAIS (or JEUNESSE GABONAISE). The first Gabonese political party, which was founded around 1922, mainly by young educated Mpongwe and other Myènè at Libreville and Port-Gentil, to secure *évolué* participation in the management of public affairs. It launched the newspaper *L'Echo Gabonais* (1922–1932), which became *La Voix coloniale* at Nice in 1932. The paper contained articles on all of Africa as well as Gabon. Its criticisms of the decisions and practices of the colonial administration led to a crackdown by the latter in 1924 and its near extinction in 1926. The group and its local committees were also plagued by personal and ethnic antagonisms. Through its brief existence, it was closely allied with the Libreville branch of the Ligue des Droits de l'Homme, to which many of its members also belonged. The program of the Jeunes Gabonais was anticolonialist but not anti-French. The group sought assimilation of the évolués and the rights that such a status carried. It wanted the creation of secondary education in Gabon, which would facilitate further integration. It rejected both Garveyism and communism. [550]

- K -

KANIGUI (or AKANIGUI or BAKANIKE). The Kanigui are an Mbédé-speaking people who have villages northwest of Franceville and east of the Ogooué. Pushed eastward from the Middle Congo by the Mbochi, they crossed the Sébé River, where they found the Shaké (q.v.), and then went on to their present locations after fighting with the Ambamba, a subgroup of the Obamba (q.v.) people. [284]

KLAINE, THEOPHILE (1840–1911). Spiritan priest who taught school at St. Mary's near Libreville from 1865 to 1911, during much of which time he had charge of the lower primary grades. He was an amateur botanist who identified and raised several dozen species of fruits and flowers in an experimental garden with the aid of his pupils. The famous species of lightwood, okoumé (q.v.), was named *Aucoumeia klaineana* in his honor by a Parisian botanist. [1029, 1045]

- L -

LABOR UNIONS. It became legally possible for both European and African workers to join unions for the first time under the French law of August 7, 1944. The French organizational model was introduced into Gabon and French Equatorial Africa with local unions (*syndicats*) grouped by profession, trade, and industry into municipal, regional, or territorial organizations (*unions locales*). These organizations then combined at the territorial, federal,and inter-African levels, depending upon the size of their membership, and established ties with both French and international labor confederations. The formation of unions among both the European and African employees of the administration, commerce, transportation, and lumbering saw the divisions between Christian and Marxist elements in the French labor movement projected into the territory. Following the split within the Marxist ranks in 1947, there would be both Communist and Socialist unions in addition to Christian and independent ones in Gabon. These divisions weakened the effectiveness of the unions in securing greater benefits and improved working conditions for their members. So also did the failure of the French Parliament to enact an Overseas Labor Code to define the legal relationship between unions and employers and to establish minimum wages until 1952. In its absence the administration refused to bargain collectively with public employees and took sanctions against civil servants involved in strikes. The first collective agreements under the labor code were negotiated throughout the federation only in 1957. By then the overseas territories had headed along a path to self-government and independence that would lead to the restructuring of the unions at the national and inter-African levels. The presence of multiple unions with different inter-African and international ties would persist until April 1969. At that time the government abolished all existing unions and created a single national confederation that would later become a special organ of the single political party.

The first union in Gabon was organized with the

encouragement of the missions on August 9, 1944, by Félix Adandé [a cousin of Prince Félix Adandé (q.v.)] among the Myènè employees of the administration to press for better salaries and working conditions. Called the Syndicat des Employés de Libreville, in 1946 it formed with other unions of a Christian orientation the Union Territoriale des Syndicats CFTC affiliated with the metropolitan Confédération Française des Travailleurs Chrétiens (CFTC). Concerned about the African direction of the organization and its militancy, the administration sponsored the formation of biracial unions affiliated with the French Marxist Confédération Générale du Travail (CGT). Among them by the end of 1945 were the Syndicat des Employés du Gouvernement of which Frédéric Moreau served as secretary and a union of private employees headed by Georges Damas (q.v.). The Union des Syndicats Confédérés (USC) included these unions and several others of CGT affiliation with Damas as secretary-general. Damas attended the first African conference of the CGT at Dakar in 1946. The CFTC and CGT unions joined forces in 1946–1947 in order to present a united front toward the administration through the Cartel des Syndicats with Paul Taty of the CGT, a civil servant, as secretary-general. When the administration refused to negotiate with the Cartel, its members launched a strike at Libreville and Port-Gentil in June 1947. The administration broke the strike by pressuring Taty to resign and by transferring other strike leaders to remote posts. The administration persuaded Félix Adandé's employer to transfer him to Port-Gentil. Also in 1947 the French CGT split, with its Communists retaining control of the organization and the Socialists forming the rival CGT-Force Ouvrière. In Gabon the CGT-FO was mainly an organization of European civil servants. The Africans in the CGT unions either remained with the older body or followed the USC into autonomy when in December 1948 Damas at the administration's request broke its CGT ties. When Frédéric Moreau decided to remain with the CGT, he was ousted from the civil service. Though the Overseas Labor Code legalized public employee membership in unions and collective bargaining, the Marxist unions never recovered from the administration's repression.

Throughout the period 1944 to 1969 the Christian unions

remained the strongest in the country. They had 3,000 members in 1953 and 13,500 in 1965. They promoted the social doctrines of the Roman Catholic Church and had considerable mission sympathy but remained under African direction. Between 1946 and 1960 they held annual congresses and study sessions to educate their membership. With the coming of self-government, the CFTC unions of the federation organized the Confédération Générale Aéfienne du Travail (CGAT) at Point-Noire, Congo, in 1957. The Union Territoriale des Syndicats CFTC thereafter was renamed Union Nationale des Syndicats Croyants (the "Croyants" in order to attract non-Christian believers), and in 1966 it became the Union Gabonaise des Syndicats Croyants (UGSC). Internationally these bodies affiliated with the International Federation of Christian Trade Unions. In 1964, after the French military restored President Mba (q.v.) to power, the Christian unions launched a general strike to protest Mba's manner of rule. Their action resulted in no political changes, but led to higher minimum salaries. The leaders of the UNSC between 1957 and 1966 were Auguste Walker-Anguilet, secretary-general, a member of the Economic and Social Council; Bernard Ntoutoume and A. Richard N'Zoghi, both employees of the Société Pétrolifière de l'Afrique Equatoriale; and Moise N'Dong, a teacher in the private schools. At the congress of 1966, when the UNSC became the UGSC, Moise N'Dong became secretary-general. The following year, N'Zoghi, who had served as *chef de cabinet* in Aubame's ministry in 1961–1963, went into voluntary exile in Europe.

With the coming of self-government, the CGT unions linked with the inter-African Confédération Générale Africaine du Travail (CGAT) between 1957 and 1962 and retained ties with the World Federation of Trade Unions. They were strongest at Libreville and Port-Gentil. In 1953 they had 1,700 members and in 1960, 3,000. Their most important leaders were Augustin Anguilet and Leon Dicky. From 1961 on, some of the CGAT leaders were in jail, charged with civil offenses, while others entered the BDG and abandoned syndicalist activities.

A third labor organization, the Confédération Nationale des Travailleurs Gabonais (CNTG), was created in 1962 and affiliated with the International Confederation of Free Trade Unions (founded in 1949 by Socialists opposing Communist domination of the World Federation of Trade Unions). Leaders of the CNTG were Laurent Essone, an employee of the CFAO, and Pierre N'Kogho, a public school teacher. Its influence extended throughout Gabon and was strongest at Libreville, Port-Gentil, and Franceville. It had 4,500 members in 1962 and 6,800 in 1969.

After the government organized a single political party, the PDG, to work for national unity and construction, in April 1969 it summoned delegates of the CATC, CGAT, and CNTG to form a single national labor federation, the Fédération Syndicale Gabonaise (FESYGA), which in 1973 became a special organ of the party. The FESYGA leaders were required to pursue the interests of the workers within the guidelines set forth by the party. Beginning in 1973 the government became more directly involved in the negotiations between the FESYGA and the organization representing private employers, UNIGABON. At the same time, divisions in the FESYGA's leadership led to its greater involvement in the selection of the organization's executive bureau and officers. Wildcat strikes by dissatisfied workers at various times, including 1975–1976, suggested the difficulties of the leaders effectively to represent the membership in such a framework. Secretary-General of the FESYGA in the late 1970s was Gaston Indassy-Gnambault and president Goba Wora.

The economic expansion linked with the oil boom of the 1970s and early 1980s brought thousands more European technicians and managers and tens of thousands of additional non-Gabonese African laborers into the country. Their presence diluted the influence of the Gabonese within the labor unions, making it more difficult for them to exert pressure on the government to secure material improvements and redress of grievances. Government requirements that Gabonese workers be paid more than foreigners benefited those who had employment. But they encouraged private employers to give preference to foreigners in hiring and retention.

During the 1980s FESYGA became COSYGA (the Confédération Syndicale Gabonaise). In 1990 Martin Allini was serving as president. During the protests against government austerity policies in the late 1980s and early 1990s, officers of COSYGA locals began to side with the workers against the government. Among the demands of protesters and strikers during the upheaval of 1990 was the right to form unions independent of government control. Those who seized the initiative, such as petroleum industry workers and university teachers, were unable at first to gain official recognition of their independent unions as bargaining agents. Then on June 6, 1991, the National Assembly passed a law restoring the right to strike and liberalizing the process for creating new labor unions. [599, 578, 550]

LANGUAGES. The official language of Gabon and the medium of instruction is French. Prior to the Second World War only a tiny portion of the population received instruction in French, but most persons employed in the market sector of the economy or by the administration learned to speak the language. In the period after the Second World War, France sought to achieve universal primary education in Africa. While a majority of young people were eventually enrolled, the average child remained only two or three years and thus did not learn French well. The 1960–1961 census revealed that only 47 percent of those over fourteen years of age spoke French, 76 percent of the males and 26 percent of the females. Only 23 percent of the males and 5 percent of the females were literate in French, that is, 13 percent of the adult population. By the early 1970s as a result of intensified efforts, including adult education, an estimated 25 percent of those over fourteen were literate, and in 1990 60 percent.

Since independence Gabon has nearly achieved universal primary education. At the same time, several thousand persons, who have obtained secondary or higher education, have learned French very well. They form part of an international Francophone elite that can communicate with the educated classes in other formerly French African states.

The indigenous languages of Gabon are Bantu, thus part of the larger group that encompasses most of central and southern Africa. They were introduced into Gabon perhaps 2,000 years ago and were further developed and differentiated there. The Bantu tongues were spoken but not written. Christian missionaries from the United States and France transcribed various languages such as Mpongwe, Dikèlè, Benga, and Fang using the Latin alphabet from the 1840s on. They translated the Bible and prepared mainly religious materials in them. French colonial policy discouraged or prevented the use of African languages for anything but religious purposes, especially beginning in the 1880s. At the same time, it promoted the study and use of the French language. Thus the Bantu languages have tended to remain mainly spoken languages transmitted in the family and not studied at school. Many Africans, especially in urban areas or in regions where many peoples are in contact, learn to communicate in several Bantu languages.

During the 1970s the government of Gabon sponsored research on indigenous languages within the Ministry of Education and at the National University. It is possible that some of these languages may eventually be used in primary instruction or studied at the primary and secondary levels. It is very unlikely that the government would seek to adopt one particular language as a national language as has been done elsewhere in Africa or Asia or that it would abandon instruction in French for its educated elite.

The 1960–1961 census indicated the following distribution of Bantu languages for those fourteen years of age or older. It omitted the Bakouélé, who were classified for some reason as Apindji, Bakèlè or Bakota. (For the peoples within the groups, *see* PEOPLES.) [1225, 1227, 1228, 1219, 65]

Group	Percentage
Omyènè	5.0
Séké	1.9
Eshira	22.0
Okandé	4.0
Bakèlè	2.0
Fang	31.0
Bakota	6.0
Mbédé	25.0
Téké	0.5
Vili	0.5

LAWLIN, CAPTAIN RICHARD E. (d. 1861). Lawlin was the leading American trader on the northern coasts from 1830 to 1861. He aided the ABCFM missionaries to locate in the Estuary in June 1842 and befriended them thereafter. But he undermined their work through the sale of rum. As the representative of various Yankee firms, he purchased ivory and rubber between the Rio Muni and Fernan-Vaz. In 1854 Lawlin received the island Adjanga on which he established a factory called "Brooklyn" from the Nkomi chief, King Rotimbo. While purchasing rubber, he undertook extensive plantations to try to develop a greater taste for commercial agriculture among the Nkomi (q.v.). They regarded him as a benevolent father and made his burial place a kind of sacred site. [300, 394]

LE BERRE, PIERRE-MARIE (1819–1891). Cofounder of the French Roman Catholic mission and second bishop. Born at Neuillac, Brittany, in the Vannes diocese on August 1, 1819, Monsignor Le Berre evangelized in Gabon from May 1846 until his death on July 16, 1891. He headed the Holy Ghost Fathers (q.v.) community near Libreville from 1859 and was named bishop in September 1877. Bishop Le Berre became an expert in the Mpongwe (q.v.) language. He prepared an excellent Mpongwe grammar and gave sermons in Mpongwe in St. Mary's Church. He initiated the second period of Catholic expansion by establishing missions among the Fang (q.v.) of the upper Estuary (1878), the Galoa (q.v.) and Fang around Lambaréné on the Ogooué (1881), and at several new points on the coasts and in the interior during the following decade. [1002, 1045]

LE COUR, CAPTAIN A. A French trader along the West African coast from 1823 and a member of the Chamber of Commerce of Nantes, Captain Le Cour attempted to grow cotton on lands of the Asiga clan of the Mpongwe (q.v.) under terms of the commercial treaty of April 4, 1844, between France and King Denis (q.v.). Denis was to provide the necessary labor. Experiments with varieties of wild cotton found in Gabon as well as with rubber, peanuts, sugar cane, and touloucouna were successful. But Le Cour failed to obtain expected subsidies from the French government, and Denis not only failed to provide labor but discouraged his people from working for the captain. Le Cour with the help of Captain J.-B. Amouroux obtained a commercial treaty with Chief Quaben or Kaka-Rapono (q.v.) in March 1846, securing land near Fort d'Aumale. He encountered some success raising coffee there, but mismanagement by his local French agents caused the failure of this attempt as well. [252]

LE ROY, ALEXANDRE (1854–1938). Spiritan priest who as vicar apostolic of Gabon from 1892 to 1896 insisted upon teaching the Gabonese children to read the catechism in their own language before teaching them French, which went counter to the official government policy of the day. Le Roy continued the Catholic advance into the interior by founding several new stations and by developing the work of the catechists who resided in the villages. While superior-general of the Holy Ghost Fathers, he wrote influential works on the Pygmies and primitives as well as the sections on Gabon and the Congo in Piolet's history of the missions (1902). [1302, 1041, 1042]

LIBREVILLE. The capital of Gabon and its largest city is located on the northern shore of the Estuary. In 1991 its population was estimated at more than 300,000. Exact figures are not available in the absence of an accurate census and fluctuations in the numbers of foreigners since the economic downturn that began in 1986. In the mid-1950s Libreville had a population of 18,000 of whom 1,500 were Europeans; in 1960–1961, 44,598; in 1970–1971, an estimated 167,394. Most of the country's more than 20,000 French (down from 26,000 in 1985) live in the Libreville area as do the bulk of the more than 100,000 non-Gabonese Africans.

Libreville (which means free town or city in French) takes its name from the settlement organized by the French navy in August 1849 for 50 freed adult slaves and two children of Vili (q.v.) origin from the Congo who had been rescued several years before from the slaving ship *Elizia*. The slaves had been taken in May 1846 to Gorée, Senegal. In Gabon they were given plots of land and huts between the lands of the Mpongwe (q.v.) clans, the Agekaza-Glass and Agekaza-Quaben. The French post, which was moved in 1850 to higher ground nearby (the so-called Plateau), the residence of the Sisters of the Immaculate Conception (q.v.), and St. Peter's Church also came to be known under the name Libreville, and ultimately the name was applied to all the settlements on the right bank of the Estuary above Owendo. Libreville at first served as the capital of the French Congo until it was moved to Brazzaville in 1904. Libreville remained the administrative capital of Gabon and an important commercial center.

Today, most of Gabon's imports arrive at Libreville and its port of Owendo, while at least half of the manganese and some of its timber are exported from there. During the years of the oil boom, Libreville acquired many multi-story buildings, which radically changed its traditional skyline of low-lying structures amid clusters of palm trees. [940, 926, 924, 251, 295, 756, 782, 921]

LIGUE DES DROITS DE L'HOMME, LIBREVILLE BRANCH. Civil servants from Guadeloupe and Martinique were instrumental in founding branches of a French civil liberties organization, the League of Human Rights, in various African colonies, including Gabon, in 1918. The presidency was vested in an educated Séké, Jean-Baptiste N'Dendé (q.v.), and most of its members were young educated Mpongwe (q.v.). Among the most active members were Mpongwe who had served as non-commissioned officers at Libreville or in the French campaigns against the Germans in northern Gabon and Cameroon, 1914–1916. Among them were Louis Bigmann (q.v.) and his cousin Laurent Antchouey (q.v.). Antchouey articulated Ligue issues in the monthly paper *l'Echo Gabonais* from Dakar and Nice, France, between 1922 and 1926. The most important figure in the Ligue between 1926 and 1930 was François-de-Paul Vané (q.v.), a Benga whose family was long settled in Libreville. In 1930 the Ligue presidency was transferred through trickery to a Frenchman who put an end to its anti-colonialist agitation. Among the issues in which the Libreville branch was active were: an appeal for the return of the Brothers of Saint Gabriel (q.v.), who had provided the highest level and quality of education before their departure in 1918 (they returned in 1924); demand for autonomy of Gabon within the federation of French Equatorial Africa (q.v.) in view of the situation where taxes on okoumé were being used to support the other territories instead of to develop Gabon; defense of traditional land rights in the courts in face of administrative encroachment and failure to provide just compensation (the decree of March 28, 1899, establishing the concessionary system had denied the existence of African property rights and had given the administration the power to control all land); demand for the end of the *indigénat* (q.v.), which had been extended to Gabon in 1910.

Among the early members of the Ligue were Antoine M'Ba, Ignace Békalé, N'Tutume Ossame, Maurice N'Gôme Obiang, Victor Obame Otsague, Paulin N'Dinga, Martin Tambané, Jean-Remy Issembé, and Léon Mba (q.v.). After 1930 the former Ligue members split between *métis* (q.v.) and full-blooded Africans in their pursuit of elite interests throughout separate organizations. [550]

LOANGO. A centralized kingdom of the Vili (q.v.) people dating from the late fourteenth or early fifteenth centuries. Its core was located in the coastal areas of today's Congo Republic but its sway extended south into the Cabinda enclave (today part of Angola) and north into present-day Gabon. Loango's sway encompassed the Ngowe (q.v.) people at Lake Iguéla, the Loumbou (q.v.) at Setté-Cama and around Mayumba, as well as some Vili along the Banio Lagoon. Though Loango's political control of the Gabon coast was only nominal, trading networks centered at Loango Bay persisted into the twentieth century. Under French colonial rule economic activity on the Loango coast was transferred to Pointe-Noire where a modern harbor was built. Pointe-Noire became the terminus of the Congo-Ocean Railroad, completed in 1934, and the point for the penetration of French Equatorial Africa. [326, 384, 846, 217]

LOUIS, KING or ANGUILE DOWE or RE-DOWE (ca. 1800–1867). Louis, the Mpongwe village headman of the Agekaza-Quaben or Agekaza w'Anwondo clan, through the treaty of March 18, 1842, ceded sovereignty over his territories on the northern shore of the Estuary to the French. He also gave them the lands on which they built their post, Fort d'Aumale, in June 1843, and the Holy Ghost Fathers (q.v.) constructed St. Mary's Church and other buildings at the village of Okolo. Louis was the nephew of King Quaben or Kaka-Rapono (q.v.) (d. 1863), head of the clan. Though a relatively weak underling of King Quaben before 1842, Louis's openness to France increased his influence immensely in the next two decades. He served on the French commission for arbitrating trade disputes. It was composed of two African traders and a French merchant who served as its president. [252, 254, 362, 394]

LOUIS BERRE MONGUITIGANA, PRINCE (1906–ca. 1974). Prince Louis Berre was a direct descendant of King Louis Dowe (q.v.), who made the treaty of 1842 with the French, which gave them the land on which they built their first fort. Louis Berre worked as an artisan. During the 1930s he became active in the movements to assert traditional Mpongwe rights, including to lands in the Estuary. With the support of the Comité Mpongwe (q.v.) he was named *chef de groupe de quartier* of the Louis section of Libreville and later sat on the governor's administrative council. In August 1958 he became active in the Parti d'Union Nationale Gabonaise (PUNGA) (q.v.), which advocated a negative vote in the referendum of September 1958 on membership in the French Community. At that time he asked for strict application of the treaties, which the Mpongwe had made with the French between 1839 and 1848. He was subsequently removed from his chiefship by the government. [550, 593, 598]

LOUMBOU or BALOUMBOU. A people of the southwest (Nyanga Province) whose territories were under the sway of the Vili kingdom of Loango (q.v.) through the nineteenth century. According to tradition the Loumbou came from Mongo near present-day Pointe-Noire in the Congo Republic via the savanna (grasslands) many centuries ago. They settled as far north as the marshy coastal areas of the Ndugu Lagoon (Setté-Cama); in the coastal savannas from Banio Lagoon north to a point beyond the Nyanga River; inland in the forested Mayombe mountain chain (300 to 600 meters above sea level), and in the savannas beyond this range, south of the Nyanga. The coastal Loumbou evaporated seawater to obtain salt for trade with the interior. The coming of the Europeans in the 1480s saw the inhabitants of Setté-Cama selling ivory and beeswax and those of Mayumba ivory and a redwood that was much sought after by both Europeans and Africans for its valuable red dye. In the sixteenth and seventeenth centuries Setté-Cama and Mayumba sent the small numbers of slaves they obtained from interior peoples to Loango. Neither place became very important in the greatly expanded slave trade centered on Loango during the eighteenth century.

The Loango kingdom, whose core lay north of the Congo River, held sway over the Gabon coast as far north as Cape St. Catherine. The various clans of the Loumbou apparently acknowledged the nominal overlordship of its Vili (q.v.) rulers and until the late eighteenth century paid them tribute. The Loumbou themselves had only territorial chiefs, called "kings" by European traders, whose main function was to settle disputes among the clans. According to tradition, during the 1760s a Vili princess called Nsoami fled from her home at Loango and established an independent kingdom among the Vili and Loumbou at Mayumba, until that time a northern province of Loango. Despite its origins, the kingdom in the late nineteenth century seems to have had a Loumbou king called Mayombo Ignondrou. His authority extended over the areas of Setté-Cama, the Mayombe mountains, and Mayumba, which had a population of 1,000 at that time, a good-sized town.

Between the 1840s and 1870s Anglo-French suppression of the slave trade in the Gabon Estuary and around Cape Lopez helped to make the Mayumba area the scene of increased slave trading under the auspices of Portuguese, Spanish, and Brazilian merchants. But by 1873 rubber had become the most important export from Mayumba, an activity from which both Loumbou and Vili traders profited. [284, 326, 384]

- M -

MADEMOISELLE. Mademoiselle is an antiwitchcraft movement that apparently was introduced into several regions of Gabon from the Middle Congo in the 1940s and acquired some importance in the 1950s. It achieved its greatest following among the Fang in the Woleu N'Tem Province but encountered strong opposition from the colonial administration and the missions. Mademoiselle, like Bwiti, can be viewed as an attempt by Gabonese to deal with the rapidly changing conditions resulting from a deterioration of traditional ethnic structures and the acculturation resulting from colonial rule. [617]

MAGANGA-MOUSSAVOU, PIERRE-CLAVER (1952–). Former presidential adviser. Maganga-Moussavou was born on April 8, 1952, at Mouila in the N'Gounié Province. After studies in economics and history at the University of Upper Brittany in Rennes, he completed his doctorate in history at the University of Paris. Thereafter he became an adviser to President Bongo. As a result of his study of French public aid to Gabon between 1960 and 1978, he urged the government to rethink the economic and financial aspects of its relationship with France. He advocated a lessening of the dependence on France for investment capital, technical and administrative expertise, and a diversification of its external ties, including expanded ones with the United States. At the congress of the Parti Social Démocratique, of which Maganga-Moussavou is president, in April 1992 he was selected as the group's candidate for president in the December 1993 elections. His wife, who is the party's vice president, is the group's only deputy in the National Assembly. [490, 491]

MAHONGWE. The Mahongwé people belong to the Bakota linguistic group. They inhabit the southern part of the Mékambo Prefecture, Ogooué-Ivindo Province. The Mahongwé originally occupied the junction of the Ivindo and the Mouniangui Rivers. Poupou's War in the nineteenth century caused them to flee to the northeast, some toward Okondja, others toward the Louaï and Liboumba Rivers. [365, 284]

MAKOUAKA, FELICIEN-PATRICE (1922–). Monsignor Makouaka is the first Catholic bishop of the diocese of Franceville, which was created on October 5, 1974. He was born at Ngomo-Boulongo in the diocese of Mouila in 1922. Following seven years of study at the major seminary in Brazzaville, he was ordained a priest on October 10, 1954. For the next 20 years he worked in clergy formation, school administration, and the pastory ministry. Thus from 1954 to 1957 he taught at the Seminary of Saint-Jean in Libreville. From 1957 to 1961 he was vicar at N'Dendé and director of the Catholic schools. After teaching in the seminary at Mouila during 1962–1963, he became vicar of Tchibanga (1963–1965), director of schools in the diocese of Mouila (1966–1969), and director of Catholic schools throughout Gabon (1969–1974). [988, 1021]

MANGANESE. Exploitation of manganese began in 1962 around Moanda in the Haut-Ogooué Province under the auspices of the Compagnie Minière de l'Ogooué (COMILOG). COMILOG had been organized several years earlier when France changed its policy of reserving its overseas territories for French investors and sought foreign partners in order to promote more rapid development. United States Steel originally owned 49 percent of the company and French interests the rest. In 1974 the Gabonese state acquired a share. By 1988 the ownership had become still more diversified. US Steel had 36.4 percent of COMILOG's shares; the Gabonese state, 30 percent; COFRAMINES of France, 17.6 percent; SAMAF of the Netherlands, 7.1 percent; Elkem of Norway, 5.7 percent; and Imetal from France, 3.2 percent. COMILOG, in turn, owned 10 percent of Elkem, a producer of ferroalloys.

Gabon's reserves, which are estimated at more than 200 million tons, have an average manganese content of 50 percent, which permits the production of the purest natural manganese dioxide in the world. Since the 1960s Gabon has been the fourth largest producer of manganese globally, over 2,500,000 tons in 1989, that is, more than one-third of the output of the non-Communist world. Stagnant market conditions during the late 1980s caused COMILOG to undertake changes that will reduce extraction costs and improve the quality of the ore. While continuing to export chiefly to the United States, France, Germany, and Japan, it sought to diversify its trading partners. Thus in 1989 it was exporting 10 percent of its output to the Soviet Union and smaller amounts to China and the Philippines. In 1991 COMILOG purchased the Belgian firm of Sadachem, which produces metallic oxides and salts. Sadachem, a leading supplier of manganese by-products for dry cell electric batteries and cathode ray tubes, also sells derivatives to agro-business and petroleum companies.

From the start of production, the ore was evacuated via an aerial cable line (*téléférique*) that carries buckets of the metal. It was constructed for this purpose over a distance of 76 km. to M'Binda in the Congo Republic. At M'Binda the Congo-Ocean Railroad transports the ore 85 km. farther west to its Atlantic terminus at Point-Noire. These arrangements, which were planned when Gabon formed part of the federation of French Equatorial Africa, have made its government dependent upon the Congo. In order to lessen this dependence and to permit the expansion of production, Gabon built the Transgabonais Railroad from the port of Owendo on the Estuary to Moanda between 1974 and 1986. COMILOG itself constructed a minerals terminal in the port, independent of the commercial facilities. Its completion in December 1988 thus permits exportation of manganese via the Transgabonais. But for the time being Gabon continues to evacuate half of the ore via the Congo. [780, 1364]

MAPAKO-GNALI, HERVE. Ponty School graduate and teacher. Mapako-Gnali belonged to a Vili (q.v.) family from Diosso on the Loango coast, some of whom were settled at Libreville in the period when their homeland formed part of Gabon. As one of the two most promising graduates of the public school in 1914, he was sent, along with Jean-Félix Tchicaya (q.v.), on government scholarship to the William Ponty School at Dakar to prepare to be an upper-primary teacher. At Ponty he was in the same class as Félix Houphouet-Boigny and Mambo Sano, and one year behind Mamadou Konaté, all future deputies in the French National Assembly. Mapako-Gnali in 1921 on his return to Libreville was appointed to the teaching staff of the public primary school. [550]

MASSANGO (or SANGOU). The Massango people, who are linguistically related to the Eshira (q.v.), inhabit a forested mountainous area of the south-central interior between the Ogoulou and Offoué Rivers. Their traditions assert a common origin with the Eshira. While the Eshira migrated toward the coast, they stayed in the interior but later transferred a bit westward to seek warmer temperatures. In the nineteenth century the Bakèlè (q.v.) made war upon them. The Massango exchanged slaves, palm cloth, iron utensils, and weapons for salt from the Bapounou.

In September 1917 a Massango called Mabiale Mabioko died in a French prison, having been jailed for what the administration judged to be the slave trade. This sparked a revolt by men who considered themselves protected from the French guns by a supernatural power. The Massango leaders organized 36 villages to fight the French and gained support among the Mitsogo (q.v.), Bakèlè, and smaller groups. The French were able to suppress the revolt only in 1918–1919 after the death of its main leader, Mayambo. [284, 201]

MBA, GERMAIN (1932–1971). Diplomat. Mba, a relative of Léon Mba, was born at Libreville on December 15, 1932. He graduated from the Institut d'Études Politiques of the University of Paris and the École Nationale des Douanes et de Législation Financière de Paris at Neuilly. Between 1962 and 1964 he served as Assistant Secretary-General of the Union Africaine et Malgache at Cotonou, Benin. He resigned this position in protest against the de Gaulle government's intervention to restore Léon Mba (q.v.) to power in February 1964. He went to Brazzaville where he helped to organize an opposition movement, first called the Mouvement Gabonais d'Action Populaire and then converted into the Mouvement de Libération Nationale du Gabon. After being expelled from the Congo, he took refuge in Kinshasa, where the Zairian authorities imprisoned him for a year. Thereafter in 1965 he became deputy editor-in-chief of *Jeune-Afrique* in Paris. Along with Mba-Ndong he protested the amendment of the constitution creating the post of Vice President of the Republic in November 1966. But after the death of Léon Mba, he rallied to the regime and in September 1968 was named economic and commercial counsellor to President Bongo.

Between 1969 and 1971 he held a number of diplomatic posts in Europe including that of ambassador to the German Federal Republic. On September 16, 1971, during a visit to Libreville before assuming a new post as ambassador to Japan, he was kidnapped and probably murdered by unidentified assailants believed to be Frenchmen. His body was never found. Pierre Péan attributes his death to the French mercenary, Bob Denard, acting on orders from Omar Bongo, who allegedly saw Mba as a dangerous rival. [599, 603, 1367]

MBA, LEON (1902–1967). Fang (q.v.) leader, first prime minister and first president of the republic (1961–1967). Mba was born at Libreville on February 9, 1902, the son of a Fang village chief. His older brother, the Abbé Jean Obame, was the first Fang to be ordained a Roman Catholic priest. The numerous Fang immigrant population of the Estuary were both held in low esteem and feared by the native Mpongwe (q.v.) and by the colonial administration in this period. At the same time they were being actively evangelized by both Catholic and Protestant missions. Léon Mba was educated in Catholic primary schools, including the Ecole Montfort (q.v.) at Libreville. Thereafter he entered the service of the colonial administration in various humble positions, including interpreter.

In the early 1920s Mba became active in the Libreville

branch of the Ligue des Droits de l'Homme. He joined the Jeunes Gabonais or Jeunesse Gabonaise (q.v.) and contributed articles to its newspaper, *L'Echo Gabonais*. He showed determination to improve both the status of the *évolués* and the Fang in relation to the Myènè (q.v.) populations with whom they frequently were disputing land rights. Mba often wrote letters for illiterate Fang who wished to protest against various administrative practices or to make requests and thereby incurred the suspicion of the administration.

In 1922 he was condemned for an offense on apparently slim evidence and fined. In December of the same year he was imprisoned arbitrarily under the *indigénat* (q.v.) for 15 days, where someone reportedly tried to poison him. But Governor-General Victor Augagneur attributed his troubles to the dislike of the governor of Gabon and came to his defense in 1922.

In the meantime Mba was becoming a specialist in Fang customary law and was frequently being called to adjudicate disputes and to give expert advice in proceedings before the customary tribunal. In 1924 the administration named Mba the Fang canton chief (*chef de canton*) at Libreville instead of Ndongo-Edzo, the son of his predecessor. But he thereafter became unpopular with elements of the administration for denouncing, in the name of the Ligue, the murder of a Gabonese by the French administrator heading the post at Akok. Mba's rigorous execution of the administration's orders made him unpopular with some of the Fang, who held him responsible for recruiting forced labor. Mba reportedly joined the Freemasons with the aid of administrators from the Antilles working in Gabon. He also encouraged the spread of Bwiti as a means of revitalizing shattered Fang society and of gaining increased authority among the Fang. He thus incurred the hostility of the mission authorities. In 1931 Mba was charged with having a role in the ritual murder of two young Fang women and the sale of their flesh in the Libreville market, human flesh being required in certain Bwiti (q.v.) ceremonies. His conviction in 1933 resulted at least as much from the hostility of the various groups he had antagonized, some of whom may have given false testimony against him, as from the evidence presented by the prosecution.

Mba was sentenced to three years in prison, spent at Birao in the Ubangi-Shari, and 10 years at Bambari in the same colony, where he remained until 1946. There he became the trusted financial agent of the administration and in August 1940 rallied to Free France. He wrote an authoritative study on Fang customs. Upon his return to Libreville in 1946 he worked for the John Holt Company and later for SE-PEMIAG. Though not a Communist, he joined the local Groupe d'Etudes Communistes (q.v.), an agency for political education that was both anti-colonialist and comparatively radical. The candidate that the GEC supported in the November 1946 elections for the French National Assembly was defeated by Jean-Hilaire Aubame (q.v.), a young Fang *évolué* who had been the protégé of Mba's priest brother and whom Mba had aided in securing employment in the colonial administration. Aubame had the support of the administration and missions as well as the northern Fang and non-Fang notables throughout the interior regions. Aubame thereafter organized the Union Démocratique et Sociale Gabonaise (q.v.) for purposes of presenting candidates for the Territorial Assembly. In early 1947 Mba and other Estuary Fang, most of whom belonged to the GEC, had formed the Comité Mixte Gabonais (q.v.), a more militant and radical anti-colonialist party, which affiliated with the inter-territorial Rassemblement Démocratique Africain. The RDA in this period was Communist-advised and linked in the French Parliament with the French Communist Party, which until March 1947 had ministers in the government. The colonial administration severely weakened the Comité Mixte Gabonais by transferring most of its members, who were civil servants, to distant points in the interior. In the meantime at the Pahouin or Fang Congress, which the administration organized at Mitzic in February 1947 to discuss Fang problems, Mba played an important role. Though the Congress was largely composed of officially appointed chiefs and local Assembly members, Mba convinced them to take some positions at odds with official wishes. He emerged from the Congress as a progres-

sive, authoritative leader with influence among both tradi-
tionalist and modernist elements. In 1951 he went along with
the RDA majority in its break with French Communism and
thereafter moderated his militant stances. He rebaptized his
Comité Mixte Gabonais as the Comité Mixte Franco-
Gabonais to point out that his orientation was not anti-
French. He failed, however, in his bid to replace Aubame as
deputy in the French National Assembly during the elections
of June 1951. Later in 1951 Mba joined forces with Senator
Paul Gondjout (q.v.), a Myènè in the Territorial Assembly,
and various southerners to oppose Aubame and his party (the
UDSG), which they accused of representing only the inter-
ests of the northern Fang. Mba, Gondjout, and Aubame all
won seats in the Territorial Assembly in the elections of
March 1952. In 1954 Gondjout organized a new party, the
Bloc Démocratique Gabonais (q.v.), to which Mba later
adhered and of which he became the secretary.

The BDG, which was avowedly antitribalist, failed to
prevent Aubame's reelection to the National Assembly in
January 1956 in which he again defeated Mba. But it helped
to secure the election of Mba as mayor of Libreville in
November 1956 following a reform that increased the powers of the elected representatives. The mayor's position
enabled Mba to place his allies and supporters in key
positions in the city government.

In the wake of the Loi-Cadre of June 23, 1956, Gabon
acquired a Territorial Assembly with some real legislative
powers and a Government Council in which Africans held
executive posts for the first time. While the elections of March
1957 gave the UDSG a majority of the popular votes, it gave
the BDG and Independents a majority of seats in the Territorial
Assembly. It enabled them to name Mba as the vice president
of the 12-member Government Council (the governor was the
president). Later in July 1958 Mba replaced the governor as
president of the council. The BDG's control of eight out of the
12 ministries presented the opportunity for placing its supporters throughout the administration. Prior to the 1957 elections,
important French lumbering firms had shifted their support
from the UDSG to the BDG whose attitudes about their
interests seemed to be more advantageous.

In the aftermath of the May 1958 revolution in Algiers, which led to the demise of the Fourth Republic and the return to power of De Gaulle, both the UDSG and the BDG supported Gabon's membership in the general's Community in the referendum of September 1958. Both parties also favored the establishment of a republic within the Community in November of that year. Thus Mba became the first prime minister under the new constitution of February 19, 1959, leading a government that contained ministers of both parties. During the 18 months of the operation of that constitution, friction developed between the executive and the legislative, with Gondjout and a majority of both the BDG and the UDSG supporting a strong parliament and a weak executive. Mba and his ministers were forced to accept an essentially parliamentary constitution for the independent republic on November 3, 1960. But ultimately these arrangements proved unworkable and after further conflicts, in which Mba utilized emergency powers against the Gondjout faction and ordered new Assembly elections, he secured the new constitution of February 17, 1961, establishing a strong presidency.

For the next two years Mba pursued a policy of national unity aimed at bringing all elements into cooperation with the government. Aubame and Gondjout and their followers were brought into the government or given responsible positions in the civil service. René-Paul Sousatte (q.v.), who in 1958 had organized a third party to oppose the Community, was awarded a ministerial post. Early in 1963 Mba sought to institute a single-party regime by forcing all of these elements to join the BDG and to accept his dominant role in that party and in the government. His actions provoked resistance and in their turn repression and new conflicts, which culminated in the coup of February 17–20, 1964 (q.v.). The coup, which toppled Mba, led to French intervention to restore him. Mba's determination to punish those opponents whom he held responsible, rightly or wrongly, even in the face of much popular discontent, led to an increasingly authoritarian regime, the violation of civil liberties, and ultimately to the end of the democratic experiment in Gabon. Holding close to absolute power and backed by French forces, a terminally ill Mba chose a talented and loyal young administrator, Albert-Bernard Bongo (q.v.), to be his successor. In November 1966 he replaced Vice President Paul-Marie Yembit (q.v.) with Bongo and then advanced the date of the presidential elections to March 1967 so that Bongo was elected as vice president and successor at the time of his own reelection as president. During the last year of his life Mba remained in Paris for medical treatment and died there on November 27, 1967. *See* COUP OF FEBRUARY 17–20, 1964; DECOLONIZATION; FOREIGN RELATIONS; POLITICS. [550, 551, 617, 593, 569, 536, 65]

MBA-ABESSOLÉ, PAUL (1939–). Leader of MORENA. The Reverend Paul Mba was born in the Estuary Province on October 9, 1939. He is a relative of the late President Léon Mba and former Prime Minister Léon Mebiame. Father Mba received his early education in Catholic schools. After joining the Holy Ghost Fathers (Spiritans) (q.v.), he studied theology at their major seminary in Chevilly, south of Paris. Following ordination in 1968, he held posts in Gabon until 1976 when he transferred to the Mother House in Paris and became a critic in exile of the Bongo regime. He attempted to present his candidacy in the presidential elections of December 1979, but was denied the possibility of appearing on the ballot under the single-party system. In Paris he joined other intellectuals and Gabonese studying in France in forming the Mouvement de Redressement National (MORENA) (q.v.). As president of the group, he advocated a multi-party system to be achieved through democratic dialogue and other peaceful means. After rejecting several appeals from President Bongo to return to Gabon, in May 1989 he returned briefly, and in November 1989 permanently to undertake discussions that led ultimately to reforms and in April 1990 to the return of multi-party democracy. He served as president of the faction known as MORENA des Bûcherons, which on January 21, 1991, became the Rassemblement National des Bûcherons. *See* MOUVEMENT DE REDRESSEMENT NATIONAL; POLITICS; INTRODUCTION. [574]

MBA-ZUÉ, EMANUEL (1931–). President of the National Council of the Evangelical Church of Gabon. Pastor Mba was born at Mbomo 60 km. from Oyem on July 3, 1931. After secondary education at the Protestant collège in Limbamba in Cameroon, he graduated from the theological school of Ndoungué in that country. Following an internship at Bitam, he began evangelistic work at Mitzic where he showed a remarkable understanding of the Bible. His election as council president in July 1989 culminated efforts to end the split of many years within the church. Conflicts between the conservative faction now headed by Mba-Zué and a more numerous reformist one led to violence during an extraordinary synod of the church at Libreville in September 1992.

MEBIAME, LEON (1934–). Former prime minister. Mébiame was born at Libreville on September 1, 1934. He studied at the Ecole Montfort (q.v.) and the Collège Moderne there. He later graduated from the Centre de Préparation aux Carrières Administratives and the Ecole Fédérale de Police at Brazzaville. Thereafter he served in the administration in Chad. After a *stage* at the National Police School in Lyons, France, in November 1960 he became commissioner of police. After further stages at police institutions in Paris, he became deputy director of the Sûreté Nationale in March 1962 and director in October 1963. He entered the government in January 1967 as Under Secretary of State for the Interior, and then in September 1967 he became Minister of State for Labor and Social Affairs. On January 25, 1968, President Bongo selected him as Vice President of the Government and Minister of Justice. Concurrently he served as mayor of Libreville from 1969 to 1975. When the position of vice president was suppressed on November 12, 1975, he became prime minister. In August 1981, as a result of further constitutional changes, the prime minister became the head of the government. Mébiame continued to exercise this function until replaced in the cabinet reorganization that followed the national conference in April 1990. [1367, 1310, 1321]

MEDIA. Since 1977 Gabon has had a daily newspaper, *L'Union,* published at Libreville by a company in which the state owns three-quarters of the stock. Nevertheless, during the last half of 1991 and 1992 the editors frequently criticized the government of Prime Minister Oyé-Mba for what they considered its failures to tackle the country's problems and its toleration of continuing administrative corruption. The restoration of press freedom in 1990 led to a proliferation of independent weeklies expressing the viewpoints of opposition parties and professional groups. The official Agence Gabonaise de Presse (AGP) publishes a daily bulletin, *Gabon Matin.* Other newspapers, mainly in French, from France and neighboring countries, also circulate throughout Gabon. Representatives of the Agence France Presse (AFP) and Reuters of London are based in Libreville to send news out of the country.

The official agency, Radiodiffusion-Télévision Gabonaise, operates radio and television stations in Libreville, Port-Gentil, and Franceville, and a radio station at Oyem, as well as smaller radio stations in the other provinces. The national and provincial radio network, called *La Voix de la Rénovation,* broadcasts 24 hours a day in French and local languages. Gabon has had black and white television since the late 1950s and color since 1975. A second network in color was inaugurated in August 1977. Originally transmissions from Libreville reached as far as Kango on the Estuary to the east and to Lambaréné on the Ogooué River. But by the late 1980s reception had been extended to the rest of the country. In March 1988 a private commercial channel, which is part of a Pan-African network, Télé-Africa, began broadcasting 24 hours a day at Libreville. In 1990 Gabon started to receive programs from the Canal France International, a subscriber enterprise that is subsidized by the French Ministry of Cooperation. CFI features fiction, culture, information, sports, and entertainment.

In 1981, at President Bongo's initiative, Gabon inaugurated Africa no. 1, the largest shortwave station on the continent and second only to the Voice of America in the world. It broadcasts to 14 Francophone states from Senegal to Zaire. In these countries it employs local correspondents.

Africa no. 1 has five transmitters of 500 kw. at Moyabi in the Haut-Ogooué Province. Within Africa by 1990 it had 40 percent of the shortwave market, ahead of both Radio France Internationale and the Voice of America. The Gabonese state owns 60 percent of the stock of Africa no. 1; the French state through the intermediary of SOFIRAD owns the remaining 40 percent. Gabonese and French advertisers supply some of its revenues, while rental of transmission time to foreign agencies provides much of the remainder. Thus a largely French staff locally produces 12 hours of daily programming, Radio France Internationale provides six hours more, and the remaining time includes programs from Radio Suisse Internationale, Voice of America and Radio Japan. In 1992 the station began broadcasting its programs on 107.6 FM to Paris. Previously, in 1987, Africa no. 1 started presenting daily news bulletins in English as a first step in expanding its English-language programming. But for the moment Africa no. 1 remains an important instrument for spreading French culture and influence. [1364]

METEGUE N'NAH, NICOLAS (1944–). Historian and educator. Métégué N'nah was born on December 6, 1944, in the Schweitzer Hospital at Lambaréné. After primary studies in his home village of Junckville, he earned the *bac* at the Lycée Léon Mba in Lambaréné in 1965. At the University of Rennes he received the *licence* and master's degree in history. Thereafter, at the University of Paris he completed another licence and master's in education. After receiving his doctorate in history from Paris, in 1975 he was appointed to the faculty of the Omar Bongo University in Libreville where subsequently he became chairman of the department of history.

Métégué N'nah was one of the first Gabonese (along with Joseph Ambouroué-Avaro [q.v.] and Ange Ratanga-Atoz) to complete a doctorate in the history of his country and to teach that subject from an African as well as a French perspective. His study, *L'Implantation Coloniale au Gabon: la Résistance d'un Peuple,* shows that the peoples of the interior often resisted the attempts of the French to impose upon them a colonial rule that interfered with their trade and required payment of various taxes, contribution of labor, and porterage. In other words, the Gabonese did not passively acquiesce to the imposition of European control as is suggested in some older French works. [340, 339]

METIS. Persons of mixed race, mainly French-Mpongwe. The presence after the mid-nineteenth century of scores of European traders, administrators, and military men, who were either unmarried or without their wives, gave rise to concubinage with Gabonese women and frequently to marriage according to local customs (*mariage à la mode du pays*). The women, in the case of the traders, were often the sisters, daughters, or slaves of trading partners or chiefs. These unions led to the creation of a class of mixed race, generally called *métis* in French, *mestiço* in Portuguese, and mulatto in English. In the latter part of the nineteenth century, the British trader and explorer R. B. N. Walker (1830–1900), fathered at least a dozen children by Mpongwe wives, the most prominent of his offspring being the Rev. André Raponda Walker (1871–1968) (q.v.). Others among R. B. N.'s descendants have played important roles in the economic and political life of the country. Like Walker, many French fathers recognized and continued to support their métis offspring. They sought preferment for them in education and employment so that by the 1920s the several hundred métis in the Estuary formed an important part of the educated elite and the civil service. Socially they were closely linked to the Mpongwe (q.v.). In late 1933 educated métis at Libreville founded the Association Amicale des Métis mainly to aid the growing number of métis orphans who had been abandoned by their fathers and rejected by the families of their mothers. Under the leadership of Joseph-Gaston Walker-Deemin, one of the few successful non-European lumbermen, the association gained a subsidy and an okoumé (q.v.) concession from the administration for this purpose.

Given the interest that Governor-General François-Joseph Reste (1935–1939) showed in their problems, the association thereafter petitioned for privileges for the métis in French Equatorial Africa (q.v.) similar to those already held by métis in other French colonies, including easy access to French citizenship. On September 15, 1936, Governor-General Reste decreed a special métis status, which allowed 400 of them to acquire French citizenship in the following years. In keeping with the special status, the association won admission for métis to the previously all-European school at Libreville, which taught the metropolitan programs necessary for secondary and higher education and, in turn, entrance to the European cadres of the civil service. The group secured creation of a special orphanage (*internat*) for métis children near the school where those aged five to seventeen received maintenance and a free education. The group also petitioned for special privileges in the civil service, military service, allotments of lands, and okoumé-cutting permits. In 1938 the association became the Libreville branch of the Amicale des Métis de l'AEF with other branches at Pointe-Noire, Brazzaville, and Bangui. In 1943 the administration built the Cercle des Métis in the Glass section of Libreville with a library and meeting room.

In the meantime the activities of the association provoked the formation of the rival Mutuelle Gabonaise (q.v.) in October 1934 by leading Mpongwe, Benga, and Séké, as well as a few métis opposed to the special status. Métis activities also created bitter resentment among the Fang of Libreville, who were excluded from events at the Cercle des Métis until after independence at a time when Myènè were welcomed there. [926, 550]

MEYE, FRANCOIS (1922–1970). Teacher, author, and politician. Meye was born on February 22, 1922, near Oyem in the Woleu-N'Tem Province. He received his early education at Samkita in the N'Djolé Prefecture where his father served as a teacher and preacher for the French Protestant mission. From 1933 to 1940 Meye attended the Ecole des Cadres Supérieurs in Brazzaville to prepare for a career in primary teaching. He thereafter served as a teacher and school administrator in the Middle Congo and Gabon. In 1947 he joined the Comité Mixte Gabonais (q.v.) and contributed articles to the RDA newspaper, *AEF Nouvelle,* at Brazzaville. He later belonged to the Bloc Démocratique Gabonais (q.v.) but was elected to the Legislative Assembly in March 1957 from N'Djolé under the banner of the Défense des Intérêts Gabonais, which thereafter allied with the Union Démocratique et Sociale Gabonaise (q.v.). He was reelected to the National Assembly in 1961 and during the period 1959–1964 held ministerial posts. In 1965 and after he served in the education and information ministries where he gathered documentation for the history of Gabon. His autobiography, *Souvenirs de Saison Sèche,* contains valuable material on his career in education, politics, and lay leadership of the Evangelical Church. [1205, 1166, 550]

MIGOLET, JEAN-STANISLAS (1920–1987). Politician. Migolet was born at Koula-Moutou in the Ogooué-Lolo Province on August 1, 1920, and was educated at Catholic mission schools. He entered the colonial administration in 1941. In 1947 he was elected to the Territorial Assembly and later to the National Assembly in which he continued to serve until 1975. Migolet was a member of the first Gabonese executive from March 1957 and continued to hold various ministerial and BDG (q.v.) party posts under presidents Mba (q.v.) and Bongo (q.v.). He represented Gabon in the Senate of the French Community from 1959 to 1961. In November 1975 he became Vice Prime Minister, a position that he held until dropped from the cabinet in late February 1980. Migolet died on July 6, 1987. [1310, 1367]

MITSOGO (or MITSHOGO or TSHOGO). The Mitsogo belong to the Okandé linguistic group. Their traditions indicate a migration from the Ivindo River southwestward into the mountainous areas between the Offoué and N'Gounié rivers as a result of wars and slave raids by the Bakèlè. When the explorer Paul du Chaillu (q.v.) visited them in 1857 they numbered several thousand and were occupying a strip of mountainous territory 150 miles long northeast to southeast and parallel to the N'Gounié. They sold slaves to the Bapounou (q.v.) and Eshira (q.v.) for salt and European merchandise. As late as 1899 the Bakèlè (q.v.) were still attacking Mitsogo settlements and taking away women as slaves. With the establishment of the French administrative post at Sindara in 1899 and of the Catholic mission not far away, the Mitsogo came under regular European influences. In December 1904 some Mitsogo rose against the exactions of the Compagnie de la Haute-Ngounié, a concessionary company to which the French had given exploitation of the region, and killed two of its most abusive European agents. French forces suppressed the revolt and the following year instituted a tax on all able-bodied persons over ten years of age. Gold was discovered in the Mitsogo areas in 1937–1938. [284, 835, 304, 893]

MOUVEMENT DE REDRESSEMENT NATIONAL (MORENA). Major party in opposition to the Bongo regime. MORENA was first organized in Paris in the 1970s by Gabonese exiles opposed to the Bongo regime. It was not able to function openly in France until after the victory of the Socialist Party in May 1981. That victory encouraged MORENA sympathizers in Gabon itself to meet clandestinely between May and November in order to prepare a number of tracts and a White Book elaborating a program of liberal democracy with strong reformist and populist tendencies. In these writings MORENA accused President Bongo of extravagance, corruption, nepotism, and tribalism. It urged the restoration of multi-party democracy, the curbing of governmental abuses, and a fairer distribution of national wealth among individuals and regions. The last goal reflected the view of the Fang of the Woleu-N'Tem Province and the Bapounou of the Ngounié Province that their regions had been disfavored while the Estuary and Haut-Ogooué Provinces had been particularly favored. During the visit of Jean-Hilaire Aubame to Libreville during the autumn, tracts were distributed and slogans hostile to the regime scribbled on the walls of the main post office. On November 27, 1981, the government arrested six civil servants and a deputy whom it accused of writing and circulating the tracts and White Book. Among them were Jules Mba (1928–), former ambassador to the United States and Egypt, and currently an inspector of administrative affairs; Simon Oyono Aba'a (1931–), a civil administrator and former ambassador; and Jérôme Nguimbi Mbina (1940–), a deputy from the Nyanga

Province. On November 29–30, tracts demanding the liberation of the seven were distributed at Omar Bongo University. Then early on the morning of December 1, a crowd of several hundred demonstrators gathered at the main bus terminal carrying placards and distributing tracts demanding the resignation of the government, formation of a new political party, and liberation of the seven. Some demonstrators also protested the increased cost of living. An hour and a half later police arrived to disperse the demonstrators and to make some arrests. Thereafter university and lycée students demonstrated on behalf of the MORENA program, to the extent that institutions had to be closed for a time. But the population of Libreville in general did not respond to the summons to opposition. The troubles in the schools led to the arrest of the university rector, Jean-Pierre Nzoghe Nguema (1932–), who was accused of having knowledge of MORENA activities and failing to report them to the authorities. Following the visit of Pope John Paul II to Libreville on February 17–18, 1982, during which MORENA tracts were distributed, there were additional arrests, including a former minister and Protestant leader, Jean-Marc Ekoh (q.v.). Also arrested were Samuel Mba Nguema, editor of the country's only daily newspaper; Francis Ondo Edou, director of national radio; and François Sima Messa (1950–), an instructor in social communications. The three were accused of participating in an interview concerning MORENA with a journalist from Radio France Internationale. A journalist for Africa no. 1, Jean-Baptiste Asse Bekale, was accused of oral propaganda for MORENA.

In all, 260 persons were arrested, of whom 37 were brought to trial between November 10 and 26, 1982. Thirty of the 37 were either Fang or Bapounou; the majority were government employees. Most of those who were arrested were mistreated in various ways, including being kept unclothed and not having proper food and medical care. Nearly all were beaten and some were tortured by means of electrical charges and submersion in water in the prison of Gros Bouquet by agents of CEDOC (Centre de Documentation), DCI (Direction de Contre-Ingérence), and the Brigade de Recherches de la Gendarmerie, often in the presence of high-level functionaries. (All three of these intelligence units were headed by Frenchmen in the service of Gabon.) (Ironically Gabon, on February 26, 1982, signed the OAU's Convention on the Rights of Man and Peoples prohibiting torture as well as cruel and degrading treatment. On January 21, 1983, it would ratify the international pact concerning civil and political rights.) Those brought to trial were not given the opportunity for proper legal defense. The special court that tried them, the State Security Court, denied their attorneys access to data essential to their defense. The government failed to present evidence to substantiate its charge that MORENA members were planning to overthrow the regime by violent means. Nevertheless on November 26, the State Security Court convicted 29 of the 37 defendants. The 13 convicted of threatening the security of the state as well as illegally constituting a political party and insulting the president were sentenced to 20 years at hard labor. Among them were Simon Oyono Aba'a, Jules Mba, Jérôme Mbina, Jean-Pierre Nzoghe Nguema, and Jean-Marc Ekoh. The remaining 16, including the journalists, received lesser sentences.

On October 5, 1982, the government arrested the Reverend Noël Ngwa-Nguema, a Catholic priest whom it suspected of editing and distributing tracts criticizing the government. Father Ngwa, who was director of the prestigious Collège Bessieux and professor of philosophy in the university, was condemned to a four-year term on June 11, 1983. He was confined with the MORENA members.

President Mitterrand, during his visit to Libreville on January 17–18, 1983, personally urged Bongo to review the sentences, which were provoking widespread criticism, even in friendly countries. Later in the year Bongo reduced the sentences. The report of Amnesty International, prepared by Maître Bacre Waly N'Diaye, an attorney who was president of the organization's chapter in Senegal, was published early in 1984. It noted the mistreatment of the defendants, the unfairness of the trial procedures, and the injustice and severity of the sentences. Concluding that the 29 had committed no crimes but had been condemned for their political opinions, the report urged their release. Between 1984 and August 1986, President Bongo reduced the sentences of the defendants further and released them.

In the meantime, MORENA-in-exile had surfaced in Paris

early in 1982, under the leadership of the Reverend Paul Mba (q.v.), a Holy Ghost Father living at his congregation's mother house since 1976. Mba emphasized the determination of the group to use nonviolent means to achieve its goals and the reliance on dialogue with the regime. Because of the greater freedom allowed to opposition groups under the Socialist government and fewer controls on state radio and television, MORENA was able to hold meetings and press conferences, and to gain access to the media, much to the consternation of the regime in Libreville.

At this point MORENA included the Parti National Gabonais under Mba-Abessolé, which represented Fang interests and favored liberal democracy and a western orientation for Gabon; a group of radical students of revolutionary Marxist orientation led by Parfait Anotho Dedonizo, who had contacts with influential French socialists; and the Association des étudiants gabonais, a moderate student group led by André Mba Obame. Dedonizo served as secretary-general of MORENA and Obame as its theoretician and spokesman.

At the Third Extraordinary Congress of the PDG in March 1983, Bongo appealed to the exiles to return to Gabon and to participate in a dialogue within the single party. Among MORENA members who defected and returned home in this era were Mba Obame and Dedonizo. (In September 1986 they would be elected to the Central Committee of the PDG. In 1990 Mba Obame became, along with Ali Bongo, a leader of the reformist elements within the PDG.) In May 1985 Bongo repeated his invitation. MORENA-in-exile responded in August by organizing a government-in-exile headed by Max Anicet Koumba-Mbadinga. The announcement led to new bomb attacks on MORENA headquarters and the homes of several of its notables. In October Simon Evouna, a prominent member, defected and returned to Gabon. Rivalries between the supporters of Father Mba and Koumba-Mbadinga, reflecting differences over personalities and strategies, surfaced at the time of the November 1986 presidential elections in Gabon and following months. Restrictions imposed on MORENA activities by the French government in order to placate the Bongo regime also weakened the movement.

Early in 1989 MORENA tracts smuggled into Gabon through Equatorial Guinea criticized the Bongo regime for the current economic problems while reiterating the party's program. Father Mba, after rejecting several appeals by President Bongo to return to Gabon, in May 1989 agreed to spend a week in Libreville discussing the country's problem with the chief executive. Mba was received in a private capacity and not as president of MORENA. Bongo nevertheless hoped to defuse the pressures building in the country because of dissatisfaction with his regime and its austerity measures. In November 1989 Mba returned permanently to undertake an extended dialogue with Bongo. These talks led to the creation of a PDG commission on democracy on January 14, 1990. On January 20, Mba gave his support to a Bongo proposal for the formation of a Rassemblement Social et Démocratique Gabonais (RSDG), a single grouping within which pluralism would be permitted. The acceptance of such arrangements under presidential control rather than insistence on multi-partyism caused Mba's exclusion from MORENA by its local committee, operating illegally but now tolerated, on January 22, and by the exiles in Paris on March 5. Joseph Mba Bekale, Simon Oyono Aba'a, and Father Noël Ngwa-Nguema from the local committee criticized Father Mba for agreeing too readily to Bongo's terms instead of pressing for the restoration of multi-partyism immediately as a condition for cooperation. The exclusion of Father Mba, widely respected for his non-violent but courageous opposition to the Bongo regime, split MORENA into two factions. Thus at the national conference in March and April 1990, Mba headed the MORENA des Bûcherons (MB), so named for its symbol of a woodcutter, and Ngwa-Nguema and Oyono Aba'a, the MORENA-Originel (MO).

Father Mba rejected the offer of a major post as Minister of Justice in the new government of April 1990. But other members of the two MORENA factions, including Oyono Aba'a, accepted minor posts.

MORENA des Bûcherons held a national congress from

June 20 to 24, 1990, in Libreville attended by 3,000 delegates. They elected Father Mba president and Professor Pierre Kombila, a cardiologist, secretary. The party initiated arrangements to present candidates in the coming legislative elections. Professor Jean-Pierre Nzoghe Nguema became the secretary of MORENA Originel.

In the first round of the elections for the National Assembly on September 16, 1990, Father Mba received 49.22 percent of the vote in a Libreville district. Thus he was required to present himself at the second round, which, because of numerous irregularities and fraud, was postponed by the government until October 21. Protesting that the absence of proper electoral procedures and interference by PDG militants would again prevent a fair contest, Mba withdrew his candidacy and urged his followers to boycott the elections. Thus in his district the PDG candidate, a well-known cabinet minister, Jean-François N'Toutoume, won by default.

A majority of the MB candidates and supporters refused to heed Mba's recommendations to boycott the second round and subsequent runoffs on October 28. Balloting in three districts in Nyanga Province was held Nov. 4. Thus MB won 20 of the 120 seats in the new Parliament, with strongest support from the Estuary and the Woleu N'Tem Provinces. MO won seven seats. But the overall effect of Mba's withdrawal and call for a boycott was to turn what might well have been an opposition victory into a narrow PDG victory. The PDG held on to only 63 seats while the opposition parties won 57. Later, on November 15, an MB deputy, Hilaire Etoughe, defected to the PDG.

After the runoffs on October 28, Father Mba urged the MORENA deputies not to participate in either the Assembly or the new cabinet, in which opposition members were offered some minor posts. Despite his preferences, all the deputies took their seats and members of both MORENA factions accepted ministries in the government of November 1990. During the organization of the Assembly, the majority offered the opposition the chairmanship of three of the seven standing committees, which they accepted. Thus an MB deputy heads one of the committees. But when the Supreme

Court invalidated the results of the elections in five districts won by two PDG, two MB, and one USG deputies, MB at Father Mba's urging decided not to compete. Thus in the March 24, 1991, elections, the PDG won four seats and the PGP one, reducing the MB's parliamentary delegation by two to a total of 17.

In the meantime, on December 28, 1990, some of the founders of MORENA assembled, minus Father Mba and Professor Nzoghe Nguema, in order to reunite the two factions into a single party. This effort failed, and on January 21, 1991, MB changed its name to Rassemblement National des Bûcherons (RNB).

The same day Father Mba told a press conference that the political situation made it impossible for the country to deal with its problems. He urged the immediate resignation of the Assembly and president, to be followed by new elections in which foreigners would help to prepare the arrangements and observe the balloting in order to ensure fairness. In early March he joined with the other opposition parties in denouncing the systematic violation of the elementary rules of democracy by the PDG regime and in calling for the resignation of the government.

On March 5, 1991, the deputies of RNB and MO joined all the others in voting unanimously for the new constitution. In May, when the regime failed to move expeditiously to implement its provisions, the two groups joined six of the seven opposition parties in the Assembly in suspending their participation until a new government was formed in conformity with the constitution. On June 5, 1991, the opposition parties called a general strike throughout Gabon to demand the immediate application of the constitution. The strike was largely effective throughout the urban areas and forced President Bongo to name a new government whose key posts, with the exception of the Ministry of Justice, were still dominated by PDG stalwarts. Thereafter the RNB, MO, and other parties formed the Coordination de l'Opposition Démocratique (COD) to press the government to implement other provisions, including the establishment of the constitutional council and the communications council that is to safeguard freedom of expression. But subsequently, cooperation between the RNB and the other parties, for whom Agondjo-Okawe of the PGP had become the most frequent spokesman, broke down over strategies. Mba-Abessolé and his party unilaterally organized an unsuccessful general strike in February 1992 and refused to join the other parties in boycotting the Franco-African summit in Libreville in October 1992.

In the meantime MORENA-Originel, which had become simply MORENA, continued to be weakened by conflicts over strategies and personalities. The party in November 1991 expelled André Nguemah Ondo, vice president of the National Assembly, and Simon Oyono Aba'a, Minister of Labor, for accepting positions in the regime. In February 1992 MORENA, the Union Socialiste Gabonaise, and the Parti Socialiste Gabonais organized the Front Africain pour la Reconstruction (FAR) within the Assembly where they collectively have nine deputies.

From Paris in 1990 and 1991 Max Anicet Koumba-Mbadinga denounced the irregularities and fraud of the various stages of electing the new National Assembly. Early in 1991 he announced that he would become his group's candidate for president in 1993.

The division of MORENA into three competing factions and the inexperience of its leaders weakened the movement's ability to bring about significant reforms in Gabon. But the elections of 1990 revealed that the movement has strong support in the northern provinces among three sometimes overlapping elements: the Fang, persons of Christian background, and the growing lower middle class in the urban areas. This support, together with the restoration of the freedoms of speech, press, and assembly enables its leaders and representatives to continue to work toward the achievement of their goals. [574, 575, 576, 544, 612, 65, 603, 605, 1364, 1407]

MPONGWE. Oldest known people to inhabit the Estuary, including the area on the northern shore that is today Libreville. Recent linguistic studies of the Bantu expansion have placed Myènè speakers (the group to which Mpongwe belongs) in the region encompassing Libreville, Port-Gentil, and Lambaréné as long as 2,000 years ago. But it is likely that Mpongwe clans began arriving or coalescing on the shores and islands of the Estuary only in the sixteenth century, quite possibly in response to the new trading opportunities offered by the coming of the Europeans. This process seems to have continued into the late seventeenth and even the early eighteenth centuries. While the Mpongwe continued to fish, hunt, and farm, they gradually became the middlemen traders between the Europeans and peoples farther inland such as the Bakèlè (q.v.) and Séké (q.v.). During the last third of the eighteenth century the Mpongwe clans of the southern shore, in particular, became increasingly involved in the slave trade; these trading networks extended overland into the Ogooué and Congo river systems and south along the Atlantic coast to Cape Lopez. In the 1830s the Mpongwe traders were transmitting slaves, dyewood, redwood, ebony, ivory, rubber, beeswax, and gum copal to European merchants in exchange for cloth strips, iron bars, firearms, powder, knives, rum, and other strong alcoholic beverages.

On the eve of the arrival of American Protestant missionaries (June 1842) and the establishment of a French naval post (June 1843), the Mpongwe communities contained 6,000 to 7,000 freemen and 6,000 domestic slaves. Four clans (a clan was formed by several patrilineages) among the two dozen identifiable clans had risen to prominence as a result of their leadership in trade, which was based in part on their geographical location. These were the Asiga and Agulamba clans on the southern shore and the Agekaza-Glass and Agekaza-Quaben clans on the northern shore of the Estuary. The Asiga, situated on the Atlantic peninsula called Point Pongara, and the Agulamba, found farther east along the Remboué River, dominated the slave trade. The two Agekaza clans, located between Owendo and Point Santa Clara, were involved in non-human commodities as well as slaves. Though by the 1840s the Mpongwe clans possessed a common language and culture, they regarded one another as rivals, especially in trade. Each clan was presided over by a head (*oga*) called a king by the European traders, but was ruled by an oligarchy of clan patriarchs that included lineage heads and the leading traders.

Weak government, inter-clan rivalries, and the absence of central political institutions hindered Mpongwe resistance to French pressures for treaties ceding sovereignty and land for installations between 1839 and 1844. The strongest resistance to French penetration was offered by King Denis, or Antchouwé Kowe Rapontchombo (q.v.), of the Asiga clan, who by diplomacy prevented the French from establishing a post on his territory, and by King Glass, or R'Ogouarowe (q.v.), of the Agekaza-Glass clan, who submitted in 1845 only as a result of a French bombardment to enforce a treaty that was probably obtained by deception. The French incorrectly attributed much of Glass's resistance to the activities of the American missionaries, who had been headquartered in his territories since June 1842. As a result of British and some American trade, Glass Town continued to grow in size and prestige after 1845 and remained the most important village in the Estuary in the mid- and late-nineteenth century.

In contrast to Denis and Glass, King Louis, or Anguilé Dowe (q.v.), a village headman of the Agekaza-Quaben clan, in 1842 freely ceded his village of Okolo to the French and established a new one. Okolo became the site of the French naval station, Fort d'Aumale, in June 1843 and the French Catholic mission in September 1844.

Under British pressure the French intermittently sought to suppress the slave trade in the Estuary from which the Mpongwe had so greatly profited. It was largely eliminated there by the 1860s. By that time the French were using their authority to protect European trading houses in their quest for direct contact with the interior peoples, thus eliminating the middleman role of the Mpongwe traders. In the same period mission education was providing young Mpongwe with literacy skills, thus equipping them to play new roles as the employees and agents of the companies and administration under the expanding colonial regime. From the Mpongwe people would come as well the first Gabonese schoolteachers and Christian clergy.

During the period from 1845–1870, the Mpongwe declined in numbers by a third to a half as a result of smallpox epidemics and a diminishing birthrate. In 1884 the total Mpongwe population was estimated at only 3,000. This decline, accompanied by their diminished status and the pressures of Fang (q.v.) migration, promoted a regrouping of the remaining Mpongwe around Libreville, particularly at Glass Town. Their ownership of much of the land of the capital, their long experience in commerce, and their continued benefits from western education enabled them to occupy a place in twentieth-century Gabonese life well out of proportion to their dwindling numbers. During the 1920s and 1930s educated Mpongwe organized to defend their traditional land rights against both French and Fang encroachments, to secure a larger role in the management of public affairs, and to gain access to quality education. At independence in 1960 1,200 of the estimated 1,800 Mpongwe inhabited the Libreville area, where their members continued to play important roles in the civil service, the professions, education, religion, and business. Prince Félix Adandé (q.v.), a descendant of King Denis on the paternal side and the Agekaza rulers on the maternal, was serving as the head of the Mpongwe collectivity of Glass. The rebuilding of the Agekaza clan foyer, or council house, in 1974 at Nomba, the historic home of the Agekaza-Glass, was the most obvious sign of the persistence of Mpongwe vitality and of determination to play an active role in public affairs. [252, 254, 362, 394, 303, 283, 332]

MUSIC. The traditional music of Gabon's Bantu peoples resembles that of the other Bantu populations of the southern half of Africa in its forms and genres. Vocal music is frequently accompanied by string instruments, wooden flutes, xylophones, and drums. Among the most notable instruments are the eight-string harp of the Bakèlè, the mouth-resonated musical bow of the Mitsogho and Myènè, and the *mvet* of the Fang. In the last named, a calabash provides the sounding chamber for the strings, which are plucked to accompany recitation of the epic of the same name. The Bantu peoples possess songs and chants in fixed form as well as traditional themes for vocal and instrumental improvisation, which are used to accompany religious rituals and social events of various kinds. The Bwiti cult, both in its older form among the Mitsogho and its contemporary form among the Fang, has liturgical ceremonies involving music and dance. The vocal music of the Pygmies has features in common with that of other hunting and food-gathering peoples in Africa, including the use of a pentatonic tonal system incorporating tetratonic forms and of a yodelling technique and polyphonic imitation.

MUTUELLE GABONAISE. A political group formed at Libreville in October 1934 by educated Mpongwe, Benga, and Séké (qq.v.) to oppose the special privileges being sought by the *métis* (q.v.). A branch formed among the Gabonese working at Brazzaville served to establish a group that was subsequently to dominate the beginnings of postwar politics. Among the latter was a young Mpongwe, George Damas (q.v.), who attacked métis privileges in the columns of the *Etoile de l'Afrique Equatoriale Française*. [550]

MVE, BASILE ENGONE (1941–). Bishop of Oyem. Monsignor Mvé was born at Nkolmelène in the Woleu-N'Tem Province on May 30, 1941. He received his baccalaureate from the minor seminary in Libreville where he studied from 1957 to 1965. Thereafter, he entered the Salesian order and undertook a novitiate in France. From 1970 to 1974 he studied at the major seminary of Lubumbashi, Zaire, and was ordained a priest in June 1973. He then served as a pastor in Pointe-Noire, Congo, studied at the Salesian Pontifical University in Rome (1976–1977), and became spiritual director of the minor seminary. He was named coadjutor bishop in April 1980. Upon the death of Monsignor François Ndong in August 1982, Mvé became the bishop of Oyem. In March–April 1990, Monsignor Moé, head of the conference of Gabonese bishops, was elected as presiding officer of the national conference called by President Bongo to plan democratic reforms, including the restoration of multi-partyism.

- N -

NANG ESSONO, SAMUEL ADRIEN (1921–). Protestant leader. Pastor Nang Essono was born in 1921 at Bileossi.

After completing his primary studies in Protestant schools, he earned his diploma as a primary-school teacher and taught in Protestant schools. Later he earned degrees in theology in the Cameroons and Switzerland. He served as president of the regional synod of the Evangelical Church of Gabon in the Woleu-N'Tem Province from 1960 to 1969. Between January 1970 and July 1989 Pastor Nang Essono was president of the National Council of the Evangelical Church and therefore head of that body throughout northern Gabon. His tenure was troubled by the formation of a dissident faction composed of the supporters of his predecessor, Pastor Basile Ndong Amvane. Pastor Nang Essono relinquished the presidency as part of the settlement of that schism in 1989.

NASSAU, ROBERT HAMILL, M.D. (1835–1921). American Presbyterian missionary among the Benga, Galoa, Bakèlè, and Fang (qq.v.), 1861–1898. Nassau was born in Lawrenceville, New Jersey, on October 11, 1835, into a family of German and Irish descent that contained several distinguished clergymen, including his father. He graduated from Princeton's University and theological seminary, and the University of Pennsylvania Medical School in 1861. He became an expert in the Benga language while working on Corsico Island and the mainland nearby between 1861 and 1871. He helped the Rev. Ibea (q.v.) prepare a history of the Benga people. He established the first Christian mission up the Ogooué River in 1874, above Lambaréné (moved there in 1876) among the Galoa and Bakèlè, and another farther upstream at Talagouga (near modern N'Djolé) among the Bakèlè and Fang in 1881. A gifted linguist and talented observer, Nassau was comparatively free of the ethnocentric bias that characterized the attitudes of his peers. His many published volumes and manuscripts form a rich source for the history of these four peoples in the last part of the nineteenth century. His works also contribute to tropical medicine and natural science. Nassau and his sister Isabella (1829–1906) also pioneered in the formation of African teachers, catechists, and pastors. They struggled to secure a meaningful role for these agents in the face of missionary paternalism and conservatism. Dr. Nassau died on May 6, 1921. [214, 1004, 1009, 1093]

N'DENDE, JEAN-BAPTISTE. N'Dendé was a Séké who studied at the Ecole Montfort (q.v.) in Libreville and taught there while a novice of the Brothers of Saint-Gabriel (q.v.). In 1918 he became the president of the Libreville branch of the Ligue des Droits de l'Homme (q.v.), which agitated a number of issues of concern to the educated elite of the Estuary. N'Dendé served in this capacity until 1930 when tricked into transferring the presidency to a Frenchman who refused to seek redress of African grievances. In 1935, at a moment when he was at odds with elite Mpongwe, Benga, and *métis* (q.v.), N'Dendé helped Fang elders of Libreville to organize *La Voix du Pays* (q.v.) for purposes of cooperative agriculture and fishing. He also intended that *La Voix du Pays* should unite the Fang community, the largest in the capital by this time, in defense of its interests vis à vis the other peoples. [550]

NDIWA. The Ndiwa are either the first of the Mpongwe (q.v.) clans to arrive in the Estuary or a separate people who preceded the Mpongwe on the southern shore (left bank) as far west as Point Pongara. Under a leader called Rogombe some Ndiwa went to live on Dambe, or Coniquet, Island where they were residing in 1698 when tradition holds that the Dutch attacked in reprisal for Mpongwe attacks on Dutch shipping. The Mpongwe assimilated the survivors as well as other Ndiwa who came directly from the southern shore to Owendo on the northern shore in the sixteenth or seventeenth century. In turn Rogombe is regarded as the creator of the Mpongwe language and laws, an "African Confucius," according to the description of Rev. William Walker, an American missionary, in 1847. [394]

NDONG, FRANCOIS (1906–1982). Monsignor Ndong was born at the Fang village of Nzamaligé in 1906 and was ordained a Catholic priest on April 17, 1938. He was named auxiliary bishop of Libreville on November 15, 1960, the first Gabonese to be appointed a bishop. In May 1969 he was named bishop of the diocese of Oyem. He died in August 1982. [987, 988]

NDONG, MENDAME. Son of a Fang (q.v.) clan head in a part of the Woleu-N'Tem Province that was transferred to Germany in 1911, he was sent to the school for chiefs in Berlin from 1912 to 1919. In 1947 Ndong played an important role in the Fang Congress at Mitzic as an advocate of the preservation of Fang culture. Between 1947 and 1961 he sat in the Territorial Assembly (later called Legislative and then National Assembly) as a member of the Union Démocratique et Sociale Gabonaise (q.v.). [617]

NDONG NTOUTOUME, PHILIPPE TSIRA (1928–). Author, editor, and politician. Ndong was born at Engongome near Oyem on September 14, 1928. He served as an instructor in the schools of the Woleu-N'Tem Province. Ndong was elected to the Legislative Assembly in March 1957. In 1959 while serving in the Ministry of Education, he founded the review *Réalité Gabonaises* to succeed the defunct cultural review *Liaison* of Brazzaville, which had served all of French Equatorial Africa. Through *Réalité Gabonaises* he sought to promote knowledge and understanding of Gabonese history and culture, particularly among teachers. Ndong held a position in the short-lived Provisional Government of February 1964, which led to his internment for several years. He was later released by President Bongo. Ndong has published *Mvett,* a study of the Fang traditional epic, as well as *Souvenirs, Edzoh, l'homme panthère,* and *Lettres gabonaises.* [565, 569, 598]

NDOUMOU (or MINDOUMOU). An Mbédé-speaking people who live along the M'Passa River in the area of Franceville. Chief Nguimi from this people gave Brazza the land on which he founded the French post of Franceville in 1880. [284]

NGOWE (or NGOVE). The Ngowe people are probably a branch of the Eshira (q.v.) who migrated from the interior plains to the coast around Cape St. Catherine and the Iguéla Lagoon possibly as early as the fifteenth century. They dispersed southward some of the Vili who were sparsely settled along the coasts north of Loango. The Ngowe in turn ceded a place at Cape St. Catherine to the Nkomi (q.v.), who arrived in the fifteenth or sixteenth centuries. The territory of the Ngowe was known in the seventeenth and eighteenth centuries to Europeans as the province or kingdom of Gobby. Gobby paid at least nominal allegiance at that time to the kingdom of Loango (q.v.). The Ngowe, who probably never numbered more than a few thousand, were middlemen traders with the interior peoples, especially the Eshira. One of the Ngowe chiefs, Ogala, made a treaty with a French administrator, Avinenc, on December 5, 1883. Ogala probably acted on his own and secretly, for the other Ngowe chiefs opposed his action when they learned about it. Today the remnants of the Ngowe at Iguéla speak Nkomi, the language of their northern neighbors. Many others have resettled at Port-Gentil (q.v.) and at Omboué near Fernan-Vaz among the Orungu and Nkomi respectively. At the same time Fang and Loumbou have settled around Iguéla Lagoon, which during the twenti-eth century became the scene of the lumbering industry. [394, 340]

NGUEMA, FRANCOIS OWONO (1939–). Scientist, educator, politician. Born at Oyem in 1939, Nguema pursued his secondary studies at Brazzaville. In France he studied at the universities of Lille and Strasbourg, earning his doctorate in nuclear physics from the latter institution in 1968. After directing a technical lycée from June 1969 to September 1971, he was named vice-rector of the university and then rector. From 1975 to 1980 and again from 1985 to 1987, he was Minister of Scientific Research, also responsible for the environment and the protection of nature. From February 1980 until December 1981, and then again from 1987 to 1990 Nguema was Minister of Culture, the Arts, and Popular Education. In between, from 1981 to 1985 he served as the secretary-general of the Agence Culturelle pour Coopération Technique (ACCT) in Paris. Nguema survived an assassina-tion attempt in 1978. The first edition of this work reported, on the basis of erroneous data, that he had been killed. [1321, 1367]

NKOMI. The Nkomi people form part of the Omyènè linguistic group. When the Portuguese first arrived along the coast in 1482, the Nkomi were already inhabiting the lagoon they called Eliwa Nkomi, or lake of the Nkomi, which became Fernan-Vaz for the Portuguese, and the river that flowed into the lagoon, the Rembo Nkomi. Nkomi traditions state that they had earlier supplanted the Vili (q.v.) at Cape Sainte Catherine and chased them beyond Lake Iguéla southward toward Loango. With the arrival of the Dutch in 1595, the Nkomi became middlemen in relation to the peoples farther inland up the Rembo Nkomi in the exchange of iron goods for ivory, polychrome fabrics, and slaves. The Nkomi also sent slaves northward to the Orungu of Cape Lopez. As a result of a war with the Orungu over the marketing of slaves, most of the Nkomi fell under the rule of King Ogoul Issogué (q.v.) (1802 or 1804 to 1840). But they thereafter regained their independence. In 1857 Chief Quinguéza, who controlled the Rembo Nkomi, facilitated Paul du Chaillu's (q.v.) access toward the N'Gounié River and Mitsogo country. Between 1854 and 1861 the American trader, Captain Richard Lawlin (q.v.), maintained a factory at the entrance of the lagoon on land given to him by King Rotimbo, where he purchased rubber. On January 18, 1868, France, which already controlled the Estuary and Cape Lopez, signed a protectorate treaty with several Nkomi chiefs or clan heads. With the decline of the slave trade and the establishment of several European trading factories on the lagoon in the 1870s and 1880s, under the protection of the French navy, rubber became the most important export.

In 1864–1868 the ABCFM of Boston had maintained an African schoolteacher among the Nkomi, but lacked staff to found a mission. In 1887 the French Holy Ghost Fathers (q.v.) established a mission, including a school. One of their priests, Rev. Marie-Georges Bichet (d. 1900) was elected as a kind of chief (*renima*) of the Nkomi in 1897, which reflected his great influence as well as the transformation of traditional institutions. During the period between the two world wars numbers of Fang, Eshira, Bapounou, and Varama began to settle on traditional Nkomi lands. Hundreds of

Nkomi, in turn, migrated to Port-Gentil, the port that the people at Fernan-Vaz supplied with fish and other foodstuffs. [300, 394, 301, 785]

NTAKA (or TOKO) TRUMAN (1840 or 1841–1894). The Reverend Ntâkâ Truman was the first Mpongwe (q.v.) to be ordained as a Presbyterian minister on January 7, 1880. He was the son of the leading trader at Glass (east of Libreville), Toko (q.v.), who had helped the ABCFM missionaries to locate at Baraka on the northern shore of the Estuary in 1842 and had given them a plot of ground. Truman excelled in his studies during his 11 years at the American Protestant school. Following his baptism on July 3, 1864, he undertook theological studies with the reverends William Walker (q.v.) and Albert Bushnell (q.v.). After working as a trader for several years, he entered the service of the Presbyterian mission on August 27, 1870. For most of the next 11 years, Truman worked at Nengenenge, an important trading intersection 60 miles east of Baraka on the Como River. There, with the assistance of his wife, Emma, and an Mpongwe teacher, he ran a boarding school for Bakèlè children. He had a Sunday congregation of white traders, Mpongwe, Bakèlè, and Fang. Truman was regarded as an eloquent speaker by both the missionaries and the Gabonese. On January 13, 1874, Truman was licensed to preach, and the following October was ordained an elder of the Baraka church. In 1878 Truman was sent to New York State to assist Bushnell in translating the Bible into Mpongwe but he became ill and returned home after a few months via Britain. Between 1873 and 1883 Truman had a running battle with most of the American missionaries over his salary and treatment, which he regarded as discriminatory. Between 1881 and 1883 he was sent to found, in cooperation with the elderly Walker, a new post on the Remboué River that did not work out. Thereafter Truman returned to Baraka where, despite complete blindness in 1887, he continued his ministry until his death on November 19, 1894. [1028]

N'TCHORERE, CHARLES (1896–1940). Military hero. Born at Libreville on November 15, 1896, the son of an Mpongwe notable, young Charles achieved an exceptional record at the École Montfort in that city. Financial necessity forced him to abandon his studies at age sixteen in order to join his father in work in the neighboring German Cameroons. Back in Libreville in 1914, he obtained a position in the governor's cabinet. Then in 1916 he enlisted in the Tirailleurs Sénégalais and fought in the First World War, distinguishing himself sufficiently to be promoted to sergeant. During the 1920s he received further training at the École Spéciale des Sous-Officiers Indigènes at Fréjus and at Saint-Maximent. He became one of the few African commissioned officers in 1927.

While commanding Tirailleurs Sénégalais in the French Sudan (now Mali), N'Tchoréré received much praise for upgrading the military training in the schools for the sons of African troops; many of these young men became non-commissioned officers and later distinguished themselves in French service. In 1937 he became a battalion chief. In 1938, after serving as commandant of the École des Enfants de Troupe at Saint-Louis, Senegal, he retired with the rank of lieutenant. At the outbreak of the Second World War, N'Tchoréré was given command of a battalion of Gabonese volunteers at Bordeaux. During the battle of the Somme, he commanded the Seventh Company of the Fifty-Third Régiment d'Infanterie Coloniale Mixte Sénégalaise, which after three days of valiant resistance against German bombardment contained only 10 African and five European survivors. The young German Panzer officer who accepted the surrender of these remnants near Amiens refused to treat N'Tchoréré as an officer and ordered him to fall in line with the black enlistees. When Captain N'Tchoréré refused the order, the German blew out his brains.

One week later N'Tchoréré's eldest son, Jean-Baptiste, who had followed his father's footsteps by becoming a soldier, was killed in action nearby on the lower Somme.

Captain N'Tchoréré's career and conduct show strong loyalty to France and French values of a kind that service in the colonial army often produced among its African members. His heroism has been memorialized through a monument erected in the village of Airaines by its people and the French Ministry of Veterans Affairs. [663, 667, 671]

NTOUTOUME-EMANE, JEAN-FRANCOIS (1939–). Politician. Ntoutoume-Emane was born at Libreville on October 6, 1939, among the Fang people. After primary studies at the Ecole Montfort, he received his *bac* from the Collège Bessieux in 1960. Following studies in letters, law and economics, and history at the universities of Rennes and Paris, he earned a doctorate in political science in Paris in 1968. His thesis dealt with the political evolution of Gabon from 1958 to 1968. In 1969 he entered government service, holding positions in finance, banking, and transportation. Concurrently he taught at the Omar Bongo University. From 1972 he also served as the editor-in-chief of the PDG newspaper, *Dialogue,* and member of the party's Political Bureau. In 1975 he became a presidential adviser for economic and financial affairs. Between 1976 and 1987 he held ministerial posts in these same fields. Between January 1987 and August 1989 he served as Minister of Commerce. From 1980 he also was Inspector-General of Finance. In October 1990 he was elected to the National Assembly from the Estuary Province. [1321]

NYONDA, VINCENT DE PAUL (1918–date of death unknown). Politician and dramatist. Nyonda was born in 1918 at Bouranga-Dibounga in the old district of Mandji where his father, an Eshira, was village chief. His mother was a Voungou from Mouila. After studies in the boarding school of Saint-Martin-des-Apindjis, in 1937 he entered the minor seminary in Libreville. Then he went on to the major seminary in Brazzaville, which he left for health reasons in 1951. Thereafter he aided the missionaries at Mouila and taught in the Catholic schools. Elected to the Legislative Assembly from the N'Gounié Province in March 1957, he entered the first Gabonese executive as Minister of Posts, Telecommunications, Transport, and Mines, a post he held until 1963 when given no further ministerial responsibilities by President Mba. Nyonda represented Gabon in the Grand Council of French Equatorial Africa from 1957 to 1959. He served in the National Assembly after independence and from December 1960 headed the executive bureau of the BDG.

As a young man, Nyonda began to produce dramas and musicals, with a choreography inspired by Bwiti ritual. Then he undertook to write his own texts, of which by the mid-1980s there were 30. In 1966 his epic of a legendary hero, *La Mort de Guykafi,* (published in 1981) in five acts was enthusiastically received at the World Federation of Negro Arts at Dakar. In 1967 OCORA produced his *Le Parricide* for a radio audience. President Bongo, who had followed Nyonda's theatrical productions, named him director of the National Theatre, where he served for five years. Subsequently, he became a cultural adviser at the Ministry of Culture and then a presidential adviser. [1199, 550]

NZABI (or BANDJABI). The Nzabi are one of the most numerous peoples in Gabon and the Congo. In the early 1970s they were spread out over a vast area of 31,000 sq. mi., about equally between the two countries. Not much is known about the Nzabi prior to the mid-nineteenth century. It is believed that at that time they had already for two centuries inhabited the heart of the forested Massif du Chaillu where they lived from hunting with nets and shifting cultivation of food crops. They formed the eastern end of trading networks that extended into the Ogooué and Nyanga rivers and into which they sent rubber, tobacco, groundnuts, red dye, and a few slaves. One branch of the Nzabi produced iron tools and weapons of good quality, which were also sold to neighboring peoples. In the late 1860s, in response to Fang (the Osyéba clan) closure of the Ogooué River near the juncture of the Ivindo River, which persisted for a decade, thousands of Nzabi began a southward and southwestward migration into a nearly uninhabited region between the Louesse River, a tributary of the Niari-Kwilou, and the Nyanga River. Through their migration they sought to move closer to the route that led to Mayumba and the Loango coast. Though predominantly peaceful, this migration brought them into conflict with the Massango (q.v.) and Ngomo. Other Nzabi remained in their older territories between the upper Ogooué and upper N'Gounié. Between 1914 and 1918 the Nzabi interrupted commerce in the course of their refusal to accept the installation of the French colonial administration. In the mid-1930s missionaries of the Christian & Missionary Alliance began evangelistic work among the Nzabi, and today a large part of their adult church members come from the Nzabi people. [290, 166, 844, 845, 852, 891, 820]

- O -

OBAMBA (or MBAMBA). The Obamba are an Mbédé-speaking people who inhabit the northern part of the Franceville Prefecture and nearly all of the Okondja Prefecture in the Haut-Ogooué Province. As a result of conflicts with the Mbochi of northwestern Middle Congo, they migrated down the Sébé River to the vicinity of Okondja. There they encountered the Kanigui (q.v.) people, who shared the area with Pygmies, fought against them, and forced them to flee westward toward the Ogooué. [284]

OBAMBA, CYRIAQUE SIMEON (1918–). Monsignor Obamba is the first Gabonese to serve as Catholic bishop of the diocese of Mouila. Born on February 28, 1918, at Oghéwa near Lambaréné, Monsignor Obamba was ordained a priest on May 12, 1946. Pope Paul VI named him to his present post as second bishop of Mouila on November 30, 1976. [988]

OGOOUE (OGOWE in English). Gabon's most important river, it is 1,200 km. long. Its basin extends over 220,000 of the 267,667 sq. km. of the country. In this volume the Ogooué is subdivided into Lower Ogooué, from its mouths to the confluence of the N'Gounié, which enters it from the south just above Lambaréné Island; Middle Ogooué from the N'Gounié River to the confluence of the Ivindo River, which enters from the north; Upper Ogooué, from the Ivindo to the source. [929]

OGOULA-M'BEYE (1860–1947). Author. Ogoula-M'Beye was a Protestant pastor who studied the traditions and history of the Galoa people. He refused to take a European first name as was the custom under Christian and French influences. Born in the Moyen-Ogooué Province, he entered the American Protestant school there at Kangwe (near Lambaréné) in 1879. Thereafter, he became a catechist, an evangelist (1890), and in 1930 was ordained a pastor by the French missionaries. As a pastor at Port-Gentil, he studied the local history of the Orungu, earlier having written *Elombè zi Galwa,* which Paul-Vincent Pounah's French translation published as *Galwa ou Edinga d'antan.* [881]

OGOUL' ISSOGOUE, KING (or ROGOMBE or PASSOL). Orungu (q.v.) monarch from ca. 1802–1804 to 1840 at the height of the kingdom's power and involvement in the slave trade. During this period the Orungu were occupying Apomande and Mandji islands and controlling the two most important mouths of the Ogooué River delta, the Nazareth and the (San) Mexias mouths as well as the course of the river for 80 miles inland, that is, halfway to Lambaréné. Ogoul' Issogoué fought a successful war with the Nkomi to the south, who were receiving slaves from the Galoa at Lambaréné, and who wished to sell them directly to Europeans, not through Orungu middlemen. The Nkomi (q.v.) remained under Orungu control until after his death, when a disputed succession gave them the opportunity to regain their independence. Ogoul' Issogoué maintained his father's capital at Point Apomande but centered the slave trade at Sangatanga to avoid surveillance by European anti-slavery patrols. The dispute over the succession among his sons at his death saw one of them abandon Orungu territory and with his followers move closer toward the Estuary. [362, 394]

OKANDE. The Okandé people inhabited both banks of the middle Ogooué east of the Okano River junction and west of Booué. The infertile soils of this grassy enclave helped to turn them to other activities in the pursuit of their livelihood. During the age of European expansion and exploration, they provided expert boatmen for many of the expeditions. In the process they came into conflict with the Chiwa, or Osyéba, now considered a branch of the Fang.

Okandé traditions relate origins along the Ivindo River, which they travelled down to reach their mid- and late-nineteenth-century locations. They apparently advanced down the Ogooué past Lambaréné and toward Lake Zilé before returning upstream to these locations. The Okandé developed a flat-bottomed canoe, decorated fore and aft, which was well-suited for maneuvering the rocky passages of the Middle-Ogooué. Unlike practically all of the rest of the peoples of Gabon, the Okandé did not hold slaves. But they bought slaves from the Shaké, Bakota, Adouma, and Nzabi (qq.v.) to exchange for salt, palm cloth, matches, and tobacco. Okandé canoes travelled the Ogooué from Lastoursville to Lambaréné and later, after the establishment of French rule, from Franceville to Port-Gentil. [283, 261]

OKOUME. Okoumé is a softwood used in the production of plywood. It comes from a tree that is usually 30 to 40 meters in height and has a trunk with a diameter of 1.5 meters. Gabon is the world's leading producer. The wood was identified by Rev. Théophile Klaine (q.v.), a Holy Ghost priest from France and an amateur botanist, and later named Aucoumea Klaineana in his honor. Okoumé had been traditionally used by the Gabonese to make canoes, and its resin was burned in torches. Fang canoers brought the first logs to Glass, then near Libreville, in July 1889. On the initiative of the lieutenant governor of Gabon, Charles de Chavannes, the local director of the SHO (q.v.), M. Sajoux, sent seven to eight tons to France where it sold well. But the merchants of Le Havre preferred to stick with the older woods of northern Europe and Canada and combined to prevent further sales at good prices. They thus delayed the use of okoumé in France for 20 years. Okoumé was sent to Hamburg in 1892 by the Woermann firm where it soon replaced Cuban cedar in the making of cigar boxes. A Dutch firm, Picus, in 1898 and various German firms thereafter began to use okoumé for plywood. During the First World War the French military began to employ okoumé for construction, including airplanes. The inter-war period saw French companies become much more involved in the production of okoumé, which could be floated down streams to ships. Okoumée production, which reached 381,000 tons in 1930 before the impact of the world depression was felt, had risen to 737,000 tons in 1960, the year of independence, and in the 1970s generally exceeded 1 million tons annually. [732, 772]

OMBAMBO-ROGOMBE, KING (or PASSOL or PASCAL). Orungu (q.v.) monarch ca. 1840 to ca. 1860. As a result of Orungu contacts with Brazilian and Portuguese traders, he stayed at Maranhão, Brazil, in 1805 and thereafter spent two years in Lisbon. He spoke Portuguese, Spanish, and French. Ombambo-Rogombe gained victory over his brothers in a succession dispute at the death of their father, Ogoul' Issogoué, in part as a result of the backing of the Spanish traders who operated the slave barracoons at Cape Lopez. Ombambo-Rogombe presided over the Orungu kingdom during a period of Anglo-French pressure to terminate the slave trade. To avoid surveillance, he moved his capital from Apomande Island to Sangatanga, two miles inland from the coast. He refused to permit the Holy Ghost Fathers (q.v.) to evangelize in his lands and was in part responsible for ousting them in 1850 from another clan that had invited them to establish a post. He refused to make a treaty recognizing French sovereignty over his territories. [362, 394]

ORSTOM. The Office de la Recherche Scientifique et Technique Outre-Mer (ORSTOM) is a French government research bureau that was organized under the Fourth Republic to undertake studies in the social and physical sciences, and to a lesser extent in the humanities, in the overseas territories. Since the independence of the African countries ORSTOM has continued its work in cooperation with their governments. In Gabon ORSTOM has undertaken systematic studies of the country's hydrology and pedology. It has sponsored the research of several social scientists, including the Gabonese sociologist, Laurent Biffot (q.v.) and the French anthropologist of the Libreville Museum, Louis Perrois.

ORUNGU. A Myènè-speaking (q.v.) people who inhabited the delta of the Ogooué River from the seventeenth century and who developed a centralized kingdom during the era of the slave trade (1760s to 1870s). The Orungu were originally called the Ombéké. They were probably an offshoot of the Eshira who moved down the lower Ogooué River early in the seventeenth century and located behind the coastal creeks, especially the upper Gange, next to several Mpongwe clans along the coast. From these locations the Orungu supplied wood and ivory to the Adyumba (q.v.) clan of the Mpongwe from whom they learned boat building and ironworking, and whose language they adopted. During the seventeenth century the Orungu gradually settled along the Nazareth River, an important mouth of the Ogooué River north of Cape Lopez, and on the Atlantic coast northward. Around 1700 they made a successful bid for control of the coast and direct access to trade with Europeans. They killed many Adyumba and chased the remnants of their clan toward Lake Azingo. They drove the Adoni and Angwengila clans of the Mpongwe northward toward Point Pongara. Thereafter, an assembly of the heads of the 20 or so Orungu clans decided that the head of the Aboulia clan should henceforth be their king. They gave him control over maritime commerce and relations with Europeans. Another clan, the Awandji, was assigned control of inland commerce.

At first the Orungu traded ivory, beeswax, honey, gum copal, dyewood, and ebony with merchants from Portugal and Britain. During the 1760s the Orungu became involved in the slave trade in which slaves drawn from the Ogooué River system were often sent to São Tomé and Príncipe for transporting to the New World. We lack precise figures for the Orungu areas alone. But we know that by 1788 the Estuary and Cape Lopez together were exporting 500 slaves annually and between 1809 and 1815, 1,500 each year. Between the late 1700s and 1860, the Orungu monarchs controlled the two most important mouths of the Ogooué, the Nazareth and the (San) Mexias, and navigation up the river for 80 miles. They grew rich and powerful from taxing and regulating the slave trade. King Ogoul' Issogoué, or Rogombe, (q.v.) (ca. 1802–1804 to 1840) and his son King Ombango-Rogombe, or Passol, (q.v.) (1840–1860) could even be described as despots, for they no longer submitted to either advice or control from the traditional council of clans.

A reduction in Brazilian slave imports in 1850 and increasing British anti-slavery patrols influenced Ombango-Rogombe to move his capital from Olibatta on the Nazareth River northward and inland to Sangatanga, where shallow waters and winding channels prevented surprise patrol raids. On February 2, 1853, Ombango-Rogombe signed a treaty with Britain agreeing to end the slave trade and to trade in various other commodities, but he did not live up to its terms. His brother and successor, Ndebulia-Rogombe (1860–1865), made a treaty on June 1, 1862, recognizing the sovereignty of the French, who were actively extending their nominal control along the coasts southward from the Estuary. Ndebulia-Rogombe thereafter moved his capital to the Ogooué delta, where he and another brother Ntchengué (1865–1882?) saw their power shrink rapidly as the slave trade sputtered to its deserved end in the late 1860s and 1870s. In this period European merchants under French protection established houses at Cape Lopez (1867) and then up the Ogooué in order to bypass the Orungu middlemen. Protests by the Orungu chiefs and a blockade of the Nazareth River failed to halt this commercial penetration. The Orungu at this time probably numbered no more than 5,000 persons. On August 6, 1873, King Ntchengué signed a second treaty with France. Under its terms the French in 1880 established posts on Mandji Island; one of them at Cape Lopez on the northwest tip of the island became the site of Port-Gentil, an important commercial center.

The Holy Ghost Fathers, whose efforts to found a mission among the Orungu in 1850 encountered the hostility of the slave trading elements and ended in withdrawal, returned only in 1927. Thus the Orungu did not benefit, as did the Mpongwe to the north, from the western education that might have permitted them to play new roles under the colonial system. Independence in 1960 found some Orungu traditional chiefs remaining on their ancestral lands in which the Orungu people had become a tiny minority. [362, 394, 229]

OWONDO, LAURENT (1948–). Novelist. Owondo was born on July 14, 1948, at Libreville where his father was an important traditional chief of the Mpongwe. He did his primary studies at the Ecole Montfort and his secondary at the Lycée National Léon Mba. After study at the University of Aix-en-Provence, he received his doctorate at the Sorbonne in Paris. Since then he has been teaching Afro-American literature at the Omar Bongo University. His novel, *Au bout du silence* (1985), won critical acclaim throughout the Francophone literary world. The work deals with a young man's struggle for self-understanding in terms of the cosmic vision of his ancestors. Since that time he has written a play, *La folle du gouverneur*. [1201]

OYE-MBA, CASIMIR (1942–). Prime Minister since April 27, 1990. Casimir Oyé-Mba was born in 1942 at Nzamaligue in the Estuary Province. He earned the baccalaureate in 1961 following primary and secondary studies at Libreville. Thereafter he studied law and economics at the universities of Rennes and Paris. His thesis at the University of Paris concerned the juridical dimensions of mining in Gabon. After specialized studies in finance and banking at the Caisse Centrale de Coopération Economique, he served a brief stint at the Banque des Etats d'Afrique Centrale. Following administrative service in Port-Gentil and Libreville between 1969 and 1973, he was once more assigned to the BEAC in Paris. In 1977 its headquarters were transferred to Yaoundé with Oyé-Mba as deputy director. In April 1978 he became the director, the first African to hold the post. There he achieved a reputation as a talented technocrat of efficiency and honesty. In April 1990 President Bongo named Oyé-Mba prime minister, heading a PDG government that included some opposition members in secondary posts. Oyé-Mba was elected to Parliament in October 1990 from Ntoum in the Estuary Province as the candidate of the PDG. Bongo reappointed him prime minister in November 1990 following elections and again in June 1991 under the terms of the new constitution. [1400]

- P -

PARTI DEMOCRATIQUE AFRICAIN (PDA). Organized by progressive elements at Libreville and Port-Gentil in late 1945 to contest the elections for the French Constituent and National Assemblies. It twice unsuccessfully supported a well-educated career civil servant, Emile Issembé (q.v.), for African representative in these bodies. But it was plagued by personal rivalries and experienced the hostility of the administration when it became the local branch of the interterritorial RDA. This anger stemmed from the fact that the RDA at this time had ties with the French Communist Party and the Communist-dominated labor confederation, the CGT. Quite a number of the PDA members also belonged to the Libreville GEC (q.v.). In the face of internal tensions and external pressures, the PDA ceased to function by the end of 1946, and much of the membership joined the CMG. [550]

PARTI DEMOCRATIQUE GABONAIS (PDG). The PDG, founded by President Bongo, served as the country's only political party between March 1968 and May 1990. The party acquired functions in government through various measures, including the law of March 12, 1968, and the constitutional revisions of 1972, 1975, and 1983. Bongo served as its secretary-general (a title later upgraded to founder president). The PDG had in theory 300,000 militants who belonged to local committees; these were in turn grouped into 71 communal and departmental sections, which were then further formed into nine provincial federations. Each local and section committee was headed by an elected secretary.

The various units of the party elected delegates to the party congresses. Ordinary congresses met periodically, usually prior to national legislative and/or presidential elections as in March 1968, November 1979, and September 1986; extraordinary ones were summoned to deal with particular problems (e.g., in January 1979, the economic crisis; in March 1983, the challenge of MORENA; and in May 1990, the return to multi-partyism). The Congress theoretically was the party's policy-making body. While delegates vented their dissatisfaction with various policies and practices with an often amazing degree of candor, smaller bodies tended in fact to formulate policies and make decisions. These bodies included the central committee (which had 297 members in 1990), the political bureau (44), and the permanent committee (13). With the return of multi-partyism, the PDG became one of several parties.

Confirming the wishes of the national conference in March–April 1990, President Bongo resigned as head of the PDG and no longer belongs to the party. The head was its secretary-general Jacques Adhiénot. The PDG won a slight majority of seats in the National Assembly elections of September–October 1990 and thus continued to control the legislature and the cabinet.

Within the PDG there developed during the early months of 1990 a reformist group called the Rénovateurs, which is composed of younger and better educated elements. Its members favored a return to liberal democracy, including multi-partyism, along with a variety of economic and social reforms. At the extraordinary party congresses held in May 1990 and August 1991, the reformist elements gained seats in the Central Committee and Political Bureau at the expense of longtime stalwarts, including some close associates of the president. But they nevertheless constituted only minorities in those bodies and in the PDG majority in the National Assembly. Thus they lacked the strength to control either the party or the third Oyé-Mba government installed in late June 1991. While they have avoided criticism of President Bongo, they have used their influence among the editors of *l'Union* to attack the alleged failure of the government to tackle the country's problems and to control corruption. Among the main figures within the Rénovateurs are Ali Bongo, deputy from the Haut-Ogooué Province; André Mba Obame, deputy secretary-general at the presidency; Léon-Paul Ngoulakia and Engongah Owono, presidential advisers; Ondo Melologoh, minister of the plan; and Ngoyo Moussavou, deputy director-general of *l'Union*. *See* INTRODUCTION; POLITICS. [636, 543, 623, 554, 557, 595, 602]

PARTI D'UNION NATIONALE GABONAISE (PUNGA).
Punga by coincidence also means "tempest" in Eshira.
PUNGA was a political party formed in August 1958 by
René-Paul Sousatte (q.v.) and Jean-Jacques Boucavel (q.v.)
to express dissatisfaction among such southern peoples as
the Eshira (q.v.) and Bapounou (q.v.) with the political
leadership of the Fang (q.v.) and Myènè (q.v.) of northern
Gabon. It opposed Gabon's membership in the French
Community in the referendum of September 28, 1958. It was
able to secure a majority against membership in only the
Nyanga Region where the Bapounou and Eshira populations
were numerous. Gabon as a whole voted 190,334 to 15,244
for entry into the Community. In September 1959, Sousatte
demanded immediate independence for Gabon only a few
months after the country had become an autonomous republic. His declaration was apparently motivated by the Mba
government's refusal to sanction new elections to the Legislative Assembly. PUNGA at this time also had a small
electoral clientele from a miscellaneous group of progres-
sives and critics of the regime (the Conseil de la Jeunesse,
students, labor leaders). After independence, the Mba regime
refused to include PUNGA in the negotiations for a government of national union. Sousatte and Boucavel took posts as
individuals, and the party itself ceased to function. [593, 617,
599, 550]

PARTI GABONAIS DU PROGRES (PGP). Important opposition
party organized in March 1990 in time for the national
conference. Its program of socialism (of a non-Marxist-
Leninist variety) includes a fairer distribution of national
income among all classes. Its first leaders were intellectuals
involved in education, public service, and business. They
included Pierre-Louis Agondjo-Okawe, president (q.v.);
Marc Saturnin Nan Nguema, vice president; and Joseph
Rendjambe (q.v.), secretary-general. Agondjo-Okawe is a
well-known attorney who heads the bar in Gabon. Both
Agondjo-Okawe and Rendjambe were university professors
from a well-known Nkomi family in Port-Gentil. Nan
Nguema is a public servant who has been secretary-general

of OPEC and the deputy director-general of Elf-Gabon. The head of the PGP section at Port-Gentil, Nang Bekalé, holds a doctorate in political science from a French university.

In the National Assembly elections of September–October 1990, the PGP won 18 seats, mainly from Port-Gentil and other coastal areas. It had strong support from urban workers and the Nkomi and other Myènè. It picked up an additional seat in the revoting in March 1991, ordered in five districts by the Supreme Court. Unlike the other six opposition parties in the Assembly, the PGP refused President Bongo's offer of ministries in the governments of April 1990, November 1990, and June 1991.

Leaders of the PGP section at Port-Gentil were accused of organizing the violent protests in the wake of the discovery of the death of Joseph Rendjambe on May 23, 1990, designed to force Bongo from office. Among those arrested when the Presidential Guard arrived to restore order were Nang Bekalé and Didier Ping. The latter is a paternal nephew of Agondjo-Okawe; son of Jean Ping, prominent businessman and one-time PDG minister as well as Agondjo-Okawe's half brother; and a close friend of Albertine Bongo, the president's younger daughter.

The PGP has not been spared the dissensions that have troubled other parties. Late in 1991, two of its deputies, Gaubert Obiang Ndong and Fidel Moudounga-Mouity, resigned from the party. Then in mid-1992, its vice president, Marc Saturnin Nan Nguema organized his own party, the Parti Libéral Démocrate. [1400, 1407]

PEOPLES. Gabon, like other African states that were brought into being as a result of European expansion and competition during the nineteenth century, contains many different peoples. A people may be defined in the sense of the Greek term *ethnos* or the Latin *natio* as a group related by biology, culture (including language), and history. While these factors serve to differentiate more than three dozen distinct peoples, various ones among them possess similarities that permit some grouping or classification. All of the peoples except the Pygmies speak Bantu languages. The Pygmies (q.v.), who are believed to be the descendants of the earliest inhabitants of Gabon, retain their own languages in some cases while frequently employing the languages of their Bantu neighbors. The basically linguistic classification of eight groups developed by the French ethnographer Marcel Soret in the 1950s, to which are added the Vili group (a majority of whom live in the neighboring Congo) and the Pygmies, is as follows:

Group	Peoples
Omyène (Myènè)	Mpongwe, Adyumba, Enenga, Galoa, Orungu, Nkomi
Séké	Séké, Benga, Bakouélé
Eshira	Eshira, Ngowe, Varama, Voungou, Bapounou, Loumbou, Babuissi, Massango
Okandé	Apindji, Mitsogo, Pove, Shimba, Okandé, Evéia
Bakèlè	
Fang	
Bakota	Bakota, Mahongwé, Shaké, Dambomo, Shamai, Mindassa, Woumbou
Mbédé	Obamba, Mbamba, Ndoumou, Kanigui, Nzabi, Batsangui, Awandji, Adouma
Téké	
Vili	
Pygmies	

National boundaries divide several of these peoples. The Vili, Bapounou, Nzabi, Téké, Bakota, and Bakouélé are also found in the Congo. The Fang are also located in Equatorial Guinea and Cameroon. The present frontiers were arbitrarily drawn, often in ignorance of the precise locations of the various peoples. Many of the peoples were fixed in their present locations only in the nineteenth century and in some cases only as a result of the installation of colonial rule. Throughout the previous centuries, relocations and migrations, most often from an eastern or northeastern direction, were a regular feature of Gabon's history. The basic unit of social organization for all these peoples was the extended family or lineage, whose members shared a common ancestry. Related lineages formed clans, and related clans composed peoples (formerly called tribes). At the same time, as a result of the constant movement of populations in search of fresh lands or in flight from warlike neighbors, some clans became divided and over the decades regrouped as parts of different peoples. In the process they gradually adopted the language of the people to which they henceforth belonged.

Economic factors in the colonial period and since independence have contributed to the relocation of numerous individuals within the various groups of peoples. The introduction of the French language and culture, and its large-scale generalization since the late 1940s, have helped to create a Gabonese people. Civic education since independence has further promoted this identity. At the same time the average person still derives a very important part of his identity from belonging to a particular extended family and people. [394, 284]

PETROLEUM. The existence of petroleum from Cape Lopez south to Mayumba, both onshore and offshore, has been known since 1929. But the exploitation dates only from 1956. By that time France had changed its policy of reserving its overseas territories for French investors and sought foreign partners in order to promote more rapid development. Thus prospecting and exploitation during the first two decades were handled by such firms as Elf-Gabon (affiliated with the French parastatal, the Société Nationale Elf-Aquitaine [SNEA]), Shell-Gabon (British), and the Mobil Oil and Gulf Oil companies (American). By 1967 spectacular growth had occurred with the coming into production of the Gamba-Ivenga deposits, onshore south of the Ndogo Lagoon and the Setté-Cama, and of the Anguillé deposits offshore just south of Port-Gentil. Port-Gentil became the site of the refinery of the Société Gabonaise de Raffinage (SOGARA). In 1976 a second refinery opened at nearby Pointe-Clairette. Petroleum production increased from 1,400,000 tons in 1966 to 11,300,000 tons a decade later, with offshore accounting for 80 percent of this total. Eighty-five percent of the production was exported overseas, the rest being used in Gabon and neighboring countries.

During the late 1960s petroleum became Gabon's leading export and source of government revenue. During the 1970s the state acquired a portion of the shares in the leading oil companies and a larger percentage of the revenues from production. In the expectation that the reserves would be exhausted by the end of the 1980s, the government gave the companies incentives to undertake new prospecting for additional deposits. In 1977 there began a downturn in world demand for petroleum, which produced a financial crisis for the state. But the government was able to secure the assistance of the International Monetary Fund for a plan that allowed it to weather the crisis by the early 1980s. Even though production levels never exceeded 9 million tons between 1980 and 1988 and sometimes fell as low as 7,650,000 tons, a strong U.S. dollar enabled Gabon to earn important revenues once more. During 1986, the high point in receipts, petroleum generated five-sixths of the country's export earnings and two-thirds of its budgetary funds. But by that time a disastrous decline in demand, coupled with a weakness in the dollar, had already begun, setting in motion a second crisis, deeper and more prolonged.

The previous year, in August 1985 Shell-Gabon had located oil reserves of 160 million tons, of which at least 60 million tons were immediately exploitable, at Rabi-Kounga in the forests 230 km. southeast of Port-Gentil. During 1987, prior to the coming-on-stream of the Rabi-Kounga deposits, production of petroleum was concentrated in four areas: (1) Port-Gentil, in which Elf-Gabon, 54 percent owned by the SNEA and 25 percent by the Gabonese state, accounted for 76 percent of the national output; (2) Setté-Cama/Gamba, in which Shell-Gabon, also partly state-owned, contributed 8 percent; (3) Mayumba, also owned by Shell-Gabon, had 7 percent; (4) Oguendjo, owned by Amoco Gabon, an affiliate of Standard Oil of the USA, had 9 percent. Six hundred millions dollars were required to develop facilities for production at Rabi-Kounga. Funding came from the CCCE and a consortium of mainly French, British, and American banks. Shell-Gabon retained 42.5 percent of the shares in this enterprise, while Elf-Gabon acquired 29.45 percent, the SNEA 13.05 percent, and the Gabonese state 15 percent. In January 1991, Gabon, in order to liquidate some of its debts to the oil companies, sold most of its shares. As a result, Elf-Gabon now has 32.92 percent, the SNEA 14.58 percent, Amerada Hess Production Gabon 6.7 percent, and the state 3.3 percent. Shell-Gabon constructed a 135 km. pipeline south to Gamba where there are storage facilities. Elf-Gabon is building a 238-km. pipeline from Rabi-Kounga north to Cape Lopez. The petroleum, which has a low sulfur, high paraffin content, has to be heated in transit so that only specialized tanks can transport it to refineries. Production costs nevertheless have proved less than for most offshore deposits.

The coming-on-stream of the Rabi-Kounga field in January 1989 has had many consequences. Exploitation of the new deposits delayed the arrival of the post-petroleum era until at least the year 2000. By February 1991 Rabi-Kounga was providing half of Gabon's petroleum output and Shell-Gabon had replaced Elf-Gabon as the leading company. Total production rose in 1989 to 10,390,000 tons and in 1990 to 13,500,000 tons (estimated), providing the government, despite depressed world market prices, additional revenues for dealing with its budgetary crisis. The Rabi-Kounga find stimulated exploration both onshore and offshore from the frontier of Equatorial Guinea southward toward Lambaréné, with quite a number of promising results. A score of companies are involved, the bulk of the investments European and American but with Japanese and Korean capital as well. (The bulk of the petroleum from Gabon as a whole is sold to France and the United States.)

A new feature in the development of the Rabi-Kounga field has been the imposition of rigorous environmental standards as required both by Gabonese law and the International Finance Corporation, the World Bank's lending arm in the private sector. This is because the oil field is situated in rain forests and marshes that are also the natural habitat of many endangered species of plants and animals.

A by-product of petroleum is natural gas production at Port-Gentil, primarily for domestic use.

The development of Gabon's petroleum resources has had far-reaching consequences for the state and society as well as the economy. While providing the government with unprecedented revenues for development, social services, and the enrichment of the ruling class, the expansion of petroleum gave rise to the creation of a variety of secondary industries. It greatly accelerated the rural exodus and an urbanization that were already under way since independence. It helped to bring into the country tens of thousands of non-Gabonese Africans as unskilled workers, traders, and transporters, and thousands of European technicians, administrative personnel, and skilled workers. By further integrating Gabon into the global economy, it made the country even more vulnerable to world market conditions, with all of their many-sided repercussions. The upheaval in Gabon from January 1990 reflected in a multiplicity of ways the very real transformations wrought by the development of petroleum during the previous quarter-century. [940, 1, 704, 717, 690, 731, 680, 693, 1364]

PHOSPHATES AND RARE ELEMENTS. During the 1980s Gabon, through the agency of a Canadian firm, undertook a mining survey over a 1,000 km. strip on either side of the Transgabonais Railroad to locate new mineral resources, in particular gold, diamonds, and uranium. Using aerial techniques in part, the survey has found dozens of indications of deposits of various metals and minerals in the first half of the 130,000 sq. km. that are to be explored. In January 1989 deposits of phosphates estimated at 50 million tons were discovered at Mabounié near Lambaréné, only 10 km. from a waterway. The deposits, which are of an exceptional quality, contain no cadmium as is sometimes the case, but have some iron, which can be removed. At the same time, 40 km. east of Lambaréné were located deposits of niobium, which is incorporated into highly specialized alloys used by the aerospace and nuclear technology industries. The estimated 50 to 80 million tons are mixed with pyrochlorine, which at the present time cannot be separated industrially. Studies are under way to ascertain how this might be accomplished. (In 1990 Brazil provided 80 percent of the 40,000 tons of niobium in world use.) Intermingled with the deposits of niobium are others of cadmium and titanium. Also discovered nearby were rare metals of the lanthanide series from Mendeleyev's table of elements that are used in small quantities in the electronics industry. In 1990 Gabon began studies of the phosphates and other elements to ascertain the economic feasibility of their development. [1364]

POLITICS. Modern politics in Gabon fall into several periods of unequal length. In a sense they begin in the aftermath of the First World War in the form of activity by the western-educated elite in the larger towns through a number of organizations that were anti-colonialist and liberal in outlook but not anti-French. From the 1840s American and French missionaries had provided a western education to handfuls of Gabonese. But the organization of Catholic boys' schools at Libreville and Lambaréné in 1900 staffed by a congregation of professional teachers, and the creation of a public day school at Libreville in 1911 staffed by professionals, greatly increased the numbers of the elite and their academic level. For the first time there were dozens of persons whose competence in French reached the upper primary levels. Members of this elite were among those who became non-commissioned officers in the French army in the Cameroons campaign against the Germans and thereby enlarged their horizons. Some of these young men received further experience in the outside world as employees in such colonies as Senegal, the Ivory Coast, and the Belgian Congo before returning to Gabon to work for European commerce or the administration.

The first political organization in the modern sense in Gabon was the Libreville branch of the French Ligue des Droits de l'Homme, which functionaries from Martinique and Guadeloupe organized in 1918. The Ligue in Europe tended to be republican, liberal, and anti-clerical, and thus had the sympathy of many of the European functionaries, who were almost entirely Freemasons or socialists in this era. The Gabonese members of the Libreville branch, however, were not anticlerical but anticolonialist. Under the leadership of Jean-Baptiste N'Dendé (q.v.), its Séké secretary, the

Libreville branch became a vehicle for the expression of the interests of the Gabonese elite. The members were gravely concerned about the departure of the Brothers of Saint-Gabriel (q.v.) from Lambaréné in 1911 and Libreville in 1918 for lack of funds (the administration having cut off subsidies in 1907 in the wake of separation of church and state in France) and staff, which meant that the quality and level of instruction reverted to their pre-1900 status under priests and African monitors. Education for the elite was a means to full equality with Frenchmen in public employment and the enjoyment of basic rights. The elite wished to cease being subjects and to become French citizens. Their aspirations extended to their own class and not to the traditionally oriented masses. They were also concerned about various aspects of colonial rule such as the *impôt* (head tax), *prestation,* forced labor, and *indigénat* (q.v.), which had been applied in Gabon really only at the end of the nineteenth and the beginning of the twentieth century, as well as the violation of customary land rights. In the latter matter, the Mpongwe (q.v.), long implanted on the northern shores of the Estuary, were also in conflict with later arrivals, particularly the thousands of Fang (q.v.) who by now formed a majority of the population. The French legislation establishing the concessionary system in 1898 had not respected indigenous land rights, and the practices of the local administration trampled upon those in the urban areas. Though the French had made treaties with various clan heads and chiefs in the process of securing recognition of their sovereignty, they failed to respect them or to live up to their terms. They had a tendency to choose the chiefs with whom they subsequently would deal rather than allow the local peoples to select their own. But they did not seek to dispense with chiefs entirely for with such a very limited number of administrators, only 1,000 for all of French Equatorial Africa in 1910, they depended upon chiefly intermediaries to assist in carrying out their orders and transmitting them to the peoples. As far as the elite were concerned, they tried to have the administration select chiefs from among the educated, and in the inter-war period were increasingly successful when such persons were available. Thus the young Léon

Mba (q.v.), a graduate of the Catholic schools, became Fang canton chief at Libreville in the early 1920s and educated Mpongwe became the *chefs de quartier* there in the 1930s. The decision of the federal administration to allow election of African representatives to the governor-general's administrative council in 1937 presented the first opportunity for the various elements to compete in an electoral process. Those of Gabon elected François-de-Paul Vané (q.v.), a Libreville resident from a Benga chiefly family and a one-time seminarian, who had played a leading role in various anticolonialist organizations since the mid-1920s. The decision to name Africans to the municipal commission of Libreville also opened the way for African representation, though of course the choices lay with the administration. But the French were not likely to select those without education or some backing. The conviction of Léon Mba in 1931 for involvement in ritual murders and his exile to Ubangi-Shari deprived the Estuary Fang of their most capable leader for the next 15 years. Mba improved his standing by rallying to Free France in 1940 and was allowed to return to Gabon in 1946.

During his absence the political situation had evolved considerably. The Second World War had arrived and the Free French had taken control of the country. In 1944 they had organized the Brazzaville Conference to plan the reform of the colonial empire in a liberal direction. Late in the war and right after, the most hateful aspects of the colonial regime were abolished—prestation, forced labor, the indigénat, and travel controls. The educated Gabonese, like their counterparts in other territories, were given representation in the two Constituent Assemblies of 1945–1946, which charted the new relationship between France and overseas. Gabon at first shared a representative with the Middle Congo. The two territories elected Félix Tchicaya (q.v.), a schoolteacher and war veteran of Vili parentage, who was born at Libreville and had family connections in the Loango area. In November 1946, when Gabon and Congo each acquired a deputy, Tchicaya was elected to the French National Assembly from the Middle Congo and Jean-Hilaire Aubame (q.v.), a Fang linked to the Woleu N'Tem, was elected from Gabon. A one-time seminarian, as a young civil servant at Brazzaville in the early 1940s Aubame had received a political education within Free French circles at the side of Félix Eboué (q.v.), the federation's black governor-general. Solid support from the missions, both Catholic and Protestant, and also from elements in the administration and European commerce, aided Aubame to win reelection to the National Assembly in June 1951 and January 1956. There he became a prominent member of several important committees to the point that he focused his attention upon politics in the metropole while rivals were devoting their entire energies at the territorial level. While Aubame was also elected to the Territorial Assembly and two other leading politicians, Paul Gondjout (q.v.) and René Sousatte (q.v.), acquired seats in the French Senate and Assembly of the French Union, respectively, Léon Mba failed to gain a seat in the metropole. He ran unsuccessfully against Aubame for deputy in 1951 and 1956. At the territorial level he organized the Comité Mixte Gabonais (q.v.) in 1947 to counter the Union Démocratique et Sociale Gabonaise (q.v.) (UDSG) of Aubame, but there were few issues of importance that really divided them. Their differences were personal and became rooted in a division between the Estuary Fang and the northern and hinterland Fang with other ethnic groups attaching themselves to the two elements. Mba affiliated his group with the progressive inter-territorial movement, the Rassemblement Démocratique Africain (RDA), which until 1949 was affiliated in the French Parliament with the Communist Party (which belonged to the government until March 1947). Aubame belonged to the parliamentary group called the Indépendants d'Outre-Mer (IOM), which included Leopold Sédar Senghor and Dr. Louis-Paul Aujoulat and altogether had a Catholic but anti-colonialist complexion. The IOM affiliated with François Mitterrand's tiny Union Démocratique et Sociale de la Résistance (UDSR) in the parliament. Back in Gabon, Senator Gondjout, a Myènè from Port-Gentil, organized the Bloc Démocratique Gabonais (BDG) (q.v.) in 1954, to rival the UDSG, and persuaded Léon Mba to drop his Comité and join it. They thus combined forces to oppose the influence of Aubame and the northern Fang and sought to group all other ethnic groups around them. Their first real victory came in November 1956 when they were able to win control of the new popularly elected municipal commission of Libreville, which chose Mba as mayor. In that position he was able to fill the city hall with his supporters. Then in the territorial assembly elections of March 1957, the BDG and independents won a bare majority of the seats, though the UDSG received a majority of the popular votes, and were able to choose a majority of the members of the first government council, that is, an embryonic cabinet instituted under the *loi-cadre* reforms, of which Mba became the vice president, with the French governor as the president.

Before the cabinet could function for very long, the Fourth Republic came to an end in the wake of the May 1958 revolution in Algiers. This situation allowed for the establishment of a new relationship between France and its overseas territories. Within Gabon, while both the UDSG and the BDG favored membership in the new French Community, probably as an overseas department or an autonomous republic, a new party called PUNGA (q.v.) campaigned for a negative vote, which would have meant complete independence. PUNGA was composed of peoples of the southwest who felt left out of the regime dominated by Fang and Myènè and centered upon René Sousatte, who had not been reelected by the Territorial Assembly to the Assembly of the French Union. While the PUNGA obtained a majority against the Community in the Nyanga Province, Gabon as a whole voted overwhelmingly in its favor. Thereafter Gabon became an autonomous republic and Léon Mba became the prime minister in a coalition government of BDG and UDSG ministers. PUNGA became reconciled to the situation, and most of its members joined the BDG. Both major parties opposed the membership of Gabon in a revived federation of Equatorial African states, and therefore as the Community rapidly evolved, Gabon found itself an independent republic on August 13, 1960. Léon Mba became president.

The next three and a half years would be characterized by a general conflict between Mba, who wished to be a strong authoritarian leader, and the other leading politicians—

Aubame, Gondjout, Sousatte—sometimes cooperating with him and sometimes in opposition. Mba's determination and the determined opposition of the others ultimately led to the coup of February 1964 overthrowing him. But the French military intervention that restored him to power provided him with the basis for virtual one-man rule of the country for the rest of his life. It allowed him to hand over his power intact to his chosen successor, President Albert-Bernard Bongo (q.v.).

Bongo, without relinquishing that power, took steps to conciliate the opponents of Mba's regime without depriving himself of the supporters. Sousatte was already in retirement. Bongo gave Gondjout and other critics of Mba positions of importance within the government and administration. In 1972 he finally released Aubame, with whom he had earlier enjoyed good personal relations. Aubame was allowed to go and live in Paris. In March 1968 Bongo gained the agreement of the National Assembly, composed by that time only of BDG deputies, to dissolve all the existing parties and to organize a single new one, the Parti Démocratique Gabonais (PDG). His justification was that Gabon could not afford a multi-party system, which was based on ethnic and regional rivalries and therefore prevented the national unity necessary for effective government. The role of the PDG in governance prior to 1972 was at first defined only by law, despite the constitutional implications of its institutional involvement.

Between 1968 and 1990 the political system thus centered upon a powerful president who also headed the PDG. He governed in consultation with a political elite of several hundred holders of the top positions in the government, administration, parastatals, parliament, and party. The members of this elite, for the most part, had received a secondary education in Gabon or France and many of them a higher education in France. But the president selected them for their posts primarily on the basis of their ethnic and regional origins as well as their loyalty to him and willingness to work within a single-party system. Though some of the appointees were highly qualified, competence took second place among the criteria for selection and advancement. In this system all discussion, dialogue, and criticism could legitimately take place only within the party. Political activities outside the party were regarded as disloyal and usually as subversive. They were severely repressed, as evidenced in the cases of the professors' plot (q.v.) in the early 1970s and MORENA (q.v.) in the early 1980s.

Because the holders of high government office also held a preponderance of the seats in the Political Bureau and Central Committee of the PDG, initiatives for policy changes or reforms came primarily from within the government and not from the party. The party tended, except in crises, to remain an organization whose central organs sent out orders and information to its local committees rather than receiving recommendations and suggestions from them. There are indications, however, that at the second Extraordinary Congress in January 1979, summoned to deal with the economic crisis of that time, delegates from the local branches transmitted their constituents' discontent with the economic policies and administrative practices of the government. The delegates also secured a larger voice for local committees in the selection of candidates for the Central Committee. The immediate result was that several senior members lost their seats. In the selection of candidates for the National Assembly in the March 1985 elections, local committees were given a larger voice. They helped to generate a list of 268 candidates from which the Political Bureau selected 111 to run for the Assembly. The president himself chose the remaining nine nominees, one from each province. As a result of these procedures, 49 of the 89 deputies who sat in the Assembly between 1980 and 1985 were not renominated. In 1985 the terms of deputies were reduced from seven to five years.

Just as the number of deputies was increased from 47 to 70 in February 1973, to 89 in February 1980, and to 120 in March 1985, the size of the Political Bureau and Central Committee was also increased. In September 1986 the Bureau was enlarged from 27 to 44 members and the committee from 245 to 297 members to permit the inclusion of more women, young people, and members of the armed forces. At the same time the president as party head retained the power to name a portion of the members of the Central Committee.

Unlike the party as a whole, the women's organization, the Union des Femmes du PDG, operated with local units forwarding their concerns to higher levels, which responded positively. This organization worked steadily to bring women's issues to the attention of the government and to increase the participation of women in political office and administrative service. In contrast, the youth organization, the Union des Jeunes du PDG, remained moribund as the most talented young people sought to prepare themselves for jobs in the bureaucracy rather than risk activities that might lead to tensions with their elders. More active was the school in Libreville to train party cadres, which was upgraded in the 1980s to the University Center of Political Studies and Development.

The hub of the single-party political system was the president and party head. Until August 1981 he headed both the state and the government. Even after the designation of the prime minister as head of the government, he continued to dominate all branches of government. He controlled the Ministry of Foreign Affairs successively through his relative Martin Bongo (1981–1989), his son Ali Bongo (1989–1991), and his daughter Pascaline Bongo (June 1991–), and the Ministry of National Defense through other close relatives.

It was President Bongo's ability and willingness to consult and dialogue with the political elite and their cooperation, to a lesser extent, that made the political system function. It was also his control of opportunities for lucrative public employment and, unfortunately, for personal enrichment that made it possible for him to incorporate the bulk of the educated elite into the system and to obtain their support or acquiescence to his policies. Most of those unwilling to work within the system withdrew from political activity and sought private employment or lived abroad, either in France or in other Francophone countries. Individuals who showed opposition to the Bongo regime or expressed criticisms risked the danger of political violence. Those who organized clandestinely were repressed with great severity.

An important group that was uneasily incorporated into the single-party system was the leadership of the trade unions, who represented the skilled and semiskilled workers in forestry, mining, transportation, communications, and commerce. Organized by the Bongo regime in 1969 into a single Fédération Syndicale Gabonaise (FESYGA) (later changed to the Confédération, or COSYGA), and then attached to the PDG as a semi-official organ, their participation was neither fully effective nor responsive to their membership. But the presence of thousands of Europeans in top- and middle-level technical and managerial positions in the economy and other thousands of non-Gabonese wage laborers diminished the relative strength of the Gabonese labor force and the potential influence of its leaders. The increased number of work stoppages and wildcat strikes under single-party rule reflected the dissatisfaction of Gabonese workers with the lack of effective representation as well as their inability to alter their situation.

During 1989 worker dissatisfaction with the austerities imposed as a result of the economic downturn since 1986 led to an increased number of strikes, despite their illegality, in both public and private sectors. Several of these actions had the support of the officers of local unions and some of them of the leaders of COSYGA. Worker unrest may have influenced President Bongo to undertake unofficial talks with MORENA and to create a commission on democracy within the PDG on January 14, 1990. But it was student demonstrations at the Omar Bongo University a few days later that, by sparking violence in other portions of the capital and a new wave of strikes during February and March, pushed the president into dialogue with all opposition groups. The strikes, larger in number and more prolonged, by workers reacting against a new series of austerity measures soon widened their scope to include long-term grievances. Thus the strikes, protests, and demonstrations brought into the open widespread popular dissatisfaction with the single-party system, the mismanagement of the economy, the inadequacy of social services, and the corruption involving the ruling class, who were appropriating one-quarter of the state revenues for their private use.

The extent of the upheaval convinced Bongo of the need to summon a national conference in March and April in which opposition groups, though technically still illegal, were asked to participate. From this conference a number of decisions emerged. The conference asked the president to serve out the rest of his term (through the end of 1993) but to place himself above parties. Thus he resigned as head of the PDG and was replaced by Jacques Adiahénot. On May 22, 1990, the constitution was amended to permit the restoration of multi-partyism in time for the forthcoming elections for the National Assembly, which were postponed until September. The death of an opposition leader, Joseph Rendjambe, in suspicious circumstances provoked an uprising in Port-Gentil aimed at ousting the Bongo regime, which degenerated into looting there and in Libreville. It brought about a French military intervention to protect French interests and ultimately the arrival of the Presidential Guard to suppress dissent and to end the disorders. The involvement of some of Rendjambe's supporters in violence may have cost his party support in the fall elections.

The calling of the national conference also involved the restoration of the freedoms of speech, press, and assembly as well as a dialogue between some PDG militants and opposition groups. Reflecting the extensive changes that Gabon had undergone since independence, the new parties had socioeconomic and ideological dimensions as well as ethnic and regional bases. The Mouvement de Redressement National (MORENA) showed the desire of the Fang and Bapounou regions for a more equitable treatment and of the growing middle class in the cities for a fairer distribution of national income. MORENA also reflected the dissatisfaction of populations of Christian background with a regime that favored Masonry and Islam. MORENA split in January 1991 into two factions over the issue of the best strategy for dealing with the Bongo regime. MORENA des Bûcherons (MB) under Father Paul Mba had a greater degree of popular support than the MORENA Originel (MO) led by former university rector Jean-Pierre Nzoghe Nguema. Also strongly committed to a democracy involving multi-partyism was the Parti Gabonais du Progrès (PGP), a party of socialist and secularist orientations led by intellectuals, particularly of Myènè background, which found its greatest support among workers at Port-Gentil. Its officers included two of the leading figures in the professors' plot of the early 1970s, Pierre-Louis Agondjo-Okawe and Joseph Rendjambe. Smaller socialist parties that found electoral support were the Association pour le Socialisme au Gabon (APSG) led by Albert Ntze Ntoutoume and the Union Socialiste Gabonaise (USG) led by Serge Mba Bekalé and Marc Ropivia.

The government allocated the 120 seats in the new Assembly without strict regard for population. The Estuary Province, which had one-third of the population, received less than one-sixth of the seats while the president's Haut-Ogooué Province received almost the same representation. Thus the Estuary Province had 18 seats; the Haut-Ogooué, N'Gounié and Woleu-N'Tem provinces 17 each; Ogooué-Maritime 13; and the others nine to 10 each.

During the electoral campaign for the National Assembly, all parties had access to *L'Union* and to the radio and television for a few minutes each day. Campaigning was fairly free. But the government of Oyé-Mba did not take steps to ensure a fair and honest election so that the first round of balloting on September 16 was marred by widespread irregularities, fraud, and intimidation, the bulk of the offenses attributable to PDG militants fearful of losing their sway. Instead of annulling the results nationwide as demanded by the opposition parties, the government decided to confirm the results in 58 districts (of which 36 had been won by the PDG), to order a second round of voting in 30 districts where no party had received a majority, and to annul the results in the remaining 32 districts (in most of which the opposition parties were leading). A second round of voting on October 21 would decide the contests in the 30 districts. In the case of the 32 districts the first round would be on October 21 and a second round, if necessary to obtain a majority, on October 28. In the light of the government's partisan action, Father Mba was convinced that no more honesty and fairness could be assured in October than had been in September. He thus withdrew his candidacy in a Libreville district and urged a boycott of the October 1990 elections. Though the other MB candidates and many MB supporters did not heed his appeal for abstention, enough of the electorate did in order to turn what very likely would have been an opposition victory into a narrow retention of power by the PDG. As a result of all the balloting the PDG and affiliates won 62 seats, the MB 19, the MO 7, the PDG 18, the APSG 6, the USG 4, and one other for a total of 117. Voting of three districts of Nyanga Province, which was postponed until November 4, added one PDG, one MB and one USG. Then on November 15 a deputy of MB defected to the PDG. Thereafter the Supreme Court invalidated the results in five districts (2 PDG, 2 MB, and one USG). In the revoting in March 1991 the abstention of the MB allowed the PDG to win four seats, while the PGP captured one. Thus after that time the PDG had 66 seats; the PGP 20; the MB 17 (called after January 1991 the Rassemblement National des Bûcherons); MO 7; APSG 6; USG 3; the Cercle pour le Renouveau et le Progrès 1 seat; and the Union pour la Démocratie et le Développement 1 seat.

As early as April 1990, following the national conference, President Bongo reorganized the government so as to include PDG ministers with greater expertise and to give some members of the opposition minor posts. After the Assembly elections, a new government was constituted in November 1990 in which members of the MB, MO, APSG, and USG held ministries. The PGP again declined to accept any posts. In June 1991 a new government conforming to the constitution of March 1991 was formed. Headed by Oyé-Mba of the PDG, it had 25 other PDG ministers, eight opposition ones, and two technocrats. For the first time an opposition deputy Serge Mba Bekalé of the USG headed a major ministry, that of justice.

During the last half of 1991 and 1992, several trends could be observed. First of all, while the 66 PDG deputies in the Assembly resisted attempts by the Opposition to secure a vote of no-confidence against the Oyé-Mba government, its reformist faction (Rénovateurs) of 17 strongly criticized the government's performance. The Rénovateurs included Ali Bongo, André Mba Obame, and Ngoyo Moussavou, deputy director-general of *l'Union,* through whose editorials the group publicly expressed their dissatisfaction. On October

12, 1991, the prime minister was castigated for his alleged softness and lack of initiative as well as "the corruption without limit in the administration that is openly maintained from the summit of the hierarchy." Though the Rénovateurs had gained greater representation in the PDG's Central Committee and Political Bureau during the fifth extraordinary congress in August 1991, conservatives opposed to basic changes still controlled the party and the government.

Secondly, the opposition parties had great difficulty in maintaining a united front in their dealings with the government in the aftermath of the successful general strike that they had organized in early June 1991 to force Bongo to name a new government in accordance with the terms of the new constitution. The Coordination de l'Opposition Démocratique (COD) which they organized in July to exert pressure on the government to create the new institutions provided under the constitution rapidly experienced very real disagreements about strategies. The RNB, in particular, went its own way throughout most of 1992. Thirdly, disagreements within the leadership of the PGP, MO, and USG weakened the effectiveness of those bodies and contributed to further fragmentation of the opposition. Fourthly, new political parties continued to be formed and to gain legal recognition under the terms of the Charter of Parties voted by the Assembly in March 1991. Among them were the Union du Peuple Gabonais headed by Pierre Mamboundou, a high civil servant in exile in Senegal and unable to return to Gabon because of his conviction in absentia for plotting the overthrow of the government in 1989; the Parti Social Démocratique led by former presidential adviser, Pierre-Claver Maganga-Moussavou; the Parti de l'Unité du Peuple of Louis Mayila, a former longtime cabinet minister and PDG stalwart; the Parti du Centre des Indépendants, including Jean-Pierre Lemboumba-Lépandou, former director of the president's cabinet, and other one-time PDG officials who feel marginalized by the Oyé-Mba government; and the Parti Libéral Démocrate of Marc Saturnin, former PGP leader and OPEC official.

Lastly, preparations got under way for the presidential election of December 1993. The government agreed to a new census to be taken with U.N. assistance as demanded by the opposition. But the new electoral code voted in July 1992 lacked the safeguards that the opposition considered as essential for securing honesty and fairness. They showed particular concern about the possibility of non-citizens voting massively for the reelection of the incumbent, who appeared to be the strongest candidate. Late in June 1991 several opposition deputies joined with the PDG to invest the new prime minister by a margin of 72 to 46. *See* CONSTITUTION; DECOLONIZATION; INTRODUCTION. [550, 551, 617, 129, 599, 65]

PORT-GENTIL. Gabon's second largest city, center of the petroleum and wood industries, and port for 80 percent of the country's exports. Its population has grown from 4,500 in 1947 to 10,000 in 1955, 21,000 in 1960, 31,000 in 1970, to an estimated 60,000 in 1985. The latter figure includes a resident European population, mainly French, estimated at 2,500, and several thousand non-Gabonese Africans.

Port-Gentil was named in 1900 for Emile Gentil, French explorer and later governor-general of French Equatorial Africa (q.v.). In 1873 the French made a treaty with the Orungu (q.v.) people that allowed them to establish at Cape Lopez on sandy Mandji Island, which is separated from the mainland by rivers that are mouths of the Ogooué River. These are the deepwater mouths of the Ogooué, in comparison with the (San) Mexias and Fernan-Vaz mouths. The French built hangars on Mandji for use by Savorgnan de Brazza's exploratory expeditions into the interior of the Ogooué River valley. In 1894 they established a customs post around which grew up commercial houses, including the British Hatton & Cookson and John Holt; the German Woermann; and the French Société du Haut-Ogooué and Compagnie d'Exploitations Forestières Africaines. Through Port-Gentil passed rubber, ivory, and especially after 1900 various woods, from the Ogooué and N'Gounié rivers and Fernan-Vaz. Port-Gentil became the center for the export of okoumé (q.v.), which was used for plywood in Europe. During the 1960s, Port-Gentil became the location for the petroleum refinery of the Société Gabonaise de Raffinage

(SOGARA), which processes most of the country's petroleum. In 1968 it became the site for the production of natural gas as well.

A deepwater port for commerce and fishing was completed in 1983. The effect of the evacuation of some of the timber of the interior via the Transgabonais instead of down the Ogooué River system to Port-Gentil has not yet been assessed. [394, 681, 760, 940, 704]

POUNAH, PAUL-VINCENT (1914–1991). Civil servant and author. Pounah was born at Lambaréné on March 24, 1914. His father, Henri Renfouévy Pounah, at that time a first deputy in the administrative services of French Equatorial Africa in the Middle Congo, was one of the first Gabonese to have acquired French nationality. Paul-Vincent received his primary education at the Catholic mission schools of Libreville and Lambaréné between 1922 and 1934. Thereafter he undertook correspondence courses for three years to perfect his French. Between September 1937 and independence in August 1960, he held a variety of administrative posts at Libreville and Port-Gentil. After a year's training in Europe for diplomatic service in 1960–1961, he returned to administrative service in Libreville, completing his long career as director of the official new agency, Agence gabonaise de Presse, from April 1967 to January 1971.

Pounah's interest in the history and folklore of the Galwa people was stimulated by contact with his teacher, the Rev. André Raponda Walker. In challenging Walker's thesis that the Galwa and Eshira have a common origin, he began a lifetime of study that has resulted in the publication of a half dozen volumes. [1197, 1205]

POVE (or PUBI). A people of the Okandé linguistic group who inhabit the forest between the Lolo and Offoué Rivers. Among them live small groups of Bakèlè (q.v.). Their traditions relate that they crossed the Ogooué from the north at about the same time in the late nineteenth century as the French were arriving. The Pove refused to participate in the Awandji revolt of 1928–1929 even though they, too, had suffered from administrative and concessionary exactions.

Men were even recruited among them to fight against the Awandji (q.v.). [284]

PRE-HISTORY. Pre-history refers to the periods for which neither written records nor oral traditions exist. The evidence about human life comes from archaeological remains, many more of which were uncovered during the 1980s, at least as many in the savannas as in the forests. Findings must be interpreted cautiously and are likely to be modified or revised as further research continues.

Bernard Clist, an archaeologist working for the International Centre for Bantu Civilization (CICIBA), established the following periodization for the regions that today form Gabon:

Middle Stone Age	(before 38,000 B.C. to 7,000 B.C.);
Late Stone Age	(around 7000 B.C. to 5000 B.C.);
Early Neolithic	(3000 B.C. to 1000 B.C.);
Late Neolithic	(600 B.C. to 200 B.C.);
Early Iron Age	(500 B.C. to A.D. 1000);
Late Iron Age	(since A.D. 1000).

The gaps between some of these periods result from lack of evidence, the overlappings from the coexistence of different technologies.

Clist believes that the oldest tools found in Gabon were made by a hunting and collecting people in a savanna area of the Middle Ogooué more than 40,000 years ago. Late Stone Age tools dating from the Estuary around 6000 B.C. during a wetter phase seem to belong to forest dwellers, who possibly were Pygmies. The oldest radiocarbon dates for stone tools found in the Ogooué-Ivindo and Estuary Provinces, 240 km. from one another, are 5670 ±80 B.C. and 5500 ±90 B.C., respectively. These and other radiocarbon dates from the Late Stone Age suggest that the tool-making industries in Gabon bear little resemblance to those in southern Congo and Zaire to the south or in Cameroon to the north in comparable periods. Evidence from the Estuary suggests that Late Stone Age hunters and gatherers may have had contacts with the first Neolithic sedentary populations between 2800

B.C. and 2400 B.C. The earliest evidence for iron smelting in the interior regions derives from the Haut-Ogooué Province between 350 and 300 B.C. and from Oyem in the Woleu-N'Tem Province between 280 and 220 B.C. The earliest evidence for the Estuary is at Kango 91 km. southeast of Libreville around A.D. 100. While arguments have been advanced for diffusion of iron skills into Gabon from the east and the south, the most probable direction seems to be the north. That these skills were brought by speakers of Proto-Bantu or Bantu languages seems possible but less certain.

Linguists tell us that the first proto-Bantu speakers spread from Nigeria and Cameroon both eastward and southeastward beginning around 1000 B.C. The neolithic villages excavated on the coasts near Libreville and dating from 400 to 200 B.C. may therefore have been inhabited by Bantu-speaking groups. Thereafter, Bantu languages were dispersed throughout the rest of Gabon, most probably through river routes and savannas far more than through forests. Recent research, which produced evidence for village settlements in the same area near Libreville from around 2000 B.C., may lead to a redating of the early Bantu migrations into Gabon. [148, 185, 154]

PRESTON, IRA (1818–1886). American missionary (1848–1867) and specialist in Dikèlè and Fang. Born at Danvers, Massachusetts, on April 21, 1818, Rev. Ira Preston was educated at Marietta College in Ohio and at Lane Seminary in Cincinnati. After ordination as a Presbyterian minister, he accepted service with the ABCFM mission in Gabon. In 1854, with the Rev. William Walker (q.v.), he made a pioneering exploration up the Nazareth mouth of the Ogooué River half way to the site of present-day Lambaréné. They were the first whites to make this voyage. Standard French works on Gabon, which did not know of their trip, credit this achievement to French naval officers in 1862 and 1867. Preston reduced Dikèlè (the language of the Bakèlè people) to writing and translated portions of the Scriptures into that language. Preston studied the Fang language and left a manuscript that served the Rev. Arthur Marling as the basis for further work after 1870 and ultimately the translation of the Scriptures into Fang. Preston's wife, Jane Sophia Woodruff (1817–1890), taught school in Gabon from 1848 to 1866 and authored *Gaboon Stories* about her experiences. Ill health forced Preston's return in 1867 to the States where he taught at Marietta College. [360]

PROFESSORS' PLOT. In 1972 the government announced that it had discovered a "professors' plot" at the new university opened just two years earlier. It claimed to have uncovered Marxist-Leninist cells, together with pamphlets violently hostile to state authorities. It held four professors and a dozen students in the central jail at Libreville on charges of plotting against the security of the state for three years before bringing them to trial. On July 7, 1975, the Court for State Security sentenced the professors (Patrice Ondo Mba, Bernard Ondo Nze, Joseph Rendjambe [q.v.], and Pierre-Louis Agondjo-Okawe [q.v.]) to terms of eight years and three of the students to lesser terms. Nine students were acquitted. In 1976 President Bongo released all but one of the condemned. Ultimately the professors were allowed to resume their posts. Agondjo-Okawe, who had been dean of the faculty of law and economic sciences, and his relative Rendjambe, a professor of economics, in 1990 became organizers of the Parti Gabonais du Progrès. [1307]

PROTESTANTISM. Protestantism in Gabon is represented by three churches that were organized around the time of independence from missions established by American and French Protestants in the nineteenth and twentieth centuries. The churches are 1) the Evangelical Church of Gabon; 2) the Christian Alliance Church; and 3) The Pentecostal Evangelical Church. In Gabon, as elsewhere in Francophone Africa, the term "evangelical" is synonymous with "Protestant" and served to differentiate the Protestant churches from the Roman Catholic.

Protestantism was first introduced into the Estuary region in June 1842 by Congregational and Presbyterian missionaries sponsored by the American Board of Commissioners for Foreign Missions of Boston. The ABCFM field was transferred to the Presbyterian Board of Foreign Missions of New

York in 1870. The PBFM had already been maintaining missionaries since 1850 on Corisco Island and the mainland opposite in what is today Equatorial Guinea. As a result of the French government's requirement of April 1883 that the schools teach only in French, the Presbyterians in 1892–1893 and 1913 transferred their work to the Société des Missions Evangéliques of Paris. The SME turned over direction of its work to the independent Evangelical Church of Gabon in 1961.

The Protestantism of these three consecutive missionary societies had its theological roots in the Reformation theologian, John Calvin, and reflects the subsequent experience of the churches of the Calvinist or Reformed tradition in Europe and America. The church organization in Gabon follows the Presbyterian and French Reformed model in which authority is vested in a synod of clergy and laymen.

Between 1842 and 1870 the ABCFM sent 35 missionaries to Gabon, the most important of whom were the Revs. John Leighton Wilson (q.v.), William Walker (q.v.), and Albert Bushnell (q.v.). Nearly half of these missionaries became victims of tropical diseases. The PBFM sent 66 missionaries between 1870 and 1913 and the SME 138 between 1887 and 1961, among whom there were also some deaths, especially before 1900.

The ABCFM initiated evangelization among the Mpongwe, Bakèlè, and Séké peoples and made contact with the Fang of the upper Estuary region. The Presbyterians extended their work among the Benga to the mainland around Cape Esterias after 1870. The Rev. Robert Nassau (q.v.), M.D., founded posts up the Ogooué River in 1874 and after, near Lambaréné Island, and on Talaguga Island (N'Djolé), among the Galoa, Fang, and Bakèlè. French pastors Elie Allégret and Urbain Teisserès took over the work on the Ogooué in 1892–1893, but the Americans retained Baraka (Libreville) until 1913. The SME extended its work in 1922 to the Fang of the Woleu-N'Tem Province, which became their most fruitful field numerically, and south to Port-Gentil. The American missionaries reduced Mpongwe, Benga, Dikèlè, and Fang to writing and translated the Bible into them, as well as preparing grammars, dictionaries, and other instructional materials. Rev. William Walker completed translation of the entire Bible into Mpongwe. Rev. Samuel Galley, a French Swiss pastor, building on the work of the Presbyterian, Rev. Arthur Marling, finished the Fang translation in the 1940s.

American Protestant insistence on monogamy, abstinence from alcoholic beverages, and a strict New England Sabbath hindered conversion and retention among the Mpongwe trading communities as did their opposition to the slave trade. Most of their converts were pupils in their schools, particularly their boarding schools. When the French Protestants arrived in 1887, they found only 300 Gabonese Protestants. By 1914 they had increased this number to 2,300 church members and 2,200 catechumens. The American Protestants had prepared African teachers, Bible readers, and catechists. The Presbyterians ordained the first indigenous pastors, Rev. Ibea Ikenga (q.v.), a Benga from Corisco in 1870, and Rev. Ntâkâ Truman (q.v.), an Mpongwe from the Libreville area, in 1880. The SME ordained 21 pastors between 1923 and 1960, seven of whom were Myènè and 14 Fang. Fourteen of these pastors were serving in 1960 along with 53 other Gabonese catechists and preachers. In 1961 the Evangelical Church of Gabon had 45,000 adherents, including 20,00 baptized adult members, that is, roughly 10 percent of Gabon's population. The church was governed by a National Council of seven members elected by the synod and headed from 1959 to 1969 by Pastor Basile Ndong Amvane. At the general synod of 1969 Pastor Ndong failed to obtain reelection to the council and therefore the presidency of the church. He was succeeded as president by Pastor Samuel Nang Essono (q.v.). Out of the rivalries between the supporters and opponents of Pastor Ndong grew a split that was formalized when the supporters selected their own national council in 1971 in opposition to the regularly constituted one headed by Pastor Nang Essono. The division was not rooted in theology but in a complex of generational, personal, regional, and ethnic factors that proved difficult to resolve despite the good offices of various African and European churches and the intervention of President Bongo. The two factions thereafter continued to coexist within a church that was still formally a single body. In 1973 the Evangelical Church had 25 Gabonese and two European pastors plus nine evangelists working in the 25 parishes throughout northern Gabon. It possessed approximately 60,000 members and adherents. It operated primary, secondary, and normal schools with some government support.

In 1978 there were renewed attempts to end the division through the good offices of Reformed bodies outside Gabon. But delegations from the two councils meeting at Yaoundé failed to resolve their differences. Reformed bodies world-wide refused to permit the participation of the two factions in their deliberations until they settled their differences. In July 1982 a national synod of the official group ousted the dissident pastors from the church.

In February 1989 President Bongo initiated new talks under the leadership of his second vice premier, Étienne-Guy Mouvagha-Tchioba, which led to an agreement on proce-dures for ending the split. Three regional synods elected a single national council of 12 pastors and 12 laymen. From among the pastors, the full council in July 1989 elected a new president, the Reverend Emmanuel Mba-Zué (q.v.). Both the official faction under Pastor Nang Essono, and the dissident one under Pastor Daniel Sima-Ndong, have 12 members on the national council, which governs the church under Mba-Zué's leadership.

In 1985 the Evangelical Church claimed 120,000 mem-bers in 30 parishes served by 60 pastors and evangelists, all Gabonese. Renewed conflicts over the leadership of the church led to the holding of an extraordinary national synod at Libreville in early September 1992. During the proceed-ings the more numerous dissident faction (the so-called Ndjolé group) led by Pastor Jean-Noël Ougouliguendé sought reforms in governance and evangelization strategies among other things. They were resisted by the official faction (the so-called Baraka group) under President Mba-Zué. On September 6, Molotov cocktails were thrown into the meet-ing place, injuring several participants, some of them seri-ously. The government thereafter took measures to protect the leaders and to maintain order. Two years earlier, a college for the formation of pastors, evangelists, teachers, and youth workers had been developed at Oyem on the foundations of the previous Bible school. During 1990 representatives of the Evangelical Church held discussions with the government on reviving their schools, which had been damaged by the long years of division.

The Evangelical Church of South Gabon grew out of the work of the Christian and Missionary Alliance since the 1930s. The CMA, which was founded in the United States in 1897 and had headquarters at Nyack, New York, is both a missionary society and a sect in the evangelical Protestant tradition. Its conservative theology includes a literal interpretation of the Bible and emphasizes the imminence of Christ's Second Coming. Its practices include anointing with oil for bodily healing. CMA missionaries began evangelization in the N'Gounié river valley of southern Gabon in 1933 among peoples not previously reached by Protestants. These include the Nzabi (Bandjabi) (1934); Bapounou (1942); Eshira (1946); Massango (1947); and Mitsogo (1948). The CMA employed indigenous languages and translated portions of the Bible into Nzabi and Ipounou. From the early 1950s it operated dispensaries, primary schools, and a secondary school at Bongolo. In 1959 the American missionaries transferred control of the Evangelical Church of South Gabon to its Gabonese members while continuing to assist them in preaching, teaching, and health care. Membership doubled between 1960 and 1970 to 7,000 adults, 84 percent of them Nzabi and 11 percent Bapounou.

During the 1980s the Evangelical Church of South Gabon was renamed the Christian Alliance Church (CAC) better to reflect its origins and its recent geographical expansion. The extensive urbanization of the Seventies and Eighties had transferred thousands of the church's members into the urban centers of northern Gabon. By the early Nineties Christian Alliance churches in Libreville and Port-Gentil had become among the largest and fastest growing. In 1991 the CAC had 13,975 baptized members and an average Sunday morning attendance of more than 40,000 in 113 organized churches and 86 preaching sites. These congregations were served by 47 ordained Gabonese ministers and 49 missionaries. Missionaries were helping to prepare ministers, evangelists, and catechists at the Bethel Bible Institute in Libreville, opened in 1975, and at the Koula Moutou Bible Institute in the Ogooué-Lolo Province. The former institution enrolled 19 full-time and 22 part-time students, and the latter enrolled 15 full-time. The CAC recently sent evangelists into the Haut-Ogooué Province, which had been closed for several years by presidential edict to any new Protestant activity. The CAC operates a modern hospital in Bongolo that in 1991 was treating 400 patients daily. The hospital was staffed by six missionaries (two doctors and four nurses) and 10 Gabonese nurses. Given the shortage of personnel and medicine at government facilities during the era of economic downturn, the Bongolo Hospital plays a vital role in providing medical care throughout the province.

The Pentecostal Evangelical Church is a product of the Great Revival of the mid-1930s. In 1935 a Swiss pastor of the French Protestant mission, Rev. Gaston Vernaud, initiated a revival involving possession by the Holy Spirit. After first affecting two Gabonese evangelists travelling in the Monts de Cristal in mid-August 1935, the revival spread to the Libreville area, to the Fang of the Woleu-N'Tem Province, the Boulou of southern Cameroon, and by February 1936 to Ngômô on the lower Ogooué River. The experience has since been known as the Great Revival. Vernaud's preaching aroused much concern among his church's authorities in Paris, who were especially troubled about the miraculous cures said to be taking place. The French administration feared the creation of an independent African movement that might become anticolonialist as Kimbanguism had done 15 years previously in the Belgian Congo. Rather than abandon the kind of work he was doing, Pastor Vernaud withdrew from the SME and founded the Pentecostal Mission, which drew most of its followers from the Fang and Myènè. The mission affiliated with the Assemblies of God (Pentecostals) in France and the United States. Today the main churches of the Pentecostal Evangelical Church are those in Owendo, southeast of Libreville, and at Médouneu in the Woleu-N'Tem. The Pentecostal church has African personnel, including pastors.

President Bongo has continued the French colonial practice of excluding foreign missionary bodies or denying legal recognition to independent sects that might disturb the peace or threaten public order. Thus he denied entrance to the Jehovah's Witnesses and the Salvation Army, both of which had been established for several decades in the neighboring Congo. In the course of the 1980s, Bongo also outlawed a number of independent African Christian sects, including Christianisme Céleste, a body of West African origin. A young military officer from Bongo's home province, Captain Alexandre Mandja Ngokouta, who was a member of Christianisme Céleste, was executed in August 1985 for his role in a plot to assassinate the president. The spread of these sects since independence often reflects the dissatisfaction of portions of the new middle class with the materialism and dishonesty of the ruling class. It also shows a desire to have a Christianity expressed in African terms and directed by Gabonese who are free from foreign associations. [1031, 1028, 1037, 1021a, 998, 1009, 1103]

PYGMIES. Pygmies numbered 3,320 in the last census. They are located in many parts of the country and are divided into several different groups such as the Bekwui, Bobinga, Babango, Okowa, Bakota, and Baka. The Pygmies of southern Gabon are quite widely dispersed throughout the forests whereas in the area of Mékambo in the northeast one thousand Bakola Pygmies are grouped in 10 adjacent villages. The Pygmies still live as their ancestors did, at least 2,000 years ago, primarily from hunting and gathering but they also raise food crops and livestock. They often have symbiotic relationships with the adjacent peoples, such as the Bakota of Mékambo.

The Pygmies are believed to be the descendants of the oldest known inhabitants of the forests. Their traditions indicate that some of them arrived in the forests from the south or east and others (such as the Baka around Minvoul in the Woleu-N'Tem Province) from the north. The traditions of most of the Bantu peoples declare that the Pygmies preceded them or guided them through the forests. All of the various Pygmy groups share common physical characteristics with the Pygmies of Cameroon and Zaire, but some among them, such as the Babango south of Lastoursville, reflect racial mixing with Negroid people. At the same time, the Babango of Dibandi near Mimongo in the N'Gounié Province bear some resemblances to the Bushmen of southern Africa, another of the aboriginal peoples of the continent. While some Pygmies, such as the Baka of Minvoul who live among the Fang (q.v.), have retained their own languages, others, such as the Babango of Dibango, who live among the Massango (q.v.), have adopted the Bantu languages of their neighbors.

A few Pygmies around Mékambo have become day laborers for the new mining enterprises. But in general the Pygmies live outside the modern sector of the economy and reject formal education. [284, 847, 848, 898, 899, 791, 851, 886]

- Q -

QUABEN, KING (or KAKA-RAPONO) (d. 1863). Head of the Agekaza-Quaben, or Agekaza w'Anwondo, clan of the Mpongwe of the northern shore of the Estuary. He signed the treaty of April 27, 1843, with the French, which allowed them to construct their post, Fort d'Aumale, on the lands of his nephew King Louis/Anguilé Dowe (q.v.). He encouraged the French political, commercial, and religious presence in the hope of rivalling the hegemony of the Agekaza-Glass clan, which rested on collaboration with British, American, and German traders. [252, 254, 394]

- R -

RAPONTCHOMBO, JEAN-FELIX (1872–1903). The first Gabonese to earn the baccalaureate or French secondary diploma. He was the grandson of King Denis (q.v.) and the eldest son of King Félix-Adandé (q.v.). After primary studies with the Holy Ghost Fathers at Libreville, he was sent in February 1892 on government scholarship to the secondary school at St. Louis, Senegal, and thereafter to Sainte-Marie Lycée at

Vitré, Brittany, in 1894. He was awarded the baccalaureate at Rennes in November of that year, coming in first out of 30 candidates. He was employed in the customs service in Africa until his death. [394]

RAWIRI, ANGÈLE NTYUGWETONDO (1954–). Novelist. Angèle Rawiri was born at Port-Gentil on April 29, 1954, to Galoa parents. Her father, Georges Rawiri (q.v.), a prominent politician, is also a poet. Her mother, who died when she was six, was a teacher. After studying at the lycée of Alès in France from which her father had previously graduated, she earned her *bac* at the girls' collège at Vanves. In Paris at the Institute Lentonnet, she obtained a second *bac* in the commercial translation of English. Thereafter, she spent two years in London to perfect her English. To help support herself, she played small roles in James Bond films and posed as a cover girl for fashion magazines. Back in Gabon since 1979, she has worked for the government and private enterprises as a translator and interpreter.

Angèle Rawiri is perhaps the first Gabonese writer to attract an international audience. Her novel, *Elonga* (1986), which means "hell" in Myènè, deals with the effects of fetishism upon a young *métis* who has returned to the country of his mother. *G'amarakano* (1983) involves the clash between an older generation's desire to safeguard traditional values and a young girl's appetite for material goods. Rawiri's third novel, *Fureur et cris de femmes,* was published in 1989. [1193, 1198, 1187]

RAWIRI, GEORGES (1932–). Politician and poet, close associate of President Bongo. Rawiri was born among the Galoa people at Lambaréné on March 10, 1932. After completing the Protestant primary school at Ngomo, he obtained the baccalaureate at the lycée of Alès in France. Thereafter he spent two years at the studio school of the French radio in Paris. After several years as director of Radio-Gabon, in 1963 he became director of Radiodiffusion-Télévision Gabonaise. In 1964 he was named Minister of Information, Tourism, and Communications (PTT). Then he served as ambassador to France (May 1965 to June 1971) while concurrently serving as ambassador to Great Britain, Switzerland, Austria, and the Holy See most of the time. In 1971 he returned to Gabon as Minister of Foreign Affairs. In April 1975 he became Minister of Transportation, a position he retained until 1989, during which time he supervised the construction of the Transgabonais and the port at Owendo. From February 1980 until April 1990, he also served as first deputy prime minister. In January 1990 President Bongo selected him to preside over the PDG's special commission on democracy, which recommended the end of the single-party system and the return to multipartyism. Rawiri is reputed to be the second most wealthy Gabonese, only the president himself having acquired greater wealth in the course of his years in office. Among Rawiri's poems, the *Chants du Gabon* (1975) are probably the best known. [1321]

REMOMBE, REMI (1852–1873). A graduate of the Holy Ghost Fathers (q.v.) school near Libreville, Rémi Remombe continued his studies for the priesthood at the Abbey of Notre Dame de Langonnet, Morbihan Department, Brittany, between 1865 and 1873. He died at Gorée en route to Gabon to restore his health. Rémi was the son of Henri Oréniga, one of the first Catholic converts at Quaben, and brother of Elisa, the first wife of King Félix-Adandé (q.v.). [1029, 394]

RENDJAMBE, JOSEPH (d. 1990). PGP leader. Rendjambe was born at Port-Gentil into an Nkomi family. While a university student in France, he headed the Association Générale des Etudiants du Gabon (q.v.). Back in Gabon, as a professor of economics at the new university in Libreville, he was implicated in the professors' plot (q.v.) of 1972. After spending several years in prison, he was released and allowed to resume his teaching duties. He also directed Sonapresse, which publishes the pro-government daily, *L'Union,* and headed the administrative council of SONA-DIG, a parastatal that manages government investments. With the return of multi-partyism in March 1990, he became the secretary-general of a new socialist party led by intellectuals and supported by workers, the Parti Gabonais du

Progrès (PGP) (q.v.). The president of the PGP was his university colleague and close relative, Pierre-Louis Agondjo-Okawe (q.v.). It was expected that Rendjambe would become the PGP's candidate for president of Gabon in 1993.

On May 23, 1991, Rendjambe was found dead in his room in the Hôtel Dowe in Libreville in suspicious circumstances. The conclusion that his death was the work of government agents seeking to eliminate an influential rival set off rioting by PGP militants in Port-Gentil, Libreville, and other cities. The disorders led to French military intervention at Port-Gentil on May 24 and to the arrival of the presidential guard there on May 29. Despite autopsies by both government and private French physicians that attributed the death to natural causes, Agondjo-Okawe and other PGP militants continued to believe that Rendjambe had been murdered. But they ultimately urged their supporters to work for the return of calm. In such an atmosphere Rendjambe's funeral was conducted at Port-Gentil in early July.

While the death of Rendjambe helped to unify the PGP and others against the Bongo regime, it also deprived the party and country of a leader known for his moderation and balanced judgment who might have become a serious contender for the presidency. [1400, 1407]

REOMBI-MPOLO, KING. Orungu (q.v.) monarch from 1790 to ca. 1802–1804. Reombi-Mpolo was the first really strong Orungu ruler, who grew rich and powerful through controlling and taxing the slave trade. He came to power with the aid of Spanish slavers, who kidnapped his brother Ndombe, his most serious rival for the throne. Reombi-Mpolo made his headquarters on Apomande Island and later on Mandji Island where he established a virtual trading monopoly at the entrances of the Ogooué River delta. [362]

ROBERT, MAURICE (1919–). French administrator and diplomat, close associate of Omar Bongo. Robert was born at Bordeaux on April 19, 1919. In the course of military service during the Second World War and in northern Indochina until 1953, he rose from the ranks to become a colonel. In 1954, he entered the special services and created the first S.E.D.E.C.E. post in

West Africa for gathering information. In 1959, at the time of
the negotiation of the cooperation agreements between France
and the Francophone African states, he organized a network of
information gathering for the S.E.D.E.C.E. Jacques Foccart, in
charge of African affairs in the French presidency under De
Gaulle, placed him at the head of the Africa section of the
S.E.D.E.C.E. He participated in the selection of Omar Bongo
as vice president and eventual successor of Léon Mba late in
1966. He was much involved in protecting French interests in
Gabon and in the security of the Bongo regime. Obliged by
Giscard d'Estaing to resign from the S.E.D.E.C.E. in 1974, he
became an employee of Elf-Aquitaine. At Bongo's insistence
and over the objections of the French Ministry of Foreign
Affairs, Giscard reluctantly named him ambassador to Libreville succeeding Maurice Delauney. He served from 1979
to 1981, the coming to power of the Socialist Party in Paris.
Ambassador Robert challenged in the French courts various
allegations made against him by Pierre Péan in his exposé,
Affaires Africaines (1983). [603, 65]

ROMAN CATHOLIC BISHOPS. The following bishops have
had jurisdiction in Gabon.

*Vicars Apostolic or Prefect Apostolic of the
  Two Guineas*:

Edward Barron (v.a.)	1842–1844
Eugène Tisserand (p.a.)	1844–1846
Benoiît Truffet (v.a.)	1846–1847

Vicars Apostolic of Gabon:

Jean-Rémy Bessieux	1848–1876
Pierre-Marie Le Berre	1877–1891
Alexandre Le Roy	1892–1896
Jean Martin Adam	1897–1914
Louis Martrou	1914–1925
Louis Tardy	1925–1947

*Vicar Apostolic, Bishops, Archbishops of Li-
  breville*:

Jean Jérôme Adam (v.a. 1947–1955; bishop 1955–1958; archbishop 1958–1969)	1947–1969

André-Ferdinand Anguilé	1969–
Auxiliary Bishop of Libreville:	
François Ndong	1960–1969
Bishop of Mouila:	
Raymond de la Moureyre	1959–1977
Cyriac Siméon Obamba	1977–
Bishop of Oyem:	
François Ndong	1969–1982
Basile Engone Mvé	1982–
Bishop of Franceville:	
Félicien-Patrice Makouaka	1974–

Notes: Edward Barron was an American from Philadelphia. Eugène Tisserand and Benoît Truffet were members of the Congregation of the Holy Heart of Mary, which in 1848 merged with the older Holy Ghost Fathers (Spiritans) (q.v.) and retained their name. All of the French bishops from 1848 to 1977 belonged to that congregation. The Gabonese bishops are members of the diocesan clergy, except Monsignor Mvé, who is a Salesian. [987, 988]

RUBBER. Natural rubber was gathered in important quantities for export to western markets at least as early as the beginning of the nineteenth century. During the 1860s, in the wake of the French penetration of the interior, rubber acquired even greater commercial importance. Between that decade and the early 1900s, annual exports of rubber averaged 500 to 600 tons but only exceeded 1,000 tons once, in 1883. Following the depletion of the reserves, prospects for commercial production proved bleak in the light of international market conditions and local labor shortages. In 1981 the Gabonese state organized a parastatal, Hévéa-Gabon, to develop commercial plantations at Mitzic and Bitam in the Woleu-N'Tem Province. Another parastatal, Agrogabon, managed plantations at Kango in the Estuary. In 1990–1991 Hévéa-Gabon produced its first 10,000 tons of natural rubber. In the late 1980s the state undertook a project for rubber production by farmers in the Woleu-N'Tem near the Hévéa-Gabon facilities, with promising results. [940]

- S -

SANMARCO, LOUIS (1912–). Sanmarco served as governor of Gabon during 1958–1959 at the time of the formation of the French Community and the organization of the Gabonese republic. Born at Marseilles on April 7, 1912, into a family of Italian origin, he was educated at the Colonial School in Paris from 1931 to 1935. His memoirs, *Le colonisateur colonisé,* contain a section on his service in Gabon, including his impressions of Léon Mba. Since 1958 Sanmarco has been involved in business with Africa. [610]

SCHWEITZER, ALBERT (1875–1965). Medical missionary, religious philosopher, and musician. Schweitzer founded and maintained an independent medical mission at Lambaréné from 1924 until his death in 1965. He was born at Kayserburg, Alsace, on January 14, 1875, the son of a pastor of the Lutheran Church. After brilliant studies in philosophy and theology at the University of Strasbourg and in organ at Paris, he became pastor of St. Nicholas Church, Strasbourg, and organist of the Bach Society of Paris. While retaining these positions, he undertook medical studies and received his M.D. in 1911. After marriage to Hélène Bresslau (1878–1957), a one-time music and art student who thereafter took courses in social work and medicine, the couple went in 1912 under the sponsorship of the Société des Missions Evangéliques of Paris as medical missionaries to Gabon. The Schweitzers worked at Lambaréné from 1913 to September 1917, when as Alsatians of questionable loyalty to France, they were interned in France for the remainder of the First World War. Back in Gabon in 1924, Schweitzer built his own hospital away from mission property and earned the operating expenses through lectures and organ concerts in Europe and the New World, and through recordings, especially of Bach's works in which he was considered an expert. He also won support from individuals and groups in Europe and America, including Unitarian-Universalists, who found his philosophical and theological views especially attractive.

Dr. Schweitzer felt that a western-style hospital had little chance of inducing suffering Gabonese to abandon fetishers and sorcerers. Therefore, he allowed them to bring members of their families and even small animals to the medical center. The families prepared the patients' food and gave them moral support for getting well. Schweitzer relaxed the standards of hygiene to this end. Schweitzer's medical methods generated controversy, mainly outside Gabon, as did his views on the capacities of the Africans, which some thought bordered on racism. In Gabon itself Schweitzer was much appreciated and beloved by many whom he aided. Some of them were aware of his views but chose to overlook them. Schweitzer died at Lambaréné in 1965 and was buried there, 12 years after receiving the Nobel Peace Prize. While Schweitzer had an impact upon Gabon for several decades, Gabon also had an impact upon him. His experiences at Lambaréné contributed to the shaping of his ethical humanism, which though still rooted in Christian traditions, now rested as well on broader and older ones, including some that were African.

After Dr. Schweitzer's death, his daughter Rhéna (1919–) and other associates continued his medical mission. An international foundation formed to build and equip the new modern Albert Schweitzer Hospital, which opened at Lambaréné in January 1981, and received support from the governments of Gabon, France, Switzerland, and the Netherlands as well as private sources. [999, 1034, 1036, 353, 1012, 55, 1071, 1014]

SEIGNON, HENRI. Settler, lumberman, and Free French (q.v.) leader. Henri Seignon as president of the Chamber of Commerce at Libreville played an important role in convincing Governor Pierre Masson to rally the colony to Free France in August 1940. Though subsequently captured by Vichy elements and sent to France, he eventually was able to return to Gabon. In September 1943 he was named to represent French Equatorial Africa in the consultative assembly at Algiers. The Gaullist regime in 1944 named him director of the Office des Bois de l'Afrique Equatoriale Française, a body that controlled the exploitation and marketing of all woods in the federation. Seignon incurred great hostility from the European lumbering interests, which saw the Office as a step toward permanent government control or even nationalization. Seignon was defeated by Gabriel d'Arboussier (q.v.) in the contest for European deputy for Gabon and Middle Congo in October 1945, but elected to the Second Constituent Assembly in June 1946. In November 1946 Maurice Bayrou defeated him in the contest for European deputy from Gabon to the French National Assembly. But he gained election to the Territorial Assembly in December 1946, where he sat for the next decade and wielded great influence. Hostility to his Office des Bois lessened in the 1950s when the drop in timber prices in world markets proved its value. [550]

SEKE. The Séké people were called Shékiani by the Mpongwe (q.v.) and Boulou by the French in the early nineteenth century. The Séké are today found on the northern coast at Cocobeach, just south of the Rio Muni, as well as in adjacent Equatorial Guinea. Some have settled at Libreville and Lambaréné. These few hundreds of Séké are all that remain of a once numerous people that played an important commercial role in many parts of northern Gabon prior to the twentieth century. Séké traditions suggest origins in the upper Ivindo River, within present-day Cameroon, from which they were driven south- and westward by pressure from Bakèlè (q.v.) hunters. Some of them arrived along the northern coasts on the Rio Muni and its tributaries (the Noya and the upper Temboni rivers) and on the estuary of Mondah Bay before the coming of the Portuguese in the 1470s and possibly as early as the fourteenth century. From these locations they traded ivory, redwood, ebony, balls of rubber, gum copal, and a few slaves with the Portuguese and later with other western traders. Other Séké, who were settled behind the Orungu (q.v.) near the lower Ogooué River and on the upper Remboué River, became involved in the Remboué-Ogooué network of the slave trade in the 1760s and after. In addition to transmitting slaves from other peoples, they sold into slavery unsatisfactory wives, unhealthy or delinquent children, and orphans from their own populations. In the 1840s American and French missionaries and traders encountered the Séké living on both sides of the Estuary behind and among the Mpongwe and the Bakèlè. These Séké collected beeswax and gum copal, and hunted elephants in the forests for ivory, which they sold to the Mpongwe. Those on the northern shore also received ivory from the Bakèlè, who both gathered it and secured it from the Fang (q.v.). By the late 1840s Fang migrations were pushing both the Séké and the Bakèlè ahead of them down the Como and Remboué rivers into the Estuary. Twenty years later Fang moving toward the Ogooué would displace the southern Séké. In the late 1850s the Franco-American explorer, Paul du Chaillu (q.v.), encountered Séké living behind the far northern coasts and as far east as the Monts de Cristal, 150 miles inland, where they too were experiencing the pressure of Fang migrations westward.

Séké and Bakèlè chiefs on the Como and Remboué rivers signed treaties recognizing French sovereignty on December 2, 1846. The Séké leader, King Kianlinwin of the Mondah, accepted French protection through a treaty of February 14, 1848.

The Holy Ghost Fathers (q.v.) in 1851–1852 attempted unsuccessfully to evangelize among the Séké, Bakèlè, and Mpongwe at Chinchoua (Ntché-Ntchuwa) on the lower Remboué. Their attempt in 1877 to establish a mission among the Séké of the Mondah River also failed. Only in 1890 did their mission on the Rio Muni, first at Kogo on the northern shore in territory eventually awarded to Spain, and then at Boutika on the southern shore, gain a modest Séké audience. By that time the trading factories of several European firms, particularly British ones, were well-established among the Séké. [394, 261]

SHAKE. The Shaké people belong to the Bakota linguistic group. Together with a closely related people, the Dambomo, they inhabit the upper Ogooué above Booué and along the road from Booué to Lalara. Other Shaké live north of Lastoursville. A third closely related people, the Shamai, live north of Okondja in the Haut-Ogooué Province. The traditions of these three peoples relate their departure from the upper Ivindo River because of Poupou's War and their passage to Mt. Ngouadi in the Okondja District where they formed three peoples. From there in the late nineteenth century they passed into the Ogooué east of Booué where they encountered a people called the Chiwa (q.v.) whom they forced toward the junction of the Ivindo River. The Chiwa had previously fought the Pygmies near Booué. The Bakèlè (q.v.), who had accompanied them toward Booué, fled during the war with the Chiwa and mounted the Lolo River as far as Koulamoutou.

The three peoples made objects both of iron and of copper. The copper came from an open pit near Minc on the upper Djidji (Dilo) River. They hunted elephants, buffaloes, and sangliers, the meat of which they sold, after the arrival of the French, to the factories of the SHO (q.v.) and to the posts at Booué and Lastoursville. Earlier they had sold slaves to the Okandé (q.v.), sometimes through Chiwa intermediaries, for transmission to the coast. [365, 284]

SHIMBA (or SIMBA). A not very numerous people of the Okandé linguistic group living in the forested lower Offoué and the upper Ikoyi River. [284]

SHO. *See* SOCIETE COMMERCIALE, INDUSTRIELLE ET AGRICOLE DU HAUT-OGOOUE.

SLAVE TRADE. Gabon was never a major site of the Atlantic slave trade as were the Niger River Delta, the Congo, and Angola, but the slave trade carried on there, above all from the 1760s to the 1860s, affected a majority of its peoples. Practically all of the peoples of Gabon engaged in the slave trade at one time or another. The most notable exception was the Fang people, who possessed few slaves and refused to become involved in the slave trade despite the opportunities that the warfare connected with their frequent migrations offered to them. While some slaves were obtained in warfare and in slave raids, most of them were exchanged by members of their own societies who were interested in securing European goods and/or getting rid of ''undesirables,'' both slave and free.

Geography helped to postpone and limit the impact of the slave trade in Gabon. Nearly 75 percent of the country is covered with tropical rain forest; slightly under 20 percent is grasslands and the remainder is coastal marshlands. The soils of the forests are generally mediocre and some of the most important food staples were introduced by the Portuguese from the New World only late in the sixteenth century and after. Thus the population tended to be sparse and scattered. Though Gabon has numerous rivers and streams, many of them contain sandbars and/or rapids, which prevent the passage of vessels. The absence of very many beasts of burden because of tropical diseases, such as that spread by the tsetse fly, meant that much of the passage inland had to be on foot.

When European traders arrived in the Estuary and along the Atlantic coasts in the sixteenth century, they found few slaves available, few especially in relation to the much larger numbers available both to the north (the Niger Delta) and to the south (the Congo and Angola). Only during the last third of the eighteenth century, in response to the increased demand from the New World, did the Mpongwe (q.v.) of the Estuary and the Orungu (q.v.) at Cape Lopez become more actively involved. Because the upper reaches of the Remboué River, which flowed northward into the Estuary, lay only a few miles north of Lambaréné Island in the Ogooué, a network was able to develop linking the Mpongwe of the southern Estuary shore with the Galoa (q.v.) suppliers around Lambaréné and other peoples beyond. The Galoa were also linked with the Orungu 160 miles downstream at the mouth of the Ogooué and peoples upstream. Trade on the Ogooué was conducted under a system in which each group along the river dominated a section and acted as middlemen for goods and slaves passing up- or downstream. The inland peoples who provided the largest numbers of slaves for these two networks had the most numerous populations: the Apindji, Adouma, Eshira, and Mitsogo (qq.v.). Slaves were also drawn from the Nzabi, Massango, Shaké (qq.v.), and other peoples.

The increased demand of the New World for slaves coincided with the Industrial Revolution in Europe, which gradually lowered the price of the now mass-produced British manufactures and thus made them even more competitive with African goods. The apparently increased supply of slaves by the 1760s may have resulted from the westward migrations of various peoples into the Ogooué River system and toward the coasts during the eighteenth and nineteenth centuries, some of them seeking increased trade with the Europeans.

Complete statistics for the slave trade are lacking, but reliable estimates for some periods are available. It is likely that 500 slaves were being exported annually from the Estuary and Cape Lopez in the 1780s and 1790s, and 1,500 annually between 1800 and 1815. Total slave exports from these two areas likely averaged several thousand a year between 1815 and 1830.

Beginning in 1815, Britain sought to terminate the slave trade, first north of the Equator, and to gain the cooperation of other nations such as France for this purpose. French cooperation was halfhearted and grudging, for the French resented British commercial supremacy on most of the western and equatorial coasts from the Gambia to Angola. They were suspicious, with some justification, of British motives. Though the French officially listed a desire to end the slave trade as one of the reasons for establishing a post in the Estuary in 1843, they wished even more to promote French commerce and thereby gain supremacy over the British. Between the 1840s and the 1860s, the French showed much more zeal in seeking cessions of sovereignty from the Gabonese peoples and in trying to restrict the activities and influence of English-speaking traders and missionaries than in combatting the nefarious slave trade. Between 1857 and 1862, the government permitted the Régis Company of Marseilles to recruit indentured servants for the West Indies using methods that frequently resembled the discredited slave trade. It would appear that French antislaving activities became important and regular only in the 1860s, that is, after they had gained formal control of the Estuary and northern coasts. In the 1840s and 1850s, they made only irregular and unsystematic efforts, and then only after prodding by the British.

After the Anglo-French convention of May 29, 1845, which provided for the involvement of French squadrons along with British and American ones in policing the coasts, the French commander in Gabon ordered the Estuary leaders to end all traffic in slaves immediately and the European slavers to leave the southern shore. Fear of British navy patrols, in particular, from the mid-1840s caused the slavers to convert a heretofore open trade into a clandestine one. Most of this was conducted by Portuguese, Spanish, and Brazilians, often using ships owned or financed by Americans. The slavers made increasing use of São Tomé and Príncipe as trans-shipment points on the way to Brazil and Cuba. The virtual closure of the Brazilian market after 1850 was only partially compensated by the agricultural boom on the Portuguese islands in 1860 and after. At that time São Tomé and Príncipe acquired cocoa plantations worked largely by slave labor. While one can cite the arrest of a Portuguese slaver in Orungu territory by the French in 1887, it appears that the slave trade had largely ended in the Estuary during the 1860s and at Cape Lopez in the 1870s.

A small slave trade was carried on along the southern mouth of the Ogooué (the Fernan-Vaz mouth) among the Nkomi (q.v.) people. It drew slaves from the Ogooué River system. It appears that the Nkomi trade was never extensive, except perhaps in the 1830s. A more extensive trade was carried on farther south in the Gabon provinces of the Loango (q.v.) kingdom, though the trade had a shorter duration than that in northern Gabon.

Loango, whose main provinces are today located in the Congo Republic, became an important center of the slave trade in the eighteenth century with French traders predominating. The northern provinces, now in Gabon, were at first involved in a minor way. The provinces of Mayumba, Setté-Cama, and Gobby from the seventeenth century exchanged salt, guns, and cloth mainly for ivory with the interior peoples of the upper Nyanga, N'Gounié, and Ogooué Rivers. In the course of this trade they received a few slaves whom they took south to Loango Bay for dispatch to the New World. These slaves came from the Bapounou (q.v.) and Voungou (q.v.) peoples and to a lesser extent from the Mitsogo, Massango, and Pove, in other words from some of the same populations that supplied northern Gabon. But in the late 1840s, as a result of British and French efforts to suppress the slave trade in the Estuary and at Cape Lopez, a much increased effort arose at Mayumba and Banda on the Banio Lagoon to secure slaves from these various interior peoples. Brazilian, Spanish, and Portuguese traders, as in northern Gabon, were the most active in search of the high profits of the Brazilian and Cuban markets. Many of the ships were American-built and owned since the United States refused until 1862 to allow other nations to search American ships. The new slave trade involved an increased number of points from which slaves were embarked and the establishment of more permanent white trading posts ashore. Through these tactics the slave traders sought to circumvent the growing threat from patrolling cruisers. Between the 1840s and 1870s most slaves from the Iguéla Lagoon and Setté-Cama were marched south to Mayumba, a town of 1,000 inhabitants. The same traders who were already operating at Loango Bay or Cabinda maintained barracoons there, which usually held 500 to 600 captives awaiting a ship. At Banda, on the coast near the southern end of Banio Lagoon, 700 to 800 captives customarily could be found. Many of the slaves were transported to São Tomé for transfer to other slaving vessels headed for the West Indies and South America. It thus appeared that several thousand slaves annually left the southern Gabon coast in the mid-nineteenth century. Taking Gabon as a whole, the bulk of the slaves went to South America, particularly to Brazil, and to the West Indies, especially to Cuba. Some were taken to São Tomé and Príncipe, but only a few reached North America.

It is difficult to evaluate the consequences of the slave trade in Gabon. Given the absence of reliable population figures, it is impossible to know the exact percentage annually captured or sold. Estimates range from 1 to 5 percent of populations numbered at 150,000 to 250,000. It should be recalled that only the young and able-bodied were generally recruited for the slave trade. A portion of those taken in the interior did not survive the trip to the coast or the stay in the barracoons. Others perished under the horrible conditions of the long voyage to the New World and of the plantations there. The past two decades have seen a number of scholars argue that this loss of manpower was not serious and was more than compensated by the economic stimulus of the European goods thus obtained. Even if one agrees with their economic conclusions, one must not forget the terrible sufferings of the victims and their families as well as the many deaths arising from the slave trade and plantation slavery. Though blacks were involved in selling other blacks to whites, the slave trade contributed to the racial attitudes and practices that have plagued black-white relations in the western world during the past four centuries. *See* FREE EMIGRANTS SCHEME. [252, 262, 326, 110, 39, 50, 123]

SOCIETE COMMERCIALE, INDUSTRIELLE ET AGRICOLE DU HAUT-OGOOUE (SHO). Most important concessionary company in Gabon. The SHO held a commercial monopoly over 104,000 sq. km. out of 267,000 sq. km. in all Gabon between 1893 and 1930. The establishment of this chartered company in eastern and southeastern Gabon predated the general French policy of developing French Equatorial Africa through some 40 concessionary companies in 1899. The SHO possessed even more extensive powers with fewer responsibilities than the later enterprises, and its sway lasted two decades longer than most of them, in part because it was better funded and directed. The SHO was founded at the urgings of Savorgnan de Brazza (q.v.) by Marius-Célestin Daumas (d. 1894), a one-time agent of the Régis firm of Marseilles who was long involved in commerce in Gabon and was the most successful French businessman there. The SHO had its own police force and administered justice in its territories. Though it eventually had to pay customs duties, it did not have to establish native reserves as the later companies were required to do, pay rent, or make plantations. It held a monopoly of trade in its vast territories, including the sale of European imports and the purchase of local products such as rubber. It took exorbitant profits from both processes. For a kilogram of rubber, which usually took an African gatherer four work days and which brought 15 francs in Europe ($3 at the time), it exchanged a kilogram of salt or two needles. Because the Ogooué River above N'Djolé and most of its tributaries were blocked by waterfalls and rapids, and because steamboat transport was impossible and portage necessary, the SHO forcibly recruited porters and demanded the sale of foodstuffs from the area's peoples. Its activities frequently involved injustice and brutality. They contributed to African resistance, including opposition led by the Fang chief Emané Tolé (q.v.) near N'Djolé in 1901–1902, on the N'Gounié among the Mitsogo and Apindji from 1903 to 1909, and by Awandji (q.v.) chiefs near Lastoursville in 1928–1929. The SHO built 100 km. of roads at an expense of 1.5 million francs to try to reduce portage, but was unable to secure the labor to maintain them. Through a subsidiary, the SHO became active in lumbering in the 1920s, especially in the okoumé whose value Daumas had perspicaciously recognized in the early 1890s. In 1930 the SHO relinquished its concession in exchange for outright title to 35,000 hectares (70,000 acres) of choice timberland. [266]

SOCIETY. The various peoples of Gabon traditionally possessed a social organization based on kinship. Members of an extended family, or lineage, shared a common ancestry. Related lineages formed clans and related clans composed peoples (often called tribes in older usage). Originally a clan was governed by its elders, heads of families, or lineages, and clan heads were spokesmen for their decisions and arbitrators of disputes. Some peoples had clan councils that handled disputes and regulated matters of common concern. Only the Orungu of Cape Lopez and the Vili of the Loango coast developed centralized monarchies, in both cases in response to external trade. (The Nkomi at Fernan-Vaz also had a monarchy in the 1830s at the height of the slave trade.) But changes in the patterns of this trade later helped to destroy these institutions. Succession to the monarchy and clan headship was generally confined to the members of a particular lineage. Within that lineage, succession was either patrilineal or matrilineal but without primogeniture. Thus the succession ordinarily went to the oldest nephew of the previous ruler or head, that is, to the son of his brother (patrilineal) or of his sister (matrilineal). There are a few cases of female heads (e.g., the princess who founded the

Vili-Loumbou kingdom at Mayumba and Enenga ''queens'' in the mid-nineteenth century).

Custom and tradition governed social behavior, and secret societies of both men and women enforced the decisions of the elders when necessary. The elders and clan heads exerted influence over the younger men through their control of the wealth of the society—use of the land, goods, and women.

Most peoples practiced domestic slavery, the slaves coming from other peoples by purchase, exchange, or warfare. Slaves did the agricultural work along with the free women, who ordinarily raised the group's foodstuffs. Peoples sold free men into slavery as a means of social control and to obtain merchandise. Ordinarily they did not sell the domestic slaves, whose labor was necessary to ensure their food supply. Free men often married slave women, and their offspring became free men. Children born to parents who were both slaves remained slaves.

Traders in these societies often achieved great influence because of their wealth, sometimes advancing ahead of others in succession for headships of villages and clans. Trade with Europeans on the coasts enriched some younger men, who gained more freedom from the control of their elders. During the colonial period, the French transformed the role of the clan heads by forcing them to become the agents of the administration. The French also created canton or territorial chiefs who had no bases in traditional society. After the Second World War, the western educated, which included some persons who belonged to the lineages of clan heads, acquired positions in the new representative institutions and administration, which further weakened the traditional organization. The extended family, or lineage, nevertheless remains primary in the social relations and loyalties of most persons, even many with a western education.

Gabon today possesses social classes based upon economic and educational factors. In 1978 there were 267,000 persons involved in agriculture; 60,000 in forestry, mining, and construction; 8,200 in commerce and industry; 8,000 in the civil service; 38,200 in other activities (military, clergy, independent professionals, students in higher education, and others). By 1990 the number of government employees had risen to 40,000, including schoolteachers and the employees of the parastatals. The FAO estimated the number of agricultural workers at 370,000 and salaried workers in the private sector at 138,000. Those in agriculture are largely subsistence farmers who own their own land, livestock, and tools. Commercial farmers, organized in cooperatives that utilize some machinery, are found mainly in the Woleu-N'Tem Province (cocoa, coffee) and around Lambaréné in the Moyen-Ogooué Province (palm products). While Gabonese provide the unskilled and some skilled labor for forestry, mining, and construction, some top-level technical and management personnel are Europeans. In the civil service French experts continue to fill many of the key technical and administrative positions, but under the direction of Gabonese executives. The well-educated Gabonese tend to form a bureaucratic class that lives through government employment. The longtime domination of the economy by Europeans prevented the development of a Gabonese bourgeoisie during the colonial period. An economically independent class has emerged mainly since independence and primarily in the area of urban real estate investments. The economic expansion of the past decades in particular has greatly increased the numbers of non-Gabonese African wage laborers, which were always a feature of the labor-short society during the colonial period. [251, 300, 795, 802]

SOUSATTE, RENE-PAUL (1913–1969). Politician. Although born at Fernan-Vaz on June 18, 1913, Sousatte's family came from the Eshira area of the N'Gounié Province. He studied at the Catholic seminaries in Libreville and Brazzaville, leaving the latter shortly before ordination. He joined the civil service at Brazzaville in 1937, where he was a colleague of Jean-Hilaire Aubame (q.v.) and Jean-Rémy Ayouné (q.v.). Sousatte supported the Free French (q.v.) movement in 1940 and under Governor-General Félix Eboué (q.v.) became head of an organization of civil servants, the Union Educative et Mutuelle de la Jeunesse de Brazzaville, which published a pro-Gaullist newspaper, *L'Education de la Jeunesse Africaine*. He also advised Eboué on African matters. In 1947 the Territorial Assembly elected Sousatte to represent Gabon in the Assembly of the French Union. Thereafter he founded the Comité Gabonais d'Etudes Sociales et Economiques (COGES) (q.v.) to foster cooperation among Gabon's peoples in order to promote modernization of society and to develop a political base for himself. COGES had sections in the main towns and found members mainly among the Eshira and Myènè. Paul Gondjout (q.v.) headed the Libreville section. Sousatte became active in various Franco-African groups as well as the African section of the Gaullist party, the Rassemblement du Peuple Français. He published a book, *L'Afrique Equatoriale Française, Berceau de l'Union Française* (1952), which discussed the Free French movement and Gabon's importance to France. He wrote articles for the RPF paper *L'Etincelle de l'AEF*. His Gaullist politics contributed to his failure to be renamed to his post in 1952 as well as to the refusal of the administration to readmit him to the civil service upon his return to Gabon. For the next five years he worked in Madagascar, returning to Gabon to reenter politics after the collapse of the Fourth Republic. Several weeks before the September 1958 referendum on the French Community, with J.-J. Boucavel, he organized a party of southern peoples, especially the Eshira and Bapounou, who were dissatisfied with the Fang and Myènè leadership of the UDSG and BDG, and urged a negative vote. The Parti d'Union Nationale Gabonaise (q.v.), or PUNGA (a name that happens to mean "tempest" in Eshira), succeeded in mobilizing a majority in the Nyanga Province, a Bapounou area, against the Community. PUNGA also had a small national following among trade unionists and students. After independence, Sousatte was arrested for his opposition to some of Mba's policies, but in 1962–1963 served as Minister of Agriculture until the breakup of the coalition government. Sousatte thereafter returned to Port-Gentil where he spent his remaining years in private business. He died on February 27, 1969. [617, 550]

- T -

TCHICAYA, JEAN-FELIX (1903–1961). Ponty School graduate and deputy from Gabon and Middle Congo to the French National Assembly. Tchicaya was born on November 9, 1903, at Libreville into a prominent Vili family from Diosso (Buali) on the Loango (q.v.) coast in a period when the Kouilou Region formed part of Gabon. His grandfather, André Portella, was one of the wealthiest Vili merchants at Diosso. As one of the two brightest graduates of the public school of Libreville, Tchicaya was sent in 1918 on government scholarship to the William Ponty School at Dakar where he was a classmate of Houphouet-Boigny and Mamba Sano and one year behind Mamadou Konaté, like him all future deputies. In 1921, upon his return to Gabon, he was appointed an upper-primary teacher at the Libreville school. In 1923–1924, after quarreling with the French principal of the school, he was dismissed. His grandfather summoned him in 1925 to Point-Noire to work with the administration in the construction of the port and the Congo-Ocean Railroad. There he organized the educated young Vili and others into a club and band, L'Harmonie de Pointe-Noire, and at the same time he formed among the Vili an informal protest committee, which succeeded through Portella's influence with the administration in winning a number of local reforms. When the Ma-Loango was imprisoned on minor charges, this committee mobilized the Vili to secure his release. When a French *chef de région* became too arbitrary and severe in his relations with the Vili, Tchicaya's committee passed letters through Portella to Governor-General Raphaël Antonetti, which won his removal. Tchicaya was instrumental in winning the election to the federal council of administration in 1937 and 1939 of Louis Oliveira, a Vili *métis* educated at Libreville.

During the Second World War, Tchicaya joined the armed forces of the Free French movement. In 1945 Gabon and Congo elected Tchicaya as their deputy to the First Constituent Assembly. Later when the Gabonese secured their own deputy, he was elected as Middle Congo's deputy to the French National Assembly, serving from 1946 to 1958.

Tchicaya became a vice president of the territorial RDA. He died at Pointe-Noire on January 15, 1961.

He was the father of the noted poet Tchicaya U'Tamsi (Gérard Tchicaya) (1931–1989), a longtime employee of Unesco in Paris. [607, 505, 96]

TEKE (or BATEKE). The Téké people inhabit the grassy plateaux east of Franceville in the Haut-Ogooué Province. They are related to the Téké or Tyo of the Congo Republic but had no political ties with the Makoko of the Pool area, who made a treaty with Brazza on September 10, 1880, recognizing French sovereignty. The Téké are also related to the Mbamba, Ndoumou, and Kanigui. According to their traditions, they were living near Ewo and Okoyo on the Alima River (a tributary of the Congo) when pressures from the Mbochi forced their transfer into the plateaux between the Alima and the Leconi Rivers (an Ogooué tributary) where they planted palm trees. As they retreated, they divided into three groups in uninhabited territories on the upper M'Passa, Leconi, and Lelani Rivers, probably in the mid-nineteenth century. At the arrival of Brazza, the Téké had two important chiefs: Ngoshama on the Leconi, and Lelani and Mbani-Lekivi on the upper M'Passa. The Téké sold slaves and raphia fabrics to the peoples of the Congo and Niari River systems (Congo Téké, Balali, Bapounou) in exchange for salt, fabrics, and goats. [284, 384, 356, 816, 865, 884, 109, 880]

TOKO (or NTOKO) RAVONYA (d. 1858). The leading trader of the Mpongwe village of Glass from 1840 until his death, who allied with British and American merchants. His opposition to the recognition of French sovereignty helped to delay the French occupation of the lands of the Agekaza-Glass or Agekaza w'Olamba clan for several years between 1842 and 1845. Toko had given the land on which the ABCFM missionaries located their Baraka station in 1842 and was their protector and friend. His son, the Rev. Ntâkâ Truman (q.v.), was the first Mpongwe to be ordained a Presbyterian minister. Toko himself headed the Agwesono clan, which lived among the Glass people. [252, 255, 362, 1031]

TRANSPORTATION. In precolonial times, the main means of transporting men and goods was canoes on waterways. Gabon has many rivers, but only 3,300 km. of them are navigable in all seasons. The presence of rapids and waterfalls, especially where they drop from plateaux to plains, made human portage a necessity. In a country that is both heavily forested and sparsely populated, neither the manpower nor the funds were available to build roads, even if the projects had been viable.

Trade and commerce remained waterborne in the colonial period even after the arrival of the steamboat and other power-driven vessels. The exploitation of woods that could be floated down streams became the chief industry. The colonial administration helped to develop the ports of Port-Gentil and Libreville to aid this industry and commerce in general, but the costs of constructing and maintaining very many all-season roads remained prohibitive. Most of the 7,513 km. of roads today are laterite and are cut by numerous creeks. A great number of them are usable only in the dry season. Five hundred and sixty-five km. of roads are asphalt, including the national highways from Libreville to Lambaréné built under FIDES (q.v.) in the 1950s. At present, one can travel by motor vehicle in the dry season on a north-south axis from Cameroon to the Congo via N'Djolé and Lambaréné (870 km.) and on a west-east axis from Libreville to Franceville via N'Djolé and Lastoursville (774 km.).

The difficulties of road travel have led since the Second World War to the construction of a rather dense air network. Libreville, Port-Gentil, and Franceville have international airports, and there are 121 smaller airports and landing fields distributed throughout the country. As of June 1977, Gabon withdrew from the inter-state Air Afrique and replaced its services with Air-Gabon, a government company that heretofore was operating only within the country. Gabon is served internationally by such lines as Air France, UTA, Sabena, and Swiss Air.

Between 1974 and 1986 the Bongo regime undertook the construction of the Transgabonais Railroad for 648 km. between Owendo on the Estuary to Franceville on the upper Ogooué River. It thereby sought to reach the forest and mineral riches of the interior where the rivers are not navigable for long stretches or where road building and maintenance are not viable or would be more expensive. Facilities to handle the timber were completed at the port of Owendo in 1979 and the manganese in 1988. Plans for constructing a section of the railroad from Booué 240 km. northeast to the iron ore of Belinga had to be postponed. Plans are nevertheless under way to revitalize the entire economic life of the regions that the Transgabonais now serves. During the late 1980s limited use of the railroad and high maintenance costs were producing annual deficits of $20 to $30 million. [929, 687, 689]

TRILLES, HENRI (1866–1949). A Spiritan priest from Clermont-Ferrand who served in Gabon from 1893 to 1907. He became an expert on the Fang (q.v.) and their language as well as the Pygmies (q.v.) of the northeast, peoples about whom he wrote many volumes. He was also an amateur botanist. [1302]

TRUMAN. *See* NTAKA TRUMAN.

- U -

UNION DEMOCRATIQUE ET SOCIALE GABONAISE (UDSG). The political party that formed around Jean-Hilaire Aubame (q.v.) in 1947 following his election as deputy to the French National Assembly in November 1946. It supported his reelection in 1951 and 1956 and presented lists of candidates in the elections for the Territorial Assembly in 1952 and 1957. The UDSG relied upon local influentials and regional groups to organize its electoral support. It had the support of the missions and between 1947 and 1956 the sympathy of the French administration. Though the UDSG won a majority of the popular votes in the Territorial Assembly elections in 1957, its opponents among the BDG and Independents were able to organize the first executive council and make Léon Mba its chief African member. BDG control of the government thereafter inhibited its actions, and in the 1964 elections it refused to present candidates. The UDSG's legal existence was terminated in March 1968 by President Bongo's decree dissolving all parties as a prelude to formation of a single party, the PDG. [550, 593]

UNION DOUANIERE ET ECONOMIQUE DE L'AFRIQUE CENTRALE (UDEAC). A customs and economic union of Gabon, Congo, the Central African Republic, and Cameroon. During the colonial period, Gabon had economic links with the other territories of French Equatorial Africa and with Cameroon, which was a French mandate and later a trusteeship territory. After the dissolution of the federation of French Equatorial Africa, Gabon and the other three states decided to remain linked in a customs union. On June 23, 1959, they signed a treaty establishing the Union Douanière Equatoriale (UDE) whose main features were 1) the free movement of goods and capital among the member countries; 2) the introduction of common import taxes; 3) the creation of a solidarity fund; and 4) the introduction of a single tax system (*taxe unique*). The solidarity tax sought to compensate the inland states (Central African Republic and Chad) for the advantages the coastal states derived from the transit trade. The single tax applied to products of the five states with a view to protecting and encouraging domestic industry. On June 22, 1961, Cameroon became an associate member of the UDE under terms that permitted retention of its separate import duties and taxes. But from July 1, 1962, the five countries established a common external tariff limited to customs duties.

Then on December 8, 1964, the five signed a treaty creating UDEAC, whereby they undertook to strengthen the customs union and transform it into a broader economic union. To this end they took steps to harmonize customs, fiscal, and investment policies. By the time UDEAC took effect on January 1, 1966, unification of import taxation had largely been achieved, while taxation of exports remained the prerogative of the individual states subject to mutual consultation. One important feature concerning import taxation retained from the UDE was exemption from customs duties of goods from the countries of the European Common Market and from the other states in the former Organization of African and Malagasy States for Economic Cooperation (Benin, Ivory Coast, Madagascar, Mauritania, Niger, Senegal, and Upper Volta). This provision had the effect of disfavoring products from non-EEC industrial nations such as the United States, Japan, and until its entrance into the EEC, the United Kingdom.

Dissatisfaction with the results of UDEAC by the inland states led to their withdrawal on April 25, 1968. On the previous February 1, the Central African Republic and Chad had joined Zaire in forming the Union des Etats d'Afrique du Centre, or UEAC, from which they hoped to achieve greater benefits. But on December 10, the CAR returned to UDEAC. Chad did not until 1984, but subsequently it made its own arrangements with Cameroon through which most of its transit trade passes.

The policies of UDEAC are determined by agreement of the heads of state meeting periodically and are implemented by a committee of their ministers of finances and economic affairs. The secretariat of UDEAC is located at Bangui, Central African Republic.

The UDEAC members on May 3, 1976, organized the Banque de Développement des Etats de l'Afrique Centrale with its seat at Brazzaville. A decade earlier they had established an oil refinery at Port-Gentil for common use. [402, 433, 444, 466, 469, 494, 507, 508, 509]

URANIUM. France began uranium exploration in Gabon in 1947 on the initiative of its Atomic Energy Commission. In 1956 important deposits were located at Mounana, 25 km. north of Moanda, that is, in the same part of the Haut-Ogooué Province where manganese is being exploited. The Compagnie des Mines d'Uranium de Franceville (COMUF), which was formed in 1958 to mine the ore, remains the sole producer. Though originally it was entirely owned by French interests, in 1990 the Gabonese state held 25 percent of the shares. Until 1978 the ore was shipped by truck to M'Binda in the Congo Republic and from there by the Congo-Ocean Railroad to the port of Pointe-Noire. At that time, a yellowcake plant started operations. The completion of the Transgabonais to Franceville in December 1986 and of the minerals port of Owendo two years later makes possible the evacuation of uranium entirely through Gabonese territory.

Under the terms of the various cooperation agreements with France, Gabon gives that country priority in the purchase of uranium and restricts sales to third countries as required in the interests of common defense. In the late 1980s, a subsidiary of the French Atomic Energy Commission, the Compagnie générale des matières nucléaires (CO-GEMA), which holds 19 percent of COMUF's shares, purchased 60 percent of the total production. The rest was exported to Japan, Belgium, and Italy. Production of uranium concentrates reached a peak of 1,850 tons in 1977, but fell to half of that total in the late 1980s as a result of diminished world market conditions. At the same time, prices, further depressed by the weakness of the U.S. dollar, declined drastically from $43 a pound in 1978 to $17 in 1986 and $8.70 in 1990.

The deposits at Mounana have become exhausted so that mining is now carried on in the same general vicinity at Mikoulougou, Boyindzi, Oklo, and Okelobondo. The short-term production capability from known reserves and existing plants is 1,500 tons per year for the period 1985 to 1995. Despite unfavorable world market conditions, French interests have been undertaking exploration for additional deposits in the vicinity of Franceville and Mounana. The Gabonese government as well as private German and Korean firms has a small portion of the investments in exploration, which totalled $6 million in 1986. Through this exploration, France is seeking not only to ensure its long-term needs for nuclear energy but also to prepare for the possible loss of uranium supplies from Namibia and South Africa. In the late 1980s, those two countries provided one-sixth of French needs, Gabon another sixth, and Niger two-thirds.

As for Gabon, in the early 1980s it discussed with both France and Argentina the possibilities of establishing its own nuclear power plant. The high costs involved led to the shelving of the proposal upon the arrival of the economic downturn of 1986. [500, 1364]

- V -

VANE, FRANCOIS-DE-PAUL (ca. 1890–1957). Estuary political leader during inter-war period. Vané was descended from a chiefly Benga family that was among the first to convert to Roman Catholicism in the 1850s. He was raised by the Holy Ghost Fathers at Libreville and educated at their seminary. Though he left in 1911 in the middle of his theological studies, he was nevertheless one of the best educated Gabonese of his day. From 1912 to 1925 Vané worked in the Ivory Coast. After his return to Libreville he became chief accountant for a Senegalese merchant and in 1926 the secretary-general and moving spirit of the local chapter of the Ligue des Droits de l'Homme. In this capacity he sought reforms that would benefit the Estuary elite and defended their traditional land rights upon which the colonial authorities and other peoples were encroaching. After the administration succeeded in dividing the elite through its support for métis interests, Vané, with various leading Mpongwe, organized the Mutuelle Gabonaise (q.v.) to oppose a special favored status for just the métis. The Mutuelle, though primarily a cultural and educational organization, brought together the older generation, which had supported the Ligue and the younger men who had studied at the Ecole Montfort and the Catholic seminary during the 1920s and early 1930s. Under the auspices of the Catholic mission, Vané in 1933 had previously organized the Cercle Catholique, which served to educate and to heighten elite awareness. In October 1937, Vané won election as Gabon's delegate to the new federal council of administration at Brazzaville, defeating the candidate appointed temporarily the previous year, Pierre-Marie Akanda, an Mpongwe lumberman. He was reelected in June 1939 and used his office to speak out in defense of elite and African interests. He thus successfully opposed measures initiated by French officials that would have had the effect of restricting Christian mission schools to catechismal instruction and therefore of lessening educational opportunities. He helped to secure the decree of

February 10, 1938, recognizing limited traditional land rights and providing a new basis for claims for compensation for land taken by the administration. In 1938 Vané was among the first two Africans named to the Libreville municipal commission.

When French Equatorial Africa rallied to Free France in August 1940, Vané and the Mpongwe elite followed the bishop of Libreville, Monsignor Louis Tardy, in support of Vichy. The Free French replaced Vané as Gabon's delegate at Brazzaville with Akanda and later Georges Damas. Though still influential, Vané was not permitted to participate in politics until 1946. In December 1946 he ran unsuccessfully for the Territorial Assembly. For the remainder of his life he worked in private business and supervised his plantations at Cape Esterias. [550]

VARAMA. The Varama are a people of the southwestern interior linguistically related to the Eshira group. They live inland from the Loumbou along the Rembo Ndogo, which flows southwest into the Ndogo Lagoon and north of the Rembo Nkomi, as well as both north and south of the Eshira proper. [284]

VILI. A people of southwestern Gabon and the adjacent coasts of the Congo Republic. The Vili language is a branch of the large Kongo family of the West Central Bantu. It is a dialect of the language spoken in Mbanza Kongo (San Salvador), the capital of the Kongo Kingdom, which is now located within Angola. Oral traditions suggest common origins for the Vili, Kongo, Téké (Tio), and Woyo peoples in an inland kingdom called Nguunu, north of the Stanley Pool, from which a dispersion occurred, perhaps as early as the eleventh century. After proceeding to the lower Congo River, the populations that became the Vili transferred by the thirteenth or fourteenth centuries to the Loango coast, where Portuguese navigators encountered them in the 1480s. By that time Vili were found along the Gabon coast as far north as Cape Saint Catherine, including the shores of the Iguéla Lagoon, Ndugu Lagoon (Setté-Cama), and the Banio Lagoon (at Mayumba and Banda). Nineteenth-century European explorers also encountered small groups of Vili on the upper N'Gounié and Ogooué rivers where they engaged as middlemen in the salt and ivory trade. These Vili may have been remnants from a period during which the power of Loango (q.v.) extended over the whole region. If this is the case, then incoming groups such as the Eshira, Bakélé, and Fang had pushed them south. Alternately, they may have been emigrants from Loango in the eighteenth century who moved away from the coast following a disagreement with their ruler.

The Vili of the coastal regions were traditionally involved in agriculture, hunting, and fishing. They made salt and palm cloth for trade as well as domestic purposes. Vili miners and coppersmiths lived part of each year at the mines inland beyond the Mayombe mountain range, and Vili porters carried the smelted ore and manufactures to the coasts. During the seventeenth century the Vili traded in ivory and in the eighteenth century in slaves with the interior peoples. Until the nineteenth century the Vili rulers controlled the terms of trade with the European merchants.

Attempts by French Catholic missionaries to evangelize the Vili and Kongo between 1766 and 1776 met with failure. The Holy Ghost Fathers (q.v.) conducted a ministry among the Vili who composed the core of Libreville, a settlement of freed slaves, in 1849 and after. From the 1870s, the Holy Ghost Fathers undertook missions on the Loango and Congo coasts, including at the town of Loango in 1883. Catholic mission work on the southern Gabon coast was based on Loango and a seminary was located at Mayumba.

With the onset of French colonial rule, the Vili became porters and agents of European firms. At the submission of the Loango monarch to French rule in 1883, the French attached the entire Loango coast as far south as the Portuguese territory of Cabinda to Gabon. It remained part of Gabon until 1918 when it was transferred to the colony of the Middle Congo. The link during several decades between Loango and the Gabon colony led to the establishment of Vili populations at both Libreville and Port-Gentil, which at independence numbered 600 persons. Gabon's first deputy to the French Constituent Assembly in 1945 was a Vili, Jean-Félix Tchicaya, a native of Libreville with family ties in Loango. [326, 384, 846, 394]

VOIX DU PAYS, LA. In 1935 the Séké leader of the Libreville branch of the Ligue des Droits de l'Homme, Jean-Baptiste N'Dendé (q.v.), helped a number of Fang (q.v.) elders to organize *La Voix du Pays* to unite the Fang populations vis à vis the Mpongwe and the French administration. This move was a reaction to the formation of the Association Amicale des Métis and the Comité Mpongwe by *métis* on the one hand, and full-blooded Mpongwe on the other, to defend and assert their traditional rights to property and influence in the Estuary. By this time the Fang were the most numerous people at Libreville and had been left without effective leadership since the conviction and exile of Léon Mba (q.v.) in 1933. According to its statutes, which were drawn to secure legal recognition, the primary aim was to encourage cooperative agriculture and fishing among the Libreville Fang, and to this end a shop was established to market Fang produce. Though the group did not become involved in the elections for a delegate to the governor-general's council of administration in 1937 and 1939, behind the scenes it worked successfully to promote the careers of several Fang civil servants, to the end that these men soon controlled key posts in the office of the French administrator-mayor of Libreville. [550]

VOUNGOU. The Voungou people of the southwestern interior are linguistically part of the Eshira group. According to their traditions they originally lived on the left bank of the upper N'Gounié River at a time when the Mitsogo (q.v.) inhabited the right bank. Warlike Bapounou (q.v.) invaders pushed them a bit to the west into the forested mountainous areas west of the Moukabala River, a tributary of the Nyanga River, where they still live. Among them habitual offenders and debtors could be reduced to slavery. The Voungou also enslaved defenseless foreigners whom they transmitted to the Eshira (q.v.) for sale to the Nkomi (q.v.) of Fernan-Vaz and to the Loumbou (q.v.) of Setté-Cama. In return they received salt and fabrics from Portuguese and British traders. In the nineteenth century they gathered and sold rubber to American traders based at Mayumba. [284, 384]

- W -

WALKER, ANDRE RAPONDA- (1871–1968). First Gabonese priest and the nation's most noted scholar to date. Monsignor Walker was the son of Robert Bruce Napoleon Walker (1830–1900), British agent for the Hatton & Cookson firm in Gabon between 1859 and 1875 and explorer of the middle Ogooué and an aristocratic Mpongwe, Agñorogoulé Ikoutu (1852–1912). She was the niece of King Georges (q.v.) and a relative of King Louis (q.v.). André Walker was educated by the Holy Ghost Fathers entirely in Gabon and was ordained a Roman Catholic priest on July 23, 1899. While serving as a pastor and teacher in many parts of Gabon during the next five decades, he became an expert on the peoples, languages, history, and botany of his country. Among the most important of his extensive publications are *Notes d'Histoire du Gabon* (1960), *Plantes utiles du Gabon* (1959), and *Rites et Croyances des Peuples du Gabon* (1962), the latter two volumes in collaboration with the French scholar Roger Sillans. Walker's unpublished autobiography is a valuable source for Gabonese history. In May 1963 he was made a domestic prelate by Pope John XXIII with the title of monsignor.

In early December 1964 Monsignor Walker clashed with President Mba (q.v.) as a result of a tract he had sent to Parisian newspapers denouncing the exactions and acts of violence committed by the president's Fang supporters during October. Mba expelled the elderly prelate from St. Peter's rectory near the presidential palace and 40 to 50 Fang from the president's Essoké clan beat him unconscious and sacked his library. [284, 569]

WALKER, WILLIAM (1808–1896). American missionary in Gabon, 1842–1870, 1879–1883, and translator of the Scriptures into Mpongwe. Rev. William Walker was born at

Vershire, Vermont, on October 3, 1808, and worked as a young man as a blacksmith, a trade he continued to practice for the ABCFM mission in Gabon. Educated at Amherst College and at Andover Seminary in Massachusetts, Walker went out to Cape Palmas (now in Liberia) in February 1842 and later that year to Gabon. Over the next 40 years he served as pastor of the church at Baraka, head of the boys' boarding school, and translator of large portions of the Old and New Testaments into Mpongwe. In 1854 Walker and the Rev. Ira Preston (q.v.) made a pioneering exploration up the Nazareth mouth of the Ogooué River halfway to the site of present-day Lambaréné, the first whites to venture there. His diaries are an important source for the history of Gabon. Walker served as a Congregationalist minister in Milton, Wisconsin, after his final return to the States until his death on December 8, 1896. [360, 1031, 1028]

WALKER-DEEMIN, HENRI (1930–). Civil servant. Walker-Deemin was born at Libreville on November 30, 1930, into a prominent *métis* (q.v.) family. Between 1936 and 1948, he did his primary and secondary studies in France. Back in Gabon he prepared to be a primary teacher and school inspector. Since 1956 he has held a variety of positions in education, culture, and information. He was the president of the national commission for Unesco (1970–1973) and since then has served as director of the Official Journal. Walker-Deemin is a gifted poet who writes in French. [1367]

WILSON, JOHN LEIGHTON (1809–1886). Founder of the American Protestant mission in the Estuary and specialist in Mpongwe (q.v.). The Rev. J. L. Wilson was born in Mount Clio, South Carolina, on March 25, 1809, into a family of prosperous Scotch-Irish landowners and prominent Presbyterians. He was educated at Union College, Schenectady, New York, and the Columbia (South Carolina) Seminary. He married Jane Bayard of Savannah, Georgia, (1809–1885), a member of a well-known aristocratic family of Huguenot origins. After ordination in 1833, he was commissioned by the American Board of Commissioners for Foreign Missions of Boston, the largest Protestant missionary society in the

United States, which represented churches of the Calvinist or Reformed traditions, to found a mission at Cape Palmas in the colony of the Maryland State Colonization Society in 1834. Disagreements between the mission and the officials of the colony led to the transfer of the ABCFM mission to Gabon in June 1842. For the next decade, until health problems forced his definitive return to the States, Wilson was the animating spirit of the Protestant mission. Using the orthography developed by John Pickering for American Indian languages, he transcribed Mpongwe into Latin characters, prepared an Mpongwe grammar, an Mpongwe-English dictionary, and translated a portion of the Gospels into Mpongwe. He had these works and religious instructional materials that he prepared printed at Cape Palmas and Gabon on the mission press. He founded the Baraka church east of Libreville and served as its first pastor. He opened schools staffed in part by English-speaking black Americans and West Africans. As part of his campaign against the slave trade, he wrote a pamphlet that was distributed throughout England and influenced members of Parliament. He befriended the young Paul du Chaillu (q.v.) whose interest in the fauna of Gabon and exploration he helped to cultivate. Wilson located the skeletal remains of a gorilla, which he brought back to the Peabody Museum in Boston, the first to reach America. After his return to the States, he published *Western Africa: Its History, Condition, & Prospects* (New York, 1856), a work influential in the anti-slavery movement and in making western Equatorial Africa known to the American public. Its information on peoples remains useful today. From 1853 Wilson served as secretary of the Presbyterian Board for Foreign Missions and, with the outbreak of the American Civil War, of the Southern Presbyterian Board until a year before his death on July 13, 1886. [1031, 250, 252, 255, 272]

WOUMBOU (or BAVUMBU). The Woumbou are a Bakota-speaking group who inhabit villages west of Franceville and south of that town on the upper Ogooué around Lebagni. Their traditions related their arrival down the Sébé River with the Mindassa (Ndasa) and the Mbahouis into an empty territory. They were pushed farther west by the Ambamba. They intermarried with the Ndoumou and the Babongo Pygmies. [365]

- Y -

YEMBIT, PAUL-MARIE (1917–1979). Vice president under Mba. Yembit was born on December 22, 1917, at Ndende among the Bapounou (q.v.) people. He was educated at local Catholic schools and at the public secondary school at Lambaréné. He was a successful businessman at Mouila between 1943 and 1952. He was elected to the Territorial Assembly from the N'Gounié Province in March 1952 and was reelected to the Legislative Assembly in March 1957, where he belonged to the Bloc Démocratique Gabonais. He was appointed Minister of Agriculture & Livestock in the first government council in March 1957. He held ministerial posts until becoming vice president of the government in February 1961 and also served in the National Assembly. President Mba replaced him as vice president in November 1966 with Albert-Bernard Bongo. [1310, 1367]

BIBLIOGRAPHY

Introduction

The best introduction to Gabon and its history in English is the recent work of James Barnes [6a]. Its sections on developments since independence and on the economy have particular value. The best introduction in French (through 1987) is François Gaulme [65]. His study outlines and interprets the main historical periods while including economic trends and foreign relations during the Bongo era. Another recent work, by Marc Aicardi de Saint-Paul [1], must be used with caution. It does not reflect an acquaintance with recent historical scholarship. It shows a strong bias in favor of the Bongo regime. Its data on recent economic and financial matters nevertheless have much value. A brief history by Ange-Ratanga-Atoz [375] summarizes events from the fifteenth century through 1960. It is extremely sketchy for the period after the Second World War. The author does not use the large body of scholarship in the English language. An excellent study by Roland Pourtier [940] provides a detailed, up-to-date introduction to the geography, demography, and economy of Gabon from a historical perspective. A geography text by two Gabonese teachers, Frédéric Meyo-Bibang and Jean-Martin Nzamba [929], is particularly strong for economic geography.

The most comprehensive works on the peoples of Gabon, including their history, are those by André Raponda Walker [394] and Hubert Deschamps [283]. Marcel Soret [384] treats the peoples of the south and southeast who also inhabit the Congo Republic. Studies by K. David Patterson [362], Henry Bucher [252], and Elikia M'Bokolo [332] ably treat the history of the northern coastal regions through 1875. Phyllis Martin [326] deals with the portions of the southern coast under the sway of Loango

321

through 1870. François Gaulme [300] analyzes the evolution of Nkomi society through the nineteenth century. Joseph Ambouroué-Avaro [229] studies the peoples of the lower Ogooué during the nineteenth century. Other works on individual peoples, which include the impact of colonial rule, are those on the Fang by Georges Balandier [795] and James Fernandez [830], and on the Bakota by Louis Perrois [365]. Ange Ratanga Atoz [377] and Nicolas Metegué N'Nah [340] have dealt with the resistance of Gabon's peoples to the establishment of French colonial rule through 1914. Michael Reed [378] has studied the political economy of N'Djolé since 1800. A chapter by Ralph Austen and Rita Headrick [232] discusses French colonial rule in French Equatorial Africa, of which Gabon formed part, during the twentieth century.

Helpful for understanding political developments from the Second World War through the end of the Mba period are works by John Ballard [550], Brian Weinstein [617], and Charles and Alice Darlington [569]. An authoritative article by Gilbert Comte [565] treats the Mba period and the early years of the Bongo regime. A much more extensive one by Michael Reed [605] concentrates upon the involvement of France and Frenchmen since independence. Indispensable for the politics of the Bongo era are the articles by N'Dong Obiang [602] and François Hervouet [636]. Useful for both the politics and economics of the period 1945–1958 are the chapters in the survey by Virginia Thompson and Richard Adloff [129]. Articles by David Gardinier [961, 962, 967, 1030, 1031] introduce educational developments since independence as well as the history of western education since 1842. Christian missionary activities during the nineteenth century have been studied by Penelope Campbell [1009, 1010] and David Gardinier [1028, 1029]. The best older work on Catholic evangelization is that of Alexandre LeRoy [1045]. André Raponda Walker and Roger Sillans [1099] treat the traditional religions and beliefs of Gabon's peoples. James Fernandez [1026] and Stanislaw Swiderski [1081] have studied the newer indigenous religion, Bwiti. O. H. Kasule [1040] surveys recent Muslim activities.

Students of contemporary affairs should start with the Gabon sections of *Africa Contemporary Record* [1305], *Année Africaine* [1317], and the *Annuaire du Tiers-Monde* [1320]. The annually updated sections in *Africa South of the Sahara* [1308] provide less data but greater perspective. Especially valuable for detailed current news is the Agence France Presse's *Bulletin Quotidien d' Afrique* [1315]. The best summary of the press is found in the *Africa Research Bulletin* [1307]. Detailed political and economic news with analyses are found in *Marchés Tropicaux et Méditerranéens* [1407], *Bulletin d'Afrique Noire* [1338], and the Economist Intelligence Unit's *Congo, Gabon, Equatorial Guinea Country Report* [1364]. Less frequent or less detailed information appears in *Africa Confidential* [1304], *Africa Report* [1306], and *West Africa* [1447]. *Jeune Afrique* [1400] has detailed interpretive articles on important developments.

Continuing bibliographical sources for books, articles, and chapters in collections include the *International African Bibliography* [1397], *Africa Bibliography* [1303], *Current Bibliography of African Affairs* [1349], and *Bibliographie des Travaux* [1363]. *Recently Published Articles* [1425] lists articles through the end of the 1980s. *Afrique Contemporaine* [1311], *Mondes et Cultures* [1413], and *Cahiers d'Etudes Africaines* [1339a] review or indicate the contents of nearly every new book on Gabon. The *Repertoire des Thèses Africanistes* [1344] lists Master's theses and doctoral dissertations completed in French universities.

A recent annotated bibliography by David Gardinier [1383a] provides descriptions or summaries of the contents of the most important works on Gabon past and present in both English and French.

Scope of the Bibliography

The bibliography includes the books, articles, reports, and theses most useful for understanding Gabon and its history. It omits outdated works as well as most political and economic ephemera. A few of the latter are included on important matters where no larger studies are available. Some citations have been briefly annotated in brackets where their titles do not indicate their contents sufficiently. Nearly all publications on Gabon are in French and English and most of the rest are in German or Spanish. The writings are grouped into 21 subject categories. In addition, each item has been numbered individually so that the most important sources for the entries in the dictionary portion of the volume can be readily identified. These references are given in brackets after each entry. The subject categories are:

I.   General Works
II.   Archaeology and Pre-History
III.   Early History and Exploration Accounts (Before 1914)
IV.   Historical Studies of Gabon and Equatorial Africa
V.   External Relations since 1960
VI.   Politics
VII.   Administration and Law
VIII.   Military Affairs
IX.   Economics
X.   Anthropology, Ethnology, and Sociology
XI.   Geography and Demography
XII.   Education
XIII.   Religion and Missions
XIV.   Physical and Natural Sciences
XV.   Health and Medicine
XVI.   Literature
XVII.   Linguistics
XVIII. Art, Music, and Dance
XIX.   Tourism
XX.   Reference and Bibliography
XXI.   Map

ABBREVIATIONS IN THE BIBLIOGRAPHY

AC	Armand Colin
AC	*Afrique Contemporaine*
AENA	*Annales de l'Ecole Nationale d'Administration*
AHA	American Historical Association
AJ	*Africana Journal*
ASA	African Studies Association
BDPA	Bureau pour le Développement de Production Agricole
Bibl.	Bibliography
BIEC	*Bulletin de l'Institut d'Etudes Centrafricaines*
BIFAN	*Bulletin de l'Institut Français d'Afrique Noire*
BIRSC	*Bulletin de l'Institut de Recherche Scientifique Centrafricaine*
B-L	Berger-Levrault
BLAMB	*Bulletin de Liaison des archéologues du monde bantu*
BMBCEAEC, ES / *BMBEAC, ES*	*Bulletin Mensuel de la Banque Centrale des Etats de l'Afrique Equatoriale et du Cameroun, Etudes Statistiques / Bulletin Mensuel de la Banque des Etats de l'Afrique Centrale, Etudes Statistiques*
BSPPG	*Bulletin de la Société Préhistorique et Protohistorique Gabonaise*
BSRC	*Bulletin de Société de Recherches Congolaises*
Bv.	Brazzaville
CEA	*Cahiers d'Etudes Africaines*
CJAS	*Canadian Journal of African Studies*
CNRS	Centre National de Recherche Scientifique

CNRST	Centre National de Recherche Scientifique et Technologique
CO-M	*Cahiers d'Outre-Mer*
CORSTOM, SSH	*Cahiers de l'Office de la Recherche Scientifique et Technique d'Outre-Mer,* série *Sciences Humaines*
CRMSASO-M / CRTSASO-M	*Comptes Rendus Mensuels des Séances de l'Académie des Sciences d'Outre-Mer / Comptes Rendus Trimestriels des Séances de l'Académie des Sciences d'Outre-Mer*
DF	La Documentation Française
Diss.	Dissertation
ed.	editor, edited
eds.	editors
Ed.	Editions
FCS	*French Colonial Studies*
G.	Geneva
G-A	*Genève-Afrique*
HA	*History in Africa*
IJAHS	*International Journal of African Historical Studies*
Impr.	Imprimerie
IN	Imprimerie Nationale
IO	Imprimerie Officielle
IPN	Institut Pédagogique National
JA / JAS	*Journal des Africanistes / Journal de la Société des Africanistes*
JAH	*Journal of African History*
JMAS	*Journal of Modern African Studies*
JRA	*Journal of Religion in Africa*
L.	London
Lv.	Libreville
MA	*Le Mois en Afrique*
MTM	*Marchés Tropicaux et Méditerranéens*
n.d.	no date
NED	*Notes et Etudes Documentaires*
no.	number
n.s.	new series, nouvelle série
N.Y.	New York

ORSTOM	Office de la Recherche Scientifique et Technique d'Outre-Mer
P.	Paris
PA	*Présence Africaine*
P&D-A	R. Pichon & R. Durand-Auzias
PB	Paul Bory
PDG	Parti Démocratique Gabonais
PFCHS	*Proceedings of the French Colonial Historical Society*
PNPA	*Peuples Noirs, Peuples Africains*
PUF	Presses Universitaires de France
RFEPA	*Revue Française d'Etudes Politiques Africaines*
RFHO-M / RHCF	*Revue Française d'Histoire d'Outre-Mer / Revue d'Histoire des Colonies Françaises*
RG	*Réalites Gabonaises*
RJP	*Revue Juridique et Politique*
RTM	*Revue du Tiers-Monde*
SME	Société des Missions Evangéliques
Tr.	Translation
U.	University
UP	University Press
v.	volume
W.	Washington, D.C.

I: GENERAL WORKS

1. Aicardi de Saint-Paul, Marc. *Le Gabon: Du roi Denis à Omar Bongo*. P.: Albatross, n.d. 183 pp. Tr. *Gabon: The Development of a Nation*. N.Y.: Routledge, 1989, 145 pp.

1a. Alexander, Caroline. *One Dry Season: In the Footsteps of Mary Kingsley*. N.Y.: Knopf, 1990. 283 pp.

2. Ansprenger, Franz. *Politik im Schwarzen Africa*. Cologne: Westdeutscher Verlag, 1961. 516 pp.

3. Ayouné, Jean-Rémy. "Occidentalisme et Africanisme," *Renaissances* (Brazzaville) (Oct. 1944).

4. ———. "Points de vue d'intellectuels d'Afrique centrale," *Renaissances* (Brazzaville) (Oct. 1944).

5. ———. "Valeurs et christianisme," *La Semaine de l'Afrique Equatoriale Française* (Brazzaville) (Jan. 29, 1955), p. 4; (Feb. 5, 1955), p. 4; (Feb. 19, 1955), p. 4.

6. Baer, Barbara. "The British Views of the Importance of French Africa to the Allied War Effort, 1940–1944," *PFCHS*, v. 2 (1977), pp. 16–23.

6a. Barnes, James F. *Gabon: Beyond the Colonial Legacy*. Boulder: Westview, 1992, 135 pp.

7. Betts, Raymond F. *Tricouleur: The French Overseas Empire*. L.: Cremona, 1978. 174 pp.

8. Binet, Jacques. "La République Gabonaise," *NED* (no. 3703, June 27, 1970). 36 pp.

9. Borella, François. *L'évolution politique et juridique de l'Union Française depuis 1946*. P.: P&D-A, 1958. 499 pp.

10. Bourgi, Robert. *Le général de Gaulle et l'Afrique noire, 1940–1969*. P.: LGDJ, 1980. 515 pp.

11. Bouquerel, Jacqueline. *Le Gabon*. P.: PUF, 2nd ed., 1976. 128 pp.

12. Broc, Numa. "Les explorateurs Français du XIXe Siècle Reconsidérés," *RFHO-M* v. 69 (no. 3, 1982), pp. 237–274; (no. 4, 1982), pp. 323–359.

13. Brownlie, Ian. *African Boundaries. A Legal & Diplomatic Encyclopedia*. L.: C. Hurst, 1979, 1355 pp. [texts].

14. Bruel, Georges. *L'Afrique Equatoriale Française*. P.: Larose, 1935. 558 pp.

15. Brunschwig, Henri. "French Exploration and Conquest in Tropical Africa from 1865 to 1898," in P. Duignan and L. H. Gann, eds., *The History and Politics of Colonialism, 1870–1914*. L.: Cambridge UP, 1969, pp. 132–164.

16. ———. *Mythes et réalités de l'impérialisme colonial français, 1871–1914*. P.: AC, 1960. 204 pp. Tr. *French Colonialism, 1971–1914; Myths & Realities*. L.: Pall Mall Press, 1966. 228 pp.

17. Buell, Raymond Leslie. *The Native Problem in Africa*. N.Y.: Macmillan, 1928. 2 v., 1049 pp.

18. Charbonneau, Jean & René. *Marchés et marchands de l'Afrique noire*. P.: Ed. du Vieux Colombier, 1961. 150 pp.

19. Charbonnier, François, ed. *Gabon, Terre d'Avenir*. P.: Encyclopédie d'Outre-Mer, 1957. 151 pp.

20. Chemery, J. *Histoire de la mise en valeur minière des territoires d'Afrique Centrale*. P.: Bureau d'Etudes Géologiques et Minières Coloniales, 1960. 175 pp.

330 / Bibliography

21. Cohen, William B. *Black Encounter: French Images of Africa, 1500–1885.* Bloomington: Indiana UP, 1979. 360 pp.

22. Cominardi, Giuliano, and Ducci, Paolo. *Gabon: République Gabonaise.* Rome: Istituto Italo-Africano, 1975. 112 pp.

23. Comte, Gilbert. *L'Empire triomphant (1871–1936).* v. 1, *Afrique occidentale et Afrique équatoriale.* P.: Denoël, 1988. 383 pp.

24. Coquery-Vidrovitch, Catherine. "Colonisation ou impérialisme: la politique africaine de la France entre les deux guerres," *Mouvement Social* (Apr.–June 1979), pp. 51–76.

25. ———. "French Black Africa," in Andrew D. Roberts, ed., *The Cambridge History of Africa.* v. 7, *From 1905 to 1940.* L.: Cambridge UP, 1986, pp. 329–392.

26. ———. "French Colonization in Africa to 1920: Administrative and Economic Development," in P. Duignan and L. H. Gann, eds., *The History & Politics of Colonialism, 1870–1914.* L.: Cambridge UP, 1969, pp. 165–198.

27. ———. "L'Afrique coloniale française et la crise de 1930: crise structurelle et genèse du sous-développement. Rapport d'ensemble," *RFHO-M,* v. 53 (no. 3–4, 1977), pp. 386–424.

28. ———. "La mise en dépendance de l'Afrique Noire: Essai de périodisation, 1800–1970," *CEA,* v. 16 (no. 1–2, 1976), pp. 7–58.

29. ———. "L'impérialisme français en Afrique Noire: Idéologie impériale et politique d'équipement, 1924–1975," *Relations Internationales* (Autumn 1976), pp. 261–282.

30. ———. "Mutation de l'impérialisme colonial français dans les années 30," *African Economic History* (Fall 1977), pp. 103–152.

31. ———, and Moniot, Henri. *L'Afrique Noire de 1800 à Nos Jours.* P.: PUF, 1974. 462 pp.

32. Corbett, Edward M. *The French Presence in Black Africa.* W.: Black Orpheus Press, 1972. 209 pp.

33. Cornevin, Marianne. *Histoire de l'Afrique contemporaine de la deuxième guerre mondiale à nos jours.* P.: Payot, 1972. 426 pp.

34. ———, and Cornevin, Robert. *Histoire de l'Afrique des origines à la deuxième guerre mondiale.* P.: Payot, 4th ed., 1974. 411 pp.

35. Cornevin, Robert. *L'Afrique noire de 1919 à nos jours.* P.: PUF, 1973. 251 pp.

36. ———. *Histoire de l'Afrique.* P.: Payot, 1962, 1966, 1975. 3 v. 453, 638, and 700 pp.

37. ———. *Histoire des Peuples de l'Afrique Noire.* P.: B-L, 1960. 715 pp.

38. ———, and Cornevin, Marianne. *La France et les Français Outre-mer: De la première Croisade à la fin du Second Empire.* P.: Tallandier, 1990. 514 pp.

39. Daget, Serge. ''L'abolition de la traite des noirs en France de 1814 à 1831,'' *CEA,* v. 11 (no. 1, 1971), pp. 14–58.

40. ———. *Répertoire des expéditions françaises à la traite illégale (1814–1850).* Nantes: Centre de Recherche sur l'histoire du monde atlantique. Comité nantais en sciences humaines, 1988. 603 pp.

41. D'Arjanse, Jean. *Les Conquérants au Gabon.* P.: Jules Tallandier, 1933. 92 pp.

42. Decourbe, Serge. *Essai de bibliographie analytique des sources imprimées concernant les explorations françaises en Afrique équatoriale de 1839 à 1914.* P.: Mémoire, EPHESS, 1979. 2 v. 977 pp.

43. Decraene, Philippe. *L'Afrique Centrale.* P.: CHEAM, 1989. 154 pp.

44. ———. ''Gabon 1968,'' *CRMSASO-M,* v. 28 (June 1968), 297–312.

45. De La Gorce, Paul-Marie. *L'Empire écartelé 1936–1944.* P.: Denoël, 1988. 511 pp.

46. Delavignette, Robert L. ''French Colonial Policy in Black Africa, 1945 to 1960,'' in P. Duignan and L. H. Gann, ed., *the History and Politics of Colonialism, 1914–1960.* L.: Cambridge UP, 1970, pp. 251–285.

47. Denis, Jacques; Vennetier, Pierre; and Wilmet, Jules. *L'Afrique Centrale et Orientale.* P.: PUF, 1971. 294 pp.

48. Deschamps, Hubert, ed. *Histoire générale de l'Afrique noire, de Madagascar et des archipels.* V. I. *Des origines à 1800;* V. II. *De 1800 à nos jours.* P.: PUF, 1970–1971. 576 & 720 pp.

49. ———. ''France in Black Africa & Madagascar Between 1920 & 1945,'' in P. Duignan and L. H. Gann, eds., *The History & Politics of Colonialism, 1914–1960.* L.: Cambridge UP, 1970, pp. 226–250.

50. ———. *Histoire de la traite des Noirs de l'antiquité à nos jours.* P.: Fayard, 1972. 338 pp.

51. ———. *Les méthodes et doctrines de colonisation de la France.* P.: AC, 1953. 222 pp.

52. ———, et al. *Afrique au XXe siècle, 1900–1965.* P.: Sirey, 1966. 908 pp.

53. Dewitte, Philippe. *Les Mouvements nègres en France, 1919–1939.* P.: Harmattan, 1985. 416 pp.

54. Duignan, Peter, and Gann L. H. *The United States and Africa: A History.* L.: Cambridge UP, 1984. 450 pp.

55. Durand-Réville, Luc. ''Albert Schweitzer ou la Coopération avant l'heure,'' *CRTSASO-M,* v. 35 (no. 2, 1975), pp. 307–318.

56. Edibiri, Unionwam. "The Cultural Dimension of the French Presence in Africa," *Nigerian Journal of Political Economy* (no. 1, 1983), pp. 178–209.

57. Fall, Mar. *Des Africains noirs en France: Des tirailleurs sénégalais aux 'Blaks'.* P.: Harmattan, 1986. 115 pp.

58. French Equatorial Africa. High Commissioner's Office. *Annuaire statistique de l'Afrique Equatoriale Française.* V. I, *1936–1950;* V. II. *1950.* Bv.: IO, 1951, 289 pp.

59. ———. Service for Coordination of Economic Affairs and the Plan. *L'Afrique Equatoriale Française économique et sociale, 1947–1958. Avec l'aide du FIDES.* P.: Ed. Alain, 1959. 112 pp.

60. *Le Gabon Après Léon M'Ba.* Special no. *Europe-France-Outre-Mer* (Nov. 1967). 60 pp.

61. *Gabon, Données statistiques sur les activités économiques, culturelles et sociales.* P.: Ministry of Cooperation, 1976. 241 pp.

62. *Gabon, République du.* P.: Office de la Coopération, DF, 1970.

63. Gadoury, Victor, and Cousinié, Georges. *Monnaies coloniales françaises, 1670–1988.* 2nd rev. ed., Monte Carlo: V. Gadourg, 1988. 552 pp.

64. Gardinier, David E. "French Equatorial Africa," *Current History,* v. 34 (Feb. 1958); pp. 105–110.

65. Gaulme, François. *Le Gabon et son Ombre.* P.: Karthala, 1988. 210 pp.

66. Gifford, Prosser, and Louis, Wm. Roger, eds. *Decolonization and African Independence: The Transfers of Power, 1960–1980.* New Haven: Yale UP, 1988. 641 pp.

67. ———. *France and Great Britain in Africa: Imperial Rivalry and Colonial Rule.* New Haven: Yale UP, 1971. 989 pp.

68. ———. *Transfer of Power in Africa: Decolonization, 1940–1960.* New Haven: Yale UP, 1982. 654 pp.

69. Goulven, J. *L'Afrique Equatoriale Française (Ancien Congo Français): Son Organisation Administrative, Judiciaire, Financière.* P.: Larose, 1911. 250 pp.

70. Great Britain. Naval Intelligence Division. *French Equatorial Africa and the Cameroons.* L.: His Majesty's Stationery Office, 1942. 542 pp.

71. Grébert, F. *Au Gabon (Afrique Equatoriale Française).* P.: SME, 3rd ed., 1948. 216 pp.

72. Hallett, Robin. *Africa to 1875: A Modern History.* Ann Arbor: U. of Michigan Press, 1970. 503 pp.

73. ———. *Africa Since 1875.* Ann Arbor: U. of Michigan Press, 1974. 807 pp.

74. Heduy, Philippe. *Histoire de l'Afrique: AOF-AEF-Madagascar (1364–1960).* P.: Henri Veyrier, 1985. 381 pp.

75. Hegba, Meinrad. *Emancipation d'Eglises sous Tutelle: Essai sur l'Ere Post-Missionnaire.* P.: *PA,* 1976. 174 pp.

76. Institut d'histoire du temps présent. *Les chemins de la décolonisation de l'empire français 1936–1946.* P.: Éditions du CNRS, 1986. 564 pp.

77. Jalloh, Abduh. *Political Integration in French-Speaking Africa.* Berkeley: Institute of International Studies, U. of California, 1973. 208 pp.

78. Kaufmann, Otto, "La protection sociale dans les pays francophones d'Afrique au sud du Sahara," *RJP* v. 92 (Jan.–Feb. 1988), pp. 61–73.

79. Lamb, David. *The Africans.* rev. ed. N.Y.: Vintage, 1987.

80. Le Vine, Victor T. "African Patrimonial Regimes in Comparative Perspective," *JMAS* v. 18 (Dec. 1980), pp. 657–674.

81. Londres, Albert. *Terre d'Ebène.* P.: Albin Michel, 1929. 268 pp.

82. Lusignan, Guy de. *French-Speaking Africa Since Independence.* N.Y.: Praeger, 1969. 416 pp. Tr. *L'Afrique Noire depuis L'Indépendance. L'Evolution des Etats francophones.* P.: Fayard, 1970. 410 pp.

83. Marseille, Jacques. *Empire colonial et capitalisme français.* P.: 1984.

84. Marshall, D. Bruce. *The French Colonial Myth and Constitution-Making in the Fourth Republic.* New Haven: Yale UP, 1973. 363 pp.

85. Martin, Gaston. *L'Ere des Negriers (1714–1774): Nantes au XVIIIe siècle d'après des documents inédits.* P.: Alcam, 1931, 452 pp.

86. ———. *Histoire de l'esclavage dans les colonies françaises.* P.: PUF, 1948. 318 pp.

87. Martin, Jean. *Lexique de la colonisation française.* P.: Dalloz, 1988. 395 pp.

88. M'Bokolo, Elikia. *L'Afrique centrale: Stratégies de développement et perspectives.* P.: Unesco, Bureau d'études et de programmation, 1987. 149 pp.

89. Mbot, Jean Émile. *Notre Gabon.* v. 2, *Hommes.* Toulouse: Éd. Universelles, 1984. 93 pp.

90. ———. *Notre Gabon.* v. 3, *Cultes.* Toulouse: Éd. Universelles, 1986, 106 pp.

91. Merle, Marcel, ed. *Les Eglises Chrétiennes et la Décolonisation.* P.: AC, 1969, 519 pp.

92. Mertz, Robert Anton, and Mertz, Pamela McDonald. *Arab Aid to Sub-Saharan Africa*. Grunewald: Kaiser, 1983. 287 pp.

93. Montagnon, Pierre. *La France Coloniale: La Gloire de l'empire. Du temps des croisades à la Seconde Guerre mondiale*. P.: Pygmalion, 1988. 508 pp.

94. Morgenthau, Ruth S., and Lucy C. Behrman. "French-Speaking Tropical Africa," in Michael Crowder, ed., *The Cambridge History of Africa*. v. 8, *From c. 1940 to c. 1975*. L.: Cambridge UP, 1984, pp. 611–673.

95. Morris-Jones, Wyndraeth, and Fischer, Georges, eds. *Decolonisation & After: The British & French Experience*. L.: Frank Cass, 1980.

96. Mortimer, Edward. *France and the Africans; 1944–1960: A Political History*. L.: Faber, 1969. 390 pp.

97. Mytelka, Lynn Krieger. "A Genealogy of Francophone West & Equatorial African Regional Organisations," *JMAS*, v. 12 (no. 2, 1974), pp. 257–320.

98. Neuhoff, Hans Otto. *Gabun*. Bonn: Schroeder, 1967. 176 pp.

99. ———. *Geschichte, Struktur und Probleme des Aufsfuhr-wirtschaft eines Entwicklungs Landes*. Berlin & N.Y.: Springer Verlag, 1967. 273 pp.

100. Obenga, Théophile. *Les Bantu, langues, peuples, civilisations*. P.: PA, 1985. 376 pp.

101. ———, ed. *Les peuples bantu: migrations, expansion et identité culturelle: Actes du colloque international de Libreville du 1–6 avril 1985*. 2 v. Lv.: CICIBA, P.: Harmattan, 1989. 598 pp. [24 papers].

102. Oliver, Roland, and Fagan, Brian. "The Emergence of Bantu Africa," in J. D. Fage, ed. *Cambridge History of Africa*. V.

2. *500 B.C. to 1050 A.D.* L.: Cambridge UP, 1978, pp. 342–409.

103. Oschswald, Pierre. *Randonnée au Gabon.* P.: SME, 1956. 48 pp.

103a. *Les pays des trois estuaires.* Lv.: Centre culturel français Saint Exupéry & Sépia, 1990. 352 pp.

104. Pedler, Frederick. *Main Currents of West African History, 1940–1978.* L.: Barnes & Noble, 1979. 301 pp. [interstate organizations].

105. Poquin, Jean-Jacques. *Les relations économiques extérieures des pays d'Afrique Noire de l'Union Française, 1925–1955.* P.: AC, 1957. 297 pp.

106. Pounah, Paul Vincent. *Concept gabonais.* Monaco: Ed. PB, 1968. 88 pp.

107. ———. *Dialectique gabonaise, pensées d'hier, opinion aujourd'hui.* Monaco: Ed. PB, 2nd ed., 1975. 144 pp.

108. Priestly, Herbert Ingram. *France Overseas: A Study of Modern Imperialism.* N.Y.: Appleton-Century, 1938. 463 pp.

109. *Province du Haut-Ogooué.* Lv.: Multipress, n.d. 195 pp.

110. Renault, François. *Libération d'esclaves et nouvelles servitudes.* Dakar: NEA, 1976. 236 pp.

111. Renucci, France. *Souvenir de Femmes au Temps des Colonies.* P.: Ballard, 1988. 255 pp.

112. "La République Gabonaise," *NED* (no. 2795, July 1961). 56 pp.

113. Richardson, David. "Slave Exports from West and West-Central Africa, 1700–1810: New Estimates of Volume and Distribution," *JAH* v. 30 (no. 1, 1989), pp. 1–22.

114. Roberts, Stephen H. *History of French Colonial Policy (1870–1925)*. L.: King, 1929. 2 v. 741 pp.

115. Saint-Martin, Y.-Y. "Un visionnaire nantais de l'expansion coloniale: Adolphe Le Cour-Grandmaison 1801–1851," in *Enquêtes et documents*. v. 7, *Nantes-Afrique-Amerique*. Nantes: Centre de Recherche sur l'histoire de la France atlantique; U. of Nantes, 1982, pp. 93–106.

116. Saintoyant, Jules. *L'affaire du Congo, 1905*. P.: Ed. de l'Epic, 1960. 162 pp.

117. Senegas, Louis. *Cher Gabon*. P.: S.O.S., 1976. 191 pp.

118. Servel, André. *L'Organisation administrative et financiére de l'Afrique Equatoriale Française*. P.: Larose, 1912. 298 pp.

119. "Le Service de la Coopération culturelle, scientifique et technique avec les Etats Francophones Africains et Malgache: Bilan et Perspectives," *NED* (no. 3787, May 4, 1971).

120. Sorum, Paul Clay. *Intellectuals and Decolonization in France*. Durham: U. of N. Carolina Press, 1977. 305 pp.

121. Sousatte, René-Paul. *L'Afrique Equatoriale Française—Berceau de l'Union Française*. P.: Brodard & Taupin, 2nd ed., 1963. 143 pp.

122. Spiegler, James S. *Aspects of Nationalist Thought Among French-Speaking West Africans, 1921–1939*. D. Phil. Diss., Oxford U., 1968. [Film, Center for Research Libraries, Chicago].

123. Stein, Robert Louis. *The French Slave Trade in the Eighteenth Century: An Old Regime Business*. Madison: U. of Wisconsin Press, 1979. 256 pp.

124. Suret-Canale, Jean. *Afrique et Capitaux: Géographie des capitaux et des investissements en Afrique tropicale*

d'expression française. P.: L'Arbre verdoyant, 1987. 2 v. 860 pp.

125. ————. *Afrique noire, Ere Coloniale (1900–1945).* P.: Ed. Sociales, 1964, 637 pp. Tr. *French Colonialism in Tropical Africa, 1900–1945.* N.Y.: Pica, 1971. 521 pp.

126. ————. *Afrique Noire occidentale et centrale.* P.: Ed. Sociales, 3rd ed., 1968. 321 pp.

127. ————. *Afrique Noire occidentale et centrale. De la colonisation aux indépendances (1945–1960).* P.: Ed. Sociales, 1972. 430 pp.

128. Susset, Raymond. *La vérité sur le Cameroun et l'Afrique Equatoriale Française.* P.: Ed. de la Nouvelle Revue Critique, 1934. 218 pp.

129. Thompson, Virginia, and Adloff, Richard. *The Emerging States of French Equatorial Africa.* Stanford: Stanford UP, 1960. 595 pp.

130. ————, and ————. "French Economic Policy in Tropical Africa," in P. Duignan and L. H. Gann., eds., *The Economics of Colonialism.* L.: Cambridge UP, 1975, pp. 95–126.

131. Trenezem, Edouard. *L'Afrique Equatoriale Française.* P.: Ed. Maritimes et Coloniales, 3rd ed., 1955. 208 pp.

132. Tudesq, A. J. *La Radio en Afrique Noire.* P.: Pedone, 1983. 312 pp.

133. Vennetier, Pierre. *L'Afrique Equatoriale.* P.: PUF, 1972. 128 pp.

133a. *Vers les plateaux de Masuku.* Lv.: Centre culturel français Saint Exupéry & Sépia, 1990. 380 pp.

134. Wall, Irwin. "Communism, Decolonisation, and the Fourth Republic," *FCS* (Spring 1977), pp. 82–99.

135. Weinstein, Brian. *Eboué.* N.Y.: Oxford UP, 1971. 350 pp.

136. White, Dorothy S. *Black Africa & De Gaulle: From the French Empire to Independence.* U. Park: Penn State U. Press, 1979. 314 pp.

137. ———. ''De Gaulle & the Decolonization of Black Africa,'' *PFCHS,* v. 1 (1976): 52–63.

138. Wodie, F. *Les institutions internationales et régionales en Afrique occidentale et centrale.* P.: P&D-A, 1970. 274 pp.

139. Yacono, Xavier. *Les Etapes de la décolonisation française.* P.: PUF, 1971. 127 pp.

140. Zieglé, Henri. *Afrique Equatoriale Française.* P.: B-L, 1952. 190 pp.

141. Ziemer, Klaus. *Politischen Parteien in frankophonen Afrika.* Meisenbeim au Glau, 1978.

II: ARCHAEOLOGY AND PRE-HISTORY

142. Allainmat-Mahine, Basile. ''Technologies traditionnelles bantu: Méthode et rituel de la construction d'une pirogue et de ses apparaux au cap Santa Clara (Gabon),'' *Muntu,* (no. 3, 1985), pp. 101–120.

143. Asseko-Ndong, A. ''Recherches en traditions orales et archéologie dans la province du Woleu-Ntem (Gabon),'' n.s. 1: *BLAMB,* (no. 4, 1988), 10–20.

144. Beauchêne, Guy de. ''La préhistoire du Gabon,'' *Objets et Mondes,* v. 3 (no. 1, 1963), pp. 3–16.

145. Blankoff, Boris. "L'état des recherches préhistoriques au Gabon," *Etudes et Documents Tchadiens, Mémoire* (No. 1, 1969).

146. ———. "Quelques découvertes préhistoriques récentes au Gabon," *Proceedings of the Pan-African Congress for Prehistory,* V. 5 (1965), pp. 191–206.

147. Clark, J. Desmond. "The Legacy of Prehistory: An Essay on the Background to the Individuality of African Cultures," in J. D. Fage, ed., *Cambridge History of Africa.* V. 2, *C. 500 B.C. to A.D. 1050.* L.: Cambridge UP, 1978, pp. 11–86.

148. Clist, Bernard. "Archaeology in Gabon, 1886–1988," *African Archaeological Review,* v. 7 (1989), pp. 59–95.

149. ———. "La campagne de fouilles 1989 du site âge du fer ancien d'Oveng, province de l'Estuaire (Gabon)," n.s. 1: *BLAMB,* (no. 5, 1989), pp. 15–18.

150. ———. "La fin de l'âge de la pierre et les débuts de la métallurgie du fer au Gabon: résultats préliminaires 1986–1987," n.s. 1: *BLAMB,* (no. 2, 1987), pp. 24–28.

151. ———. "Le néolithique en Afrique centrale: État de la question et perspectives d'avenir," *Anthropologie* v. 90 (no. 2, 1986), pp. 217–232.

152. ———. "Travaux archéologiques récentes en République du Gabon: 1985–1986," n.s. 1: *BLAMB,* (no. 1, 1987), pp. 3–12.

153. ———, Oslisly, Richard, and Peyrot, Bernard. "Métallurgie ancienne du fer au Gabon. Premières éléments de synthèse," *Muntu,* (no. 3, 1985), pp. 41–68.

154. Collomb, Gérard. "Métallurgie du cuivre et circulation des biens dans le Gabon précolonial," *Objets et Mondes,* v. 18 (Spring 1978), pp. 59–68.

155. ———. "Quelques aspects techniques de la forge dans la bassin de l'Ogooué," *Anthropos,* v. 76 (nos. 1–2, 1981), pp. 50–66.

156. Credland, Arthur G. "The Crossbow in Africa," *Journal of the Society of Archer-Antiquaries,* v. 32 (1989), pp. 37–45.

157. Des Hermens, Roger de Bayle. "Recherches préhistoriques au Gabon. Mission 1986," *Anthropologie,* v. 91 (No. 2, 1987), pp. 699–704.

158. ———, and Peyrot, Bernard. "Premières séries de pierres taillées du Paléolithique inférieur découvertes au Gabon, Afrique Centrale," *Anthropologie,* v. 91 (no. 2, 1987), pp. 693–698.

159. Digombe, Lazare, and Diop, Abdoulaye Sokhna. "La recherche archéologique au Gabon: État actuel et perspectives," in *Archéologie africaine et sciences de la nature appliquées á l'archéologie.* P.: ACCT, 1986, pp. 413–422.

160. ———, Locko, Michael, and Emejulu, James. "Nouvelles recherches archéologiques à Ikengué (Fernan-Vaz, Province de l'Ogooué-Maritime, Gabon): Un site datant de 1,300 B.C." *Anthropologie,* v. 91 (no. 2, 1987), pp. 705–710. Also *Afrika Zamani,* (nos. 18–19, 1987), pp. 4–8.

161. ———, et al. "Recherches archéologiques au Gabon, année académique 1986–1987," n.s. 1: *BLAMB,* (no. 2, 1987), pp. 29–31.

162. ———, et al. "L'âge du fer ancien au Gabon," *Anthropologie,* v. 91 (no. 2, 1987), pp. 711–717.

163. Farine, B. "Le Néolithique de Moanda," *BSPPG* (no, 5, 1966), pp. 79–94.

164. ———. "Note sur une poterie ancienne de l'Ile Biembo," n.s. 1: *BLAMB,* (no. 3, 1988), pp. 60–61.

165. ———. *Sites préhistoriques Gabonais.* Lv., Ministry of Information, 1964. 64 pp.

166. Guillot, B. "Note sur les anciennes mines de fer du Pays Nzabi dans la région de Mayako," *CORSTOM, SSH* v. 6 (no. 2, 1969), pp. 93–99.

167. Hadjigeorgiou, C., and Pommeret, Yvan. "Présence du Lumpembien dans la région de l'Estuaire," *BSPPG* (no. 3, 1965), pp. 111–131.

167a. Lanfranchi, Raymond, ed. *Aux origines de l'Afrique Centrale.* Lv.: Sépia & Centre culturel français d'Afrique Centrale, 1991. 268 pp.

168. Lanfranchi, Raymond. "Esquisses archéologiques des régions Téké," *Muntu,* (no. 7, 1987), pp. 73–107.

169. ———. "Prospection dans le Haut-Ogooué (Région de Léconi, Franceville, Boumango): Résultats préliminaires," n.s. 1: *BLAMB,* (no. 4, 1988), pp. 28–32.

170. Locko, Michel. "Nouvelles dates pour le site paléolithique de Ndéndé (Gabon)," n.s. 1: *BLAMB,* (no. 5, 1989), pp. 19–22.

171. ———. "Préhistoire du Gabon: Deux types d'outils du paléolithique inferieur découverts dans la région de Kango, aux environs de Libreville," *Nyame Akuma,* (no. 29, 1987), pp. 21–23.

172. ———. "La recherche archéologique à l'Université Omar Bongo: Bilan scientifique," *Muntu* (no. 8, 1988), pp. 26–44.

173. ———. "Recherches préhistoriques au Gabon," *Bulletin de la Société Préhistorique française,* v. 85 (no. 7, 1988), pp. 217–223.

174. ———. "Les sources archéologiques de la métallurgie du fer au Gabon," *Nyame Akuma,* (no. 29, 1987), pp. 23–26.

175. ———. "Un campement paléolithique sur les rives du lac noir," *Nyame Akuma*, (Dec. 1988), pp. 9–10.

176. Maret, Pierre de. "Archéologie bantu," *Muntu*, (no. 1, 1984), pp. 37–60.

177. ———. "Ceux qui jouent avec le feu: La place du forgeron in Afrique centrale," *Africa* (London), v. 50 (no. 3, 1980), pp. 263–279.

178. ———. "New Survey of Archaeological Research and Dates for West-Central and North-Central Africa," *JAH*, v. 23 (no. 1, 1982), pp. 1–15.

179. ———. "Recent Archaeological Research and Dates from Central Africa," *JAH*, v. 26 (nos. 2–3, 1985), pp. 129–143.

180. Oslisly, Richard. "Gravures rupestres au Gabon: les pétroglyphes d'Elarmekora," *Anthropologie*, v. 92 (no. 1, 1988), pp. 373–374. Also *Nyame Akuma* (no. 29, 1987), pp. 26–27.

181. ———, and Peyrot, Bernard. *L'Art Pré-historique Gabonais: 1887–1987. Centenaire de la recherche pré-historique au Gabon.* Lv.: Rotary Club of Libreville-Okoumé, 1987. 93 pp.

181a. Oslisly, Richard, and Peyrot, Bernard. "Synthèse des données archéologiques des sites de la moyenne vallée de l'Ogooué (provinces du Moyen Ogooué et de l'Ogooué-Ivindo)," n.s. 1: *BLAMB*, (no. 3, 1988), pp. 63–68.

182. Perrusset, André-Christian. "Aperçu de la préhistoire du littoral au Gabon," *CO-M*, v. 36 (no. 142, 1983), pp. 175–183.

183. Peyrot, Bernard, and Oslisly, Richard. "Paléoenvironnement et archéologie au Gabon (1985–1986)," n.s. 1: *BLAMB*, (no. 1, 1987), pp. 13–15.

184. ———, and ———. "Recherches récentes sur le paléoenvironnement du Gabon, 1982–1985," *Anthropologie,* v. 90 (no. 2, 1986), pp. 201–216.

185. Pommeret, Yvan. *Civilisations préhistoriques au Gabon.* Lv.: Ministry of National Education, 1966. 2v. 65 & 45 pp.

186. Ropivia, Marc. "L'âge des métaux Chez les Fang Anciens: Relations avec l'histoire générale et la chronologie absolue," *MA,* (Aug.–Sept. 1984), pp. 152–163.

187. ———. "Les Fang dans les Grands Lacs et la Vallée du Nil," *PA,* (no. 4, 1981), pp. 46–58.

188. ———. "Migrations Bantu et tradition orale des Fang," *MA,* (Aug.–Sept. 1983), pp. 121–132.

189. Telefair, Peter. "Techniques de pointe Chez les Bakota," in *Aethiopia, vestige de gloire.* P.: Dappert, 1987, pp. 71–74.

III: EARLY HISTORY AND EXPLORATION ACCOUNTS (BEFORE 1914)

190. Adams, J. *Remarks on the Country Extending from Cape Palmas to the River Congo.* L.: 1847.

191. Ancel, Jacques. "Etude historique: La formation de la colonie du Congo français (1843–1882)," *Renseignements Coloniaux et Documents, Afrique Française,* (no. 4, 1902), pp. 79–94; (no. 5, 1902), pp. 99–120; (no. 6, 1902), pp. 132–134.

192. Barbot, John [Jean]. *A Description of the Coasts of North and South-Guinea and of Ethiopia Inferior, Vulgarly Angola.* L. 1732.

193. Bosman, William [Willem]. *A New and Accurate Description of the Coast of Guinea: Divided into the Gold, Slave, and Ivory Coasts.* L.: Frank Cass, 1967. 577 pp. [Tr. of Dutch ed. of 1704].

194. Bouët-Willaumez, Louis-Edouard. *Commerce et Traite des Noirs aux Côtes Occidentales d'Afrique.* P.: IN, 1848. 227 pp. Reprint, Geneva: Slatkin Reprints, 1978.

195. ———. *Description Nautique des Côtes de l'Afrique Occidentale, comprises entre la Sénégal et l'Equateur.* P.: Paul Dupont, 2nd. ed., 1849. 98 pp.

196. Bowdich, Thomas Edward. *Mission from Cape Coast Castle to Ashantee.* L.: J. Murray, 1819. 3rd. ed. L.: Frank Cass, 1966. 512 pp.

197. Burton, Richard Francis. *Two Trips to Gorilla Land & the Cataracts of the Congo.* L.: Marston, Low & Searle, 1876. 355 pp. Reprint, N.Y.: Johnson Reprints, 1967.

198. Compiègne, Louis Victor Dupont. *L'Afrique Equatoriale Française; Gabonais, Pahouins, Gallois.* P.: Plon, 2nd ed., 1876. 359 pp. Reprint, P.: Plon, 1976.

199. ———. *L'Afrique Equatoriale Française: Okanda, Bangouens, Osyéba.* P.: Plon, 3rd. ed., 1885. 360 pp.

200. Dapper, Olfert. *Description de l'Afrique.* Amsterdam: Wolfgang Waesberge, 1686. 534 pp. [Tr. of Dutch ed. 1668].

201. Du Chaillu, Paul B. *A Journey to Ashango-land and Further Penetration into Equatorial Africa.* N.Y.: Harper, 1874. 501 pp.

202. ———. *Exploration and Adventures in Equatorial Africa.* N.Y.: Harper , 1861. 531 pp. Reprint, N.Y.: Negro UP, 1969. Tr. *Voyages et Aventures dans l'Afrique Equatoriale (1856–1859).* P.: Michel Levy, 1863. 546 pp.

203. ———. *My Apindji Kingdom.* N.Y.: Harper, 1871. 254 pp.

204. ———. *Stories of the Gorilla Country.* N.Y.: Harper, 1899. 292 pp.

205. ———. *The Country of the Dwarfs.* N.Y.: Harper, 1872. 314 pp. Reprint, N.Y.: Negro UP, 1969.

206. ———. *Wild Life Under the Equator.* N.Y.: Harper, 1868. 231 pp.

207. Isert, P. E. *Voyages en Guinée et dans les Caraïbes,* P.: 1783.

208. Kingsley, Mary H. *Travels in West Africa—Congo Français, Corisco & Cameroons.* N.Y.: Macmillan, 1897. 743 pp. Reprint, L.: Frank cass, 1965.

209. Le Cour, A. *Projet d'un établissement.* Nantes: 1844.

210. ———. *Rapport sur la colonisation du Gabon et de l'Afrique centrale.* Nantes: Impr. William Busseuil, 1848. 16 pp.

211. Marche, Alfred. *Trois Voyages dans l'Afrique Occidentale. Sénégal-Gambie, Casamance, Gabon-Ogooué.* P.: Hachette, 1882. 376 pp.

212. Morel, Edward Dene. *The British Case in the French Congo.* L.: Heinemann, 1903. 215 pp.

213. Nassau, Robert Hamill. *Fetichism in West Africa: Forty Years' Observations of Native Customs and Superstitions.* N.Y.: Scribner, 1904. Reprint N.Y.: Negro UP, 1965.

214. ————. *My Ogowe: Being a Narrative of Daily Incidents During Sixteen Years in Equatorial West Africa.* N.Y.: Neale, 1914. 708 pp.

215. Ney, Napoleon, ed. *Conférences et lettres de Pierre Savorgnan de Brazza sur ses trois explorations dans l'Ouest Africain.* P.: Maurice Dreyfous, 1887.

216. Payeur-Didelot, N. *Trente Mois au Continent Mystérieux: Gabon-Congo et la Côte Occidentale de l'Afrique.* P.: B-L, 1889. 403 pp.

217. Proyart, Liévain Bonaventure. *Histoire de Loango, Kakongo et autres Royaumes d'Afrique.* P.: Berton and Craport, 1776. 393 pp. Tr. *History of Loango, Kakongo, and Other Kingdoms in Africa* in John Pinkerton, ed. V. 16, *A General Collection of the Best and Most Interesting Voyages and Travels,* L., 1808–1814.

218. Romer, L. F. *Le golfe de Guinée: Récit d'un marchand d'esclaves sur la côte ouest-africaine.* P.: Harmattan, 1988. 236 pp.

219. Rouget, Fernand. *L'Expansion coloniale au Congo Français.* P.: Larose, 1906, 942 pp.

220. Trader Horn, pseud. [Horn, Alfred Aloysius, or Smith, Alfred Aloysius.] *The Ivory Coast in the Earlies?* N.Y.: Library Guild of America, 1928. Tr. *La Côte d'Ivoire aux temps héroiques.* P.: 1932.

221. Van Linschoten, Jan Huygen. *Beschryvinghe van de gantsche custe van Guinea.* Amsterdam, 1594.

222. Wilson, John Leighton. *Western Africa: Its History, Condition & Prospects.* N.Y.: Harper, 1856. 527 pp. Reprint, Negro UP, 1970.

IV: HISTORICAL STUDIES OF GABON AND EQUATORIAL AFRICA

223. *Actes du Colloque Félix Éboué.* P.: Institut des Hautes Études de Défense Nationale et Académie des Sciences d'Outre-mer, 1985. 128 pp.

224. Ahavi, Rose. *Les Bouleversements de la société gabonaise au contact de l'Occident 1900–1939.* Doctoral Thesis, U. of Provence, 1984.

225. Aissi, Antoine-Marie. "Les peuples de l'Afrique Équatoriale Française face au système jurisdictionnel coloniale," in *Centenaire de la Conférence de Berlin, 1884–1885.* P.: *PA,* 1987, pp. 363–387.

226. Akelaguelo, Aganga. "Esquisse d'Histoire Ethnique du Gabon," *PA,* (no. 4, 1984), pp. 3–32.

227. Alexandre, Pierre. "Proto-histoire du groupe beti-bulu-fang: essai de synthèse provisoire," *CEA,* v. 5 (no. 4, 1965), pp. 503–560.

228. Allegret, Marc. *Carnets du Congo: Voyage avec Gide.* P.: Presses du CNRS, 1987. 295 pp.

229. Ambouroué-Avaro, Joseph. *Un peuple gabonais à l'aube de la colonisation: Le Bas Ogooué au XIXe siècle.* P.: Karthala, 1981. 285 pp.

230. Annet, Armand. *Aux heures troublées de l'Afrique française, 1939–1947.* P., 1952.

231. Aubry, Fernand. *Don Fernando.* P.: Robert Laffont, 1972. 428 pp. [1919–1929].

232. Austen, Ralph A., and Headrick, Rita. "Equatorial Africa Under Colonial Rule," in David Birmingham and Phyllis M. Martin, eds., *History of Central Africa,* v. 2. L. and N.Y.: Longman, 1983, pp. 27–94.

233. Autin, Jean. *Pierre Savorgnan de Brazza, un prophète du Tiers monde.* P.: Librairie Académique Perrin, 1985. 320 pp.

234. Avelot, R. "Notice historique sur les Bakalé," *Anthropologie,* v. 24 (1913), pp. 197–240.

235. Balesi, Charles J. "A 19th-century Anglo-French Dispute: The Issue of African Free Laborers," *PFCHS,* v. 2 (1977), pp. 75–86.

235a. Bemba, Léon. *L'Afrique Équatoriale Française dans la première guerre mondiale.* Doctoral Thesis, U. of P., 1984. 293 pp.

236. Berger, Augustin. "Le premier et désastreux voyage du Père Bessieux vers le Gabon (1843–1844)," *CRTSASO-M,* v. 36 (no. 2, 1976): pp. 257–268.

237. Berre, R. *L'Extension du pouvoir colonial français à l'intérieur du Gabon (1883–1914).* Doctoral Thesis, U. of P., 1979.

238. Birmingham, David. "Central Africa from Cameroun to the Zambezi," in R. Gray, ed. *Cambridge History of Africa.* V. 4. *From c. 1600 to c. 1790.* L.: Cambridge UP, 1975, pp. 325–383.

239. ———. "Central Africa from Cameroun to the Zambezi," in R. Oliver, ed. *Cambridge History of Africa.* V. 3, *From c. 1050 to c. 1600.* L.: Cambridge UP, 1977, pp. 519–566.

240. ———. "The Forest and Savanna of Central Africa," in J. Flint, ed., *Cambridge History of Africa.* V. 5, *C. 1790 –C. 1870.* L.: Cambridge UP, 1976, pp. 222–269.

241. Bouche, Denise. *Les Villages de Liberté en Afrique Noire Française, 1887–1910.* P.: Mouton, 1968. 280 pp.

242. Brazza, Pierre Savorgnan de. *Conférences et lettres sur les trois explorations dans l'Ouest africain de 1875 à 1886*. G.: Slatkine, 1930. 479 pp. Reprint of edition of P., 1887.

243. Brunschwig, Henri, ed. *Brazza explorateur: L'Ogooué 1875–1879*. P.: Mouton, 1966. 215 pp.

244. ———. "Expéditions punitives au Gabon (1875–1877)," *CEA*, v. 2 (no. 3, 1962), pp. 347–361.

245. ———. "Les factures de Brazza, 1875–1878," *CEA*, v. 4 (no. 1, 1963), pp. 14–21.

246. ———. *Noirs et blancs dans l'Afrique noire française, ou comment le colonisé devient colonisateur (1870–1914)*. P.: Flammarion, 1983. 243 pp.

247. ———. "La troque et la traite," *CEA*, v. 2 (no. 3, 1962), pp. 339–346.

248. Bucher, Henry H. "The Atlantic Slave Trade and the Gabon Estuary: The Mpongwe to 1860," in Paul Lovejoy, ed., *Africans in Bondage: Studies in Slavery and the Slave Trade*. Madison: African Studies Program, U. of Wisconsin, 1986, pp. 136–154.

249. ———. "Canonization by Repetition: Paul du Chaillu in Historiography," *RFHO-M*, v. 66 (nos. 1–2, 1979), pp. 15–32.

250. ———. "John Leighton Wilson and the Mpongwe: The 'Spirit of 1776' in Mid-Nineteenth-Century Africa," *Journal of Presbyterian History*, v. 54 (Fall 1976), p. 291–316.

251. ———. "Liberty and Labor: The Origins of Libreville Reconsidered," *BIFAN*, série B., v. 41 (July 1979), pp. 478–496.

252. ———. *The Mpongwe of the Gabon Estuary: A History to 1860*. Ph.D. Diss., U. of Wisconsin, Madison, 1977. 455 pp.

253. ———. "Mpongwe Origins: Historiographical Perspectives," *HA,* v. 2 (1975), pp. 59–90.

254. ———. "The Settlement of the Mpongwe Clans in the Gabon Estuary: An Historical Synthesis," *RFHO-M,* v. 64 (no. 1, 1977), pp. 149–175.

255. ———. "The Village of Glass and Western Intrusion: An Mpongwe Response to the American & French Presence in the Gabon Estuary," *IJAHS,* v. 6 (no. 3, 1973), pp. 363–400.

256. Capperon, L. "Bouet-Willaumez en Afrique Occidentale et au Gabon (1836–1850)," *Revue Maritime,* n.s. (Sept. 1953), pp. 1085–1103.

257. Carnus, Marcel. "Il y a cent ans . . . un explorateur espalionnais (Aveyron), Léon Guirnal mourait à Libreville," *Revue du Rouergue,* v. 39 (n.s. 3, 1985), pp. 219–224.

258. Catala, René. "La question de l'échange de la Gambie britannique contre les comptoirs français du Golfe de Guinée de 1866 à 1876," *RHCF,* v. 35 (1948), pp. 114–137.

259. Chamberlin, Christopher. "Bulk Exports, Trade Tiers, Regulation and Development: An Economic Approach to the Study of West Africa's Legitimate Trade," *Journal of Economic History,* v. 39 (June 1979), pp. 419–438.

260. ———. "The Migration of the Fang into Central Gabon During the Nineteenth Century: A New Interpretation," *IJAHS,* v. 11 (no. 3, 1978), pp. 429–456.

261. ———. *Competition and Conflict: The Development of the Bulk Export Trade in Central Gabon During the 19th Century.* Ph.D. Diss., U. of California at Los Angeles, 1977.

262. Chaveau, Jean Pierre. "Une histoire maritime africaine est-elle possible? Historiographie et histoire de la navigation

et de la pêche africaines à la côte occidentale depuis le XVe Siècle," *CEA,* v. 26 (no. 1–2, 1986), 173–235.

263. Clarence-Smith, Gervais. "The Effects of the Great Depression on Industrialisation in Equatorial and Central Africa," in I. Brown, ed., *The Economies of Africa and Asia in the Interwar Depression.* L.: Routledge, 1989, pp. 170–202.

264. Cookey, S. J. S. "The Concession Policy in French Congo and the British Reaction, 1897–1906," *JAH,* v. 7 (no. 2, 1966), pp. 263–278.

265. Coquery-Vidrovitch, Catherine, ed. *Brazza et la prise de possession du Congo. La Mission de l'Ouest Africain, 1883–1885.* P.: Mouton, 1969. 502 pp.

266. ———. *Le Congo au Temps des Grandes Compagnies Concessionnaires, 1898–1930.* P.: Mouton, 1972. 598 pp.

267. ———. "De Brazza à Gentil: la politique française en Haute-Sangha à la fin du XIXe siècle," *RFHO-M,* v. 52 (1965), pp. 22–40.

268. ———. "L'échec d'une tentative économique: L'impôt de capitation au service des compagnies concessionnaires du 'Congo français' (1900–1909)," *CEA,* v. 8 (no. 1, 1968), pp. 96–109.

269. ———. "French Congo and Gabon, 1886–1905," in Roland Oliver and G. N. Sanderson, eds., *Cambridge History of Africa.* v. 6, *From 1870–1905.* L.: Cambridge UP, 1985, pp. 298–315.

270. ———. "Les idées économiques de Brazza et les premières tentatives de compagnie de colonisation au Congo Français, 1885–1898," *CEA,* v. 5 (no. 1, 1965), pp. 57–82.

271. ———. "L'intervention d'une société privée à propos du contesté franco-espagnol dans la Rio Muni. La Société d'exploration coloniale, 1899–1924," *CEA,* v. 3 (no. 1, 1962), pp. 22–68.

272. ———. "Investissements privés, investissements publics en AEF, 1900–1940," *African Economic History,* (no. 12, 1983), pp. 13–31.

273. ———. "Le Pillage de l'Afrique equatoriale," *Histoire,* (no. 3, 1978), pp. 43–52.

274. ———. "Wango ou la révolte d'un chef gabonais contre l'impôt et le travail forcé," in *Les Africains,* v. 11. P.: Jeune Afrique, pp. 267–286.

275. Cordell, Dennis D. "Extracting People from Precapitalist Production: French Equatorial Africa from the 1890s to the 1930s," in D. D. Cordell and J. W. Gregory, eds., *African Population and Capitalism: Historical Perspectives.* Boulder: Westview, 1987, pp. 137–152.

276. Couture, Claude-Paul. *Le Commandant Emile Dubos, héros de Sheï Poo (1852–1935).* Rouen: Author, 1963.

277. Dantzig, Albert van. "Willem Bosman's *New and Accurate Description of the Coast of Guinea*: How Accurate Is It?" *HA,* v. 1 (1974), pp. 101–108.

278. Decraene, Philippe. "Barthélémy Boganda ou du projet d'état unitaire central africain à celui d'États-Unis d'Afrique latine," *Relations internationales,* (Summer 1983), pp. 215–226.

279. ———. "Les États-Unis de l'Afrique latine," *Afrique et Asie modernes,* (no. 161, 1981), pp. 42–50.

280. Delobeau, Jean-Michel. "Les Pygmées dans la colonisation," *Afrika Zamani,* (no. 14–15, 1984), pp. 115–135.

281. Denis, Martin J. M., ed. *Histoire militaire de l'Afrique Equatoriale Francaise.* P.: IO, 1931. 516 pp. [Gabon, pp. 84–124].

282. Dermigny, Louis, and Serre, Gérard. "Au Gabon, le district du 'bout du monde,'" *CO-M,* v. 7 (July–Sept. 1954), pp. 213–224.

283. Deschamps, Hubert. *Quinze Ans de Gabon: Les débuts de l'établissement français, 1839–1853.* P.: Société française d'histoire d'outre-mer, 1965. 98 pp.

284. ———. *Traditions orales et archives au Gabon.* P.: B-L, 1962, 172 pp.

285. Dieye, Cheikh Abdoulaye. *L'exil au Gabon: Période coloniale 1895–1902: Sur les traces de Cheikh Ahmadou Bamba.* P.: Art media international, 1985. 127 pp.

286. Dravo, Louis de. *Le Problème de la main d'oeuvre gabonaise et ses conséquences, au lendemain de la deuxième guerre mondiale, 1945–1956.* Mémoire, U. of Reims, 1980.

287. ———. *L'Exploitation forestière au Gabon de 1896 à 1930.* Master's Thesis, U. of Reims, 1979.

288. Dubois, Collette. "La double défi de l'AEF en guerre (1914–1918)," *Africa* (Rome), v. 44 (no. 1, 1989) pp. 25–49.

289. ———. *Le prix d'une guerre: Deux colonies pendant la première guerre mondiale (Gabon-Oubangui-Chari), 1911–1923.* Aix-en-Provence: U. of Provence, Institut d'histoire des pays d'outre-mer, 1985. 792 pp.

290. Dupré, G. "Le commerce entre sociétés lignagères: les nzabi dans la traite à la fin du XIXe siècle (Gabon-Congo)," *CEA,* v. 12 (no. 4, 1972), pp. 616–658.

291. Ebiatsa, Hopiel-Opiele. "Les Teke: Définition historique des hommes et de leur espace (avant de XVIIIe siècle)," *Muntu,* (no. 7, 1987), pp. 33–47.

292. Eboué, Félix. *La Nouvelle Politique Indigène (pour l'Afrique Equatoriale Française)*. P.: Office Français d'Ed., 1944, & Bv.: Afrique Française Libre, 1941. 61 pp.

293. Fernandez, James W. "The Sound of Bells in a Christian Country: The Quest for the Historical Schweitzer," *Massachusetts Review*, v. 5 (Spring 1964), pp. 537–562.

293a. Framis, Ricardo Majó. *Las Generosas y Primitivas Empresas de Manuel Iradier Bulfy en la Guinea Española: El Hombre y sus Hechos*. Madrid: Consejo Superior de Investigaciones Científicas, Instituto de Estudios Africanos, 1954.

294. *Franceville, 1880–1980*. Lv.: Éd Multipress Gabon, 1981. 63 pp.

295. Fyfe, Christopher. "Freed Slave Colonies in West Africa," in J. Flint, ed., *Cambridge History of Africa, V. 5, C. 1790–C. 1870*. L.: Cambridge UP, 1976, 170–199.

296. Gardinier, David E. "France in Gabon Since 1960," *PFCHS*, v. 6–7 (1982), pp. 65–75.

297. ———. "Overseas Empire: Equatorial Africa and Cameroon," in Patrick H. Hutton, ed., *Historical Dictionary of the Third French Republic, 1870–1940*. v. 2, *M–Z*. N.Y. and Westport: Greenwood 1986, pp. 717–720.

298. ———. "The Path to Independence in French Africa: Recent Historiography," *AJ*, v. 15 (1989): 15–38.

299. Garfield, Robert. *A History of SãoTomé Island, 1470–1665*. Ph.D. Diss., Northwestern U., Evanston, 1971. 337 pp.

300. Gaulme, Franéois. *Le pays de Cama: Un ancien État côtier du Gabon et ses origines*. P.: Karthala, 1981. 269 pp.

301. ———. "Un problème d'histoire du Gabon. Le sacre du Père Bichet par les Nkomi en 1897," *RFHO-M*, v. 61 (no. 3, 1974), pp. 395–416.

302. ———. "Vingt-ans d'indépendance du Gabon: La fin des pionniers," *MTM,* v. 41 (Aug. 1985), pp. 1975–1981.

303. Gautier, Jean M. *Etude historique sur les Mpongoués et tribus Avoisinantes.* Montpellier: Impr. Lafitte-Lauriol for the Institut d'Etudes Centrafricaines, 1950. 69 pp.

304. Gollnhofer, Otto. *Bokodu. Ethno-histoire ghetsogho: Essai sur l'histoire générale de la tribu après la tradition orale.* Doctoral Thesis, U. of P, 1967. Mimeographed, 1971.

305. ———; Noel, Bernard; and Sillans, Roger. "L'historicité des paroles attribuées au premier évêque du Gabon à propos du maintien du comptoir entre 1871 et 1873," *RFHO-M,* v. 59 (no. 4, 1972), pp. 611–644.

306. Government-General of French Equatorial Africa. *Souvenirs sur le Gabon.* Bv.: IO, 1950. 21 pp.

306a. Hahs, Billy Gene. *Spain and the Scramble for Africa: The Africanistas and the Gulf of Guinea.* Doctoral Diss., U. of New Mexico, 1980.

307. Headrick, Rita. *The Impact of Colonialism on Health in French Equatorial Africa, 1880–1934.* Doctoral Diss., U. of Chicago, 1987.

308. Heiser, E. *Émile Gentil, 1866–1914.* P.: Notices Biographiques, 1976. 110 pp.

309. Ikele, P. "La guerre de Wongo dans l'Ogooué-Lolo," *RG* (no. 34, 1969), pp. 17–23.

310. Isaacman, Allen, and Vansina, Jan. "Initiatives et résistances africaines en Afrique centrale de 1880 à 1914," in Boahen, A. A. ed., *Histoire générale de l'Afrique* v. 7, *Afrique sous domination 1880–1945.* P.: Unesco, 1987, pp. 191–216.

311. Jewsiewicki, Bogumil, and Mumbanza Mwa Bawele. "The Social Context of Slavery in Equatorial Africa During the 19th

and 20th Centuries,'' in Paul E. Lovejoy, ed., *The Ideology of Slavery in Africa*. Beverly Hills: Sage, 1981, pp. 72–98.

312. Kouambila, Juste-Roger. *La guerre de Wongo au Gabon (1928–1930)*. Doctoral Thesis, U. of P., 1984.

313. ————. *La révolte des Awandji, Gabon, 1928*. Memoir for the Master's, U. of P., 1975.

314. Koumba-Manfoumbi, Monique. *Les Punu du Gabon, des origines à 1899: Essai d'étude historique*. Doctoral Thesis, U. of P., 1987.

315. Labat, René. *Le Gabon devant de gaullisme*. Bordeaux: Delmas, 1941. 79 pp.

316. Lagarde, Georgette. *La migration pahouine au Gabon*. Doctoral Thesis, U. of P., 1966.

317. Lasserre, Guy. ''Bordeaux et les origines de Libreville,'' *Actes du VIIIe Congrès d'Etudes Régionales. Bordeaux et sa Région dans le Passé et dans le Présent*. Bordeaux: Bière for the Fédération Historique du Sud-Ouest, 1956, pp. 159–168.

318. Leterrier, R. P. ''A propos du sacre du Père Bichet,'' *RFHO-M*, V. 62 (no, 4, 1975), p. 674.

319. Le Testu, Georges. ''La soumission des Bawandji,'' *BSRC* (no. 14, 1931), pp. 11–28.

320. Liniger-Goumaz, Max. ''Le Gabon au XIXe Siècle: Peuples et Historiens Manipulés,'' *G-A*, v. 21 (no. 1, 1983), 114–127.

321. Loungou, Théophile, and Tshinyoka, Alike. ''Les Gabonais et la Première guerre mondiale (1914–1918),'' in *Les Réactions Africaines à la colonisation en Afrique centrale*. Kigali: U. nationale du Rwanda, 1985, pp. 243–272.

322. Magang-Mambuju, Wisi, and Mbumb Bwas, F. *Les Bajags du Gabon: Essai d'étude historique et linguistique*. n.p.: Imprimerie St. Michel, 1974.

323. Mamfoumbi, Christian. *Contribution à l'étude du travail forcé en Afrique Equatoriale Française dans l'entre-deux-guerres (1914–1939): L'exemple du Gabon.* Doctoral Thesis, U. of P., 1984.

324. Mangongo-Nzambi, A. "La délimitation des frontières du Gabon (1885–1911)," *CEA,* v. 9 (no. 1, 1969), pp. 5–53.

325. ————. *La pénétration française et l'organisation administrative du Nord-Gabon.* Doctoral Thesis, U. of P., 1968. 377 pp.

326. Martin, Phyllis M. *The External Trade of the Loango Coast, 1576–1870: The Effects of Changing Commercial Relations on the Vili Kingdom of Loango.* Oxford: Clarendon, 1972. 193 pp.

327. ————. "Power, Cloth and Currency on the Loango Coast," *Muntu,* (no. 7, 1987), pp. 135–147.

328. M'Bokolo, Elikia. "Du commerce licite au régime colonial: L'Agencement de l'idéologie coloniale," in D. Nordman and J.-P. Raisons, eds., *Science de l'homme et conquête coloniale: Constitution et usages des sciences humaines en Afrique (XIXe et XXe siècles).* P.: Presses de l'ENS, 1980, pp. 205–221.

329. ————. "Forces sociales et idéologies dans la décolonisation de l'A.E.F." *JAH,* v. 22 (no. 3, 1981), pp. 393–407.

331. ————. "French Colonial Policy in Equatorial Africa in the 1940s and 1950s," in P. Gifford and Wm. Roger Louis, eds., *The Transfer of Power in Africa: Decolonization 1940–1960.* (New Haven: Yale UP, 1982), pp. 173–210.

332. ————. *Noirs et Blancs en Afrique Équatoriale: Les societés côtières et la pénétration française (vers 1820–1874).* P.: Mouton, 1981, 302 pp.

333. ———. "La résistance des Mpongwe du Gabon à la création du comptoir français (1843–1845)," *Afrika Zamani* (Dec. 1978), pp. 5–32.

334. ———. "Le Roi Denis," in Charles-André Julien, ed., *Les Africains,* v. 6. P.: Ed. Jeune Afrique, 1977, pp. 69–95.

335. ———. *Le Roi Denis: la première tentative de modernisation du Gabon.* P.: Afrique Biblioclub & Dakar: Nouvelles Ed. Africaines, 1976. 94 pp.

336. Mbouku, Jean-Hubert. "La Conquête de Mayumba par le Général de Gaulle," *Afrique Littéraire,* (no. 1–2, 1984), pp. 116–120.

337. Ménier, Marie Antoinette. "Conceptions politiques et administratives de Brazza, 1885–1898," *CEA,* v. 5 (no. 1, 1965), pp. 83–95.

337a. Merlet, Annie. *Autour de Loango, XIVe–XIXe siècle: histoire des peuples du sud-ouest du Gabon au temps du royaume de Loango et du Congo français.* Lv.: Centre culturel français Saint-Exupéry & Sépia, 1991. 550 pp.

338. Merlet, Annie. *Légendes et histoire des myéné de l'Ogooué.* Lv.: Centre Culturel Français St. Exupéry, 1989. 163 pp.

339. Métégué, N'Nah Nicolas. *Économies et sociétés dans la première moitié du XIXe siècle.* P.: Harmattan, 1979. 97 pp.

340. ———. *L'implantation coloniale au Gabon.* v. 1, *Résistance d'un peuple.* P.: Harmattan, 1981. 120 pp.

341. Meye, François Charles. *L'Éveil politique des populations gabonaises du Moyen-Ogooué des origines à 1961.* Memoir, Omar Bongo U., 1979. 79 pp.

342. ———. *La fondation de Madiville, 1883 (futur Lastoursville).* Master's Thesis, U. Omar Bongo, 1985.

343. Meyo-Bibang, Frédéric. *Aperçu historique du Gabon.* Lv.: IPN, 1973. 171 pp.

344. Miller, Joseph C. "Lineages, Ideology and the History of Slavery in Western Central Africa," in Paul P. Lovejoy, ed., *The Ideology of Slavery in Africa.* Beverly Hills: Sage, 1981, pp. 40–71.

345. Minlamèze, E. "La grande famine de trois ans au Woleu-N'tem (1925–1928)," *RG* (no. 25, 1965), pp. 47–49.

346. Miquel, Annick. "La fin d'un voyage: le 'Mauritius' coule au cap Lopez," *La Recherche,* (Nov. 1987), pp. 1400–1402.

347. Myer, Valerie Grosvenor. *A Victorian Lady in Africa: The Story of Mary Kingsley.* Southampton: Ashford Press, 1989. 221 pp.

348. N'Doume-Assembe. *Emane-Tole et la résistance à la conquête française dans le Moyen-Ogooué.* Memoir for the Master's, U. of P., 1973.

349. Neuhoff, Hans-Otto. "German-Gabonese Relations from the Mid-19th Century to the Present Day," *Afrika,* (Aug. 1964), pp. 122–127.

350. ———. "Les rapports germano-gabonais depuis la seconde moitié du XIXe siècle jusqu'au présent," *Africa* (Rome) v. 20 (June 1965), pp. 200–202.

351. Ngoua, Bonjean Aba, et al. *Millénaire de Mulundu: Centenaire de Lastoursville.* Lv.: Multipress Gabon, 1986. 116 pp.

352. Nimbi, Eugène. *L'Évolution Économique et Sociale des Banzabi de Divenié (1910–1940).* Master's Thesis, U. Marien Ngouabi, Brazzaville, 1980. 98 pp.

353. Nkoghve-Mve, Moïse. "Le docteur Albert Schweitzer et la colonisation," *RG* (Jan.–Mar. 1977), pp. 21–26.

354. Nzoghe, Anselme. *L'exploitation forestière et les conditions d'exploitation des peuples de la colonie du Gabon de 1920 à 1940: Le Travail forcé.* Doctoral Thesis, U. of Aix, 1984.

355. Ortoli, Charles. "L' A.E.F. pendant la Seconde Guerre mondiale," *Histoire,* v. 508 (Apr. 1989) pp. 43–53.

356. Oudima Epigat, G. *Franceville (Gabon) des origines à la deuxieme guerre mondiale.* Memoir for the Master's, U. of P., 1974.

357. Pambo-Loueya, C. Félix. [Pambo, Félix.] *La Colonie du Gabon de 1914 à 1939: Étude economique et sociale.* 2 v. Doctoral Thesis, U. of P., 1980.

358. ———. *La crise de 1929 au Gabon.* Memoir, U. of P., 1974.

359. ———. "La crise de 1930 fut catastrophique pour le Gabon: La chute de l'exploitation de l'okoumé entraine l'effondrement de toute l'économie," *Afrique histoire,* (no. 8, 1983), pp. 49–54.

360. Patterson, K. David. "Early Knowledge of the Ogowe River and the American Exploration of 1854," *IJAHS,* v. 5 (no. 1, 1972), pp. 75–90.

361. ———. "Paul B. Du Chaillu & the Exploration of Gabon, 1855–1865," *IJAHS,* v. 7 (no. 4, 1974), pp. 648–667.

362. ———. *The Northern Gabon Coast to 1875.* Oxford: Clarendon, 1975. 167 pp.

363. ———. "The Vanishing Mpongwe: European Contact and Demographic Change in the Gabon River," *JAH,* v. 16 (no. 2, 1975), pp. 217–238.

364. Perrois, Louis. "Tradition orale et histoire: intérêt et limites d'une enquête de terrain sur les migrations Kota (Gabon)," *CORSTOM, SSH,* v. 13 (no. 2, 1976), pp. 143–146.

365. ———. ''Chronique du pays kota (Gabon),'' *CORSTOM-SSH* v. 8 (no. 2, 1970), pp. 15–110.

366. Postma, Johannes Menne. *The Dutch in the Atlantic Slave Trade, 1600–1815.* L.: Cambridge UP, 1990. 428 pp.

367. Pouchet, Gaston. *Vieux Gabon, Vieilles Missions: Histoire et Souvenirs.* P.: The author, 1984. 380 pp.

368. Pounah, Paul Vincent. *Carrefour de la discussion.* Coulonges sur l'Antize: Impr. Reynaud, 1971. 101 pp. [Galoa origins].

369. ———. *Notre passé.* P.: Société d'impressions techniques, 1970. 105 pp. [Galoa].

370. ———. *La recherche du Gabon traditionnel: hier Edongo, aujourd'hui Galwa.* P.: Impr. Loriou, 1975. 277 pp.

371. Pourtier, Roland. ''De Franceville à Masuku: Ontogenèse d'une ville centenaire,'' *Bulletin de l'Association Géographique.* v. 57 (Nov.–Dec., 1980), pp. 349–355.

372. Rabut, Elisabeth. ''Le Mythe Parisien de la Mise en Valeur des Colonies Africaines à l'aube du XXe Siècle: La Commission des Concessions Coloniales, 1898–1912,'' *JAH,* v. 20 (1979), pp. 271–288.

373. Ratanga-Atoz, Ange. ''Commerce, économie et société dans le Gabon du XIXe siècle—début XXe siècle,'' *AENA* v. 3 (1979), pp. 83–96.

374. ———. ''Fang et Miènè dans le Gabon du XIXe siècle,'' *RG* (Jan.–Mar. 1977), pp. 9–20.

375. ———. *Histoire du Gabon: Des Migrations historiques à la République, XVe–XXe Siècle.* Dakar: NEA, 1985. 95 pp.

376. ———. "L'Immigration Fang, ses origines et ses conséquences," *Afrika Zamani,* (June 1984), pp. 73–81.

377. ———. *Les Résistances Gabonaises à l'Imperialisme de 1870 à 1914.* Doctoral Thesis, U. of P., 1973. Microfiche ed. P.: CNRS; N.Y.: Clearwater Publishers.

378. Reed, Michael C. *An Ethno-Historical Study of the Political Economy of Ndjolé, Gabon.* Doctoral Diss., U. of Washington, 1988. 456 pp.

379. Renwomby, Michel. *La politique administrative de la France et ses conséquences de 1899 à 1934.* Doctoral Thesis, U. of Aix-Marseilles, 1982.

380. Reynard, Robert. "Notes sur l'activité économique des côtes du Gabon au début du XVIIe siècle," *BIEC,* n.s., (no. 13–14, 1957), pp. 49–54.

381. ———. "Recherches sur la présence des Portugais au Gabon XVe–XIXe siècles," *BIEC,* n.s. (no. 9, 1955), pp. 15–66 & (no. 11, 1956), pp. 21–27.

382. Schnapper, Bernard. *La politique et le commerce français dans la Golfe de Guinée.* P.: Mouton, 1961. 286 pp.

383. Smith, André. *Le Gabon et rivalités européennes, 1870–1914.* Doctoral Thesis, U. of P., 1983.

384. Soret, Marcel. *Histoire du Congo. Capitale Brazzaville.* P.: B-L, 1978. 237 pp. [peoples of Gabon also].

384a. Timmermans, P. "Voyage à travers le Gabon et le Sud-Ouest du Congo Brazzaville," *Africa-Tervuren* v. 10 (no. 3, 1964), pp. 69–78.

385. Tutenges, Émile. "Souvenirs sur le ralliement du Cameroun et du Gabon," *Espoir,* (no. 59, 1987), pp. 20–28.

386. Vansina, Jan. "L'Afrique équatoriale et l'Angola: Les migrations et l'apparition des premiers États," in D. T.

Niane, ed., *Histoire Générale de l'Afrique,* v. 4. Unesco, 1985, pp. 601–628.

387. ———. "Do Pygmies Have a History?" *Sprache Geschichte Afrika,* v. 7 (1986), pp. 431–445.

388. ———. "Equatorial Africa before the 19th Century," and "A Trade Revolution in Equatorial Africa," in P. Curtin, et al., eds., *African History.* Boston: Little, Brown, 1978, pp. 249–276, 419–443.

389. ———. "Esquisse historique de l'agriculture en milieu forestier (Afrique Équatoriale)," *Muntu,* (no. 2, 1985), pp. 5–34.

390. ———. "Finding Food in the History of Pre-Colonial Equatorial Africa: A Plea," *African Economic History* (Spring 1979), pp. 9–20.

391. ———. "Lignage, idéologie et histoire en Afrique Équatoriale," *Enquêtes et documents d'histoire africaine,* (no. 4, 1980), pp. 133–155.

392. ———. "The People of the Forests," in David Birmingham and Phyllis M. Martin, eds., *History of Central Africa,* V. 1. L. and N.Y.: Longman, 1983, pp. 75–117.

393. Vaucaire, Michel. *Paul du Chaillu: Gorilla Hunter.* N.Y.: Harper, 1930. 322 pp. Tr. from French.

394. Walker, André Raponda. *Notes d'histoire du Gabon.* Montpellier: Impr. Charité for the Institut d'Etudes Centrafricaines, 1960. 158 pp.

395. ———. "Toponymie de l'Estuaire du Gabon et de ses environs," *BIRSC* (no. 2, 1963), pp. 87–116.

396. ———, and Reynard, Robert. "Anglais, Espagnols et Nord-Américains au Gabon au XIXe siècle," *BIEC,* n.s. (no. 12, 1956); pp. 253–279.

397. West, Richard. *Brazza of the Congo: European Exploration & Exploitation in French Equatorial Africa.* L.: Cape, 1972. 304 pp.

V: EXTERNAL RELATIONS SINCE 1960

398. Abelin, Pierre. *Rapport sur la politique française de coopération.* P.: DF, 1975, 78 pp.

399. Adda, Jacques, and Smouts, Marie-Claude. *La France face au Sud: Le miroir brisé.* P.: Karthala, 1989. 363 pp.

400. Alibert, Jacques. "Le zone franc: Intelligence et réalisme," *AC,* v. 22 (Apr.–June 1983), pp. 3–13.

401. Alting von Geusau, Franz A. M., ed. *The Lomé Convention and a New International Order.* The Hague, 1977.

402. Anguilé, André-Gustave, and David, Jacques. *L'Afrique sans Frontières.* Monaco: Ed. PB, 1965, 311 pp.

403. Aurillac, Michel. *L'Afrique à coeur: La coopération: Un message d'avenir.* P.: B-L, 1987. 264 pp.

404. Bach, Daniel. "La politique africaine de Valéry Giscard d'Estaing: Contraintes historiques et nouveaux économiques," *Travaux et Documents, Centre d'Études d'Afrique Noire* (Talence), v. 6 (1984), pp. 1–29.

405. Barnery, Jean. "Gabon: Une politique étrangère active," *Géopolitique africaine,* (Mar. 1986), pp. 147–152.

406. Bayart, Jean-François. *La politique africaine de François Mitterrand.* P.: Karthala, 1984. 149 pp.

407. Bencheikh, Madjid. "Les conventions de Lomé—CEE—ACP: Nouvel ordre et sous-développement," *Revue algérienne de sciences juridiques, économiques et politiques,* v. 25 (June 1987), pp. 347–351.

408. Biteghe, Moïse-Nsole. *Les relations franco-gabonaises depuis 1960.* Doctoral Thesis, U. of P., 1981.

409. Bon, Daniel, and Mingst, Karen. "French Intervention in Africa: Dependence or Development," *Africa Today,* (no. 2, 1980), pp. 5–20.

410. Boukinde, Agathe Manomba. *Relations entre le Gabon et la Guinée équatoriale du temps de Macias Nguema.* Doctoral Thesis, U. of P., 1984.

411. Boundoukou-Latha, Paul. *Aide internationale et développement au Gabon.* Doctoral Thesis, U. of Poitiers, 1982.

412. Bourges, Yvon. *La politique française d'aide du développement.* P.: DF, 1971. 30 pp.

413. Bourrinet, Jacques. *La coopération économique eurafricaine.* P.: PUF, 1976. 189 pp.

414. Bouvier, Paule. *L'Europe et la coopération au développement: Un bilan: La Convention de Lomé.* Brussels: 1980.

415. Bridier, Amnuel. "Bilan et perspectives de l'aide financière aux pays africains: l'expérience de la Caisse Centrale de Coopération économique," *Mondes et Développement,* v. 14 (no. 53, 1986), pp. 105–136.

416. Buttoud, Gérard, and Kouame, Amani J. "L'évolution du commerce international des bois africaines," *AC,* v. 24 (Apr.–June 1986), pp. 3–20.

417. Cadenat, Patrick. *La France et le Tiers monde: Vingt ans de coopération bilatérales.* P.: DF, *NED,* 1983. 204 pp.

418. Cathala, Michel. *La politique étrangère de la République gabonaise.* Doctoral Thesis, U. of Toulouse, 1975. 169 pp.

419. Chipman, John. *The French in Africa.* Oxford: Basil Blackwell, 1989, 288 pp.

420. Codo, Léon. "L'Afrique noire et Israël," *Politique Africaine,* (July 1988), pp. 50–68.

421. "La Convention de Lomé III," *Revue du Marché Commun,* (Apr. 1986), pp. 183–235.

422. "La coopération entre la France, l'Afrique Noire d'Expression française et Madagascar," *NED* (no. 3330, Oct. 25, 1966). 47 pp.

423. Cot, Jean-Pierre. *A l'épreuve du pouvoir: Le tiers-mondisme, pourquoi faire?* P.: Seuil, 1984. 218 pp.

424. ———. "France and Africa: What Change?" *Africa Report,* v. 28 (May–June 1983), pp. 12–16.

425. Decraene, Philippe. "Esquisse d'une nouvelle politique étrangère gabonaise," *RFEPA,* (June 1972), pp. 58–66.

426. De Guiringaud, Louis. "La politique africaine de la France," *Politique étrangère,* v. 47 (June 1982), pp. 441–456.

427. Délégation de la Commission des Communautés Européennes en République Gabonaise. "Le Gabon et la Communauté européenne," *Économie et Finances,* (Jan. 1986), pp. 35–48.

428. Deniau, Xavier. *La Francophonie.* P.: 1983.

429. Des Jardins, Thierry. *François Mitterrand: Un socialiste gaullien.* P.: 1978.

430. Diagne, Pathé. "Mitterrand, la Gauche, l'Afrique et le Tiers-Monde," *PNPA,* v. 5 (May–June 1982), pp. 5–20.

431. Distelhorst, Lynn Harris. *Impact of American Aid and Trade on Resource Development of Gabon.* M.A. Thesis, George Washington U., 1969. 260 pp.

432. *Dix ans d'économie gabonaise, août 1963.* Lv.: Chamber of Commerce, 1964. 43 pp.

433. Dreux-Brezé, Joachim de. *Le Problème de Regroupement en Afrique Equatoriale. Du Régime Colonial à l'Union Douanière et Economique de l'Afrique Centrale.* P.: P&D-A, 1968. 214 pp.

434. Duhamel, Olivier. "L'AUPELF et la coopération universitaire ou de la francophonie au dialogue des cultures," *RFEPA* (Feb. 1976); pp. 30–59.

435. Durand-Réville, Luc. *L'assistance de la France aux Pays insuffisamment développés.* P.: ed. Génin, 1962. 128 pp.

436. Forrest, Tom. "Brazil and Africa: Geopolitics, Trade and Technology in the South Atlantic," *African Affairs* (London), v. 81 (Jan. 1982), pp. 3–20.

437. Foudoup, Kengné. "Le commerce frontalier dans le département du Ntem au Cameroun," *CO-M,* v. 40 (no. 158, 1987), pp. 127–148.

438. "La France contre l'Afrique," *Tricontinental,* special number, 1981. 271 pp.

439. Frediani, Lorenzo. *The Banking System of Gabon and the Central Bank of Equatorial Africa & Cameroon.* Tr. *Système Bancaire du Gabon.* Milan: Casse di Risparmio della Provincie Lombarde, 1974. 343 pp.

440. Freud, Claude. *Vingt-cinq Ans de coopération en chiffres.* P.: Ministère de la Coopération, 1987.

441. "Gabon, Guinée équatoriale: le conteste insulaire," *RFEPA* (Jan. 1973), pp. 25–27.

442. *Gabon, politique étrangère: Textes et documents.* Lv.: Direction de la presse et de l'information, 1987.

443. Gamet, Bernard, and Grellet, Gérard. "La politique française de coopération en Afrique noire," *Temps modernes,* v. 39 (Apr. 1983), pp. 303–314.

444. Gaudio, Attilio, ed. "L'Industrialisation des Etats de l'Union Douanière et Economique de l'Afrique Centrale (UDEAC)," *NED* (no. 3830, Oct. 25, 1971). 43 pp.

445. Gaulme, François. "Le Gabon de 1984 et ses relations avec la France: La Prosperité et les malentendus," *MTM,* v. 40 (Feb. 17, 1984), pp. 359–367.

446. Gautron, Jean Claude. "La convention de Lomé III," *Année africaine* (1984) pp. 137–162. Also *Cahiers de Droit Européen,* v. 22 (no. 1, 1986), pp. 21–43.

447. ———. "La politique africaine de la France," in *L'Afrique noire depuis la Conférence de Berlin.* P.: CHEAM, 1985, pp. 139–162.

448. Georgy, Guy. "La politique africaine de la France," *AC,* v. 18 (Mar.–Apr. 1979), pp. 1–6. Also in *Mondes et Cultures* v. 39 (no. 2, 1979), pp. 109–117.

449. Gerth-Wellman, Hella, and Kayser, Dorothée. *Die industrielle Zuammenarbeit zwischen der EG und den AKP-Staaten im Rahmen der Lomé: Politik empirische Analyse und Versuch einer Einschätzung.* Munich: 1980.

450. Goybet, Catherine, and Morrison, Jane. *La deuxième convention de Lomé: L'Aide de la CEE aux ACP (1981–1985).* Brussels: Bureau d'informations éuropéennes SPRL, 1982. 341 pp.

451. Guillemin, Jacques. "L'importance des bases dans la politique militaire de la France en Afrique noire francophone et à Madagascar," *MA,* v. 16 (Aug.–Sept. 1982), pp. 31–44.

452. ———. "L'intervention extérieure dans la politique militaire de la France en Afrique noire francophone et à Madagascar," *MA,* v. 16 (June–July 1981), pp. 43–58.

453. Harshe, Rajen. "French Neo-Colonialism in Sub-Saharan Africa," *India Quarterly,* v. 36 (Apr.–June 1980), pp. 159–178.

454. Hayter, Teresa. *French Aid.* L.: Overseas Development Institute, 1966. 230 pp.

455. Hessel, Stéphane. *Les relations de la France avec les pays en développement.* P.: DF., 1990.

456. Hewitt, A. "The Lomé Conventions: Entering a Second Decade," *Journal of Common Market Studies,* v. 23 (no. 1, 1984), pp. 95–115.

457. Hill, Tony. "Whither Lomé? A Review of the Lomé III Negotiations," *Third World Quarterly,* v. 7 (July 1985), pp. 661–662.

458. Hippolyte, Mirlande. *Les Etats du groupe de Brazzaville aux Nations Unies.* P.: AC, 1970. 333 pp.

459. Hofmeier, Rolf. "Aid from the Federal Republic of Germany to Africa," *JMAS,* v. 24 (Dec. 1986), pp. 577–602.

460. Hugon, Philippe. "L'Afrique noire francophone: l'enjeu économique pour la France," *Politique africaine,* v. 2 (Feb. 1982), pp. 75–94.

461. ———. "L'Afrique subsaharienne face au Fonds monétaire international," *AC,* v. 25 (July–Sept. 1986), pp. 3–19.

462. ———. "La politique française de coopération et la crise financière des pays d'Afrique sub-saharienne," *Mondes et Développement,* v. 15 (no. 53, 1986), pp. 35–68.

463. ———. "Les stratégies comparées des pays africains du golfe de Guinée à l'épreuve du contre-choc pétrolier," *Tiers-Monde,* v. 30 (no. 120, 1989), pp. 755–778.

464. Issembé, Georges. *Constantes Variables et Tendances de la Politique Extérieure des jeunes Etats Africains: Les Exemples du Congo et du Gabon.* Memoir, U. of P., 1978. 128 pp.

465. Jakobeit, Cord. "The CFA Franc Zone After 1973: Burden or Benefit for the African Members," *Afrika Spectrum,* v. 21 (no. 1, 1986), pp. 257–272.

466. Jalloh, Adbul Aziz. "Foreign Private Investments & Regional Political Integration in UDEAC," *Cahiers Economiques et Sociaux,* v. 17 (June 1979), pp. 174–197.

467. Jeanneney, Marcel. *La politique de coopération avec les pays en voie de développement.* P.: DF, 1963.

468. Journiac, Henri. "Vingt ans de coopération sanitaire et sociale avec l'Afrique, 1960–1980," *AC,* v. 19 (Nov.–Dec. 1980), pp. 19–23.

469. Jua, Nanang. "UDÉAC: Dream, Reality or the Making of Subimperial States," *Afrika Spectrum,* v. 21 (no. 2, 1986), pp. 211–223.

470. Kabongo-Kongo, Kola. *Traité des rapports franco-africains.* Kinshasa: Office national de la recherche et du développement, 1972. 295 pp.

471. Kamto, Maurice. "La Communauté économique des États d'Afrique centrale (C.E.E.A.C.): Une Communauté de plus," *Annuaire français de droit international,* v. 33 (1987), pp. 833–862.

472. Kessler, Marie-Christine. "La politique française des symboles aux faits," *Revue française d'administration publique,* (Apr.–June 1989), pp. 23–26.

473. Khapoya, Vincent B. "The Rupture in African-Israeli Relations," *Transafrica Forum,* v. 4 (Fall 1986), pp. 77–79.

474. Klintberg, Robert. *Equatorial Guinea-Macias Country.* Geneva: International U. Exchange Fund, 1978. 89 pp.

475. Kouame, Amani J. "L'évolution du commerce international des bois africains," *AC,* v. 24 (Apr.–June 1985): 3–20.

476. Kuhne, Winrich. "France's Africa Policy," *International Affairs Bulletin,* v. 5 (no. 2, 1981), pp. 60–72.

477. Langhammer, Rolf. *Die Zentralafrikansche Zoll-und Wirtschaftunion.* Tübingen: J.C.B. Mohr, 1978. 268 pp.

478. Lavroff, D.-G., ed. *La politique africaine du général de Gaulle (1958–1959).* P.: Pedone, 1980. 421 pp.

479. Leduc, Michel. *Les Institutions monétaires africaines des pays francophones.* P.: Pedone, 1965. 397 pp.

480. Leymarie, Philippe. "L'Agence de coopération culturelle et technique ou la francophonie institutionnelle," *RFEPA,* (Feb. 1976); pp. 13–29.

481. Liebenow, J. Gus. *Crises and Challenges.* Bloomington: Indiana UP, 1986. 305 pp. [U.S. policy].

482. Ligot, Maurice. *Les accords de coopération entre la France et les Etats africains et malgache d'expression française.* P.: DF, 1964. 187 pp.

483. Liniger-Goumaz, Max. *Comment on s'empare d'un pays,* v. 1, *La Guinée Équatoriale.* G.: Éditions du Temps, 1989. 367 pp.

484. ———. *De la Guinée Équatoriale Nguémiste: Éléments pour le Dossier de l'Afro-Fascisme.* G.: Éditions du Temps, 1983. 261 pp.

485. ———. "Le 'Fardeau-Africain' de la France," *G-A,* v. 21 (no. 1, 1983), pp. 108–113.

487. ———. "Un problème en suspens: La Frontière entre Gabon et Guinée Équatoriale (Essai bibliographique)," *G-A,* v. 26 (no. 1, 1988), pp. 113–125.

488. Luckham, Robin. "French Militarism in Africa," *Review of African Political Economy,* (May–June 1982), pp. 55–84. Also "Le Militarisme français," *Politique africaine,* v. 2 (Feb. 1982), pp. 55–110, (May 1982), pp. 45–71.

489. Lukusa, Théophile. "Intégration économique et données nationales: la création de l'Union des Etats d'Afrique Centrale," *Etudes Congolaises,* v. 11 (Apr.–June 1968), pp. 68–119.

490. Maganga-Moussavou, Pierre-Claver. *L'aide publique de la France au développement du Gabon depuis l'indépendance (1960–1978).* P.: Publications de la Sorbonne, 1982. 303 pp.

491. ———. "Economic Development—Does Aid Help? A Case Study of French Development Assistance to Gabon," *African Bibliographical Center: Current Reading List Series,* v. 14 (no. 2, 1983), pp. 1–243.

492. Maganza, Giorgio. *La convention de Lomé.* Brussels: Université libre de Bruxelles, 1990. 406 pp.

493. Makoundzi-Wolo, Nestor. "Le droit international africain de l'intégration économique est-il porteur d'autonomie (souveraineté) collective? L'exemple de la Communauté Économique des États d'Afrique Centrale?" *Revue Congolaise de Droit,* (June 1987), pp. 15–34; (Dec. 1987), pp. 8–24.

494. Marasinghe, N. L. "A Review of Regional Economic Integration in Africa with Particular Reference to Equatorial Africa," *International and Comparative Law Quarterly,* v. 33 (no. 1, 1984), pp. 39–56.

495. Martin, Guy. "L'Afrique face à l'Idéologie de l'Eurafrique: Néo-Colonialisme ou Pan-Africanisme?" *Africa Develop-

ment, v. 7 (no. 3, 1982), pp. 5–21. Also "Africa and the Ideology of Eurafrica: Neo-Colonialism or Pan-Africanism?" *JMAS,* v. 20 (June 1982), pp. 221–238.

496. ———. "The Franc Zone: Underdevelopment and Dependency in Francophone Africa," *Third World Quarterly,* v. 8 (Jan. 1986), pp. 205–235.

497. ———. "Les fondements historiques, économiques, et politiques de la politique africaine de la France: Du colonialisme au néocolonialisme," *G-A,* v. 21 (no. 2, 1983), pp. 31–68.

498. ———. "The Historical, Economic and Political Bases of France's African Policy," *JMAS,* v. 23 (June 1985), pp. 189–208.

499. ———. "Les relations économiques Europe-Afrique dans le cadre de la Convention de Lomé: Néo-colonialisme ou nouvel ordre économique international," *Africa Development,* v. 4 (no. 1, 1979), 56–69.

500. ———. "Uranium: A Case Study in Franco-African Relations," *JMAS,* v. 27 (Dec. 1989), pp. 625–640.

501. Masquet, Brigitte. "France-Afrique: Dépasser des contradictions," *AC,* v. 21 (Jan.–Feb. 1982), pp. 9–24.

502. Mba Allo, Emmanuel. "Le Gabon à l'ONU," *M'Bolo,* (no. 15, 1986), pp. 30–41.

503. Mbaku, John M., and Kamereschen, David R. "Integration and Economic Development in Sub-Saharan Africa: The Case of the Customs and Economic Union of Central African States (UDEAC)," *Journal of Contemporary African Studies,* v. 7, (no. 1–2, 1988), pp. 3–21.

504. M'Bouy-Boutzit, Édouard Alexis. "The Road to Cooperation: Gabon's Standpoint," in *OPEC and Future Energy Markets.* L.: Macmillan, 1980, pp. 18–21.

505. Midiohouan, Guy O. "Portée idéologique et fondements politiques de la francophonie," *PNPA,* v. 8 (Jan.–Feb. 1985), 12–36.

506. Nadelmann, Ethan A. "Israel and Black Africa: A Rapprochement?" *JMAS,* v. 19 (June 1981), pp. 183–220.

507. N'Djoga, Jean-Bernard. *Le Gabon et les investissements d'origine étrangère: Une asymétrie caractérisée de 1960 à 1980.* Master's Thesis, U. of Québec at Montréal, 1981. 291 pp.

508. Ndongko, Wilfred A. "Central African Regional Cooperation in the Context of the Lagos Plan of Action," *Africa Development,* v. 7 (no. 1–2, 1982), pp. 43–59.

509. ———. "The Future of the Central African Customs and Economic Union," in R. I. Onwuka, and A. Sesay, eds., *The Future of Regionalism in Africa.* L.: Macmillan, 1985, pp. 96–109.

510. ———. "Trade and Development Aspects of the Central African Customs and Economic Union (UDEAC)," *Cultures et Développement,* v. 8 (no. 2, 1975), pp. 339–356.

511. Ngango, Georges. *Les Investissements d'origine extérieure en Afrique Noire francophone: leur statut et incidence sur le développement.* P.: *PA,* 1973. 451 pp.

512. Nouaille-Degorce, Brigitte. *La politique française de coopération avec les États africains et malgache au sud du Sahara (1958–1978).* Talence, Centre d'étude d'Afrique noire, I.E.P., 1982. 567 pp.

513. Nyang, Suleiman. "Strengths and Challenges of French Influence in Africa," *Transafrica Forum,* v. 5 (Spring 1988), pp. 61–80.

514. Omrana, A. "The role of the IMF in Africa," *Finafrica,* (no. 2, 1985), pp. 143–174.

515. Owona, Joseph. "Les Doctrines de sécurité en Afrique centrale," *MA*, (Aug.–Sept., 1985), pp. 3–15; (Oct.–Nov. 1985), pp. 43–56.

516. *La Politique africaine du général de Gaulle, 1958–1969.* P.: 1981.

517. Porter, R. S. "Arab Economic Aid," *Development Policy Review*, v. 4 (Mar. 1986), pp. 44–68.

518. Quantin, Patrick. "La vision gaullienne de l'Afrique noire: Permanences et adaptations," *Politique africaine*, v. 2 (Feb. 1982), pp. 8–18.

519. Rajana, Cecil. "The Lomé Convention: An Evaluation of E.E.C. Economic Assistance to the A.C.P. States," *JMAS*, v. 20 (June 1982), pp. 179–220.

520. ———. "Lomé II and ACP-EEC Relations: A Preliminary Assessment," *Africa Quarterly*, v. 20 (Jan.–June 1980), pp. 71–95.

520a. Robarts, Richard. *French Development Assistance: A Study in Policy & Administration.* Beverly Hills: Sage, 1974. 82 pp.

521. Rondos, Alex. "France and Africa: Mitterrand's Two-Year Record," *Africa Report*, v. 28 (May–June 1983), pp. 8–11.

522. Sicé, André. *L'Afrique Equatoriale Française et le Cameroun au service de la France, 26–27–28 août 1940.* P.: PUF, 1946. 200 pp.

523. Spero, Joan Edelman. *Dominance-Dependence Relationship: The Case of France and Gabon.* Ph.D. Diss., Columbia U., N.Y., 1973.

524. Staniland, Martin. "Francophone Africa: The Enduring French Connection," *Annals of the American Academy of Political and Social Sciences*, (Jan. 1987), pp. 51–62.

525. Suret-Canale, Jean. "Difficultés du néo-colonialisme français en Afrique tropicale," *CJAS,* v. 8 (no. 2, 1974), pp. 211–234.

526. Tenreiro, Francisco. *A Ilha de São Tomé.* Lisbon: Junta de Investigaçoãs do Ultramar, 1961.

527. Tixier, Gilbert. "Les conventions fiscales passées par la France avec les pays en voie de développement," *RJP,* v. 29 (Apr.–June 1975): pp. 252–262.

528. Twitchett, Carol Cosgrove. *Europe and Africa: From Association to Partnership.* Brookfield, Vt. 1979.

529. ———. *A Framework for Development: The EEC and the ACP.* L.: 1981.

530. ———. "Lomé II: A New ACP and EEC Agreement," *World Today,* v. 36 (Mar. 1980), pp. 113–120.

531. Van Grevenynghe, Michel. "L'action culturelle de la France en Afrique," *Mondes et Cultures,* v. 51 (no. 3, 1983), pp. 501–528.

532. Vaudiaux, Jacques. *L'Evolution politique de la coopération franco-africaine et malgache.* P.: Pedone, 1971. 47 pp.

533. Vignes, Daniel. *L'Association des Etats Africains et Malgache à la C.E.E.* P.: AC, 1970. 224 pp.

534. Vinay, Bernard. "L'organisation monétaire en Afrique," *AC,* v. 16 (May–June 1978), pp. 1–12.

535. Voss, Harald. *Kooperation in Afrika: Das Beispiel Aquatorials-Afrikas.* Hamburg: Verlag-Weltarchiv, 1965. 87 pp.

536. Weinstein, Brian. "Léon Mba: The Ideology of Dependence," *GA,* v. 6 (no. 2, 1967), pp. 49–63.

537. Yakemtchouk, Romain. *La Convention de Lomé: Nouvelles formes de la coopération entre la C.E.E. et les états d'Afrique, les Caraïbes et du Pacifique.* Brussels, 1977.

538. Zang, Laurent. "L'Intégration économique en Afrique centrale: De nouvelles perspectives avec la CEEAC," *MA,* v. 22 (Mar. 1987), pp. 67–80, 97–99.

539. Zarour, Charbel. *La coopération arabo-africain: Bilan d'une décennie.* P.: Harmattan, 1989. 415 pp.

540. Zartman, I. William. "Africa and the West: The French Connection," in Bruce Arlinghaus, ed., *African Security Issues.* Boulder: 1984, pp. 39–58.

541. ———. "Europe and Africa: Decolonization or Dependency," *Foreign Affairs,* v. 54 (Jan. 1976), pp. 325–343.

542. ———. *The Politics of Trade Negotiations Between Africa and the European Community.* Princeton: Princeton UP, 1971. 243 pp.

VI: POLITICS

543. Ajami, S. M. "Le rôle prédominant du parti unique institutionaliste au Gabon," *RJP,* v. 30 (Jan.—Mar. 1976), pp. 114–129.

544. Amnesty International. *Gabon: Déni de justice au cours d'un procès.* P.: Éditions francophones l'Amnesty International, 1984. 112 pp.

545. Anchouey, Michel. *La vie politique du Gabon de 1960 à 1965.* Memoir, U. of Poitiers, 1965.

546. Assam, Aristote. *Omar Bongo ou la racine du mal gabonais.* P.: La Pensée universelle, 1985. 142 pp.

547. Association Générale des Étudiants du Gabon. *L'A.G.E.G. appuie la juste lutte des peuples: Recueils de quelques messages adressés par le Comité Exécutif de l'A.G.E.G. à divers partis révolutionnaires et organisations de jeunesse (1977–1979).* Lv.: 1979. 44 pp. [Mimeographed].

548. Aubame, Jean-Hilaire. "La conférence de Brazzaville," in E. Guernier, ed. *L'Afrique Equatoriale Française,* P.: Ed. Coloniales et Maritimes, 1950, pp. 183–186.

549. ———. *Renaissance gabonaise. Programme de regroupement des villages.* Bv.: IO, 1947. 12 pp.

550. Ballard, John A. *The Development of Political Parties in French Equatorial Africa.* Ph.D. Diss., Fletcher School, Tufts U., Medford, Mass., 1964.

551. ———. "Four Equatorial States," in Gwendolyn Carter, ed., *National Unity and Regionalism in African States.* Ithaca: Cornell UP, 1966, pp. 231–336.

552. Bernault-Boswell, Florence. "Le rôle des milieux coloniaux dans la décolonisation du Gabon et du Congo-Brazzaville (1945–1964)," Paper, Aix-en-Provence, April 1990, 25 pp.

553. Beti, Mongo. "Jacques Vergès ou comment tuer enfin l'increvable Ponce-Pilate [Pierre Péan]," *PNPA,* (Nov.–Dec. 1983), pp. 1–6.

554. Bongo, Albert-Bernard. *Dialogue et participation: avec Bongo aujourd'hui et demain.* Monaco: Ed. PB, 1973. 117 pp.

555. ———. *Gouverner le Gabon.* Monaco: Ed. PB, 1968. 139 pp.

556. ———. *Pensée et action sociales.* Monaco: Ed. PB, 1974. 127 pp.

557. ———. Rénovation, avec Bongo aujourd'hui et demain. [1983]. 63 pp.

558. ———. *Rénovation: pensées politiques.* Lv.: PDG, 1973. 63 pp.

559. Bongo, Omar. *Les années qui viennent: Faut-il avoir peur de l'an 2000.* Lv.: Multipress Gabon, 1987.

560. ———. *Le dialogue des nations: L'Afrique dans le nouvel ordre politique et économique mondiale.* P.: Ed. ABC, 1977. 130 pp.

561. ———. *El Hadj Omar Bongo.* Lv.: Édition Multipress Gabon, 1986. 257 pp.

562. ———. *Au Service du Gabon.* Lv.: Ed. Multipress Gabon, n.d. 148 pp.

563. Bory, Paul. *The New Gabon.* Monaco: 1978.

564. Boussoughou Bou Bound, Emmanuel. *A propos des fondements structurels de l'identité nationale au Gabon.* Master's Thesis, Laval U., Quebec, 1983. 125 pp.

565. Comte, Gilbert. "La république gabonaise: treize années d'histoire," *RFEPA,* (June 1973), pp. 39–57.

566. *Conférence africaine française.* Bv.: IO, 1944, & Algiers, IO, 1944. 122 pp.

567. Coulon, Christian. "Gabon," in *Année africaine, 1964.* P.: Pedone, 1966, pp. 213–230.

568. Da Gambeg, Y. N. "Le Président Bongo, le Gabon et le socialisme," *MA,* (Mar.–Apr. 1982), pp. 30–47.

569. Darlington, Charles F. and Alice B. *African Betrayal.* N.Y.: David McKay, 1968. 359 pp.

570. Dayez, Cl. "Triste retour de Gabon (nouvelle)," *PNPA*, v. 4 (Sept.–Oct. 1981), pp. 98–108.

571. Decalo, Samuel. "Modalities of Civil-Military Stability in Africa," *JMAS*, v. 27 (Dec. 1989), pp. 547–578.

572. Delauney, Maurice. *De la casquette à la jaquette ou de l'administration coloniale à la diplomatie africaine.* P.: La pensée universelle, 1982. 319 pp.

573. ———. *Kala-Kala: De la grande à la petite histoire, un ambassadeur raconte.* P.: Éditions Robert Laffront, 1986. 319 pp.

574. Doey, François. "Entretien avec Paul Mba-Abessolo," *Politique africaine*, v. 3 (Sept. 1983), pp. 17–21.

575. ———. "Gabon: Les Visages d'une opposition," *Politique africaine*, v. 3 (Sept. 1983), pp. 13–16.

576. ———. "Programme de gouvernment du MORENA," *Politique africaine*, v. 3 (Sept. 1983), pp. 22–29.

577. Duhamel, Olivier. "Le parti démocratique gabonais: étude des fonctions d'un parti unique africain," *RFEPA* (May 1976), pp. 24–60.

578. Essone-Ndong, Laurent-Thierry. "Les syndicats au Gabon," *AENA*, v. 3 (1979), pp. 45–54.

579. Eyeghe-Ndong, Jean. *L'État gabonais.* Doctoral Thesis, U. of P., 1980.

580. Filippi, Jean-Michel. *L'Evolution politique du Gabon depuis 1958.* Memoir, U. of Nice, 1967, 66 pp.

581. Gabon. Ministry of Information. *Hommage à Léon Mba.* Lv., 1971. 100 pp.

582. ———. *L'Oeuvre du Président Léon Mba, 1900–1965.* Lv., 1965. 70 pp.

582a. Gaulme, François. "Le Gabon à la recherche d'un nouvel ethos politique et social," *Politique Africaine* (Oct. 1991), pp. 50–62.

583. Hughes, Anthony. "Interview with Omar Bongo, President of the Republic of Gabon," *Africa Report,* v. 22 (May–June 1977), pp. 2–5.

584. Interafrique Presse. *Le "putsch du Gabon" à travers la presse parisienne & quelques notes sur le processus d'un coup d'Etat.* P., 1964. 16 pp.

585. Janot, M. F. "Démocratie à la Gabonaise," *PNPA,* v. 5 (May–June 1982), pp. 29–33.

586. ———. "Le Gabon, îlot de prosperité? Réponse à Ph. Decraene du 'Monde.'" *PNPA,* v. 4 (Mar.–Apr. 1981), pp. 65–72.

587. Koueli, Nguembi. *Le syndicalisme ouvrier au Gabon des origines à l'horizon 80.* Doctoral Thesis, U. of P., 1984.

588. Latappy, Denis. *Le système politique gabonais.* Memoir, U. of Bordeaux, 1973. 197 pp.

589. Ledaga-Leounda, Julien. *Les institutions politiques traditionnelles Ombaga (du Gabon): Face au fait colonial.* Master's Thesis, U. of Québec at Montréal, 1982. 183 pp.

590. LePointe, Philippe Marc. *Politique et Culture du Gabon: De l'unité culturelle à l'unité nationale dans un État pluriethnique.* P.: Memoir, EHESS, 1987.

591. *Livre blanc sur l'affaire Jean-Bernard Eyi: Enlèvement, séquestration et violences corporelles.* Lv.: Gabonese Republic, 1971. 21 pp.

592. Matongo, Julien. *Les assemblées législatives dans les Etats de l'ancienne Afrique Equatoriale Française.* Doctoral Thesis, U. of P., 1968. 436 pp.

593. Mauric, Alain. *Gabon de la Loi-Cadre au Référendum.* Memoir, Ecole Nationale de la France d'Outre-Mer, Paris, May 1959. 121 pp.

593a. M'Ba, Charles. "La 'conférence nationale' gabonaise: du congrès constitutif du Rassemblement Social Démocratique Gabonais (RSDG) aux assises pour la démocratie pluraliste," *Afrique 2000,* no. 7 (Nov. 1991), pp. 75–90.

594. Mba, Léon. *Le Président Léon Mba vous parle.* P.: Ed. Diloutremer, 1960. 102 pp.

595. Mba Andeme, Théophile. *Le Parti Démocratique Gabonais.* Doctoral Thesis, U. of Bordeaux, 1982.

596. Mba-Obame, André. *Société politique au Gabon: Contribution à l'étude de la nature patrimoniale du système politique gabonais.* Doctoral Thesis, U. of P., 1984.

597. MORENA. Mouvement de Redressement National (Gabon). *La Nullité de l'élection présidentielle du 9 novembre 1986 au Gabon.* Lv.: Multipress Gabon, 1986.

597a. Nsole Biteghé, Moïse. *Echec aux militaires au Gabon en 1964.* P.: Editions Chaka, 1990. 159 pp. [Contains important documents.]

598. N'Toutoume, Jean-François. *La crise politique gabonaise en 1964.* Memoir, U. of P., 1966. 199 pp.

599. ———. *L'Evolution de la vie politique gabonaise de 1958 à 1968.* Doctoral Thesis, U. of Rennes, 1969. 342 pp.

600. ———. "Expérience gabonaise: Le progressisme démocratique et concerté," *Géopolitique africaine,* (Feb.–Mar. 1987), pp. 105–115.

601. Nze-Ekekang, Timothée. *La "Rénovation." Analyse du Contenu des Idées Politiques du Président A. B. Bongo.* Memoir, U. of P., 1973. 125 pp.

602. Obiang, N'Dong. "Le Parti Démocratique Gabonais et l'État," *Penant,* v. 93 (Apr.–June 1983), pp. 131–152.

602a. Parti Démocratique Gabonais. *Le Deuxième Congrès Extraordinaire du P.D.G.* Special No., *Dialogue* (no. 62, August 17, 1979). 104 pp.

603. Péan, Pierre. *Affaires africaines.* P.: Fayard, 1983. 340 pp.

604. Peter, Jean E. "Gabon 1975: Le new deal," *RJP,* v. 29 (July–Sept. 1975), pp. 328–335.

605. Reed, Michael C. "Gabon: A Neo-Colonial Enclave of Enduring French Interest," *JMAS,* v. 25 (June 1987), pp. 283–320.

606. Remondo, Max. "L'administration gabonaise," *Bulletin de l'Institut d'Administration Publique,* (July–Sept. 1973), pp. 443–464.

607. Republic of Congo. Ministry of Information. *Félix Tchicaya. Premier Parlementaire Congolais (1903–1961). In Memoriam.* Bv.: IO, 1961. 23 pp.

608. Ropivia, Marc-Louis. *Les capitales politiques des États anciennement colonisés d'Afrique et les fondements actuels de leur relocalisation: Le cas du Gabon.* Master's Thesis, Laval U., Quebec, 1981. 241 pp.

609. Rosenblum, Mort. *Mission to Civilize.* N.Y.: Doubleday, 1988. 480 pp.

610. Sanmarco, Louis. *Le Colonisateur colonisé.* P.: ABC, 1983. 229 pp.

611. Séry, Patrick. "Le grand retour des barbouzes: Le noeud de Vipères au Gabon," *PNPA,* (July–Aug. 1986), pp. 21–40.

612. Trautmann, Frédéric. "Pages Gabonaises," *Journal des Missions Évangéliques,* v. 159 (Apr. 1984), pp. 23–38. [MORENA].

613. *Un homme, un pays: El-Hadj Omar Bongo, le Gabon.* Dakar: NEA, 1984. 221 pp.

614. Vermel, Pierre. "Le Parti Démocratique Gabonais," *MA,* v. 15 (Aug.–Sept. 1980), pp. 9–19.

615. Vidaud, P. "Gabon: Un pays en équilibre instable," *Aujourd'hui l'Afrique,* (no. 17, 1979), pp. 34–42.

616. Wadlow, Rene. "Après un coup d'état à rebours," *La Tribune de Genève* (Mar. 1–2, 1964).

617. Weinstein, Brian. *Gabon: Nation-Building on the Ogooué.* Cambridge, Mass.: M.I.T. Press, 1966. 287 pp.

618. Young, Crawford. "The Northern Republics, 1960–1980," in David Birmingham and Phyllis Martin, eds., *History of Central Africa,* v. 2. L.: Longman, 1983, pp. 291–335.

VII: ADMINISTRATION AND LAW

619. Agondjo-Okawe, Pierre-Louis. "Les droits fonciers coutumiers au Gabon," *RJP,* v. 24 (Oct. 1970), pp. 1135–1152.

620. ———. "Les Droits Fonciers Coutumiers au Gabon (Société Nkomi, Groupe Myènè)," *Rural Africana* (Fall 1973), pp. 15–30.

621. ———. "L'enseignement du droit au Gabon," in *La connaissance du droit en Afrique.* Brussels: Académie Royale des Sciences d'Outre-Mer, 1984, pp. 328–346.

622. Ajami, S. M. *Les Institutions Constitutionnelles de la République Gabonaise.* Lv.: Faculté de Droit et Sciences Economiques, Mar. 1976. 118 pp.

623. ———. "Les institutions constitutionnelles du présidential-isme gabonais," *RJP,* v. 29 (Oct.–Nov. 1975), pp. 436–466.

624. Ambouroué, M.-A. "La femme en droit coutumier gabon-ais," *RJP,* v. 28 (Oct.–Dec. 1974), pp. 673–680.

625. Anderson, Howard William. *The Limits of Development Management: An Analysis of Agricultural Policy Implementation in Gabon.* Doctoral Diss., Indiana U., 1987. 287 pp.

626. Andrieux, Jean-Pierre, and Lecat, Jean-Jacques. *Afrique centrale: Cameroun, Centrafrique, Congo, Gabon: Guide juridique et fiscal.* P.: F. Lefebvre, 1987. 386 pp.

626a. Biyeghe-Bi-Ovale, Jeannot. *L'Immigration clandestine, une atteinte à la sécurité du Gabon.* Memoir, IAES, Lv., 1988. 117 pp.

627. Boumah, Augustin. "Un Nouveau Code de Procédure Civile Gabonais," *Penant,* v. 89 (Oct.–Dec. 1979), pp. 373–378.

628. Brard, Yves. "Réflexions sur le code gabonais des juridic-tions administratives (loi no. 17 1984 du 29 décembre 1984)," *RJP,* v. 39 (July–Dec. 1985), pp. 916–932.

629. Buffelan, Jean-Paul. "La création d'un pouvoir régional au Gabon," *Penant,* v. 92 (Mar. 1982), pp. 49–57.

630. Cadène, Jean. "Institutions administratives Gabonaises," *Annales de l'École nationale d'Administration* (Gabon), (no. 4, 1980), pp. 7–24.

631. ———. "Les textes Législatifs et Réglementaires au Ga-bon," *Annales de l'École nationale d'Administration,* (Ga-bon), (no. 4, 1980), pp. 25–50.

632. "Document: Loi constitutionnelle no. 6/81 [22 août 1981] modifiant la Constitution de la République gabonaise," *AC,* v. 20 (Nov.–Dec. 1981), pp. 23–26.

633. Essimengane, Simon. "Le contentieux administratif gabonais," in Gérard Conac and Jean de Gaudusson, eds., *Les Cours suprêmes en Afrique*, v. 3, *La jurisprudence administrative*. P.: Economica, 1988, pp. 226–245.

633a. Francoul, André. *Commentaires sur le régime fiscal des entreprises au Gabon.* Le Vesinet: EDIENA, 1984. 185 pp.

633b. ———. *Précis fiscal du Gabon.* Le Vesinet: EDITM, 1984. 94 pp.

634. Guermann, M. *Tables des textes gabonais publiés au Ier juillet 1975 dans les journaux officiels des années 1967 à 1975,* Lv.: U. nationale gabonaise, 1976. 102 and 37 pp.

635. Hardoff, Pellegrin. "Brèves notes sur la preuve de l'état civil au Gabon," *Penant,* v. 96 (Jan.–June 1986), pp. 90–96.

636. Hervouet, François. "Le Processus de Concentration des Pouvoirs par le Président de la République au Gabon," *Penant,* v. 93 (Jan.–Mar. 1983), pp. 5–35; (Apr.–June 1983), pp. 200–215.

637. Kombila, J. P. "Les communes, les assemblées départementales et provinciales gabonaises: Une décentralisation territoriale effective?" *Penant,* v. 100 (no. 803, 1990), pp. 236–245.

637a. Lepointe, Eric. "De l'histoire du droit au droit comparé: l'exemple du droit commercial applicable au Gabon," *Penant,* v. 101 (June–Oct. 1991), pp. 214–236.

638. Luchaire, Yves. "La Chambre administrative et la Cour suprême du Gabon," in Gérard Conac and Jean de Gaudusson, eds., *Les Cours suprêmes en Afrique,* v. 3, *La jurisprudence administrative.* P.: Economica, 1988, pp. 192–225.

639. Mba, Casimir Oyé. *Les problèmes juridiques posés par l'exploitation de sous-sol au Gabon.* Doctoral Thesis, U. of P., 1969. 348 pp.

640. Mébiame, Léon. "La commune et la collectivité rurale au Gabon," *RJP,* v. 22 (July–Sept. 1968), pp. 909–918.

641. Mengue Me Engouang, Fidèle. "La Publicité des Lois et Règlements au Gabon," *Penant,* v. 95 (July–Dec. 1985), pp. 262–276.

642. Mercier, Jean-Louis. "La condition juridique des personnels de la Fonction publique au Gabon," *AENA,* v. 3 (1979), pp. 97–110.

643. Ndaot Rembogo, Séraphin. *Les institutions judiciaires du Gabon.* Yaoundé: CEPER, 1981. 165 pp.

644. Nguema, Isaac. "Aspects traditionnels de la nationalité gabonaise," *RJP,* v. 25 (no. 4, 1971), pp. 503–511.

645. ———. *Le nom dans la tradition et la législation gabonaise (Essai de droit coutumier).* Doctoral Thesis, U. of P., 1969.

646. ———. "Réalités Gabonaises, Justice et Développement, La Preuve du Droit et le Droit de la Preuve," *RJP,* v. 39 (Jan.–Mar. 1985), pp. 148–169.

647. ———. "La terre dans le droit traditionnel Ntumu," *RJP,* v. 24 (Oct. 1970), pp. 1119–1134.

648. ———. "Les voies nouvelles de la codification des coutumes gabonaises," *RJP,* v. 40 (no. 3–4, 1986), pp. 319–364.

648a. Nkogué-Nguema, Pierre. *La sous-administration au Gabon.* Doctoral Thesis, U. of Clermont-Ferrand, 1986.

649. Obame Essono, Jean-Clair. "La protection des droits de la personne sur le plan administratif et judiciaire au Gabon," *RJP,* v. 36 (Jan.–Mar. 1982), pp. 126–146.

650. Oliveira, Antoine. "Le Rôle du Juge dans l'Administration de la Preuve en Droit Privé gabonais," *RJP,* v. 39 (Jan.–Mar. 1985), pp. 170–177.

651. Pambou Tchivounda, Guillaume. "La Chambre des Comptes au Gabon," *RJP,* v. 34 (Apr.–June 1980), pp. 600–616.

652. ———. "Le Délégué Ministériel au Gabon," 90 (Jan.–Mar. 1980), pp. 49–68.

653. ———, and Moussavou-Moussavou, Jean Bernard. *Éléments de la pratique gabonaise en matière de traités internationaux.* P.: LGDJ: R. Pichon and R. Durand Auzias, 1986. 191 pp.

654. Pie, F. *Les politiques pénales en Afrique noire francophone: Le Cas du Gabon.* Bordeaux: Institut d'Études Politiques, 1989. 155 pp.

655. Pugeault, Serge. "L'administration territoriale décentralisée au Gabon," *Annuaire des collectivités locales,* (no. 5, 1985), pp. 43–56.

656. Remondo, Max. *L'Administration gabonaise.* P.: B-L, 1974.

657. ———. *Le droit administratif gabonais.* P.: LGDJ: R. Pichon and R. Durand-Auzias, 1987. 303 pp.

658. ———. "Réflexions sur le système juridictionnel gabonais," *Penant,* v. 91 (no. 771, 1981), pp. 5–21.

VIII: MILITARY AFFAIRS

659. Ammi-Oz, Moshe. "L'évolution de la place et du rôle des forces publiques africaines," *MA,* (Mar. 1977), pp. 59–76.

660. ———. "Les impératifs de la politique militaire française en Afrique Noire à l'époque de la décolonisation," *RFEPA,* (Feb. 1977), pp. 65–89.

661. ———. *Les interventions extra-militaires des forces armées nationales dans les états d'Afrique noire francophone.* Doctoral Thesis, U. of P., 1984. 484 pp.

662. Bangoura, Dominique. "La Contribution des Forces Armées et de Securité à la Stabilité de l'État Gabonais de 1967 à 1989," *Cahiers de l'Institut Pan-Africain de Géopolitique,* (Dec. 1989), pp. 6–38.

663. Bigmann, Louis. *Le Capitaine Charles N'Tchoréré.* Abidjan: NEA, 1983, 131 pp.

664. Chaigneau, Pascal. *La politique militaire de la France en Afrique.* P.: CHEAM, 1984. 147 pp.

665. Chipman, John. *Ve République et défense de l'Afrique.* P.: Éditions Bosquet, 1986. 151 pp.

666. ———. *French Military Policy and African Security.* L.: International Institute for Strategic Studies, Adelphi Papers, no. 201, 1985. 51 pp.

667. Echenberg, Myron. *Colonial Conscripts: Tirailleurs Sénégalais in French West Africa, 1857–1960.* Portsmouth, N.H.: Heinemann, 1991. 236 pp. [N'Tchoréré].

668. Ngari, Idriss. "La spécifité de l'armée gabonaise," in *Institut Africain d'Études Stratégiques de Libreville (IAES). Les Armées africaines.* P.: Economica, 1986, pp. 51–55.

669. N'Tchoréré, Charles. "Le problème des jeunes générations africaines," *Revue des troupes coloniales,* (1938), pp. 1117–1131.

670. Ongouya, Jean-Félix. "La Présence militaire de la France en Afrique," *PA,* (no. 4, 1980), pp. 43–63.

671. Rougier, Émile. "Le Capitaine [Charles] N'Tchoréré: Un héros de la guerre," *M'Bolo,* (June 1984), pp. 48–51.

672. Yakemtchouk, Romain. "La coopération militaire de l'Afrique noire avec les Puissances (1) avec la France; (2) avec l'U.R.S.S. et les États-Unis," *AC,* v. 22 (July–Sept. 1983), pp. 3–18; (Oct.–Dec. 1983), pp. 3–22.

IX: ECONOMICS

673. Abodo, Tabi. *Étude Monographique sur l'Emploi et la Formation au Cameroun, au Gabon, en République Centrafricaine.* Abidjan: Centre Interafricain pour le Développement et Formation Professionnelle, Sept. 1984. 61 pp.

674. Authié, Xavier. "Le pétrole en Afrique noire," *AC,* v. 19 (July–Aug. 1980), pp. 1–8.

675. Balandier, Georges. "Les problèmes du travailleur africain au Gabon et au Congo," *Bulletin International des Sciences Sociales,* v. 6 (no. 3, 1954), pp. 504–513.

676. Baranger, M. "Transgabonais à mi-chemin," *Rail monde,* Mar. 1983), pp. 29–40.

676a. "Le barrage de Kinguélé," *BMBEAC, ES* (Mar. 1974), pp. 135–146.

676b. Barro Chambrier, Hugues Alexandre. *L'Economie du Gabon: Analyse, Politiques d'Ajustement, et d'Adaptation.* P.: Economica, 1990, 355 pp.

677. Bertin, A. *Les Bois du Gabon.* P.: Larose, 1929. 306 pp.

678. Binet, Jacques. "Activité économique et prestige chez les Fangs du Gabon," *RTM,* v. 33 (Jan.–Mar. 1968), pp. 25–42.

679. Bouanga, Jean-Christophe. *L'Absorption du Capital au Gabon.* Memoir, U. of P., 1977. 180 pp.

680. Bouquerel, Jacqueline. "Le pétrole au Gabon," *CO-M,* v. 20 (Apr.–June 1967), pp. 186–199.

681. ———. "Port-Gentil, centre économique du Gabon," *CO-M,* v. 20 (July–Sept. 1967), pp. 247–274.

682. Boussiengul, Raymond Mondjo. *Modèles alternatifs de localisation d'activités secondaires complémentaires à intégration verticale dans les régions minières des pays de la périphérie: Application au développement de la région du Haut-Ogooué au Gabon.* Master's Thesis, U. of Sherbrooke, 1979.

683. Brard, Yves. "Les conventions dans la fiscalité pétrolière gabonaise," *RJP,* v. 41 (no. 3, 1987), pp. 151–167.

684. Brochet, Christine, and Pierre, Jacques. *Industrialisation des pays d'Afrique sub-saharienne: Le cas du Gabon.* P.: SEDES, Ministère de la Coopération, 1986. 31 pp.

685. Cabrol, Claude. "Le Ministère des Transports et de la Marine Marchande, une création récente, un avenir prometteur," *Annales de l'École Nationale d'Administration* (Gabon), (no. 4, 1980), pp. 51–58.

686. ———. "Perspectives de réalisation du chemin de fer Transgabonais," *AC,* (Mar.–Apr. 1973), pp. 2–6.

687. ———. "Les transports au Gabon. Le Transgabonais, historique des réalisations dans le temps, situation actuelle," *AENA* (no. 2, 1978), pp. 77–92.

688. Carouet, Bernard. "Activités immobilières et travaux d'urbanisme au Gabon," *BMBCEAEC, ES* (May 1972), pp. 309–320.

689. Chauput, Jean-Louis. "Les voies navigables au Gabon," *BMBEAC, ES* (June–July 1974), pp. 368–378.

690. "Contre-choc pétrolier: Le cas gabonais," *Géopolitique africaine,* (Dec. 1986), pp. 5–60.

691. Courbot, Roger. *Le Mouvement Commercial du Gabon de 1928 à 1939*. Memoir, Ecole Nationale de la France d'Outre-Mer, Paris, 1944–1945.

692. Dangeard, Alain-Louis, and Papon, André. "Les Perspectives de l'industrie minière de l'Afrique en développement," *AC,* v. 23 (July–Sept. 1984), pp. 3–16. [Includes Gabon].

693. Daverat, Geneviève. "Un producteur africain de pétrole, le Gabon," *CO-M,* v. 30 (Jan.–Mar. 1977), pp. 31–56.

694. Dialogue. *5e Plan de Développement économique et sociale, 1984–1988.* Lv.: Dialogue, 1985. 159 pp.

695. Direction Générale de l'économie minecofin. "L'Économie gabonaise en 1985," *Économie et Finances,* (Jan. 1986), pp. 17–27.

696. "Dossier: Le Gabon," *Afrique industrie infrastructures,* (Oct. 15, 1980), pp. 30–89.

697. Doupamby-Matoka. *Les Investissements Etrangers et la Politique Gabonaise du Développement.* Memoir, U. of P., 1970. 81 pp.

698. *L'Économie gabonaise.* Special no., *Bulletin de l'Afrique Noire.* P.: Ediafric, 1976. 163 pp.

699. ———. 4th ed. P.: Édiafric, 1985. 259 pp.

700. Ekagha-Assey, Jean. *L'économie moderne et les relations inter-ethniques dans la région de Lambaréné (Gabon).* Doctoral Thesis, U. of P., 1974.

701. Engonga-Bikoro, Albert. "L'impact des groupes industriels sur les pays sous-développés: La cas de Elf au Gabon," in *Entreprises et Entrepreneurs en Afrique, XIXe et XXe Siècles,* v. 2. P.: Harmattan, 1983, pp. 507–517.

702. Essie-Emane. *Agriculture traditionnelle dans la province de la Nyanga (Gabon): Une phase de son modernisme, création*

du Groupement à Vocation Coopérative de Mougoutsie. P.: Memoir, EHESS, 1979.

703. "Évolution de la Fiscalité dans 13 Pays d'Afrique Noire Francophone," *Études et Documents,* (no. 48, July 1989).

704. Fair, Denis. "The Ports and Oil Terminals of Nigeria, Cameroon, and Gabon," *Africa Insight,* v. 19 (no. 3, 1989), pp. 153–159.

705. Frélastre, Georges. "Devant la chute des revenus pétroliers et miniers, le Gabon cherche à améliorer son agriculture," *MA,* (Feb.–Mar. 1987), pp. 59–67.

706. "Gabon, 1960–1980." *MTM* (no. 1646, 1977), pp. 1246–1467.

707. *Gabon, 1960–1970. Dix ans d'Expansion Economique.* Monaco: Société nouvelle de l'Impr. nationale de Monaco, 1970.

708. "Gabon 1981: L'économie gabonaise de 1970 à 1981, un redressement indéniable, des perspectives diversifiées," *MTM,* (1981), pp. 2977–3151.

709. "Gabon 1981: The Gabonese Economy from 1970 to 1981," *MTM,* v. 33, 1981. 119 pp.

710. *Gabon horizon 1983: Les objectifs du Plan triennial intérimaire, 1980–1982.* P.: Éditions d'Iéna, 1981. 70 pp.

711. *Le Gabon, Afrique de Demain. Session d'Etude 15 août–8 Septembre 1971. Rapport des Participants.* Brussels: Centre Interuniversitaire de Formation Politique Indépendant de Tout Parti, 1971. 297 pp.

712. Gabon: Le plan triennial intérimaire 1980–1982. *Afrique industrie infrastructures,* v. 11 (Mar. 15, 1981), pp. 33–58.

713. "Gabon: La nouvelle politique économique," *Eurafrica,* v. 21 (Jan.–Mar. 1976), pp. 61–67.

714. *Gabon: Octobre 1981: Analyses et conjecture.* P.: Ministère des Relations Extérieures, n.d. 176 and 75 pp.

715. *Gabon: La réussite du plan de redressement économique et financier.* P.: Europe Outremer, 1980. 48 pp.

716. Galley, Y.-G. "Le bananier plantain: Une culture commerciale paysanne au Fernan-Vaz, Gabon," *Muntu,* (no. 6, 1987), pp. 153–169.

717. Gaulme, François. "Le Gabon face à la crise pétrolière," *MTM,* v. 42 (June 27, 1986), pp. 1686–1689.

718. Givelet, Noël. "L'économie post-pétrolière: Le Gabon compte les fruits amers du pétrole," *Céres Revue FAO,* v. 15 (Aug. 1982), pp. 26–32. [abandonment of food crops].

719. Grosset, Janin M. "L'économie Gabonaise en 1978, première approche," *Annales de l'École nationale d'Administration* (Gabon), (no. 4, 1980), pp. 59–90.

720. Hance, William, and Van Dongen, Irene S. "Gabon and Its Main Gateways: Libreville and Port-Gentil," *Tidjschrift voor Economischen en Sociale Geografie,* v. 52 (no. 11, 1961), pp. 286–295.

721. Haubert, Maxime; Frelin, Christiane; and Nguyen Trong Nam Tran. *Politiques alimentaires et structures sociales en Afrique noire.* P.: PUF, 1985. 287 pp.

722. *Les intérêts nationaux et étrangers dans l'économie africaine.* P.: Édiafric and La Doc. Afric, 1978. 305 pp.

723. International Monetary Fund. *Surveys of African Economies.* V. 1. *Cameroon, CAR, Chad, Congo (Brazzaville) & Gabon.* Tr. *Etudes générales sur les économies africaines.* V. 2. *Cameroun, République Centrafricaine, Tchad, Congo*

(Brazzaville) & *Gabon.* W.: International Monetary Fund, 1968. 365 & 393 pp.

724. Jacquemot, Pierre. ''Les enjeux économiques du Gabon à la veille du Plan 1984–1988,'' *AC,* v. 23 (Apr.–June 1984), pp. 31–43.

725. ———, and Assidon, Elsa. *Politiques de change et ajustement en Afrique: L'expérience de 16 pays d'Afrique subsaharienne et de l'océan Indien.* P.: Ministère de la Coopération et du Développement, 1988. 218 pp.

726. Kalfayan, Ph., and Mba, P. ''Le Gabon à l'aube de l'agro-industrie,'' *BMBEAC, ES,* (May 1982), pp. 138–161.

727. Kalflèche, Jean-Marc. ''Pour la Coopération, le Gabon Reste un Solide banc d'Essai,'' *Géopolitique africaine,* (no. 4, 1986), pp. 7–25.

728. Kamara, Mamdi. ''Franceville (Gabon): Activités et rôle dans l'organisation de son arrière-pays,'' *CO-M,* v. 36 (July–Sept. 1983), pp. 267–292.

729. Koenig, Gérard. ''La construction de chemin de fer transgabonais,'' *Revue génerale des chemins de fer,* (Feb. 1987), pp. 5–19.

730. Koumba-Mombo, Charles. *Le coût de la main d'oeuvre étrangère et son incidence sur le développement économique et éducation du Gabon.* Master's Thesis, Laval U., Quebec, 1985. 120 pp.

731. Labey, Antoine, and Nkouka, Jean-Marie. ''Le pétrole au Gabon, le deuxième souffle en 1990,'' *Afrique Industrie, Infrastructures,* v. 17 (July 20, 1988), pp. 26–44.

732. Lasserre, Guy. ''Okoumé et chantiers forestiers au Gabon,'' *CO-M,* v. 8 (Apr.–June 1955), pp. 118–160.

733. Lebigre, Jean-Michel. "Production vivrière et approvisionnement urbain au Gabon," *CO-M,* v. 33 (Apr.–June 1980), pp. 167–185.

734. Leret, S. "Le manganèse au Gabon," *CO-M,* v. 19 (Oct.–Dec. 1966), pp. 354–363.

735. Lotito, Gaston. "Le développement économique de Gabon," *CO-M,* v. 23 (Oct.–Dec. 1970), pp. 425–439.

736. Mamder, Josué Sandjiman. *Politique de développement rural en Afrique: Impacts sur l'emploi et les revenus: Le cas du Gabon.* Addis Ababa: BIT, PECTA, 1985. 110 pp.

737. M'Boumba, E. "La loi de finances, 1986," *Économie et Finances,* (Jan. 1986), pp. 28–34.

738. Meli, Marcel. "L'industrie forestière dans l'économie du Gabon," *BMBEAC, ES* (Feb. 1976), pp. 69–87.

739. *Mémorial du Gabon: 1960–1985.* Monaco: Société Internationale d'édition et de diffusion, 1985. 349 pp.

740. Mengue Me Engouang, Fidèle. "Réflexions sur les régimes fiscaux privilégiés du code des investissements au Gabon," *MA,* (no. 233–234, 1985), pp. 52–68.

741. Minko, Henri. *La fiscalité gabonaise du développement.* P.: LGDJ and Abidjan: NEA, 1981. 341 pp.

742. ———. "Le régime domanial de la République gabonaise," *RJP,* v. 24 (Oct. 1970), pp. 775–782.

743. ———. "Le régime foncier et la République gabonaise: l'immatriculation," *RJP,* v. 24 (Oct. 1970), 695–698.

744. Monferrer, Dante. "L'introduction de l'agriculture capitaliste et ses conséquences: Le cas du Gabon," in Maxime Haubert, et al., eds., *Politiques alimentaires et structures sociales en Afrique noire.* P.: PUF, 1985, pp. 263–278.

745. Morineau, Raymond. "L'épopée du transgabonais," *Demain l'Afrique,* v. 16 (Dec. 18, 1978), pp. 35–42, 47–54.

746. Moto-Ossou, S. "La mobilisation et le drainage de l'épargne nationale: Pour un développement auto-entretenu," *Économie et Finances,* (Jan. 1986), pp. 49–62.

747. Muet, Pierre-Alain. *Un modèle macroéconomique intégrant les comptes nationaux, le budget, l'endettement et la balance des paiements: Le modèle MEGA de l'économie gabonaise.* P.: Office Français des Conjonctures économiques, 1987. 31 pp.

748. Nyingone, Pauline. "Les sociétés d'économie mixte et le développement économique du Gabon," *RJP,* v. 32 (Jan.–Mar. 1978), pp. 85–96.

748a. Nze-Nguema, Fidèle Pierre. *Modernité Tiers-Mythe et Bouc-Hémisphère.* P.: Editions Publisud, 1990. 172 pp. [Gabon].

749. Ovono-N'Goua, Fabien. *La politique fiscale comme instrument de développement économique dans les pays sous-développés: le cas du Gabon: appréciation.* Memoir, U. of P., 1976. 167 pp.

749a. Peter, J. E. "Le Transgabonais," *Afrique Industrie Infrastructures* (May 1, 1975), pp. 29–76.

750. Peting, Isaac. *Fiscalité et développement: le cas du Gabon.* Memoir, U. of Paris, 1977. 86 pp.

751. "Les Pétroles au Gabon," *Géographie recherches,* v. 51 (Oct. 1984), pp. 69–77.

752. Ping, Jean. *Quelques facteurs externes de freinage de la croissance et du blocage du développement au Gabon.* Memoir, U. of P., 1970. 70 pp.

753. Pourtier, Roland. "Agro-industrie et développement rural au Gabon: Une contradiction," in C. Blanc-Parmard, et al., eds., *Le Développement rural en question: Paysages, es-*

paces ruraux, systèmes agraires: Maghreb, Afrique noire, Mélanesie. P.: Orstom, 1984, pp. 447–459.

754. ———. ''La crise de l'agriculture dans un État minier: Le Gabon,'' *Études rurales,* v. 77 (Jan.–Mar. 1980), pp. 39–62.

755. Prats, R. *Le Gabon: La mise en valeur et ses problèmes.* Doctoral Thesis, U. of Montpellier, 1955. 272 pp.

756. Rapontchombo, Gaston, and M'Bouy Boutzit, E. A. *Libreville, capitale de la République gabonaise.* Lv.: Société gabonaise d'éd., 1973. 131 pp.

757. Republic of Gabon. *Plan de Développement Economique et Sociale, 1966–1970.* Lv.: IO, 1966. 3 v. 555 pp.

758. Rey, Pierre Philippe. *Colonialisme, néo-colonialisme, et transition au capitalisme. Exemple de la ''Comilog'' au Congo-Brazzaville.* P.: Maspero, 1971. 526 pp. [Loango].

759. Rocq, J. ''L'aviation au Gabon,'' *Annales de l'Université nationale du Gabon, série Lettres et Sciences Sociales,* v. 1 (Dec. 1977), pp. 88–99.

760. Roumegous, M. ''Port-Gentil: Quelques aspects sociaux du développement industriel,'' *CO-M,* v. 19 (Oct.–Dec. 1966), pp. 321–353.

761. ''Le rush sur le Gabon,'' *RTM,* v. 18 (Jan.–Mar. 1977), pp. 155–157.

762. Sabolo, Y. ''Some Comments on Foreign Private Investments and the Economic and Social Development of Gabon,'' *African Development* (no. 4, 1975), pp. 499–534.

763. ———. *Quelques Réflexions sur les investissements privés étrangers et le développement économique et social du Gabon.* Geneva: B. I. Travas, 1975. 58 pp.

764. Saint-Aubin, G., de. *La forêt du Gabon.* Nogent-sur-Marne: Ed. du Centre technique forestier tropical, 1963. 208 pp.

765. Schaetzen, Y., de. "L'économie gabonaise," *RFEPA,* (June 1973), pp. 67–94.

766. Schissel, Howard. "Gabon: The Economic Outlook," *Africa Report,* v. 30 (Jan.–Feb. 1985), pp. 27–29.

767. Sinsou, Jean-Paul. "L'aviation intérieure et l'envol du Gabon," *Transports,* (Jan. 1986), pp. 27–34.

768. ———. "L'étonnante potentialité des transports fluviolagunaires par cabotage au Gabon," *Transports,* (no. 322, 1987), pp. 83–90.

769. "La situation de l'économie gabonaise," *Afrique industrie infrastructures,* v. 16 (no. 345, 1986), pp. 12–39.

770. Sobotchou, J. F. "Les modes normaux de dissolution du contrat de travail à durée indéterminée au Gabon," *Penant,* v. 92 (no. 776, 1982), pp. 9–40.

771. Souna, Jean-Baptiste. *Le développement agricole au Gabon: Discours politique, contraintes et perspectives.* Master's Thesis, U. of Sherbrooke, 1985. 106 pp.

772. Stern, M. *L'Okoumé au Gabon, 1930–1960.* Memoir for the Master's, U. of P., 1977.

773. *Stratégies et perspectives de l'emploi au Gabon.* Addis Ababa: BIT-PECTA, 1983. 305 pp.

774. "Le Troisième Plan du Gabon, 1976–1980," *MTM,* v. 32 (Nov. 5, 1976), pp. 3061–3064.

775. Vennetier, Pierre. "Les ports du Gabon et du Congo-Brazza," *CO-M,* v. 22 (Oct.–Dec. 1969), pp. 337–355.

776. Verheve, D. "Les ressources minières des états d'Afrique centrale (CEEAC)," *Tiers-monde,* v. 27 (no. 106, 1986), pp. 457–465.

402 / Bibliography

777. Viel, Hughes. "Le transgabonais et l'économie du Gabon," *MTM*, v. 42 (Dec. 13, 1986), pp. 3219–3250.

778. Villien, François. "Les Consommations d'Énergie à Libreville," *CO-M*, v. 37 (Apr.–June 1984), pp. 109–134.

779. ———. "Énergie traditionnelle et énergie moderne dans le monde gabonais," *CO-M*, v. 34 (July–Sept. 1981), pp. 233–255.

780. Villien-Rossi, Marie-Louise. *La Compagnie de l'Ogooué. Son Influence Géographique au Gabon et au Congo.* P.: Honoré Champion, 1978. 700 pp.

781. Waller, Peter P. "Petrodollars und Entwicklungsstrategie—der Fall Gabun," *Afrika Spectrum*, v. 11 (no. 1, 1976), pp. 187–196.

782. Walter, R. *Le Développement de Libreville.* Doctoral Thesis, U. of Aix-Marseilles, 1976.

X: ANTHROPOLOGY, ETHNOLOGY, AND SOCIOLOGY

783. Aboughe Obame, Jean. *Acculturation et sous-développement au Gabon.* Doctoral Thesis, U. of P., 1975.

784. Adam, Jean-Jérôme. "Sagesse obamba (Haut-Ogooué), *Muntu*, (no. 7, 1987), pp. 109–119.

785. Agondjo-Okawe, Pierre-Louis. *Structures Parentales et Développement au Gabon: Les Nkomis.* Doctoral Thesis, U. of P., 1967.

786. Akendengué, Pierre. *Religion et éducation traditionnelle en*

pays nkomi au dix-neuvième siécle. Doctoral Thesis, U. of P., 1986.

787. Akwa, Dikwa Guillaume Betoté. *Bible de la sagesse Bantu: Choix d'aphorisme, devinettes et mots d'esprit du Cameroun et du Gabon.* P.: Centre artistique et culturel camerounais, 1955. 147 pp.

788. Alexandre, Pierre, and Binet, Jacques. *Le Groupe dit Pahouin: Fang-Boulou-Beti.* P.: PUF, 1958. 152 pp.

789. Alihanga, M. *Structures communautaires traditionnels et perspectives coopératives dans la société altogovéenne (Gabon).* Doctoral Diss., St. Thomas Aquinas U. of Pontifical Studies, Rome, 1976. 625 pp.

790. Allogho Oke, Ferdinand. *Biboubouah chroniques équatoriales: Suivi de Bourrasques sur Mitzic.* P.: Harmattan, 1985. 157 pp.

791. André, L. J. "Étude d'un groupe de pygmées 'Babinga' dans la région de Mékambo (Gabon)," *Médecine d'Afrique Noire,* v. 34 (Oct. 1987), pp. 783–798.

792. Avaro, A. "La notion d'Anyambie (Dieu) dans les civilisations claniques du Gabon avant les blancs," *PA* (no. 4, 1969), pp. 96–102.

793. Bahuchet, S. "Développement des recherches sur les Pygmées d'Afrique Centrale: Septembre 1986," *Bulletin d'ethnomédecine,* (no. 4, 1986), pp. 159–170.

794. Balandier, Georges. *Afrique Ambigue.* P.: Plon, 1957. 294 pp. Tr. *Ambiguous Africa.* N.Y.: Pantheon, 1966. 276 pp.

795. ———. *Sociologie actuelle de l'Afrique Noire.* P.: PUF, 2nd ed., 1963. 532 pp. Tr. *Sociology of Black Africa.* L.: Deutsch, 1970, 540 pp.

796. ———, and Pauvert, Jean-Claude. *Les villages gabonais.* Bv.: Institut d'Etudes Centrafricaines, 1952. 90 pp.

797. Bascou-Brescane, R. *Etude des conditions de vie à Libreville (1961–1962)*. Lv.: INSEE-Coopération, 1969. 142 pp.

798. Biffot, Laurent. *Articles et communications sociologiques (1962–1972)*. Lv.: CNRST, 1977. 219 pp.

799. ———. *Comportements et attitudes de la jeunesse scolaire gabonaise*. Doctoral Thesis, U. of P., 1971. 146 pp.

800. ———. *Contribution à la connaissance et compréhension des populations rurales du Nord-Est du Gabon*. Lv.: Collection "Sciences Humaines Gabonaises," July 1977. 239 pp.

801. ———. *Facteurs d'intégration et de désintégration du travailleur gabonais à son entreprise*. P.: ORSTOM, 1960–1961. 153 pp.

802. ———. "Genèse des classes sociales au Gabon," *AENA*, (no. 1, 1978), pp. 31–48, & (no. 2, 1978), pp. 17–32.

803. ———. *Genèse des classes sociales au Gabon*. Lv.: CNRST, 1977. 51 pp.

804. ———. "La jeunesse gabonaise face au monde rurale et au monde urbain," *L'Enfant en Milieu Tropical*, v. 20 (1966), pp. 21–34.

805. Binet, Jacques. *Afrique en question de la tribu à la nation*. Tours: Mame, 1965. 252 pp.

806. Bissielo, Anaclé. *La montée de l'encadrement dans les processus socio-contemporains au Gabon*. Doctoral Thesis, U. of P., 1987.

807. Bodinga-Bwa-Bodinga, S. *Traditions orales de la race Eviya*. P.: T.M.T., 1969. 56 pp.

808. Bongo, Omar. "Message à l'occasion de la Première con-

férence des Ministres de la Culture de la zone bantu,''
Muntu, (no. 1, 1984), pp. 5–20.

809. Bôt Ba Njock, H. M. ''Préeminences sociales et systèmes
politico-religieux dans la société traditionnelle bulu et
fang,'' *JSA,* v. 30 (No. 2, 1960), pp. 151–172.

810. Bouet, Claude. ''Pour une introduction à l'étude des migrations modernes en milieu sous-peuplé: situation actuelle du
salariat et de l'emploi au Gabon,'' *CORSTOM, SSM,* v. 10
(no. 2–3, 1973), pp. 295–306.

811. ———. ''Problèmes actuels de main d'oeuvre au Gabon:
conditions d'une immigration controlée,'' *CO-M,* v. 31
(Oct.–Dec. 1978), pp. 375–394.

812. Bourdès-Ogouliguendé, Jules. *L'évolution du statut de la
femme gabonaise.* Doctoral Thesis, U. of P., 1972.

813. Boussoukou-Boumba. ''L'organisation de la chefferie indigène à Ntima et à Divenie (Congo) (1923–1941),'' *PA* (no.
3, 1978), pp. 111–134.

814. Breitengross, Jens P. ''Sozio-ökonomische Aspekte der
Bevölkerungsentwicklung in Zentralafrika,'' *Afrika Spectrum,* v. 10 (no. 2, 1975), pp. 119–140.

815. Briault, Maurice. *Dans la fôret du Gabon.* P.: Grasset, 1930,
195 pp.

816. Cabrol, Claude, and Lehuard, Raoul. *La civilisation des
peuples batéké.* Lv.: Multipress, & Monaco: Ed. PB, 1976.
96 pp.

817. Cavalli Sforza, L. L., ed. *African Pygmies.* Orlando: Academic Press, 1986. 461 pp.

818. *La civilisation des peuples Batéké.* Lv.: Multipress Gabon
and Monaco: P. Bory, 1976. 95 pp.

819. Collomb, Gérard. ''Fragments d'une Cosmologie Banzébi,'' *JA*, v. 53 (no. 1–2, 1983), pp. 107–118.

820. ———. ''Les Sept fils de Nzébi: Un mythe cosmogonique des Banzébi du Gabon,'' *JA*, v. 49 (no. 2, 1979), pp. 89–139.

821. Dupré, Georges. *Un ordre et son destruction-graphisme de la cour?* P.: ORSTOM, 1982. 446 pp. [Nzabi].

822. Dupuis, Annie. ''Être ou ne pas être: Quelques sociétés de femme au Gabon,'' *Objets et Mondes,* v. 23 (no. 1–2, 1983), pp. 79–90.

823. ———. ''Quelques représentations relatives à l'enfant de la conception au sevrage chez les Nzébi du Gabon,'' *JA*, v. 51 (no. 1–2, 1981), pp. 117–132.

824. Eckendorff, Jean. ''Note sur les tribus des subdivisions de Makokou et de Mékambo (Gabon),'' *BIEC*, n.s., v. 1 (no. 1, 1945), pp. 87–95.

825. Edzang, S. ''Gabon's Population Policy,'' *African Population Newsletter* (Dec. 1976), pp. 4–6.

826. Enonga Bikora, Blandine. ''Cosmologie bantu: Origine de la vie, du monde, et de Dieu chez les Fang,'' *Muntu,* (no. 6, 1987), pp. 105–119.

827. Fernandez, James W. ''Affirmation of Things Past: Alar Ayong & Bwiti as Movements of Protest,'' in R. Rotberg and Ali Mazrui, eds., *Protest and Power in Black Africa.* N.Y.: Oxford UP, 1970, pp. 427–457.

828. ———. ''Christian Acculturation and Fang Witchcraft,'' *CEA,* v. 2 (no. 2, 1961), pp. 244–270.

829. ———. ''Fang Representations Under Acculturation,'' in P. Curtin, ed., *Africa and the West: Intellectual Responses to European Culture.* Madison: U. of Wisconsin Press, 1972, pp. 3–48.

830. ———. *Redistributive Acculturation and Ritual Reintegration in Fang Culture.* Ph.D. Diss., Northwestern U., Evanston, 1963. 346 pp.

831. Fromaget, Michel. "Aperçu sur la thérapeutique du conjoint invisible chez les Myènè du Gabon," *JA,* (1986), pp. 105–112.

832. ———. "Contribution du Bwiti mitsogho à l'anthropologie de l'imaginaire à propos d'un cas de diagnostique divinatoire au Gabon," *Anthropos,* v. 81 (no. 1–3, 1986), pp. 87–107.

833. ———. "Projet d'étude pour le Gabon: Évaluation et dynamique des changements de valeur dans les différents pays de la zone bantu," *Cahiers de sociologie économique et culturelle,* (June 1984), pp. 133–140.

834. Gautier, J. F. "Sagesse politique de la tradition bakota," *Annales de l'université nationale du Gabon, série Lettres et Sciences Sociales,* v. 1 (Dec. 1977), pp. 69–76.

835. Gollnhofer, Otto, and Sillans, Roger. "Aperçu sur les pratiques sacrificielles chez les Mitsogho," *Systèmes de Pensée en Afrique Noire,* (no. 4, 1979), pp. 167–174.

836. ———, and ———. "Essai d'approche du concept et du mécanisme des 'objet-médiateurs' chez les Mitsogho (Gabon)," in S. Garay, et al., eds., *Ethnologiques: Hommages à Marcel Griaule.* P.: Hermann, 1987, pp. 151–165.

837. ———, and ———. "Le mythe de la découverte du génie de l'eau chez les Mitsogho," *Ethnographie,* v. 77 (no. 1, 1981), pp. 37–46.

838. ———, and ———. "Phénoménologie de la possession chez les Mitsogho: Aspects psychosociaux," *Psychopathologie Africaine,* v. 10 (no. 2, 1974), pp. 187–210.

839. ———, and ———. "Phénoménologie de la possession

chez les Mitsogho (Gabon). Rites et techniques.'' *Anthropos,* v. 74 (no. 5–6, 1979), pp. 737–752.

840. ———, and ———. ''Pratiques sacrificielles chez les Mitsogho du Gabon,'' *Systèmes de pensée en Afrique noire,* (no. 7, 1984), pp. 175–186.

841. Gruat, J. V. ''The Extension of Social Protection in the Gabonese Republic: Consolidating the Development Process,'' *International Labour Review,* v. 123 (Aug. 1984), pp. 457–472. Also, ''L'extension de la protection sociale en République gabonaise: Consolidation du développement,'' *Ibid.,* v. 123 (Aug. 1984), pp. 499–514.

842. ———. ''The Social Guarantee in the Gabonese Republic: A New Kind of Social Protection in Africa,'' *International Social Security Review,* (no. 2, 1985), pp. 157–171.

843. Guillaume, Henri. ''Pygmées en fôret d'Afrique centrale,'' *Politique africaine,* (no. 34, 1989), pp. 74–82.

844. Guillot, B. ''Le Village de Passia: Essai sur le Système Agraire Nzabi,'' *CORSTOM, SSH,* v. 7 (no. 1, 1970), pp. 47–94.

845. ———. ''Le Pays Bandzabi au Nord de Mayoko et les déplacements récents de population provoqués par l'axe COMILOG (Cie. Minière de l'Ogooué),'' *CORSTOM, SSH,* v. 4 (no. 3–4, 1967), pp. 37–56.

846. Hagenbucher-Sacripanti, Frank. *Les fondements spirituels du pouvoir au Royaume de Loango, République du Congo.* P.: ORSTOM, 1973. 214 pp.

847. Hartweg, R. *La vie secrète des pygmées.* P.: Ed. du Temps, 1961. 118 pp.

848. Hauser, André. ''Les Babingas,'' *Zaïre,* v. 7 (Feb. 1953), pp. 146–179.

849. ———. "Notes sur les Omyènè du bas Gabon," *BIFAN,* v. 16 (1954), pp. 402–415.

850. Hervo-Akendengué, A. "Social Security in Gabon," in *African Social Security.* G.: 1967, pp. 3–56.

851. Heymer, Armin. "Eco-éthologie des Pygmées Bayaka," *Objets et Mondes,* v. 21 (Summer 1981), pp. 53–72.

852. Jean, Suzanne. *Organisation sociale et familiale et problèmes fonciers des populations banjabi et bapunu de la N'Gounié-Nyanga.* P.: BDPA, 1960.

853. Laburthe-Tolra, Philippe. *Minlaaba: Histoire et société traditionnelle chez les Beti du Sud-Cameroun,* 3 vols. P.: Honoré Champion, 1977. 1912 pp. [Fang Origins].

854. Lansler, Marie. *Socialisation des jeunes enfants Vili du Gabon.* Master's Thesis, Laval U., Quebec, 1980.

855. Leblanc, Loïc. "L'évolution du Code du travail gabonais," *AENA* (no. 2, 1978), pp. 45–66.

856. Le Testu, Georges. *Notes sur les coutumes bapounou de la circonscription de la Nyanga.* Caen: J. Haulard la Brière, 1920, 212 pp.

857. Maclatchy, A. R. "L'organisation sociale des populations de la région de Mimongo (Gabon)," *BIEC,* n.s., v. 1 (no. 1, 1945), pp. 53–86.

858. Mba, Léon. "Essai de droit coutumier pahouin," *BSRC,* (no. 25, 1938), pp. 5–51.

859. Mba Allogho, Daniel. *La formation de la classe ouvrière au Gabon.* Doctoral Thesis, U. of Nantes, 1981.

860. Mba-Obame, André. *Modernité et société en Afrique Noire: Essai sur la formation et l'insertion socio-culturelle de l'état gabonais.* Master's Thesis, Laval U., Quebec, 1980. 165 pp.

861. Mbah, Jules. *Coutumes gabonaises et civilisation française.* Memoir, Ecole Nationale de la France d'Outre-Mer, Paris, 1958–1959. [Fang].

862. Mbot, Jean Emile. *Binga dzi dzi akong: "Nous mangions la lance" (comportements de guerre chez les Fang du Gabon).* Memoir for the Master's, U. of P., 1971.

863. M'Boumba Moulambo. *Mythes et cultures: Réflexion sur les aspects et les fondements socio-éducatifs et historiques de certains rituels africains.* Doctoral Thesis, U. of Lille, 1983.

864. Mboukou, Jean-Hubert. "Ethnologie Criminelle du Gabon," *RJP,* v. 39 (Jan.–Mar. 1985), pp. 178–187.

865. Miletto. "Notes sur les ethnies de la région du Haut-Ogooué," *BIEC,* n.s., (no. 2, 1951), pp. 19–48.

866. Milligan, Robert H. *The Fetish Folk of West Africa.* N.Y., 1912. 328 pp. Reprint, N.Y.: AMS Press, 1970. [Mpongwe, Fang].

867. Mondzo, Jean Chrisostom. "Une vision non hégelienne de la dialectique du maître et de l'esclave," *Milieux,* (no. 27, 1983), pp. 13–23. [Nzébi].

868. Moniot, Henri, and Felice, J. "Un exemple de destructuration sociale: Les Fang du Gabon," *Information Géographique,* v. 45 (no. 2, 1981), pp. 81–89.

869. Moukagni-Mounguengui, José-Marcel. *Aléas et perspectives de développement rural intégré dans la province de la Nyanga (Gabon).* Memoir, EHESS, 1980.

870. Mudry, René. *Migration urbaine et structures sociales (l'exemple des Fangs de Minivoul).* Memoir, EHESS, 1986.

871. Mve-Ondo, Bonaventure. "Les jeux de calcul gabonais," *M'Bolo,* (no. 16, 1986), pp. 54–64. [Fang].

872. Nassau, Robert Hamill. *Fetichism in West Africa: Forty*

Years' Observations of Native Customs and Superstitions. N.Y.: Scribners, 1904, 389 pp. Reprint, N.Y.: Negro UP, 1969.

873. Ndombet, Marie-Augustine. "La femme et la pratique de droit coutumier au Gabon: baptême, mariage, decès," in Société Africaine de culture, *La civilisation de la Femme dans la tradition africaine.* P.: *PA,* 1975, pp. 328–336.

874. Nguema, Isaac. "Divinités Gabonaises, Droit et Développement," *RJP,* v. 38 (Apr.–June 1984), pp. 95–132.

875. ———. "Les voies nouvelles du développement de la femme gabonaise," *Droit et Cultures,* (no. 1, 1981), pp. 64–90.

876. Nguema-Eyegue, Pierre Nestor. *Essai sur l'histoire, l'origine des tribus et le mouvement de regroupement clanique (élarayong) du groupe linguistique mazôna (Fang et apparentés) d'Afrique centrale.* Memoir, U. of P., 1987.

877. *Nnanga Kon.* Ebolowa, Cameroon: American Presbyterian Mission Press, 1948. [In Fang].

878. Nzaou-Mabika, Jeanne. "Initiative et pouvoir créateur de la femme. L'exemple du Gabon," in Société Africaine de Culture, *La civilisation de la Femme dans la tradition africaine.* P.: *PA,* 1975, pp. 286–295.

879. Nze-Nguema, Fidéle P. *Mirage de la modernité: État et monde rural: Le cas du Gabon.* Master's Thesis, Laval U., Quebec, 1980. 266 pp.

880. Obenga, Théophile, "Le peuple teke en Afrique centrale," *Muntu,* (no. 7, 1987), pp. 11–32.

881. Ogoula-M'Beye, Pastor. *Galwa ou Edonga d'antan.* P.: Impr. Loriou, 1978. 214 pp.

882. Ondoua, Engute, ed. *Dulu Bon be Agin Kara* [*The Journey of*

the Children of Africa]. Ebolowa, Cameroon: American Presbyterian Mission Press, 194?. [In Fang].

883. Panyella, Augusto. *Esquema de etnología de los Fang Ntumu de la Guinea Española.* Madrid: Consejo superior de investigaciones cientificas, 1959. 79 pp.

884. Papy, Louis. "Les populations batéké," *CO-M,* v. 2 (Apr.–June 1949), pp. 112–134.

885. Perrois, Louis. "La circoncision Bakota (Gabon)," *COR-STOM, SSH,* v. 5 (no. 1, 1968), pp. 1–109.

886. Philippart de Foy, Guy. *Les Pygmées d'Afrique centrale.* Roqueville: Éd. Parenthèses, 1984. 127 pp.

887. "Des Pygmies," *Ethnies,* (Aug. 1987), pp. 20–32.

888. Rey, Pierre Philippe. "Articulation des modes de dépendances et des modes de réproduction dans deux sociétés lignagères (Punu et Kunyi du Congo-Brazzaville)," *CEA,* v. 9 (no. 3, 1969), pp. 415–440.

889. Sautter, Gilles. "Les Paysans noirs au Gabon sepentrional. Essai sur le peuplement et l'habitat du Woleu-N'tem," *CO-M,* v. 4 (Apr.–June 1951), pp. 119–159.

890. Sauvageot, Jean-Pierre. "Martin Alihanga, L'Apôtre du 'Communautarisme,'" *M'Bolo,* (no. 14, 1985), pp. 23–31.

891. Shank, Floyd Aaron. *Nzabi Kinship: A Cognitive Approach.* Ph.D. Diss., Indiana U., 1974. 512 pp.

892. Sillans, Roger. *L'approche du Milieu Ethnique Gabonais de 1843 à 1891.* P.: n.d. 762 pp. [Mimeographed].

893. ———. *Motombi. Mythes et Enigmes initiatiques des Mitsoghos du Gabon Central.* Doctoral Thesis, U. of P., 1967.

894. Siroto, Leon. *Masks and Social Organization Among the*

Bakwele People of Western Equatorial Africa. Ph.D. Diss., Columbia U., N.Y., 1969. 325 pp.

895. Soret, Marcel. "Carte ethno-démographique de l'Afrique Equatoriale Française. Note préliminaire," *BIEC* n.s., v. 11 (1956), pp. 26–52.

896. Swiderski, Stanislas. "Les Chants Rituels en les Chansons Populaires chez les Apindji," *Cahiers du Musée National d'Ethnographie à Varsovie,* (nos. 4–5, 1963–1964), pp. 164–181.

897. Trenezem, Edouard. "Notes ethnographiques sur les tribus Fan du Moyen-Ogooué (Gabon)," *JSA,* v. 6 (no. 1, 1936), pp. 65–93.

898. Trilles, Henri. *L'Ame du Pygmée d'Afrique: Au Coeur de la Fôret Equatoriale.* P. Le Cerf, 1945. 262 pp.

899. ———. *Les Pygmées de la Fôret Equatoriale.* P.: Blonde & Gay, 1932. 530 pp.

900. Van Dan Audenaerde, F. E. Thys. *Les Tilapia du Sud Cameroun et du Gabon.* Tervuren: Musée Royal d'Afrique Centrale, 1968. 98 pp.

901. Walker, André Raponda. "Remarques sur les noms propres gabonais," *BIEC,* n.s. (no. 11, 1956), pp. 81–90.

902. ———. "Les Tribus du Gabon," *BSRC* (no. 4, 1924), pp. 55–101.

XI: GEOGRAPHY AND DEMOGRAPHY

903. Adassan, Félix. "Évolution des espaces péri-urbains à Libreville (Gabon): Le long de la route de Kango," in Pierre

Vennetier, ed., *Le Péri-urbanisation dans les pays tropicaux.* Talence: CEGET, 1989, pp. 175–186.

904. Adiwas-Kouerey, Gervais. *La vie rurale dans les pays myènè du delta intérieur de l'Ogooué (Gabon).* Doctoral Thesis, U. of Bordeaux, 1986.

905. Agondjo-Okawe, Pierre-Louis. ''Représentations et organisations endogènes de l'espace chez les myéné du Gabon (Nkomi et Mpongwe),'' *Bulletin de liaison de l'Équipe de recherche en anthropologie juridique,* (Jan. 1981), pp. 103–122. Also in E. Le Roy and F. Leindorger, eds., *Enjeux, fonciers en Afrique noire.* Bondy: ORSTOM and P.: Karthala, 1982, pp. 101–114.

906. *L'Agriculture africaine.* P.: Ediafric and Documentation africaine, 5th ed., 1982. 271 pp.

907. Association de la Maison de l'Afrique. Rencontres Africaines. *Dossier Gabon.* P.: ATN Maison de l'Afrique. La Défense: Les éditions fiduciaires France-Afrique, 1985. 155 pp.

908. Bouet, Claude. ''Agriculture et déforestation au Gabon,'' in C. Blanc-Pamard, et al., eds., *Le développement rural en question. Paysages, espaces ruraux, systèmes agraires: Maghreb, Afrique noire, Mélanesie.* P.: ORSTOM, 1984, pp. 381–387.

909. ———. ''Pour une géographie de l'habitat rural du Gabon,'' *CO-M,* v. 33 (Apr.–June 1980), pp. 123–144.

910. Boukoulou, Mbana. *Les Aspects de la diffusion des innovations dans le programme de developpement rural de la zone de Ntoum au Gabon.* Master's Thesis, U. of Ottawa, 1984.

911. Catrisse, Benoit. ''Une agriculture pour l'après-pétrole,'' *Afrique agriculture,* (Oct. 1, 1982), pp. 38–48.

912. Djeki, Jules. *L'évolution récente de Port-Gentil (Gabon).* Doctoral Thesis, U. of Montpellier, 1985.

913. Ekarga Mba, Emmanuel. "Esquisse d'une étude urbaine des principales agglomérations de la province du Haut-Ogooué," *Muntu,* (no. 7, 1987), pp. 49–72.

914. ———. "Régime foncier et structures agraires dans le Moyen-Ogooué," *Muntu,* (no. 8, 1988). pp. 74–101.

915. Esteve, H. "Enquête démographique comparative en pays Fang, District d'Oyem," *Médicine Tropicale,* v. 17 (1957), pp. 85–105.

916. François, Michel D. "Gabon," in *L'Evaluation des effectifs de la population des pays africains,* vol. 2. P.: Group de démographie africaine-IDP-INED-INSEE-MINCOOP-ORSTOM, 1984, pp. 135–148.

917. ———. "Gabon," in John C. Caldwell, ed., *Population Growth and Socio-Economic Change in West Africa.* N.Y.: Columbia UP, 1975, pp. 630–656.

918. Gabon. National Statistical Service. *Recensement général de la population, 1969–1970. Méthodologie. République Gabonaise.* Lv.: IO, 1971. 59 pp.

919. Gabon. *Enquête démographique au Gabon, 1960–1961.* P.: Ministry of Cooperation, 1963. 32 pp.

920. Gabon. *Recensement et enquête démographiques, 1960–1961. Ensemble du Gabon. Résultats définitifs.* P.: Ministry of Cooperation, 1965. 148 pp.

921. Ghenassia, Jean-Claude, ed. *Libreville, capitale de la république gabonaise.* Lv.: Société gabonaise, d'éd., 1973. 130 pp.

922. Goulphin, Fred. *Les veillées de chasse d'Henri Guizzard.* P.: Flammarion, 1987. 237 pp.

923. Hamono, B., and Chauliac, G. "La situation démographique des districts du Franceville, Leconi, et Moanda dans le

département du Haut-Ogooué (Gabon)." *Médicine Tropicale,* v. 31 (no. 21, 1971), pp. 215–224.

923a. Headrick, Rita. "The Population of French Equatorial Africa," in Bruce Fetter, ed. *Demography from Scanty Evidence: Central Africa.* Boulder and L.: Lynne Rienner, 1990, pp. 273–298.

923b. Hodder, P. W. "Equatorial Africa," in D. R. Harris, ed. *Africa in Transition.* L.: Methuen, 1967, pp. 259–291.

924. Indoumou, Darnabé. "Les effets de l'urbanisation au Gabon," *Acta Géographica,* (no. 1, 1982), pp. 11–20.

925. Koechlin, Jean. *Les savanes du Sud-Gabon.* Bv.: ORSTOM, 1957.

926. Lasserre, Guy. *Libreville: la ville et sa région, Gabon, Afrique Equatoriale Française: étude de géographie humaine.* P.: AC, 1958. 347 pp. Microfiche, P.: CNRS, and N.Y.: Clearwater.

927. ———. "Les mécanismes de la croissance et les structures démographiques de Libreville (1953–1970)," in *La Croissance Urbaine en Afrique Noire et Madagascar.* P.: CNRS, 1972, pp. 719–738.

928. ———. "Le paysage urbain des Libreville noires," *CO-M,* v. 9 (Oct.–Dec. 1956), pp. 363–388.

929. Meyo-Bibang, Frédéric, and Nzamba, Jean-Martin. *Notre Pays. Le Gabon. Géographie.* P.: Edicef, 1975. 80 pp.

930. Neuhoff, Hans Otto. *Contribution à la connaissance géographique du Gabon.* Bonn: Ed. Schroeder, 1967. 177 pp.

931. Nguemah-Ondo, Adrien. *Le village, structure et tradition.* P.: La pensée universelle, 1983. 173 pp.

932. Pandolfi, Massino. *Les forêts équatoriales d'Afrique.* P.: Larousse, 1986. 126 pp.

933. Perrusset, André-Christian. "Aménagements routiers en zone équatoriale forestière et accidentée: l'Exemple des Monts de Cristal (Gabon)," *CO-M,* v. 30 (Oct.–Dec. 1977); 404–411.

934. ———. "Aperçu de la géomorphologie du Gabon," *Bulletin de l'Association Géographique,* v. 58 (Jan.–Feb. 1981), pp. 83–89.

935. ———. *Le Gabon: Géographie physique équatoriale.* L.: U. Nationale du Gabon, 1977. 170 pp.

936. Piermay, Jean-Luc. "Le détournement d'espace: Corruption et stratégies de détournement dans les pratiques froncières urbaines en Afrique centrale," *Politique africaine,* (Mar. 1986), pp. 22–36. Also in B. Ganne, and Philippe Haeringer, eds., *Formes parallèles de régulations urbaines.* Lyon: U. of Lyon, 1987, pp. 7–23.

937. Pourtier, Roland. "La dialectique du vide: Densité de population et pratiques foncières en Afrique centrale forestière," *Politique africaine,* (Mar. 1986), pp. 10–21.

938. ———. "Encadrement territorial et production de nation: Quelques propositions illustrées par l'exemple du Gabon," in Emmanuel Terray, ed., *L'État contemporain.* P.: Harmattan, 1987, pp. 341–358.

939. ———. "Les états et le contrôle territoriale en Afrique centrale: Principes et pratiques," *Annales de Géographie,* v. 98 (no. 547, 1988), pp. 286–301.

940. ———. *Le Gabon,* v. 1, *Espace-Histoire-Société,* v. 2, *États et développement.* P.: Harmattan, 1989. 2 v., 254 pp. and 344 pp.

941. ———. "Nommes l'Espace: L'Émergence de l'État Territorial en Afrique noire," *Espace Géographique.* v. 12 (no. 4, 1983), pp. 293–304.

942. ———. "Stratégie Ferroviaire et Politique de l'Espace: Le Transgabonais," *Hérodote,* (no. 25, 1982), pp. 105–128.

943. ———. "Ville et espace en Afrique noire: L'exemple du Gabon," *Espace géographique,* v. 8 (Apr.–June 1979), pp. 119–130.

944. *Résultats de l'enquête agricole au Gabon.* P.: INSEE Coopération, 1969. 139 pp.

945. Saint-Vil, J. "Les climats au Gabon," *Annales de l'Université Nationale du Gabon, série Lettres et Sciences Sociales,* v. 1 (Dec. 1977), pp. 101–125.

946. Sala-Diakanda, Mpembele. "Démographie africaine: Tendances et perspectives," *AC,* v. 27 (no. 1, 1988), pp. 3–27.

947. Sautter, Gilles. *De l'Atlantique au Fleuve Congo. Une Géographie de Sous-Peuplement.* P.: Mouton, 1966. 2 v. 1102 pp.

948. Verdier, Raymond, and Rochegude, A., eds., *Systèmes fonciers à la ville et au village: Afrique noire francophone.* P.: Harmattan, 1986. 298 pp.

949. Vivien, J., and Faure, J. J. *Arbes des forêts denses d'Afrique centrale.* P.: Ministère des Relations extérieures, coopération et Développement: ACCT, 1985. 565 pp.

950. Yaya, C., et al. "Consommations alimentaires individuelles en milieu 'Galwa' urbain et rural (Gabon)," in D. Lemonnier, and Y. Ingenbleer, eds., *Les Malnutritions dans les pays du Tiérs-monde.* P.: Éd. INSERM, 1986, pp. 513–522.

XII: EDUCATION

951. Ango, E. Moure, and Becquelin, J. *Les Besoins Futurs en Ressources à la Lumière des Perspectives du Développement de l'Education au Gabon.* P.: Unesco, June 1978. 28 pp.

952. Banga, Luther. *Proverbe et éducation chez les Bulu-Fan-Beti: Une Etude socio-éducative des proverbes.* Doctoral Thesis, U. of P., 1972. 479 pp.

952a. Bipecka, Louis-Charles. "Le problème de la pédagogie et de la réforme des programmes dans les institutions de la formation professionnelle au Gabon: le cas de l'ENA," *Cahiers africains d'administration publique* (no. 33, 1989), pp. 139–152.

953. Bosworth, William. "The Rigid Embrace of Dependency: France and Black African Education Since 1960," *Contemporary French Civilization,* v. 5 (Spring 1981), pp. 327–346.

954. Botti, Marc, and Venizet, Paul. *Enseignement au Gabon.* P.: SEDES, 1965. 351 pp.

955. Cappelle, Jean. *L'éducation en Afrique noire à la veille des Indépendances.* P.: Karthala, 1980. 326 pp.

955a. "Clés en mains: le lycée technique national Omar Bongo," *Moniteur Construction Afrique* (June 1979), pp. 88–93.

956. Davesne, André. *Croquis de Brousse.* Marseilles: Ed. de Sagittaire, 1962. 321 pp.

957. Engone-Nguema, Calixte. *Essai d'analyse de l'évolution de la formation professionnelle des adultes vue dans le contexte gabonais.* Master's Thesis, Laval U., Quebec, 1984. 94 pp.

958. Erny, Pierre. *L'Enfant et son milieu en Afrique Noire. Essais sur l'éducation noire.* P.: Payot, 1972. 311 pp.

959. French Equatorial Africa. Government-General. *Histoire et organisation générale de l'enseignement en Afrique Equatoriale Française.* Bv.: IO, 1931. 97 pp.

960. Gamerdinger, George William. *Occupational Andragogy and the Informal Working Sector in Gabon.* Doctoral Diss., Oklahoma State U., 1981. 90 pp.

961. Gardinier, David E. "Education in French Equatorial Africa, 1842–1945," *PFCHS,* v. 3 (1978), pp. 121–137.

962. ———. "Education in French Equatorial Africa, 1945–1960," *Cultures et Développement,* v. 16 (1984), pp. 303–334.

963. ———. "Education in the States of Equatorial Africa: A Bibliographical Essay," *Africana Journal,* v. 3 (no. 3, 1972), pp. 7–20.

964. ———. "The French Impact on Education in Africa, 1817–1960," in G. Wesley Johnson, ed., *Double Impact: France and Africa in the Age of Imperialism.* Westport, Conn.: Greenwood, 1985, pp. 333–344.

965. ———. "Gabon," in Asa Knowles, ed. *International Encyclopedia of Higher Education.* San Francisco: Jossey-Bass, 1977, pp. 1789–1795.

966. ———. "Les Recommendations de la Conférence de Brazzaville sur les problèmes de l'éducation," in *Brazzaville, Janvier-Février 1944, Aux Sources de la décolonisation.* P.: Plon, 1988. pp. 170–180.

967. ———. "Schooling in the States of Equatorial Africa," *CJAS,* v. 8 (no. 3, 1974), pp. 517–538.

968. ———. "Vocational and Technical Education in F.E.A., 1842–1960," *PFCHS,* v. 8 (1982), pp. 113–123.

969. Kurian, George Thomas, ed. *World Education Encyclopedia.* v. 3. N.Y. and Oxford: Facts on File, 1988.

970. Labrousse, André. *La France et l'aide à l'Education dans 14 Etats africaines et Malgache.* P.: International Institute of Educational Planning, 1971. 166 pp.

971. Mboumi, René. *Le phénomène d'inadaptation de l'enseignement au contexte socio-culturel et aux exigences du développement en Afrique: Le Gabon.* Master's Thesis, U. of Montréal, 1978.

972. Ministry of National Education. "Reforme et rénovation de l'enseignement au Gabon," *Recherche, Pédagogie, et Culture* (May–Aug. 1976), pp. 16–24.

973. N'Doume Assebe, J. *L'Enseignement missionnaire au Gabon, 1842–1960.* Doctoral Thesis, U. of P., 1978.

974. Nguema, Isaac. "Université, société et développement en Afrique centrale," *PA,* (no. 143, 1987), pp. 31–90.

975. Ogden, John. "The Africanization of the Curriculum in Gabon," *French Review* (Champaign), v. 55 (May 1982), pp. 855–861.

976. ———. "French in Gabon," *Contemporary French Civilization,* v. 8 (Spring 1984), pp. 339–348.

977. Rawiri, Georges, and Cohen, Michèle. *Le train de la fôret vierge ou l'Épopee de Transgabonais.* P.: B-L, 1985. 29 pp. [for students].

978. Richmond, Edmun B. *New Directions in Language Teaching in Sub-Saharan Africa: A Seven-Country Study of Current Policies and Programs for Teaching Official and National Languages and Adult Functional Literacy.* Washington: U. Press of America, 1983. 66 pp.

979. Smith, Jasper K. *A Planning Model for Educational and*

Economic Development: Educational Requirements of Economic Development. M.A. Thesis, Howard U., Wash., 1966.

980. Soumah, Mesmin-Noël. *Objectifs de l'enseignement primaire et contenu des manuels de lecture: Contribution à une étude sociologique du curriculum au Gabon.* Doctoral Thesis, U. of P., 1987.

981. Swiderski, Stanislas. "Les agents éducatifs traditionnels chez les Apindji," *Revue de Psychologie des Peuples,* v. 21 (no. 2, 1966), pp. 194–220.

982. Swiderski, Stanislaw. "Education traditionnelle chez les Apindji," *Lu-Polsko* (no. 52, 1968), pp. 27–63. [In Polish; French summary].

983. Tedja, Paul. *Enseignement supérieur en Afrique Noire francophone: La Catastrophe?* P.: Harmattan, 1988. 223 pp.

984. Touré, Sékou. *La fédération des étudiants d'Afrique noire en France. (F.E.A.N.F.).* P.: 1985.

985. "L'Université Omar Bongo," *Eduafrica,* (Dec. 1986), pp. 149–155.

986. Weiland, Heribert. *Erziehung und Nationale Entwicklung in Gabun.* Munich: Weltforum Verlag, 1975. 245 pp.

XIII: RELIGION AND MISSIONS

987. *Annuaire de l'Archdiocèse de Libreville et du Diocèse de Mouila.* Lv., 1964. 54 pp.

988. *Annuaire de l'Eglise Catholique en Afrique Francophone (Missions Catholiques), 1978–1979.* V. 2. P.: ONPC-R.F., 1978. 688 pp.

989. *Annuaire de l'Eglise Evangélique du Gabon.* Lv.: Apr. 1973. 15 pp.

990. *Annuarium Statisticum Ecclesiae.* Rome: Secretaria Status Rationarum Generale Ecclesiae, 1987. 439 pp.

991. Babel, Henry. *Schweitzer tel qu'il fut.* P.: Payot, 2nd ed., 1970. 198 pp.

992. Berger, Augustin. "Le gouverneur-général Félix Éboué, la franc-maçonnerie et les missions catholiques," in *Actes du Colloque Félix Éboué,* P.: Institut des Hautes Études de Défense nationale et Académie des Sciences d'Outre-mer, 1985, pp. 113–117.

993. Bernault-Boswell, Florence. "Un journal missionnaire au temps de la décolonisation: *La Semaine de l'A.E.F.* (1942–1960)," *RFHO-M,* v. 74 (no. 274, 1987), pp. 5–25.

994. Bessuges, J. *Lambaréné à l'ombre de Schweitzer.* Limoges: Dessagne, 1968. 152 pp.

995. Binet, Jacques. "Drogue et mystique: les bwiti des Fangs," *Diogènes,* v. 86 (Apr.–June 1974), pp. 34–57. Tr. "Drugs and Mysticism: The Bwiti Cult of the Fang," *Diogenes,* v. 86 (Summer 1974), pp. 31–54.

996. ———; Gollnhofer, Otto; and Sillans, Roger. "Textes religieux du Bwiti-Fan et de ses confréries prophétiques dans leurs cadres rituels," *CEA,* v. 46 (1972), pp. 197–257.

997. Birinda, M. [Birinda de Boudieguy]. *La Bible secrète des Noirs selon le Bouity.* P.: Omnium Littéraire, 1952, 141 pp.

998. Blanc, René; Blocher, Jacques; and Kruger, Etienne. *Histoire des Missions Protestantes Françaises.* Flavion, Belgium: Ed. Le Phare, 1970. 448 pp.

998a. Boumba-Mavoungou, Mwiny Mbumb Tszchycaola.

Mayumba: Dernières années d'action missionnaire coloniale de 1939 à 1960. Memoir, Omar Bongo U., 1981. 91 pp.

999. Brabazon, James. *Albert Schweitzer: A Biography.* N.Y.: Putnam, 1975. 509 pp.

1000. Brasseur, Paule. "A la recherche d'un absolu missionnaire: Mgr. Truffet, vicaire apostolique des Deux Guinées," *CEA,* v. 15 (no. 2, 1975), pp. 259–286.

1001. ———. "Missions catholiques et administration française sur la côte d'Afrique de 1815 à 1870," *RFHO-M,* v. 62 (no. 3, 1975), pp. 415–446.

1002. Briault, Maurice. *Le Vénérable Père François Marie Pierre Libermann: La Reprise des Missions d'Afrique au Dix-neuvième Siècle.* P., 1946.

1003. ———. *Sur les pistes de l'Afrique Equatoriale Française.* P.: Ed. Alsatia, 1945. 285 pp.

1004. Brown, Arthur Judson. "One Hundred Years. N.Y.: Revell, 1936. [Presbyterian missions].

1005. Bureau, René. "'Connais-tu la mort?' Les trois nuits rituelles du Bwiti fang," *Annales de l'U. d'Abidjan,* Série D, v. 6 (1973), pp. 231–303.

1006. ———. "Le Harrisme et Le Bwiti: Deux Réactions Africaines à l'Impact Chrétien," *Recherches de Sciences Religieuses,* v. 63 (Jan.–Mar. 1975), pp. 83–100.

1007. ———. *La Religion d'Eboga. 1. Essai sur le Bwiti-Fang. 2. Lexique du Bwiti-Fang.* Lv.: Service de Réproduction des Thèses, 1972. 562 & 241 pp.

1007a. Bywana-Ndangou, Lin Brice. *La Mission Notre-Dame de Mbigou (des origines à 1950).* Memoir, Omar Bongo U., 1980. 61 pp.

1008. Cadier, Charles. *Lumière sur l'Ogooué. Formation de la Jeune Eglise de Samkita.* The Author, 196?. 149 pp.

1009. Campbell, Penelope. "American Protestant Evangelism and African Responses: The American Presbyterians in Gabon & Equatorial Guinea, 1850–1925," Paper, AHA, Dallas, Dec. 1977. 22 pp.

1010. ———. "Presbyterian West African Missions: Women as Converts and Agents of Social Change," *Journal of Presbyterian History,* v. 56 (Summer 1978), pp. 121–133.

1011. "Centenaire de la naissance d'Albert Schweitzer," *Communautés et Continents,* v. 67 (Jan.–Mar. 1975), pp. 3–36.

1012. Clark, Henry. *The Philosophy of Albert Schweitzer.* L.: Methuen, 1964. 241 pp.

1013. Clémenceau, Macaire. "Saint Gabriel au Gabon: Ecole Montfort (1900–1948)," *Chronique de Saint-Gabriel* (Oct. 1949), pp. 45–73.

1014. "Les Collaborateurs d'Albert Schweitzer: Madame Albert Schweitzer, Mathilde Kottmann, Emma Haussknecht," *Cahiers Albert-Schweitzer,* (June 1983), pp. 3–27.

1015. Cornevin, Robert. "Éloge du Révérend Père Augustin Berger (1908–1984)," *Mondes et Cultures,* v. 48 (no. 2, 1987), pp. 141–152.

1016. Coulon, Paul, and Brasseur, Paule, eds. *Libermann 1802–1852 Une pensée et une mystique missionnaire.* P.: Cerf, 1988. 938 pp.

1017. Delcourt, J. *Au Congo Français. Monseigneur Carrie, 1842–1904.* P.: The Author, n.d. 2 v. 459 pp. [Loango].

1018. DuFourcq, Élisabeth. "Approche démographique de l'implantation hors d'Europe des Congrégations religieuses féminines d'origine française,'' *Population,* (no. 1, 1988), pp. 45–76.

1019. Duhamelet, Geneviève. *Les Soeurs Bleues de Castres.* P.: Grasset, 1934, 241 pp.

1020. Durand-Réville, Luc. ''Albert Schweitzer: le grand docteur blanc,'' *Revue des Deux Mondes* (Nov. 15, 1965), pp. 230–241.

1021. *L'Église Catholique en Afrique Occidentale et Centrale: Répertoire des Missions Catholiques. Catholic Church.* P., 1989. 1100 pp.

1021a. *Eglise Evangélique du Gabon, 1842–1961.* Alençon: Impr. Corbière et Jugain, 1962. 52 pp.

1022. *Eglise Evangélique de Gabon. Constitutions, après les modifications adoptées par le Synode extraordinaire de Janvier 1970 à Libreville.* Oyem, Ed. CLE, 1970. 39 pp.

1023. Fanguinoveny, Thérèse. *A History of American Protestant Missions in Gabon, 1842–1893.* Memoir for the Master's, Faculty of Protestant Theology, P., 1978. 56 pp.

1024. Faure, Félix. *Christ in the Great Forest.* N.Y.: Friendship Press, 1936. 181 pp. Tr. *Le Christ dans la grande Fôret.* P.: SME, 2nd ed., 1953. [1st ed., 1934].

1025. Fernandez. C. *Misiones y Misioneros en La Guinea Española.* Madrid: Editorial Co. Cul. S.A., 1962. 817 pp. [Ibea].

1026. Fernandez, James W. ''The Body in Bwiti: Variations on a Theme by Richard Werbner,'' *JRA,* v. 20 (no. 1, 1990), pp. 92–111.

1027. ———. *Bwiti, an Ethnography of the Religious Imagination in Africa.* Princeton: Princeton UP, 1982. 731 pp.

1028. Gardinier, David E. ''The American Presbyterian Mission in Gabon: Male Mpongwe Converts and Agents, 1870–1883,'' *American Presbyterians: Journal of Presbyterian History,* v. 69 (Spring 1991), pp. 61–70.

1029. ———. ''The Beginnings of French Catholic Evangelization in Gabon and African Responses, 1844–1883,'' *FCS,* (no. 2, 1978), pp. 49–74.

1030. ———. ''Les Frères de Saint-Gabriel au Gabon, 1900–1918: La naissance d'une nouvelle élite africaine,'' *Mondes et Cultures,* v. 46 (no. 3, 1986), pp. 593–606.

1031. ———. ''The Schools of the American Protestant Mission in Gabon, 1842–1870,'' *RFHO-M,* v. 75 (no. 2, 1988), pp. 168–184.

1032. Gaulme, François. ''Anyambye: Note sur l'évolution religieuse en Afrique centrale,'' *Ethnographie,* v. 75 (no. 3, 1980), pp. 263–283.

1033. ———. ''Le Bwiti chez les Nkomi: Association culturelles et évolution historique sur le littoral gabonais,'' *JA,* v. 49 (no. 2, 1979), pp. 37–88.

1034. Goettman, Alphonse. *L'Evangile de la Miséricorde. Hommage au Dr. Schweitzer.* P.: Ed. du Cerf, 1964. 448 pp.

1035. Gollnhofer, Otto, and Sillans, Roger. ''Recherche sur le mysticisme des Mitsogho—peuple de montagnards du Gabon Central (Afrique Equatoriale),'' in *Réincarnation et Vie mystique en Afrique Noire.* P.: PUF, 1965, pp. 143–173.

1036. Gross, Helmut. *Albert Schweitzer, Grösse und Grenzen.* Munich: Ernst Reinhardt Verlag, 1974. 841 pp.

1037. Hamilton, Benjamin A. *The Environment, Establishment and Development of Protestant Missions in French Equatorial Africa.* Ph.D. Diss., Grace Theological Seminary, Goshen, Indiana, 1959. 352 pp.

1038. Haygood, William Converse. ''With Schweitzer at Lambaréné: Noel Gillespie's Letters from Africa,'' *Wisconsin Magazine of History* (Spring 1971), pp. 167–203.

1039. Hermann-Delin, Colette. "Le processus syncrétique comme dynamique culturelle: La Bwete, société secrète du Gabon: L'oeuvre de Joseph Beuys," *Revue d'histoire des arts,* (no. 6, 1985), pp. 39–48.

1040. Kasule, O. H. "Muslims in Gabon, West Africa," *Journal of the Institute of Muslim and Minority Affairs,* v. 6 (no. 1, 1985), pp. 192–206.

1041. Koren, Henry J. *Les Spiritains, trois siècles d'histoire religieuse et missionnaire.* P.: Beauchêne, 1982. 633 pp.

1042. ———. *To the Ends of the Earth: A General History of the Congregation of the Holy Ghost.* Pittsburgh: 1983. 548 pp.

1043. Lavignotte, Henri. *L'Evur, croyance des Fan du Gabon.* P.: SME, 3rd ed., 1952. 118 pp.

1044. Leperdriel, A. "Colonisation et évangélisation au Gabon," *Missions Catholiques,* (Jan. 1960), pp. 62–72.

1045. Le Roy, Alexandre. "Missions d'Afrique: le Congo Français, le Gabon," in J. B. Piolet, ed., *Les Missions Catholiques Françaises au XIXe Siècle.* V. 5. P.: AC, 1902, pp. 219–254.

1046. Luneau, René. *Laisse aller mon peuple! Églises africaines au-delà des modèles?* P.: Karthala, 1987. 196 pp.

1047. Makosso, Sylvain M. *Spiritualité africaine et catholicisme en Afrique Centrale de l'Ouest de 1945 à 1969.* Doctoral Thesis, U. of Poitiers, 1974. 245 pp.

1048. Mallo, Eugène. "Les difficultés de l'Eglise Evangélique du Gabon," *Flambeau* (May 1971), pp. 128–130.

1049. Marie-Germaine, Sister. *Le Christ au Gabon.* Louvain: Museum Lessianum, 1931. 170 pp.

1050. Marschall, George, and Poling, David. *Schweitzer: A Biography.* N.Y.: Doubleday, 1971. 342 pp.

1051. Mary, André. "L'alternative de la Vision et de la Possession dans les Sociétés Religieuses et Thérapeutiques du Gabon," *CEA,* v. 23 (no. 3, 1983), pp. 281–310.

1052. ———. *La naissance à l'envers: Essai sur le rituel du Bwiti Fang au Gabon.* P.: Harmattan, 1983. 386 pp.

1053. ———. "Le schème de la naissance à l'envers: Scénario initiatique et logique de l'inversion [Fang Bwiti]," *CEA,* v. 28 (no. 2, 1988), pp. 233–263.

1054. Mayer, R. "Églises et médias du Gabon," *Lumière et vie,* v. 30 (Oct.–Dec. 1981), pp. 28–34.

1055. Mba Zoo, Joseph-Edison. *Le Peuple 'Fang' des Traditions Paiennes à l'Évangile.* Master's Thesis, Aix-en-Provence: Faculté Libre de Théologie Réformée, 1981. 100 pp.

1056. Mboumba-Bouassa, Florent. *Genèse de l'Eglise du Gabon: Etude Historique et Canonique.* LL.D. Diss., U. of Strasbourg, 1972. 335 pp.

1057. Minder, Raynold, ed. *Rayonnement d'Albert Schweitzer. Le Livre du Centenaire.* P.: Ed. Alsatia, 1975. 301 pp.

1058. *Mission de Frère Macaire [Clémenceau], 1905–1980.* P.: Éd. Saint-Paul, 1983. 63 pp.

1059. Mvé-Ondo, Bonaventure. "Le Bwiti Fang," *M'Bolo,* (no. 11, 1984), pp. 24–35.

1060. Ndaot, Séraphin. *Le procès d'un prix Nobel ou le médecin du fleuve.* P.: La Pensée universelle, 1983. 285 pp. [Novel].

1060a. N'Diaye, Josette. *La mission protestante de Ngomo des origines à 1961.* Memoir, Omar Bongo U., 1980. 63 pp.

1061. Ndjave, Elie Ndjoya. *Henri Ndjave: Un témoins du Christ au Gabon, 1883–1962.* Strasbourg: Éd. Oberlin, 1973. 24 pp.

1062. Ndong, Amvame. "L'Eglise Evangélique du Gabon au lendemain de son Autonomie," in C. Bonzon, et al., *L'Appel.* P.: SME, 1962, pp. 61–72.

1063. Nguema-Obam, Paulin. *Aspects de la religion Fang: Essai d'interprétation de la formule de bénédiction.* P.: ACCT and Karthala, 1983. 94 pp.

1064. Perrier, André. *Gabon, un reveil religieux, 1935–37.* P.: Harmattan, 1988. 240 pp.

1065. "Persécutions religieuses en Guinée Equatoriale," *Parole et Société,* v. 87 (no. 3, 1979), pp. 184–189.

1066. Preston, Jane S. *Gaboon Stories.* N.Y.: American Tract Society, 1872.

1067. Pujadas, Tomás Luis. *La Iglesia en la Guinea Ecuatorial: Fernando Po.* Madrid: I. de Paz, 1968. 528 pp.

1068. Roques, L. *Le Pionnier du Gabon. Jean-Rémi Bessieux.* P.: Ed. Alsatia, 1971. 176 pp.

1069. Roux, André "Églises protestantes de langue française en Afrique: Évolution des missions aux Églises. Problématique actuelle," *AC,* (July–Aug. 1979), pp. 10–18.

1070. Schuffenecker, Gérard. *Lambaréné: Hôpital de brousse.* P.: Istra, 1980. 144 pp.

1071. Schweitzer, Albert. *On the Edge of the Primeval Forest.* London, 1926. 180 pp. Reprinted 1955. Tr. *A l'orée de la forêt vierge.* P.: Payot, 1929. 231 pp.

1072. ———. *From My African Notebook.* L.: Allen & Unwin, 1938. 132 pp.

1073. ———. *Histoire de la forêt vierge.* P.: Payot, 1950. 174 pp.

1074. ———. *More from the Primeval Forest.* L.: A.&.C. Black, 1931. 173 pp.

1075. Swiderski, Stanislaw. "Aperçu sur la trinité et la pensée triadique chez les Fang au Gabon," *CJAS,* v. 9 (no. 2, 1975), pp. 235–258.

1076. ———. "Le Bwiti, société d'initiation chez les Apindji au Gabon," *Anthropos,* v. 60 (no. 1–6, 1963), pp. 541–576.

1077. ———. "La conception psycho-religieuse de l'homme dans la religion syncrétique Bouiti au Gabon," *Africana Marburgensia,* v. 9 (no. 2, 1976), pp. 32–66.

1078. ———. "La cosmogonie et l'ontologie selon la religion bouiti au Gabon," *JRA,* v. 19 (no. 2, 1989), pp. 125–145.

1079. ———. "Ekany Ngoua, réformateur religieux au Gabon," *Anthropos,* v. 79 (no. 1–6, 1984), pp. 627–635.

1080. ———. "La fonction psychologique et socio-religieuse des drogues sacrées au Gabon," *JRA,* v. 8 (no. 2, 1976), pp. 123–132.

1081. ———. *Histoire de la religion Bouiti.* Saarbrücken: Homo et Religion, 1978. 138 pp.

1082. ———. "Meyo Me Nguema Minko: Réformateur Oecuméniste de la Religion Bouiti," *JRA,* v. 17 (Feb. 1987), pp. 32–43.

1083. ———. "Le Mouvement Oecuménique dans la Religion Bouiti au Gabon," *JRA,* v. 18 (June 1988), pp. 125–140.

1084. ———. "Nguema Mba Evariste, fondateur de la communauté Église Romaine de Saint Pierre de Jérusalem," *JRA,* v. 14 (no. 1, 1983), pp. 74–83.

1085. ———. "Notions théologiques dans la religion syncrétique Bouiti au Gabon," *Eglise et Théologie,* v. 6 (Oct. 1975), pp. 391–394.

1086. ———. "Nzé Ndong Rémy, fondateur de la communauté Erendzi Duma," *JRA,* v. 12 (no. 3, 1981), pp. 178–190.

1087. ———. "Les récits bibliques dans l'adaptation africaine," *JRA,* v. 10 (no. 3, 1979), pp. 174–233.

1088. ———. "Remarques sur la philosophie religieuse des sectes syncrétiques au Gabon," *CJAS,* v. 8 (no. 1, 1974), pp. 43–54.

1089. ———. "Le rite de mortuaire pour un initié au Bouiti," *Anthropos,* v. 77 (no. 5–6, 1982), pp. 741–754.

1090. ———. "Le rite de la renaissance spirituelle chez les Bouiti, Gabon," *Anthropos,* v. 73 (no. 5–6, 1978), pp. 845–886.

1091. ———. "Synretyzm religijny w Gabonie," *Przeglad Sojologie* (no. 26, 1975), pp. 133–174.

1092. ———. "Les visions d'éboga," *Anthropos,* v. 76 (no. 3–4, 1981), pp. 393–424.

1093. Teuwissen, Raymond W. *Robert Hamill Nassau, 1835–1921: Presbyterian Pioneer Missionary to Equatorial West Africa.* M. Th. Thesis, Louisville Theological Seminary. 1973.

1094. Tornezy, Odette. "Les travaux et les jours de la mission Sainte-Marie-du-Gabon (1845–1880). Agriculture et modernisation," *RFHO-M,* v. 71 (no. 3–4, 1984), pp. 147–180.

1095. Vernaud, G. *Etablissement d'une mission du plein Evangile au Gabon.* Pesseux-NE: Ed. Evangéliques, 1957.

1096. ———. *Reveil au Gabon.* Les Andelys, Eure: Viens et Vois, n.d. 69 pp.

1097. Wadlow, René V. L. "An African Church and Social Change (Eglise Evangélique du Gabon)," *Practical Anthropology,* v. 16 (Nov.–Dec. 1969), pp. 257–264.

1098. Walker, André Raponda. "Frère Dominique Fara: Religieux Gabonais," *Revue du Clergé Africain,* v. 9 (Nov. 1954), pp. 600–609.

1099. ———, and Sillans, Roger. *Rites et croyances des peuples du Gabon.* P.: *PA,* 1962. 377 pp.

1100. Werbner, Richard P. "Bwiti in Reflection: On the Fugue of Gender," *JRA,* v. 20 (no. 1, 1990), pp. 63–91.

1101. Woytt-Secretan, M. *Albert Schweitzer construit l'hôpital de Lambaréné.* Strasbourg: Dernières Nouvelles de Strasbourg, 1975. 111 pp. [Tr. of *Albert Schweitzer baut Lambaréné*].

1102. Ze-Meka. *L'Instauration du christianisme chez les populations Beti, Boulou, et Fang, (1892–1957).* P.: Memoir, EHESS, 1980.

1103. Zorn, Jean-François. *Une mission protestante à la Belle Époque: L'Action de la Société des missions évangeliques de Paris des origines à 1914.* P.: Karthala, 1993. 791 pp.

XIV: PHYSICAL AND NATURAL SCIENCES

1104. Antoine, Philippe, & Cantrelle, Pierre. "Enregistrement des decès et étude de mortalité urbaine. Etat civil de Libreville, Gabon," *CORSTOM, SSH,* v. 13 (no. 3, 1976), pp. 267–281.

1105. Aubreville, A. *Etude sur les Fôrets d'Afrique Equatoriale Française et du Cameroun.* Nogent-sur-Marne: Section technique agricole tropicale, May 1948. 131 pp.

1106. ———, ed. *Flore du Gabon.* P.: Musée National D'Histoire Naturelle, 23 v., 1961–1973.

1107. Bensaid, Anita. "Niveau nutritionnal des pays gabonais: une analyse factorielle en componantes principales," *Bulletin de l'Institut National de la Statistique et des Etats Economiques* (Paris) (May–Sept. 1970), pp. 11–44.

1108. Bernard, Pierre A. *Coquillages du Gabon/Shells of Gabon.* Lv.: Privately printed, 1984, 140 pp.

1109. Boltenhagen, Eugène. *Paylnologie du Crétace supérieur du Gabon.* P.: Bibliothèque nationale, 1980. 191 pp.

1110. Caballé, G. "Essai phytogéographique sur la forêt dense du Gabon," *Annales de l'Université nationale du Gabon* (Sciences), (no. 2, 1978), pp. 87–101.

1111. *Contributions aux études ethnobotaniques et floristiques du Gabon.* P.: ACCT, 1984. 294 pp.

1112. Eloumi-Ropivia, Jacqueline. *Contribution à l'étude phytochimique d'une espèce du Gabon: Artabotrys lastoursvillensis, Annonacées.* Master's Thesis, U. of Montréal, 1982.

1113. No entry.

1114. Fontes. "Les Formations herbeuses au Gabon," *Annales de l'Université nationale du Gabon* (Sciences), (no. 2, 1978), pp. 127–153.

1115. Girardin, N., and Lebigre, J. M. *Éléments de géomorphologie du Gabon.* Lv.: MEN, IPN, 1980. 29 pp.

1116. Hladik, Annette, et al. "Les Plantes à tubercules de la forêt dense d'Afrique centrale," *Revue d'écologie,* v. 39 (no. 3, 1984), pp. 249–290. [Makoukou].

1117. Leroy-Deval, J. R. *Biologie et sylviculture de l'okoumé; Aucoumea klaineana Pierre.* Nogent-sur-Marne: Centre technique forestier tropical, 1976. 2 v. 355 and 76 pp.

1118. Le Testu, Georges. "Notes sur les cultures indigènes dans l'intérieur du Gabon," *Revue de botanique appliquée et d'agriculture tropicale,* (Aug.–Sept. 1940), pp. 540–556.

1119. Martin, D. et al. *Les sols du Gabon, Pédogenèse Répartition et Aptitudes, Cartes à 1: 2,000,000.* P.: ORSTOM, 1981.

1120. Naudet, Roger. "The Oklo Nuclear Reactors: 1800 Million Years Ago," *Interdisciplinary Scientific Review* (Mar. 1976), pp. 72–84.

1121. Silou, Thomas. "Étude des plantes aromatiques d'Afrique centrale," *Muntu,* (No. 6, 1987), pp. 121–136.

1122. Walker, André Raponda, and Sillans, Roger. *Les plantes utiles au Gabon.* P.: Paul Lechevalier, 1961. 614 pp.

XV: HEALTH AND MEDICINE

1123. Ambonguilat, Colette Lydia. *Santé publique et problèmes sanitaires au Gabon.* Doctoral Thesis, U. of Lille, 1986.

1124. Bensaid, Georges. *Economie et Nutrition: Essai à partir d'une enquête alimentaire sur deux régions du Gabon. 1963.* P.: INSEE Coopération, 1970, 2 v. 288 and 554 pp. [Woleu-N'Tem & N'Gounié Provinces].

1125. Caperan. "Notes sur l'état sanitaire des populations M'Fangs du Woleu-N'Tem," *BSRC,* v. 12 (1930), pp. 103–125.

1126. Derrien, Françoise. *Les filarioses: Contexte écologique et problèmes de répartition: L'exemple du Gabon.* P.: Memoir, EHESS, 1979.

1127. Ford, Henry A. *Observations on the Fevers of the West Coast of Africa.* N.Y.: Edward Jenkins, 1856.

1128. Gollnhofer, Otto, and Sillans, Roger. "Aspects des consensus dans le psychothérapie ghetsogho," in *La notion de personne en Afrique noire.* P.: CNRS, 1971, pp. 545–563.

1129. Jeannel, Camille. *La Sterilité en République Gabonaise.* G.: Offenberg Press, 1962.

1130. Le Bigot, P., et al. "Problèmes, posés par la lutte contre la trypanosomiase au Gabon," *Médecine d'Afrique noire,* v. 31 (Jan. 1984), pp. 31–40.

1131. Makaya, Hilaire Jidy. *Contribution à l'étude de la santé en Afrique Équatoriale Française: Médecines traditionnelle et occidentale. Le cas du Gabon (1910–1945).* Doctoral Thesis, U. of Reims, 1984.

1132. *Médecine traditionnelle et pharmacopée: Contribution aux études ethnobotaniques et floristiques au Gabon.* P.: ACCT, 1984. 294 pp.

1133. Mezu, Julien. "Évolution de l'alimentation infantile au Gabon: Influence de l'urbanisation," *Médecine d'Afrique noire,* v. 34 (Aug.–Sept. 1987), pp. 735–742.

1134. Mori, Jean. "Le CIRMF Phare de la Recherche Médicale en Afrique," *M'Bolo,* (no. 16, 1986), pp. 20–31.

1135. Sauvageot, Jean-Pierre. "Un air du Futur: Avenir Santé," *M'Bolo,* (no. 7, 1983), pp. 30–37.

1136. Wagner, Alain. *Aspects des médecines traditionnelles du Gabon.* Toulouse: Éd. universelles, 1985. 329 pp.

1137. Walter, P. R. et al. "Dept. of Pathology, U. Centre for Health Sciences, Libreville, 1978–1984," in D. M. Parkin, ed., *Cancer Occurrence in Developing Countries.* Lyon: International Agency for Research on Cancer, 1986, pp. 43–46.

1138. Waltisperger, D. "La mortalité au Gabon," *Démographie en Afrique d'expression française. Bulletin de Liaison,* Special no. 9 (Nov. 1976), pp. 5–80.

XVI: LITERATURE

1139. Abessolo, Jean-Baptiste. *Les Aventures de Biomo.* Lv.: IPN, 1975. 36 pp.

1140. ———. *Contes de gazelle. Les Aventures de Biomo. L'Arbre du voyageur.* P.: L'Ecole, 1975. 63 pp.

1141. ———. *Contes du Gabon.* P.: Clé international, 1981. 112 pp.

1142. Adam, J.-J. *Folklore du Haut-Ogooué, proverbes, devinettes, fables mbédé.* Issy-les-Moulineaux: Impr. Saint-Paul, 1971. 360 pp.

1143. Alexandre, Pierre. "Introduction to a Fang Oral Art Genre: Gabon & Cameroon Meet," *Bulletin of the School of African & Oriental Studies, U. of London,* v. 37 (no. 1, 1974); pp. 1–7.

1144. Assoumou-Ndoutoume, Daniel. *Du Mvett: Essai sur le Dynastie Ekang Nna.* P.: Harmattan, 1986. 181 pp.

1145. Bachy, Victor. *Le cinéma au Gabon.* Brussels: OCIC, 1986. 156 pp.

1146. Bidzo, Hauban. *Poèmes choisis.* Lv.: IPN, Apr. 1975. 19 pp.

1147. Boyer, Pascal. *Barricades mystérieuses et pièges à pensée: Introduction à l'analyse des épopées fang.* P.: Laboratoire d'ethnologie et de sociologie comparative, 1988. 190 pp.

1148. ———. "Les épopées Mvet Ekang," in Jocelyne Fernandez, ed., *Kalevale et Tradition orale au monde.* P.: CNRS, 1987, pp. 441–447.

1149. Brouillet, Jean-Claude. *L'Avion du Blanc.* P.: Robert Laffront, 1972, 330 pp.

1150. Bruce, Josette. *Bagarre au Gabon pour OSS 117.* P.: Presses de la Cité, 1978. 192 pp.

1151. Charnay, René. *La terre des adieux.* P.: Olivier Orban, 1983. 323 pp.

1152. *Contes.* Special no., *L'Educateur Gabonais* (Dec. 1970). 94 pp. [93 stories].

1153. Cornevin, Robert. *Littératures d'Afrique noire de langue française.* P.: PUF, 1976. 273 pp.

1153a. Damas-Aleka, Georges. *L'Homme Noir.* Monaco: Ed. PB, 1970.

1153b. Daninos, Guy. "La mort de Guyhafi de Vincent de Paul Nyonda ou les méfaits du tribalisme," *Culture française,* (no. 3–4, 1982, no. 1, 1983), pp. 79–82.

1154. Danton, C. P. *Antilope N'Tcheri.* P.: Robert Laffont, 1976. 390 pp.

1155. Dedet, Christian. *La mémoire du Fleuve: L'Afrique aventureuse de Jean Michonet*. P.: Éditions Phébus, 1984. 540 pp.

1156. De Wolf, P. P. *Un Mvet de Zwé Nguema*. P.: AC, 1972. 492 pp.

1157. Eno Belinga, Samuel Martin. "La littérature orale du Mvet (A travers les pays d'Afrique centrale: Cameroun, Gabon, Guinée Équatoriale)," *Africana Budapest.* (no. 2, 1986), pp. 70–75. Also, in *La tradition orale de la littérature contemporaine.* Dakar: NEA, 1985, pp. 139–149.

1157a. Fonteneau, Jean-Marie. *Les Papillons de Makaba.* P.: Grasset, 1973. 237 pp.

1158. Goyonneau, Christine H. "Francophone Women Writers from Sub-Saharan Africa: A Preliminary Bibliography," *Callaloo,* v. 8 (no. 2, Spring-Summer 1985), pp. 453–483.

1159. Habay, E. *Fille du Soleil.* [n.p., n.d.] 330 pp.

1160. Kama-Bongo, Josephine. *Abali.* Lv.: 1974. 64 pp.

1161. Koumba Koumba, Rufin. *Poèmes choisis.* L.: IPN, Apr. 1975. 11 pp.

1162. Leyimangoye, Jean-Paul. *Olende ou le chant du monde. Légende populaire traduite et adaptée par l'auteur.* Lv.: Ministry of National Education, 1976. 67 pp.

1163. Lima, Josette. *Poèmes.* Dakar: Ed. Florilège, 1966.

1164. Mace, Jean-Claude. *Le Vagabond de la brousse.* P.: Pensée universelle, 1976. 247 pp.

1165. Mbot, Jean-Emile. "La Tortue et le léopard chez les Fang du Gabon (Hypothèse de travail sur les contes traduits)," *CEA,* v. 14 (no. 4, 1974), pp. 651–670.

1166. Meye, François. *Les récits de la forêt.* Monaco: Ed. PB, 1970. 93 pp.

1167. Ministry of National Education. *Anthologie de la littéra-ture gabonaise.* Montréal: Ed. Littéraires, 1976. 357 pp.

1168. Misere-Kouka, Raphaël. *Magie noire au bord de l'Ivindo.* P.: Saint-Germain-des-Prés, 1986. 98 pp.

1169. Mongaryas, Quentin Ben. *Choix de poèmes.* P.; Para-graphes littéraires de Paris, 1978. 144 pp.

1170. ———. *Itinéraire d'un jeune guerrier gabonais ou voyage au coeur de la plèbe: Poèmes.* Lv.: Bibliothèque nationale, 1985. 98 pp.

1171. ———. *Voyage au coeur de la plèbe.* P.: Silex Ed., 1986. 92 pp. [novel].

1172. Moubembé-Mbanimbongo. *Bruits de mars (poèmes),* v. 1 and 2. P.: La Pensée universelle, 1981. 64 pp.

1173. Moubouyi, Richard, comp. *Proverbes, légendes, et totems gabonais.* Lv.: Ministère de l'Information, Postes, et Télécommunications, Direction Générale de R.T.G., 1986. 119 pp.

1174. Mousessian, S. *Départ du Bourget pour Lambaréné.* P.: Éd. La Source d'Or, 1971. 163 pp.

1175. Mubumbila, Mfika. *Sur les Sentiers Mystérieux des Nom-bres Noirs.* P.: Harmattan, 1988. 166 pp.

1176. Ndaot, Séraphin. *Le Dissident.* P.: Éd. Silex, 1986. 171 pp.

1177. Ndong Ndoutoume, Tsira. *Essais.* Lv.: Ministry of Na-tional Education, 1975. 33 pp.

1178. ———. *Lettres gabonaises.* Lv.: MNE, 1975. 46 pp.

1179. ———. *Le Mvett.* P.: PA, 1970. 157 pp; 1975. 311 pp.

1180. Ndouna-Depenaud. [Ndouna-Okogo, Dieudonné Pascal]. *Elle ne l'épousera pas: Théâtre.* n.d. 29 pp. [Mimeographed].

1181. ———. *Passages.* Lv.: IPN, May 1975. 24 pp.

1182. ———. *La plaie.* n.d. 19 pp. [Mimeographed].

1183. ———. *Rêves à l'aube.* Lv.: IPN, May 1975. 13 pp.

1184. Ndzoungou, Jérôme. "L'aide au Tiers Monde vue dans *Elonga* [de N. Rawiri]," *PA,* (no. 1–2, 1985), pp. 241–247.

1185. Nkoghe-Mve, Moïse. *Fables et poèmes choisis.* Lv.: IPN, May 1975. 19 pp.

1185a. Notre Librairie. *La littérature gabonaise.* P.: CLEF, 1991. 173 pp.

1186. Nyonda, Vincent de Paul. *La Mort de Guykafi.* P.: Harmattan, 1981. 199 pp.

1186a. Odounga. *Poèmes.* Lv.: Multipresse, 1989.

1187. Ojo-Ade, Femi. "La romancière africaine face à la réalité socio-politique: L'exemple d'*Elonga* de N. Rawiri," *Conjonction: Revue franco-haïtienne,* (no. 165, 1985), pp. 61–86.

1188. Okoumba-Nkoghe. *La mouche et la glu: Roman.* P.: *PA,* 1984. 268 pp.

1189. ———. *Olendé: Une épopée du Gabon.* P.: Harmattan, 1989. 123 pp.

1190. ———. *Siana: Aube nouvelle.* P.: Silex, 1980. 110 pp.

1191. Owondo, Laurent. *Au bout du silence.* P.: Librairie Hatier, 1985. 127 pp.

1192. Pounah, Paul Vincent. *Chant du Mandola alias Pégase.* Fontenay-le-Comte: Impr. Loriou, 1978. 132 pp.

1193. Rawiri, Angèle Ntyugwetondo. "La clarté de la pénombre," *Nouvelles Sud,* (no. 9–10, 1988), pp. 103–104.

1194. ———. *Elonga: Roman.* P.: Éditaf, 1980. 261 pp.

1195. ———. *Fureurs et cris de femmes: Roman.* P.: Harmattan, 1989. 175 pp.

1196. ———. *G'amàrakano au carrefour.* P.: ABC, 1983. 197 pp.

1197. Sauvageot, Jean-Pierre. "Littérature gabonaise: Paul-Vincent Pounah à la recherche de la poésie perdue," *M'Bolo,* (no. 1, 1980), pp. 22–31.

1198. ———. "Ntyugwetondo Rawiri, romancière gabonaise," *M'Bolo,* (no. 10, 1984), pp. 20–29.

1199. ———. "Vincent-de-Paul Nyonda: Un des pères du théâtre gabonais," *M'Bolo,* (no. 8, 1983), pp. 49–53.

1200. Swiderski, Stanislaw, and Girou-Swiderski, Marie-Laure. *La poèsie populaire et les chants religieux du Gabon.* Ottawa: Ed. de l'U. d'Ottawa, 1981. 291 pp. [Fang, Penda, Bwiti].

1201. Tolopon, André Hountondji. "Mythe et tradition dans *Au Bout du Silence* de Laurent Owondo," *Afrique Littéraire,* v. 29 (no. 83–84), pp. 50–53.

1202. Towo-Atangana, G. "Le mvet, genre majeur de la littérature orale des populations Pahouines (Bulu, Beti-Fang, Ntumu)," *Abbia* (July–Aug. 1965), pp. 163–179.

1203. Trilles, Henri. *Contes et légendes pygmées.* Bruges: Librairie de l'Oeuvre St. Charles, 1935. 186 pp.

1204. Walker, André Raponda. *Contes gabonais.* P.: *PA,* 1968. 384 pp.

1205. Walker-Deemin, Henri, ed. *Ecrivains, artistes et artisans gabonais.* Monaco: Ed. PB for the IPN, 1966. 93 pp.

1206. Ze Lecourt, Moïse Nkoa. *Le Mvet: Une recherche des traditions culturelles en Afrique (zone du Sud Cameroun, Gabon et Guinée).* P.: Memoir, EHESS, 1972.

1207. Zotoumbat, Robert. *Histoire d'un enfant trouvé.* Ed. CLE, 1971. 59 pp.

XVII: LINGUISTICS

1208. Adam, J. J. "Dialectes du Gabon—la famille des langues téké," *BIEC,* n.s. (no. 7–8, 1954), pp. 33–107.

1209. ———. *Grammaire composée Mbédé, Adumu, Duma.* Montpellier: Impr. Charité, 1954. 173 pp.

1210. Alexandre, Pierre. "Aperçu sommaire sur le Pidgin Afo du Cameroun," *CEA,* v. 3 (no. 4, 1963), pp. 577–582.

1211. Barreteau, D., ed. *Inventaire des études linguistiques sur les pays d'Afrique noire d'expression française et sur Madagascar.* P.: CILF, 1978, pp. 493–503.

1212. Bates, George L. *A Grammar of the Fang Language as Spoken on the Como and Benito Rivers.* Libreville-Baraka: 1899. 113 pp.

1213. Blanchon, J. A. "Présentation du Yi-Lumba dans ses rapports avec le Yi-Punu et la Ci-Vili à travers un conte traditionnel," *Pholia,* (no, 1, 1984), pp. 7–35.

1214. Bonneau, J. *Grammaire Pounou et Lexique Pounou-Français.* Montpellier: Impr. Charité, 1956. 177 pp.

1215. ———. "Grammaire pounou," *JAS,* v. 10 (1940), pp. 131–162; v. 17 (1947), pp. 23–50; v. 22 (1952), pp. 43–94.

1216. Couvert, Claude. *La Langue française en République gabonaise.* P.: Haut comité de la langue française, 1982.

1217. Dalby, David. *Language Map of Africa and the Adjacent Islands.* L.: International African Institute, 1977. 63 pp.

1218. Galley, Samuel. *Dictionnaire français-fang, fang-français.* Neuchâtel: Ed. Henri Messeiller, 1964. 588 pp.

1219. Guthrie, Malcolm. *The Bantu Languages of Western Equatorial Africa.* L.: Oxford UP for the International African Institute, 1953. 94 pp.

1220. ———. *Comparative Bantu: An Introduction to the Comparative Linguistics & Pre-History of the Bantu Languages.* L.: Gregg, 1967–1970. 4 v.

1221. ———. "Notes on Nzabi (Gabon)," *Journal of African Languages,* v. 7 (no. 2, 1968), pp. 101–129.

1222. ———. "The Western Bantu Languages,"in Thomas A. Sebok, ed., *Linguistics in Sub-Saharan Africa.* P.: Mouton, 1971, pp. 357–366.

1223. Hombert, J. M., and Mortier, A-M. "Bibliographie des langues du Gabon," *Pholia,* (no. 1, 1984), pp. 165–187.

1224. International Institute of African Languages and Cultures. *Practical Orthography of African Languages.* L.: Oxford UP for the IIALC, 1930. 24 pp.

1225. Jacquot, André. *Les classes nominales dans les langues bantoues des groupes B. 10, B. 20, B. 30, (Gabon-Congo).* P.: ORSTOM, 1983. 360 pp. [Myène, Kele, Tsogho].

1226. ———. *Étude de phonologie et morphologie Myène.* P.: Société d'études linguistiques et anthropologiques de France, 1976, pp. 13–78.

1227. ———. "Langue national et langues nationales. Commentaire sur un projet de langue commune au Gabon," *CORSTOM, SSH,* v. 24 (no. 3, 1988), pp. 403–416.

1228. ———. "Quelques réflexions à propos de l'enseignement en langue vernaculaire," *CORSTOM, SSH,* v. 21 (no. 2–3, 1985), pp. 355–360.

1229. Jouin, Michel. *La terminologie de parenté Mpongwe.* Lv.: ORSTOM, 1973. 187 pp.

1230. Kwenzi-Mikala, Jérôme T. "L'identification des unités-langues bantu gabonaises et leur classification interne," *Muntu,* (no. 8, 1988), pp. 54–64.

1231. Mbot, Jean-Emile. *Ebughi bifia "Démonter les expressions" (Enonciation et situations sociales chez les Fang du Gabon).* P.: Institut d'Ethnologie du Musée de l'Homme, 1975. 150 pp.

1232. Muroni, Jean-Marc. *Petit dictionnaire bantou du Gabon: français/ndjabi, ndjabi/français.* P.: Harmattan, 1989.

1233. Nsuka-Nkutsi, Franéois, ed. *Élements de description du punu.* Lyons: U. of Lyon II, 1980. 247 pp.

1234. Perrou, R. P. *Lexique français-ikota.* Makoukou: Mission Catholique, 1964. 2 v.

1235. Preston, Ira M., and Best, Jacob, eds. *A Grammar of the Bakele Language with Vocabularies.* N.Y.: Prall, 1854. 117 pp.

1236. Trenezem, Edouard. "Vocabulaire Inzabi," *JAS,* v. 2 (1932), pp. 75–84.

1237. Tucker, A. N. "Orthographic Systems & Conventions in Sub-Saharan Africa," in Thomas A. Sebok, ed., *Linguistics in Sub-Saharan Africa.* P.: Mouton, 1971, pp. 618–653.

1238. Walker, André Raponda. *Dictionnaire Français-Mpongwe suivi d'Eléménts de Grammaire.* Bv.: Ed. St. Paul, 1961.

1239. ———. *Dictionnaire Mpongwe-Français suivi d'Eléments de Grammaire.* Metz: La Libre Lorraine, 1934. 640 pp.

1240. ———. *Essai de grammaire tsogo.* Bv.: Impr. du Gouvernement, 1937, 37 pp.

1241. Wilson, John Leighton. *A Grammar of the Mpongwe Language with Vocabularies.* N.Y.: Snowden and Prall, 1847. 94 pp.

XVIII: ART, MUSIC, AND DANCE

1242. Anquetil, Jacques. *L'artisanat créateur au Gabon.* P.: ACCT, 1983. 72 pp.

1243. Binet, Jacques. *Sociéte de Danse chez les Fang du Gabon.* P.: ORSTOM, 1972. 162 pp.

1244. *Catalogue des Documents Sonores Conservés au Musée National des Arts et Traditions du Gabon.* Lv.: Le Musée, 1987. 215 pp.

1245. Chaffin, Alain, and Chaffin, Françoise. *L'art kota: Les figures de reliquaire.* Meudon: A. and F. Chaffin, n.d. 351 pp.

1246. Cornet, Joseph. "Introduction à la musique africaine," *Etudes Scientifiques* (Dec. 1977), pp. 2–37.

1247. Dupré, Marie-Claude. "L'art kota est-il vraiment kota?" *Ethnographie,* v. 75 (no. 3, 1980), pp. 343–355.

1248. Farr, Francine Deewilla. *The Segmentation of Form in Pahouin Reliquary Figures.* Master's Thesis, University of California at Los Angeles, 1983. 72 pp.

1249. Fernandez, James W. *Fang Architectonics.* Philadelphia: Institute for Study of Human Issues, 1977. 41 pp.

1250. ———. "Principles of Opposition and Vitality in Fang Aesthetics," *Journal of Aesthetics and Art Criticism,* v. 25 (1966), pp. 53–64.

1251. ———, and Fernandez, R. L. "Fang Reliquary Art: Its Quantities and Qualities," *CEA,* v. 15 (no. 4, 1975), pp. 723–746.

1252. Gollnhofer, Otto; Sallée, Pierre; and Sillans, Roger. *Art & Artisanat Tsogho.* Lv.: Musée des Arts et Traditions du Gabon & ORSTOM, 1975. 126 pp.

1253. Grébert, F. "L'art musical chez les Fang du Gabon," *Archives suisses d'anthropologie générale,* v. 5 (1928), pp. 75–86.

1254. Grimaud, Yvette. *Notes sur la musique des Bochiman comparée à celle des Pygmees Babinga.* P.: Musée de l'Homme, 1957. 20 pp. [text in French & English].

1255. Hall, H. U. "Two Masks from French Equatorial Africa," *The Museum Journal* [U. of Pennsylvania] (Dec. 1927), pp. 381–409.

1256. Lefeburé, Thérèse. "Les instruments de musique au Gabon," in *LUTO (Laboratoire universitaire de la tradition orale). Revue gabonaise des sciences ethnomusicologie. Actes du séminaire ethnomusicologie 14–30 Avril 1988.* Lv.: U. Omar Bongo, 1988, pp. 87–89.

1256a. Lehuard, Raoul. "Le musée de Libreville," *Arts d'Afrique Noire,* v. 11 (1974), pp. 5–8.

1257. Maisonneuve, André. *Une Figure de reliquaire Kota: Nord-est du Gabon.* Chevilly-Larue: Ed. Regarder, 1987. 6 pp.

1258. Maquet, Jacques. ''Sculpture traditionnelle et classes sociales,'' *Bulletin des Séances de l'Académie Royale des Sciences d'Outre-Mer,* (no. 3, 1976), pp. 452–467. [Fang].

1259. M'Bokolo, Elikia. *L'épopée teke au Gabon: Traditions musicales teke au Gabon.* P.: Radio France Internationale 1989. [33 rpm record and booklet with text. Archives sonores de l'oralité 37].

1260. Mbot, Jean Émile. *Un siècle d'histoire du Gabon raconté par l'iconographie.* Lv.: Ministère de la Culture et des Arts, 1977. 193 pp.

1261. McKesson, John. ''Réflexions sur l'évolution de la sculpture des reliquaires Fang,'' *Arts d'Afrique noire,* v. 63 (Autumn 1987), pp. 7–21.

1262. Meyer, Laure. ''Art africain: Pouvoirs magiques des reliquaires,'' *L'Estampille,* v. 199 (Jan. 1987), pp. 54–58.

1263. Mvé-Ondo, Bonaventure. ''L'Architecture au Gabon,'' *M'Bolo,* (no. 13, 1985), pp. 26–35.

1264. Ndong-Ntoutoume, Philippe Tsira. ''Le rôle de la musique dans le mvet,'' in *LUTO (Laboratoire universitaire de la tradition orale). Revue gabonaise des sciences de l'homme. Actes du séminaire ethnomusicologie 14–30 Avril 1988.* Lv.: U. Omar Bongo, 1988, pp. 219–232.

1265. Nguema, Zwé. *Un mvet. Chant épique fang.* P.: AC, 1972. 473 pp. [plus three 45 rpm records].

1266. Nidzgorski, Denis. *Arts du spectacle africain: Contributions du Gabon.* Badundu: Ceeba, 1980, 373 pp.

1267. Obiang, Ludovic. ''Études de l'arc musical,'' in *LUTO (Laboratoire universitaire de la tradition orale). Revue gabonaise des sciences de l'homme. Actes du séminaire ethnomusicologie 14–30 Avril 1988.* Lv.: U. Omar Bongo, 1988, pp. 245–256.

1268. Pepper, Herbert. *Archives culturelles gabonaises: Catalogue des collections audiovisuelles.* Lv.: Centre OR-STOM, Service ethno-musicologique, 1964–1967. 2 v. 159 and 107 pp.

1269. ———. "Répertoire des enregistrements sonores effectués en Afrique équatoriale française (territoires du Moyen-Congo et du Gabon)." Brazzaville: ORSTOM, IEC, 1957. 109 pp.

1270. Perrois, Louis. "L'art Kota-Mahongwe. Les figures funéraires du Bassin de l'Ivindo (Gabon-Congo)," *Arts d'Afrique Noire,* v. 20 (1976), pp. 15–37.

1271. ———. *Art ancestral du Gabon.* P.: Nathan, 1985. 239 pp.

1272. ———. "Aspects de la sculpture traditionnelle du Gabon," *Anthropos,* v. 63–64 (1968–1969), pp. 869–888.

1273. ———. "Basin de l'Ogooué," in *Masques et sculpture d'Afrique et d'Océanie.* P.: Musée d'art moderne de la ville de Paris, 1986, pp. 106–118.

1274. ———. *Le Bwélé des Kota-Mahongwe du Gabon: Note sur les figures funéraires des populations du bassin de l'Ivindo.* Lv.: ORSTOM, 1969. 50 pp.

1275. ———. *Les chefs-d'oeuvres de l'art gabonais au Musée des arts et traditions à Libreville.* L.: Rotary Club of Libreville, 1986. 154 pp.

1276. ———. *Gabon: L'ordre du sacré, masques et statues des peuples de l'Ogooué.* P. and N.Y.: H. and Ph. Leloup, 1988. 58 pp.

1277. ———. *Problèmes d'analyse de l'art traditionnel au Gabon.* P.: Institut d'Ethnologie, U. of P., n.d. 75 pp.

1278. ———. "Le statuaire des Fang du Gabon," *Arts d'Afrique Noire,* v. 7 (1973), pp. 22–42.

1279. ———. *Le Statuaire Fan. Gabon.* P.: ORSTOM, 1972. 421 pp.

1280. ———, et al. *Gabon. Cultures et Techniques. Catalogue du Musée des Arts et Traditions.* Lv.: ORSTOM, 1969. 84 pp.

1281. "Pierre Akendengué, musicien gabonais," *Agecop-Liaison,* (May–June 1983), pp. 20–22.

1282. Rawa, Claude. "L'Artisanat Gabonais," *M'Bolo,* (no. 7, 1983), pp. 55–59.

1283. Roy, Claude. *Le M'Boueti des Mahongoué.* P.: Galerie Jacques Kerache, 1967. 79 pp.

1284. Sallée, Pierre. *L'arc et la harpe: Contribution à l'histoire de la musique du Gabon.* Doctoral Thesis, U. of P., 1986.

1285. ———. *Deux Études sur la musique du Gabon.* P.: OR-STOM, 1978. 87 pp.

1286. ———. *Étude d'une harpe à 8 cordes des populations gabonaises dans contexte socio-culturel.* Doctoral Thesis, U. of P., 1969.

1287. ———. "Gabon," in *The New Grove Dictionary of Music and Musicians,* v. 7. L.: Macmillan, 1980, pp. 45–54.

1288. ———. "Improvisation et/ou information: Sur trois exemples de polyphonies africaines," [Mitsogho, Kabre Pygmies] in Bernard Lortat-Jacob, ed., *L'improvisation dans les musiques de tradition orale.* P.: SÉLAF, 1987, pp. 93–104.

1289. ———. *Un aspect de la musique des Batéké du Gabon: Le*

Grand Pluriarc Ngwomi et sa Place dans la Danse Onkila: Essai d'Analyse Formelle d'un Document de Musique Africaine. Lv.: ORSTOM, 1971. 53 pp.

1290. Segy, Ladislav. "Bakota Funerary Art Figures," *Zaire,* v. 6 (May 1952), pp. 451–460.

1291. Siroto, Leon. "The Faces of Bwiti," *African Arts* (Spring 1968), pp. 22–27.

1292. Swiderski, Stanislaw. "Tradition et nouveauté des concepts religieux dans l'art sacré contemporain au Gabon," *Anthropos,* v. 74 (no. 5–6, 1979), pp. 803–816.

1293. ———. "La harpe sacrée dans les cultes syncrétiques au Gabon," *Anthropos,* v. 65 (no. 5–6, 1970), pp. 833–857.

1294. Vulysteke, M. *Musique du Gabon.* P.: Office de Coopération Radiophonique, 1968. 12 pp. [plus record no. 41, OCR].

XIX: TOURISM

1295. D'Herville, François. *Le Gabon.* P.: Solar, 1976. 63 pp.

1296. Eyraud, Arlette. *Centrafrique, Congo, Gabon.* P.: Hatier, 1979. 144 pp.

1297. Fendeler, Gérard. *Guide de Libreville et du Gabon.* Dakar: Société africaine d'ed., 1975. 96 pp.

1298. *Gabun gestern und heute.* Hildesheim: Roemer-Pelizaeus Museum, 1973. 72 pp. [German and French texts].

1299. Houlet, Gilbert, ed. *Afrique Centrale. Les Républiques d'Expression Française.* P.: Hachette, 1962. 533 p.

1300. Ngabissio, N. N. *Découvrir le Gabon touristique.* P.: Novafric, 1976. 166 pp.

1301. Rémy, Mylène. *Le Gabon Aujourd'hui.* P.: Ed. Jeune Afrique, 1977. 263 pp.

XX: REFERENCE AND BIBLIOGRAPHY

1302. Académie des Sciences d'Outre-Mer. *Travaux et Mémoires,* n.s. *Hommes et Destins. Dictionnaire Biographique d'Outre-Mer.* P.: V. 1, 1975; V. 2 in 2 parts, 1977.

1303. *Africa Bibliography.* Manchester: International African Institute, 1985+.

1304. *Africa Confidential.* Semi-monthly.

1305. *Africa Contemporary Record.* L.: African Research/Rex Collins, 1968+.

1306. *Africa Report.* N.Y.: African American Institute. Bimonthly, 1957+.

1307. *Africa Research Bulletin.* Series A. *Political, Social, Cultural.* Series B. *Economic, Financial, Technical.* Exeter, England, monthly, Jan. 1964+.

1308. *Africa South of the Sahara.* L.: Europa Publications, 1971+.

1309. *Africa Year Book & Who's Who.* L.: Africa Journal Ltd., 1976+.

1310. *African Biographies.* Bonn: Research Institute of the Friedrich-Ebert Stiftung, 1967+. [Loose-leaf].

1310a. *Africana Journal.* N.Y.: Africana Publishers, quarterly, 1970+.

1311. *Afrique Contemporaine.* P.: DF, Bi-monthly, 1959+.

1312. *L'Afrique Noire de A à Z.* P.: Ediafric, 1975.

1313. *L'Afrique noire politique et économique,* 5th ed. P.: Ediafric—Documentation africaine, 1983.

1314. Agence de Coopération culturelle et technique. *Répertoire des sources d'information francophones pour le développement.* P.: ACCT, 1987. 557 pp.

1315. Agence France-Presse. *Bulletin quotidien d'Afrique,* Paris, Daily, 1960+.

1316. Alalade, F. O. ''French-Speaking Africa-France Relations: A Critical Bibliographic Survey with Particular References to the Ivory Coast,'' *CBAA,* v. 9 (no. 1, 1976–1977), pp. 84–93.

1317. *Année africaine.* P.: Pedone, 1963+.

1318. *Année Politique Africaine.* Dakar: Société Africaine d'Ed., 1966+.

1319. *L'annuaire d'Afrique noire,* v. 2, 34th ed. P.: Ediafric, Documentation africaine, 1985. 625 pp.

1320. *Annuaire du Tiers-Monde.* P.: B-L, 1976+.

1321. *Annuaire national de la République gabonaise.* Lv.: 1987, 228 pp.

1322. Asamani, J. O., Comp. *Indexus Africanus.* Stanford: Hoover Institution Press, 1975. 659 pp.

1323. Baker, Philip, comp. *International Guide to African Studies Research,* 2nd ed. L.: Hans Zell and K. G. Sauer, 1987. 264 pp.

1324. Balandier, Georges, and Maquet, Jacques, eds. *Dictionnaire des Civilisations Africaines*. P.: Hazan, 1968. 448 pp. Tr. *Dictionary of Black African Civilization*. N.Y.: Leon Amiel, 1974. 350 pp. [Fang and Mpongwe].

1325. Ballard, John C. "Politics and Government in Former French West and French Equatorial Africa: A Critical Bibliography," *JMAS*, v. 3 (Dec. 1965), pp. 589–605.

1326. Barret, Jacques. *Géographie et cartographie du Gabon, atlas illustré*. P.: EDICEF, 1983. 135 pp.

1327. Barrett, David B. *World Christian Encyclopedia*. Oxford UP, 1982.

1328. Belinga, Thérèse Baratte-Eno, Comp. *Bibliographie. Auteurs africains et malgache de langue française*. P.: Office de Radiodiffusion et Télévision française, 4th ed., 1979.

1329. Berman, Sanford. *Spanish Guinea: An Annotated Bibliography*. M.L.S. Thesis, Catholic U. of America, W, 1961. 2 v. 597 pp. [chronologies; Fang].

1330. *Bibliographie ethnographique de l'Afrique sud-saharienne*. Tervuren: Musée Royal de l'Afrique centrale, 1981. 487 pp.

1331. Boston U. *Gabon: Selected Bibliography*. Boston: Boston U. African Studies Press, 1965.

1332. Bouscarle, Marie Elizabeth. *Les bibliothèques au Gabon: Note de synthèse présentée par M.E.B.* P.: Memoir, École nationale supérieure des bibliothécaires, 1982. 51 pp.

1333. Brasseur, Paule, and Maurel, Jean-François. *Les sources bibliographiques d'Afrique de l'Ouest et de l'Afrique Equatoriale d'expression française*. Dakar: Bibliothèque de l'U. de Dakar, 1970. 88 pp.

1334. Bruel, Georges. *Bibliographie de l'Afrique Equatoriale Française*. P.: Larose, 1914. 326 pp.

1335. Brune, Stefan, and Weiss, Christine. *Die Französische Afrikapolitik Auswahlbibliographie. La politique africaine de la France: Bibliographie selectionnée.* Hamburg: Deutsches Ubersee Institut, 1988. 142 pp.

1336. Bucher, Henry H. "Archival Resources in Gabon," *HA,* v. 1 (1974), pp. 159–160.

1337. ———. "The Robert Hamill Nassau Collection in Gabon's National Archives: A Bibliographical Essay," *JA,* v. 47 (no. 1, 1977), pp. 186–195.

1338. *Bulletin de l'Afrique noire.* P.: Ediafric weekly, 1957+.

1339. *Bulletin de la Société Préhistorique et Protohistorique Gabonaise.* Lv., Irregular, 1965+.

1339a. *Cahiers d'Etudes Africaines.* P.: Quarterly, 1960+.

1340. Cailloux, S. *Le Gabon: repertoire bibliographique des études de sciences humaines (1970–1974).* Lv.: Ministry of Culture and the Arts, 1975. 43 pp.

1341. Carson, Patricia. *Materials for West African History in French Archives.* L.: Althone Press, U. of London, 1963. 170 pp. [includes Gabon].

1342. Centre d'Analyse et de Recherche Documentaires pour l'Afrique Noire (CARDAN). *Bulletin d'information et de liaison: Recherche, enseignement, documentation africaniste francophone.* P., 1969–1977.

1343. Centre de Recherche, d'Étude et de Documentation sur les institutions et les législations africaines (Dakar). *Répertoire alphabétique des textes législatifs et réglementaires du Gabon (1961–1974).* Dakar: CREDILA, 1976. 192 pp.

1344. Centre d'Études Africaines-Cardan-École des Hautes Études en Sciences Sociales. *Répertoire des thèses africanistes françaises.* P.: CEA-CARDAN, 1977+.

1345. *Chroniques d'Outre-Mer.* P.: Ministry of Overseas France, 10 times a year, 1951–1958.

1346. *Chronologie politique africaine.* P.: Fondation Nationale des Sciences Politiques, bimonthly, 1960–1970.

1347. Couret, René, ed. *Guide bibliographique sommaire d'histoire militaire et coloniale française.* P.: IN, 1969. 522 pp.

1348. Cros, Anne, comp. *Ouvrages sur le Gabon.* Lv.: Centre Saint-Exupéry, 1978. 81 pp.

1349. *Current Bibliography of African Affairs.* W.: African Bibliographic Center, N.S., quarterly, 1968+.

1350. *Current Contents Africa.* Oxford: Hans Zell, 1978+. [Formerly published at Frankfurt, 1975–1977].

1351. Darch, Colin, and Mascarenhas, O. C. *Afrika Index to Continental Periodical Litterature.* Oxford: Hans Zell, 1976+. [Annual].

1352. Darkowska-Nidzgoroka, L. Olenka. *Connaissance du Gabon: Guide Bibliographique.* Lv.: U. Nationale du Gabon, 1978. 151 pp.

1353. Delancey, Mark, comp. *African International Relations: An Annotated Bibliography.* Boulder: 1981.

1354. D'Hertefelt, Marcel, and Bouttiaux-Ndiaye, Anne-Marie. *Bibliographie de l'Afrique sud-saharienne, sciences humaines et sociales 1984–1985: Périodiques.* Tervuren: Musée royale de l'Afrique centrale, 1989. 986 pp.

1355. Dokumentations-Leitstelle Afrika. Special Bibliography no. 9. *Economic & Social Policy in Central Africa* (Gabon, Cameroon, Congo, Chad, CAR). Hamburg: Deutsche Institut für Afrika-Forschung, 1974.

1356. Draguet, Zoé. *Le Gabon: Repertoire bibliographique des Etudes de Sciences Humaines* (1967–1970). Lv.: OR-STOM, Feb. 1971. 33 pp.

1357. Duffy, David, ed. *A Survey of the United States Government's Investments in Africa.* Waltham, Mass.: ASA, 1978. 112 pp. Also published as *Issue,* v. 8 (no. 2–3, 1978), pp. 1–112.

1358. Duignan, Peter, ed. *Guide to Research and Reference Works on Sub-Saharan Africa.* Stanford: Hoover Institution Press, 1971. 1102 pp.

1359. ———, and Gann, L. H., ed. *A Bibliographical Guide to Colonialism in Sub-Saharan Africa.* L.: Cambridge UP, 1977. 552 pp.

1360. Dutailly, Henri. "Les sources de l'histoire coloniale dans les dépôts d'Archives du Ministère de la Défense," *PFCHS,* v. 5 (1980), pp. 1–5.

1361. Easterbrook, David L. "Bibliography of Africana Bibliographies, 1965–1975," *AJ,* v. 7 (no. 2, 1976), pp. 101–148.

1362. ———. "Bibliography of Africana Bibliographies, 1975–1976," *AJ,* v. 8 (no. 3, 1977), pp. 232–242.

1363. Ecole des Hautes Etudes en Sciences Sociales. Centre d'Etudes Africaines. *Bibliographie des travaux en langue française sur l'Afrique au Sud du Sahara.* Paris, 1977+.

1364. Economist Intelligence Unit. *Congo, Gabon, Equatorial Guinea. Country Report.* L.: Quarterly, 1985+.

1365. ———. *Quarterly Economic Review of Gabon, Congo, Cameroon, CAR, Chad and Madagascar.* L.: 1976–1984. [Also] *Quarterly Economic Review of former French*

Equatorial Africa, Cameroon and Madagascar, 1968–
1975, and *Quarterly Economic Review of former French
Tropical Africa,* 1960–1967.

1366. *Les élites africaines. Cameroun—Gabon.* P.: Ediafric,
1971. 298 pp.

1367. *Les élites gabonaises: Who's Who in the Republic of
Gabon.* P.: Ediafric, 1977. 217 pp.

1368. *Etudes Africaines: Liste mondiale des périodiques spécial-
isés.* P.: Mouton, 1969. 214 pp.

1369. *Europe-France-Outre-Mer.* P., Monthly, 1923–1987.

1370. Fontvieille, J. R. *Gabon: Activités opérationnelles dans le
domaine de l'information: Création d'une infrastructure
nationale des archives, des bibliothèques et de la
documentation.* P.: UNESCO, 1979. 103 pp.

1371. Founou-Tchuigoua, Bernard. "Bibliographie [sur les relations économiques arabo-africaines]," *Africa Development,* v. 11 (no. 2–3, 1986), pp. 31–68.

1372. Gabon. *Annuaire International.* Lv., Irregular, 1960+.

1373. Gabon. *Annuaire national officiel de la République gabonaise.* Lv.: Agence Havas, 1973+.

1374. Gabon. *Bulletin Mensuel de la Chambre de Commerce,
d'Agriculture, d'Industrie et des Mines du Gabon.* Lv.,
1960+.

1375. Gabon. *Journal Officiel.* Lv., Semimonthly, Apr. 1959+.

1376. Gabon. Ministry of Finances. *Budget de l'Etat.* 1959+.
[also *Budget local,* 1949–1958].

1377. Gabon. Ministry of Information. *Annuaire national.* P.:
1966+.

1378. Gabon. Ministry of National Education. *Statistiques de l'Enseignement au Gabon.* Annual.

1379. Gabon. National Statistical Service. *Bulletin mensuel de statistique.* Apr. 1959+.

1379a. "Gabon," in George T. Kurian, ed. *Encyclopedia of the Third World.* V. 1. N.Y.: Facts on File, 1978, pp. 500–510.

1380. "Gabon," in S. Taylor, ed. *The New Africans.* N.Y.: Putnam, 1967, pp. 128–145.

1380a. *Gabon Matin.* Lv., Daily newspaper, 1977+.

1381. Gardinier, David E. "Bibliographical Essay: Decolonization in French, Belgian, and Portuguese Africa,"in Prosser Gifford and W. Roger Louis, eds., *Transfer of Power in Africa,* New Haven: Yale UP, 1982, pp. 515–566.

1382. ———. "Decolonization in French, Belgian, Portuguese, and Italian Africa: Bibliography," in Prosser Gifford and W. Roger Louis, eds., *Decolonization and African Independence: The Transfers of Power, 1960–1980.* New Haven: Yale UP, 1988, 573–635.

1383. ———. "French Colonial Rule in Africa [1914–1962]: A Bibliographical Essay," in P. Gifford & Wm. Roger Louis, eds., *France and Britain in Africa: Imperial Rivalry and Colonial Rule.* New Haven: Yale UP, 1971, pp. 787–902.

1383a. ———. *Gabon.* Oxford: Clio Press, 1992. 179 pp.

1384. ———. "Resources for the History of Gabon in French Missionary Archives in Rome," *HA,* v. 8 (1981), pp. 323–325.

1385. ———. "Resources in Paris Missionary Archives and Libraries for the History of Gabon," *HA,* v. 7 (1980), pp. 159–160.

1386. Gaulme, François. "Bibliographie critique pour servir à anthropologie historique du littoral gabonais (époque précoloniale XVIe–XIXe siècles)," *JA,* v. 47 (no. 1, 1977), pp. 157–175.

1387. Gosebrink, Jean E. Meeh, ed. *African Studies Resources Directory.* Oxford: Hans Zell, 1986. 572 pp.

1388. Gray, Beverly Ann, and Batiste, Angel. *Japanese-African Relations: A Selected List of References.* Washington, D.C.: Library of Congress, 1988. 24 pp.

1389. Gray, John, comp. *African Music: A Bibliographical Guide to the Traditional, Popular, Art, and Liturgical Musics of Sub-Saharan Africa.* Westport, Conn.: Greenwood, 1991. 500 pp. [Includes nine recordings from Gabon].

1390. Gregory, Joel W.; Cordell, Dennis, D.; and Gervais, Raymond. *African Historical Demography: A Multidisciplinary Bibliography.* Los Angeles: Crossroads, 1984.

1391. Griffith, Nancy Snell, and Person, Laura. *Albert Schweitzer: An International Bibliography.* Boston: G. K. Hall, 1981. 600 pp.

1392. Guernier, Eugène, ed. *L'Afrique Equatoriale Française* (V. 5 of *L'Encyclopédie de l'Union Française*). P.: Ed. Coloniales et Maritimes, 1950. 590 pp.

1393. Guichard, Edmond. *Liste bibliographique des travaux des chercheurs et techniciens-ORSTOM en République gabonaise, de 1949 à 1977.* Lv.: Mission ORSTOM, 1978. 73 pp.

1394. Henige, David, and Gardinier, David. "Bibliographical Aids for the Historical Demographer," in Bruce Fetter, ed. *Demography from Scanty Evidence: Central Africa in the Colonial Era.* Boulder and L.: Lynne Rienner, 1990, pp. 29–36.

1395. Henige, David P., comp. *Colonial Governors from the 15th Century to the Present: A Comprehensive List.* Madison: U. of Wisconsin Press, 1970. 401 pp.

1396. Hoover Institution. *United States and Canadian Publications on Africa.* Stanford: Hoover Institution Press, 1961–1966.

1397. *International African Bibliography.* L.: Mansell, quarterly, 1971+.

1398. International Council for Archives (UNESCO). *Guide to the Sources of the History of Africa.* Multi-volume. French volumes: *Sources de l'Histoire de l'Afrique au Sud du Sahara dans les Archives et Bibliothèques françaises.* V. 1 *Archives.* V. 2 *Bibliothèques.* Switzerland: Interdocumentation Co., A. G. Zug, 1971 & 1976.

1399. International Institute for Strategic Studies. *The Military Balance: 1987–1988.* L.: IISS, 1987. 240 pp.

1400. *Jeune Afrique.* Paris, weekly, 1960+.

1401. Kirchherr, Eugene C. *Place Names of Africa, 1935–1986: A Political Gazetteer.* Metuchen, N.J. and L.: Scarecrow Pr., 136 pp.

1402. Kouassi, E. Kwam. *Organisations internationales africaines.* P.: B-L, 1987. 485 pp.

1403. Lafont, Francis. *Petit Atlas du Gabon.* P.: Ed. Alain, 1958. 46 pp.

1404. Lauer, Joseph J.; Larkin, Gregory, V.; and Kagan, Alfred, comps. *American and Canadian Doctoral Dissertations and Master's Theses on Africa, 1947–1987.* Atlanta: African Studies Association, 1989. 377 pp.

1405. Library of Congress. *U.S. Imprints on Subsaharan Africa: A Guide to Publications catalogued at the Library of*

Congress, v. 1, *1985.* Washington: Library of Congress, 1986. 105 pp.

1407. *Marchés tropicaux et méditerranéens.* P., Weekly, Nov. 1945+.

1408. Maurel, Jean-François. "Le Centre des archives d'outre-mer d'Aix-en-Provence," *AC,* v. 27 (no. 1, 1989), pp. 60–63.

1409. Mbah, Jean Ferdinand. *La recherche en sciences sociales au Gabon.* P.: Harmattan, 1987. 189 pp.

1410. Miller, Joseph. *Equatorial Africa.* W.: American Historical Association, 1976. 70 pp. [historiography].

1411. Ministry of Cooperation. Service of Studies and International Questions. *République Gabonaise.* P.: Dec. 1978.

1412. ———. *Gabon. Données Statistiques sur les Activités Economiques, Culturelles, et Sociales.* P.: Sept. 1976, 241 pp.

1413. *Mondes et Cultures* [formerly *Comptes Rendus de l'Académie des Sciences d'Outre Mer.*] Paris, quarterly, 1941+.

1414. Nicholas, Blaise, and Costisella, Monique, comp. *Bibliographie des auteurs gabonais.* Lv.: IPN, Mar. 1975. 17 pp.

1415. Notre Librairie. *2500 titres de littérature: Afrique subsaharienne.* P.: CLEF, 1988. 198 pp. Also *Notre Librairie,* (July–Sept., 1988).

1416. Panofsky, Hans E. *A Bibliography of Africana.* Westport, Conn.: Greenwood Press, 1975. 350 pp.

1417. Pansini, G. *Gabon. Réorganisation des archives nationales.* P.: UNESCO, 1973. 20 pp.

1418. Patterson, K. David. "Disease and Medicine in African History: A Bibliographical Essay," *HA,* v. 1 (1974), pp. 141–148.

1419. ———, comp. *Infectious Diseases in Twentieth-Century Africa: A Bibliography of Their Distribution and Consequences.* Waltham, Mass.: Crossroads Press, 1980.

1420. Perrois, Françoise. *Le Gabon: Repertoire Bibliographique des Etudes de Sciences Humaines, 1960–1967.* Lv., OR-STOM, 1969. 58 pp.

1421. Perrot, Claude. *Le Gabon: Repertoire Bibliographique relatif aux Sciences Humaines.* P.: BDPA, 1962. 44 pp.

1422. *Personnalités publiques de l'Afrique Centrale: Cameroun, RCA, Congo, Gabon, Tchad.* P.: Ediafric, 1968. 373 pp.

1423. Porgès, Laurence. *Sources d'information sur l'Afrique noire francophone et Madagascar: Institutions, répertoires, bibliographies.* P.: Ministère de la Coopération, DF, 1988. 389 pp.

1424. *Réalités Gabonaises: Revue Pédagogique et Culturelle du Gabon.* Lv., Apr. 1959+.

1425. *Recently Published Articles.* W.: AHA, Three times a year, 1976–1990. [Africa section].

1426. *Répertoire de l'information en Afrique et dans l'Océan Indien.* P.: Radio France Internationale, 1989. 245 pp.

1427. Republic of Gabon. *Annuaire, 1966.* Brussels, 1966. [trade statistics].

1428. Sanner, P. *Bibliographie ethnographique de l'Afrique Equatoriale Française, 1914–1948.* P.: IN, 1949. 107 pp.

1430. Scheven, Yvette. *Bibliographies for African Studies, 1970–1986.* L.: H. Zell, 1988. 615 pp.

1431. ———. "Bibliographies in African Literature since 1970," *Research in African Literature,* v. 15 (Fall 1984), pp. 405–419.

1432. Sims, Michael, and Kagan, Alfred, comp. *American and Canadian Doctoral Dissertations and Master Theses on Africa, 1886–1974.* Waltham, Mass.: ASA, 1976. 365 pp.

1433. South, Aloha P., ed. *Guide to Federal Archives and Manuscripts Relating to Africa.* Waltham, Mass.: Crossroads Press, 1977. 556 pp.

1434. ———. *Guide to Non-Federal Archives and Manuscripts Relating to Africa.* L.: Hans Zell, 1989. 2 v. 1250 pp.

1435. Standing Conference on Library Materials on Africa. *United Kingdom Publications & Theses on Africa.* Cambridge: Heffer, 1963+.

1436. Statistical Office of the European Communities. *République du Gabon. Annuaire, 1951–1966.* Brussels, 1968. 134 pp.

1437. U. of London. School of Oriental and African Studies. Library. *Library Catalogue.* Boston: G. K. Hall, 1963. 29 v. Supplement, 1968.

1438. United Nations Non-Governmental Liaison Service. *Non-Governmental Organizations and Sub-Saharan Africa: Profiles of Non-Governmental Organizations Based in W. Europe, Australia and N.Z. and Their Work for the Development of Sub-Saharan Africa.* G.: U.N. Non-Governmental Liaison Service, 1988. 284 pp.

1439. *The U.N. System and Sub-Saharan Africa: Profiles of U.N. System Agencies, Funds, Programmes and Services and Their Work for the Development of the Sub-Saharan Africa.* G.: U.N. Non-Governmental Liaison Service, 1990. 145 pp.

1440. U.S. Library of Congress. African Section. *Africa South of the Sahara: Index to Periodical Literature, 1900–1970.* Boston: G. K. Hall, 1971. 4 v. Supplement, 1973.

1441. ———. *Sub-Saharan Africa. A Guide to Serials.* W.: 1970. 409 pp.

1442. ———. *United States and Canadian Publications on Africa in 1960.* W.: 1962. 98 pp.

1443. U.S. Office of Geography. Gabon. *Official Standard Names approved by the U.S. Board of Geographic Names.* W.: GPO, 1962. 113 pp.

1444. Van Der Bent, Hans Joachim, ed. *Handbook. Member Churches. World Council of Churches.* G.: Rev. ed. 1985.

1445. Weiss, Marianne, comp. *Nicht-konventionelle Literatur aus Zentral-Afrika: Gabon, Congo, Zaïre, Burundi, Rwande.* Hamburg: Institut für Afrika-Kunde, 1982. 63 pp.

1446. Welsch, Erwin K., ed. *Research Resources France: Libraries & Archives in France.* N.Y.: Council for European Studies, 1979. 146 pp.

1447. *West Africa.* Weekly, 1917+.

1448. Witherell, Julian W., ed. *The U.S. and Africa: Guide to U.S. Official Documents & Government Sponsored Publications on Africa, 1785–1975.* W., 1978. 949 pp.

1449. ———, comp. *French-Speaking Central Africa. A Guide to Official Publications in American Libraries.* W., 1973. 314 pp.

1450. ———, comp. *Official Publications of French Equatorial Africa, French Cameroons & Togo, 1946–1958.* W., 1964. 78 pp.

1451. Zell, Hans M. *Livres africains disponibles: index par auteurs, matières et titres.* P.: Ed. France Expansion, 1978. 2 v. 322 & 895 pp.

1452. ———, ed. *The African Book Publishing Record: A Directory.* Oxford: Hans Zell, 1977. 296 pp.

1452a. ———, and Silver, Helene, ed. *A Reader's Guide to African Literature.* N.Y.: Africana Publishers, 1971. 218 pp.

XXI: MAP

1453. Soret, Marcel. *Afrique centrale. Esquisse ethnique générale.* Bv.: Institut Géographique National, 1962.

ABOUT THE AUTHOR

DAVID E. GARDINIER (A.B. SUNY-Albany; M.A., Ph.D., Yale University) is a Professor of History at Marquette University in Milwaukee, Wisconsin, where he formerly served as department chairman. He makes frequent research trips to France where he was a Fulbright scholar at the University of Paris in 1958–1959 and a Fulbright professor at the French Ministry of Cooperation in 1979. He has published several dozen articles and chapters on colonial rule and decolonization in Francophone Africa, including several on the history of education and Christian missions in Gabon. He is also the author of *Cameroon: United Nations Challenge to French Policy* (Oxford U. Press, 1963). Between 1964 and 1990, he compiled the Africa section of *Recently Published Articles* for the American Historical Association. He also prepared the bibliographies and historical essays on French Africa in three of the volumes of the Yale U. Press colonialism series edited by Prosser Gifford and Wm. Roger Louis (1971, 1982, 1988). Most recently he wrote the chapter on Gabon in *Africa Contemporary Record, 1989–1990* (Africana, 1992), "Gabon" in the 1991 edition of the *Encyclopaedia Britannica,* and presented a paper, "France's Relations with Gabon during the Mitterrand Presidency" in Montreal in May 1992 at the French Colonial Historical Society, an organization of which he is a past president.